WHITE LIES

Books by A. J. Baime

Dewey Defeats Truman
The Accidental President
The Arsenal of Democracy
Go Like Hell
Big Shots

Walter F. White, 1929

WHITE LIES

The Double Life of

WALTER F. WHITE

and America's Darkest Secret

A. J. BAIME

MARINER BOOKS

Boston   New York

marinerbooks.com

Library of Congress Cataloging-in-Publication Data has been applied for.
ISBN 978-0-358-44775-7 (hardcover)
ISBN 978-0-358-43966-0 (e-book)
ISBN 978-0-358-58193-2 (audio)

Book design by Greta Sibley
Frontispiece from Afro American Newspapers / Gado / Getty Images

1 2021
4500844785

No state shall . . . deprive any person of life, liberty, or property, without due process of law; nor deny to any person within its jurisdiction the equal protection of the laws.

— Fourteenth Amendment to the US Constitution (1868)

The right of citizens of the United States to vote shall not be denied or abridged by the United States or by any State on account of race, color, or previous condition of servitude.

— Fifteenth Amendment to the US Constitution (1870)

As my father lay dying in a jimcrow hospital in Atlanta he put into words for my brother and me the faith which had sustained him throughout his life. "Human kindness, decency, love, whatever you wish to call it," he said, "is the only real thing in the world. . . . It's up to you two, and others like you, to use your education and talents to make love as positive an emotion in the world as are prejudice and hate. That's the only way the world can save itself."
— Walter White, *A Man Called White*

Contents

Author's Note

IN TELLING THE STORY of Walter Francis White, I have attempted to use primary sources as much as possible—his letters, his papers, his diaries and memoirs, as well as those of the figures around him. All quotations in this book—and the spellings and terminologies in them—are original to those sources. They include, at times, racial slurs such as the N-word. All other language in this book conforms to current-day nomenclature according to the AP Stylebook, including the capitalization of the word Black when used to describe race.

WHITE LIES

Introduction

AT THE RISK OF GETTING AHEAD OF MYSELF, I want to say: Many readers will find in this book occurrences that will feel impossible to believe, events that you may think could never have happened in the United States of America. For others, this story will hit closer to home. The difference between these two readers is exactly what *White Lies* is about.

White, Black, and the shades in between.

The central figure is Walter Francis White, born in Atlanta in 1893 and raised there as well. Both of Walter's parents came from enslaved families in Georgia, and while they were African American, they had skin so pale, they and their children could have passed for white. "I am a Negro," Walter himself explained. "My skin is white, my eyes are blue, my hair is blond. The traits of my race are nowhere visible upon me."

The family's complexion represented a shameful truth: that generations of enslaved families were born out of illicit encounters between Black women who had no rights to their bodies and white male slave owners, who had full legal impunity. Walter's great-grandmother on his mother's side, in fact, birthed six children in the 1830s, fathered by her owner, William Henry Harrison, who later became president of the United States.

Walter was raised as a Black child. He went to a Black school, attended a Black church, and graduated from all-Black Atlanta University in 1916. A chance occurrence led him to race activism, and through that, he was plucked from obscurity at twenty-four years of age and brought to New York City to work for the National Association for the Advancement of

Colored People (NAACP), a small organization made up of a handful of white and Black intellectuals that was, at the time, new and struggling to gain a foothold.

Walter's move northward coincided with a wave of racial violence, and within days he began to live a double life: as an undercover investigator, posing as a white man in the South while cracking racially charged murder cases, but also as a budding Black intellectual in New York. He was uniquely gifted in moving from one world to the other and switching racial identities when it suited his investigative work. As a *New Yorker* writer later described him in 1948, he "was the perfect economy-size double duty package. He was young, spry, fearless, perceptive, glib, and, above all, reversible."

Working as an undercover investigator in the South from 1918 to 1930, Walter infiltrated secret societies, discovering an underbelly of fear and sadism, and he wrote about his findings in reports that made sensational national headlines, exposing some of the most shocking crimes in American history. So many of the darkest chapters of America's past—the Red Summer of 1919, the Tulsa massacre of 1921, the Lowman lynchings in South Carolina in 1926, as a few examples—Walter investigated firsthand, and many of his notes from those investigations exist in his papers today, documenting it all in profound detail.

After these investigations, Walter headed north by train over the Mason-Dixon Line (which he sarcastically called "the Smith & Wesson Line"), shed his white persona, and lived openly as a Black man again, rising in the ranks of the NAACP. He moved to Manhattan at the perfect time to help found the Harlem Renaissance and emerge as one of its central figures. He became an internationally famed novelist and a fixture in Harlem's nightclub scene during the Roaring Twenties. At parties in Walter's Harlem apartment, Black and white audiences first heard the singing of Paul Robeson and the verse of Langston Hughes. Broadway hit maker George Gershwin debuted *Rhapsody in Blue* on Walter's piano.

"Walter White was a New York celebrity," David Levering Lewis wrote in his Harlem Renaissance history, *When Harlem Was in Vogue*. "His apartment at 90 Edgecombe Avenue [was] a stock exchange for cultural commodities, where interracial contacts and contracts were sealed over bootleg spirits and the verse or song of some Afro-American who was then the rage of New York. . . . At 32, short, incomparably gregarious, White was already a legend in Harlem."

In an era before TV, he could live as a famous Black man in New York and as a white undercover crime fighter in the South. When his fame transcended, however, and he became chief executive of the NAACP in 1931 — which by then was the most powerful and militant race organization that had ever existed — Walter left his undercover work to focus the fight for civil rights where he believed it would be most effective in the future: politics. He became a regular guest in the Oval Office of FDR and Harry Truman. Arguably, he was the nation's most powerful driving force in the historic realignment of Black political power, from the Party of Lincoln, the Republicans, to the Democrats, where it remains for the most part today.

Never was it lost on the poor or the powerful the bizarre twist of Walter's skin color. In his own words, he was the "enigma of a black man occupying a white body." When he died in 1955, the *New York Times* stated in his obituary, "White, the nearest approach to a national leader of American Negroes since Booker T. Washington, was a Negro by choice."

All of which begs the question: Why is his story so obscure today?

Walter spent his life exposing secrets. But he also had a secret of his own. When, late in life, he could no longer keep this secret, he let go of it, and the explosive scandal shattered his reputation. But that was not all. Soon after he died a new generation of African American leaders emerged, and for these leaders his pale complexion was an inconvenience. Walter was not Black enough, especially in the new era of television. His story faded into oblivion.

This book is a character study of Walter's odyssey and an exploration of the essence of identity. His story *is* the story of race in America. It is also a story aimed at the conscience of America. As the Nobel Peace Prize–winning political scientist Ralph Bunche said of Walter, he was "a man whose life, in fuller measure than that of any I have known, was devoted to making American democracy a complete and equal reality for the black as well as the white citizen. . . . He lived that struggle for three decades. In a symbolic sense, he was that struggle of our times."

Now is an apt time to unearth Walter White's story. America is once again experiencing a surge of white supremacy, Black protest, and racial bloodshed. And once again, the country is being divided in two. Perhaps the lessons that need to be learned are not to be found in the present or future but in the past.

— A. J. Baime

July 2021

I

Have you ever witnessed the transformation of human beings into savage beasts? Nothing can be more terrible.

—James Weldon Johnson, *The Autobiography of an Ex-Colored Man*

"MY FIRST INTRODUCTION to the race question was in September 1906, when, with my father, I saw the beginning of the Atlanta Race Riot," Walter White wrote many years later, looking back on his childhood. "In the course of that disturbance he and I saw seven men killed."

The date was September 22, 1906, a Saturday. Walter was thirteen years old. The afternoon began with a discussion in the White family home, which stood on Houston Street behind a carefully painted white picket fence. Both Black and white families lived on this street. The White family consisted of nine "light-skinned Negroes," as Walter put it — father George, mother Madeline, five sisters, an older brother, and Walter himself (he was the fourth-born). On most days Walter attended the nearby Gate City Colored School, after which he returned home to help his father — a mail carrier who worked from 3 p.m. to 11 p.m. — on his route. On this particular day, however, there were rumors that violence was going to break out on the streets of Atlanta, that it would not be safe. Walter wanted to go. His father was against it, but his mother interjected.

It would be all right, Madeline said, as long as the boy was home before dark. "I don't think they would dare start anything before nightfall," she added.

George kept a rickety mail cart in a shed behind the family home, and a horse that pulled it. As they had on so many other days, father and son set out into the streets of Atlanta.

TRAVELING THROUGH THE CITY, Walter held the reins commanding the horse, so his father could jump in and out, piling mail bags into the back of the cart. All his life Walter would remember the smell of those mail bags, like glue and canvas. He often talked with his father during these rides about prayer and God, their voices punctuated by the sound of the horse's hoofs and the wooden wheels rolling over macadam. Walter: "If God is omnipotent as you say He is, why doesn't He just decree that each of us be free of sin and weakness?" George: "That is just my point. God *is* omnipotent, but He *chooses* to work through human instruments like you and me and every other human being on earth. Never forget that He needs your brain and heart to work His will."

On this Saturday, however, Walter's father spoke nervously of what might happen in Atlanta that night. The newspapers had been warning of a race riot for some time.

The cause of the trouble was rooted in a battle for Georgia's statehouse, a gubernatorial primary election that was reaching its climax. Two candidates—Hoke Smith and Clark Howell—were locked in a political brawl with the vote nearing. Both candidates were Democrats; here in the "Solid South" of the Democratic Party, no Republican stood a chance. Thus the primary would decide which candidate would be the next governor. Each controlled one of the city's major newspapers—Howell, the *Atlanta Constitution* and Smith, the *Atlanta Journal*—and both candidates were using the pages to enflame voters, in hopes of a big turnout.

Recently, the papers had begun to publish inflammatory reports of attacks by Black men on white women. Some of the stories were likely unfounded, some not. That very morning the *Atlanta Constitution*—Georgia's most widely read newspaper—printed a front-page piece about a young white girl who allegedly had been assaulted by a Black man. The story began with a quotation: "I am the girl's father, and there are few men who can appreciate my feelings who have not experienced what I have. I know the negro is now in the hands of the law out of my reach. If it possibly can be done, I beg that I be allowed to settle this case with the negro here and now."

Atlanta was on the verge, but of what exactly, no one yet knew. Walter later recalled what he was seeing on the streets: "At first it was a gentle murmur of hatred. Then it began to swell. Papers were snatched eagerly from panting newsboys. Over the shoulders of each purchaser hung a group, standing on tiptoe to grasp the story of the latest outrage. The grumbling grew. Little flames of violent words shot up. . . . The entire city was as a huge boil."

As the sun began to set, Walter was steering the cart toward a mailbox at the corner of Peachtree and Houston Streets when he heard a roar coming from nearby. Turning the corner, he saw a mob of white men chasing a limping Black figure. This is when he witnessed murder for the first time. He later described this moment: "Down he went, and a great bellow of hatred, of passion, of sadistic exultation filled his ears as he died."

It was over in seconds. One person in the mob yelled, "There goes another nigger!" And the mob disappeared, giving chase.

Walter could hear screaming voices and shattering glass. He saw men rushing by bearing rifles and clubs. The horse pulling the cart grew twitchy and unnerved. By his own count, Walter saw six more men murdered on those streets. In the process, he experienced a kind of transformation, as the knowledge was born in him of the human capacity for blind rage and violence.

He and his father were struck by a searing irony. They were carrying mail, which might have helped to protect them, because even as the lawless mobs murdered without conscience, they were unlikely to injure government property. But what really protected George and Walter was their complexion. To the mob, especially in the fading sunlight, George and Walter appeared Caucasian. The color of their skin kept them safe.

When the streets turned dark, gunshots could be heard. All night Atlanta burned. At 11 p.m., for the first time in the city's history, a "riot call" sounded — eleven strokes on the main fire bell summoning every policeman to duty. At midnight the fire bell rang again. "The fifteen slow successive strokes on the big bell were heard in all parts of the city," the *Atlanta Constitution* reported.

In the morning Walter would remember waking safely in his home and hearing the sound of church bells. It was Sunday. The White family had a strict Sunday routine: 8 a.m. prayers in the family's parlor, followed by a home-cooked feast for breakfast and services at the First Congregational Church. But this Sunday was different, for they knew the violence was not over. Morning newspapers across the country featured front-page banner headlines and eyewitness accounts of the bloodletting. The *St. Louis Post-Dispatch*: 20 BLACKS SLAIN IN ATLANTA RACE RIOTS. The *Los Angeles Times*: 30 NEGROES SLAIN, STREETS RUN BLOOD.

In the afternoon a friend of George White's came to the house to warn that a mob was going to amass downtown and march down Houston Street, that night. The mob would be moving right past the Whites' home.

"We turned out the lights early," Walter remembered, "as did all our neighbors." The family waited out the hours, the night strangely silent. Then they heard it coming. George told his wife to take their daughters — the youngest of whom was six — to the rear of the house, for protection in case stones or bullets came through the front windows. Walter's older brother, George Jr., was away, so Walter and his father were the only males at home.

For the rest of his life Walter would tell the story of this moment. It was the springboard for his life's purpose, and he would use it to create a mythology around himself. Sometimes the details would change, and sometimes the words in the dialogue would alter. But always there was a gun in his hands, given to him by his elder. "My father," he recalled in one letter written in 1926, "who is an intensely religious man and who had never permitted a firearm in our home until that day, stood with me at the front window."

When the mob appeared on Houston Street, Walter could see the white faces flickering in the flames of burning torches. A leader stepped forward in front of the family's picket fence. When this man spoke, Walter recognized his voice; he was the son of a local grocer, from a store where the Whites had shopped for years.

"That's where that nigger mail carrier lives!" the man yelled. "Let's burn it down! It's too nice for a nigger to live in!"

Walter remembered his father turning to him and speaking "in a voice as quiet as though he were asking me to pass him the sugar at the breakfast table."

"You're not to fire until they cross the edge of the lawn. When they get that close shoot and go on shooting as long as you can."

WALTER WAS TOO YOUNG to understand what was happening in Atlanta, but he was wise enough to know that he was going to come of age in a new and more terrifying America than he had imagined. The world around him was changing, and as a thirteen-year-old, he would soon be forced to find his place in it. One can see him looking in the mirror, exploring the contours of his face, his blond hair and blue eyes. He knew he had a choice: to live his future as a Black man or a white one.

His parents were of the last generation of African Americans who could speak of the slave era from memory. His father was from Augusta, Georgia, his mother from the cotton-mill town of LaGrange. When they wed and had their first child, they settled in Atlanta, where, as Walter put it, "Mother characteristically plunged in on her lifelong war against every vestige of dust and dirt within range."

At the time Walter was born in 1893, Atlanta was experiencing a relatively progressive racial harmony. African Americans could vote, and southern states had elected nearly two dozen of them to the US House of Representatives during the post–Civil War years, every one of them a Republican. As one of Walter's older sisters later recalled, "Then, in Atlanta, as in many other Southern cities, white and colored people often were neighbors . . . good neighbors, too."

Atlanta was the South's booming unofficial capital. It was here, on September 18, 1895 (when Walter was two), that Booker T. Washington gave his Atlanta Exposition Speech, which came to be known as the Atlanta Compromise. As head of the Tuskegee Institute and the leading representative of Black America, Booker T. Washington struck a deal with white leaders: in exchange for basic education and due process of the law, African Americans would submit to a system of white supremacy and learn skills and trades that would make them useful to society. At the time, it was heralded as the key to a harmonious racial future.

The prevailing notion at the time was that people in Atlanta were making too much money to have time to worry about race. The historian Thomas Martin wrote in 1902 of Atlanta, "The white man and the negro have lived together in this city more peacefully and in a better spirit than in any other city, in either the north or the south." When Walter walked Atlanta's streets as a boy, he was struck by the affluence. Three blocks from his home stood the city's first skyscraper, the recently completed Candler Building, named for the tycoon Asa Candler, founder of Coca-Cola. Nearby was Alonzo Herndon's Barber Shop, owned by Atlanta's wealthiest Black man, and the Gate City Drug Store, owned by the state's first Black licensed pharmacist. Walter's mother shopped at Rich's, the city's largest department store, where employees addressed her politely as Mrs. White.

The forces that would destroy the progressive South and spark the Atlanta riot of 1906 had already taken root, however. In rural communities across numerous states, an agrarian depression set in. At first it was rarely reported in newspapers, but as the depression grew worse, and as the upheaval threatened to encroach on cities like Atlanta, rural communities grew desperate. Some 90 percent of the roughly ten million Black Americans (about 9 percent of the nation's population) lived in southern states, where white and Black families were now thrown into competition for basic resources. "I call that particular change a revolution," wrote the Alabama historian William Garrott Brown, who lived through this depression. "And I would use a stronger term if there were one; for no other political movement — not that of 1776, not that of 1860–1861 — ever altered Southern life so profoundly."

At the same time, the US Supreme Court's *Plessy v. Ferguson* decision established the so-called "separate but equal" law, in 1896, when Walter was three. Homer Plessy was a mixed-race man who was removed from a whites-only train car. He sued, and the case rose to the Supreme Court, where justices created the separate but equal doctrine. *Plessy v. Ferguson* gave legal sanction to segregation. Soon there appeared separate public schools for whites and Blacks. Separate hospitals. Separate taxis, public halls, even cemeteries. In Atlanta the Grant Park Zoo, where Black families had taken their children for years, was suddenly off-limits.

Laws segregating streetcars appeared in North Carolina and Virginia in 1901 and in Louisiana in 1902. Soon the entire South followed. Walter's parents were so light-skinned, Atlanta's streetcars presented a challenge. When entering a streetcar, white people were to sit from the front to the rear, while Blacks were to sit from the rear to the front. Walter would remember seeing his parents wither under insults flung by strangers if they sat in the rear. But if they sat in the front, friends and acquaintances would accuse them bitterly of "passing."

As far north as the nation's capital, Whites Only and Colored Only signs appeared next to bathrooms, drinking fountains, and entrances to buildings. In courtrooms bailiffs used a "colored" Bible and a "white" Bible, depending on whose hand would be placed upon it. Many smaller stores and restaurants barred Black customers. At bigger department stores, Black people could no longer try on clothing or shoes; one had to draw an outline of a foot on a brown paper bag, so a clerk could choose the right shoe size, and all sales were final, because if a shoe was returned to a store after being worn by a "colored" person, it could no longer be sold to a white one.

The Jim Crow* era had arrived. The eminent twentieth-century Black attorney Charles Houston summed up this cultural shift in a memory from his childhood: "I recall the first time my mother was refused service in one of the local drug stores where the family had been dealing for many years. . . . For ten or fifteen years my mother had shopped in the city [Washington, DC] and weekly had closed her shopping at the soft

---

* As C. Vann Woodward notes in his book *The Strange Career of Jim Crow,* "The origin of the term 'Jim Crow' applied to Negroes is lost in obscurity. . . . The first example of 'Jim Crow law' listed by the *Dictionary of American English* is dated 1904. But the expression was used by writers in the 1890's." (Oxford: Oxford University Press, p. 7n)

drink counter in the drug store. The habit was assumed and the refusal came as a distinct shock."

As Walter later described the situation: "Compounded of fear, guilt, greed and humiliation, the South was developing a psychosis."

White supremacists had taken control, and the key to keeping it was the ballot box. "Those who have been determined to maintain a degraded status for the Negro," Walter later wrote, "have shrewdly concentrated on taking from him his most potent weapon and defense — the right to vote." The purging of the Black American — given the constitutional right by the Fifteenth Amendment in 1870 — began in Mississippi at a state political convention in 1890. "There is no use to equivocate or lie about the matter," James K. Vardaman (elected governor of Mississippi in 1903) explained. "Mississippi's constitutional convention of 1890 was held for no other purpose than to eliminate the nigger from politics." Variations of the "Mississippi Plan" appeared in South Carolina in 1895, Louisiana in 1898, North Carolina in 1900, Alabama in 1901, and Virginia in 1902. Loopholes and special clauses appeared on state registration forms (grandfather clauses, poll taxes, literacy tests), disenfranchising Black voters.

As Georgia came upon its 1906 gubernatorial election, it was still legal — though difficult, even dangerous — for African Americans to vote. And herein lay the real reason why the two brawling candidates for the governorship, Hoke Smith and Clark Howell, used their podiums and the newspapers they controlled to enflame white voters in Georgia. They aimed to "whiten" the vote and make it "pure," by law, and in promising to do so, they knew they could draw white voters to the ballot boxes.

"This is white man's country," Clark Howell said in an Atlanta speech in 1906, "and it must be governed by white men! . . . If the dark day should ever come in Georgia when the black man, blind to his own best interest, should seek to wrest the control of Georgia from the hands of the Anglo-Saxon, I'd rather stand at the polls . . . and man to man protect my own people with my life. . . . The clothing of the Negro with the right of suffrage was a crime against the people of the South."

• • •

FEW ATLANTANS were surprised by the race riots in 1906. On September 23, the second night of violence, when Walter and his father stood at their windows looking out at a torch-bearing mob intending to harm them, they knew the law would not protect them. Walter remembered the moment in these words:

> As a boy there in the darkness amid the tightening fright, I knew the inexplicable thing — that my skin was as white as the skin of those who were coming at me. The mob moved toward the lawn. I tried to aim my gun, wondering what it would feel like to kill a man. . . . In that instant there opened up within me a great awareness; I knew then who I was. I was a Negro. . . .

> . . . There were white men who said Negroes had no souls, and who proved it by the Bible. Some of these now were approaching us, intent upon burning our house.

Suddenly a volley of gunshots rang out. The mob hesitated. More shots pierced the silence, coming from the window of another home on the block. The mob quickly dispersed. George, Walter, and the rest of the White family were safe in their home — for the moment. It left Walter with an overwhelming sensation.

"After that night I knew I never wanted to be a white man," he concluded. "I knew which side I was on."

2

We claim for ourselves every right that belongs to a free-born
American — political, civil and social — and until we get these
rights, we shall never cease to protest and assail the ears of America
with the story of its shattered deeds toward us.
— W.E.B. Du Bois, cofounder of the NAACP

IN 1908 Georgia's new governor, Hoke Smith, fulfilled his promise to dis-
enfranchise Black voters, using state constitutional amendments. Some
forty years would pass before African Americans would effectively vote
in the state again.

That same year Walter White walked through the doors of Atlanta
University for the first time. He attended high school and college there
and found it to be a magical place. Founded by a Yale graduate student
in 1865, Atlanta University had been designed to look like it was plucked
out of New England, a green ivy oasis set atop Georgia's red clay. It was
built for the relatively small number of Black Georgians who could afford
its tuition — which George White barely could, for his son Walter. Atlanta
University's tuition-based high school was in fact the only high school education available to African Americans in the city.

At Atlanta University, Caucasian teachers dined with students and
treated them as equals. The school was a little bubble in the South, where
the race of the students was secondary to their social status. The term
ivory tower took on a special irony. "Atlanta University was a school you
couldn't just walk into and make it part of you," noted Walter's childhood

friend Lucy Rucker. "You had to have credentials and get into Atlanta University, and when you got in, you found why. Because everybody was high class out there. . . . They were just superior in every way."

Students nicknamed Walter "Fuzzy" because of his wavy blond hair. He was meticulously neat, and unable to resist a peek at himself if he passed a mirror. He liked expensive clothing so much so that his mother jokingly called him "Mr. Astor." His grades were good but not great. He played baseball and football and joined the debate team. In his spare time he got a job working as a bellhop in a tony Atlanta hotel for whites only, but was let go when his boss learned of his identity.

The summer before his senior year, while still living at home, Walter took a job selling policies for the Standard Life Insurance Company, one of the largest Black-owned businesses in the country, and it was at this point that he began venturing into rural Georgia on door-to-door sales excursions. "There I talked with and learned to know white and colored people of all classes," he later wrote. He grew accustomed to the dialects of Georgians in communities where people lived their entire lives without venturing far from home, and where school might mean a creaky church with a single teacher for an entire community. Walter grew to understand the suspicion of rural Black families when a stranger who looked white knocked on their doors. The familiarity with all these sensibilities would become crucial for survival when he began to live his undercover life, in just a couple years' time.

One Saturday in the fall of 1916 Walter learned that the Atlanta Board of Education had come up with a program to save money to build a new high school for white students by eliminating seventh grade for Black ones. Two years earlier, the board had eliminated eighth grade for Black students for a similar reason. No one had protested then, so it was assumed that no one would protest now. The next day, a Sunday afternoon, in the offices at Standard Life, Walter sat with his colleagues talking bitterly about the news. "Despair and consternation had descended on Negro Atlanta," he remembered.

To Walter and his friends, the hypocrisy seemed so blatant. Atlanta's Black population made up a third of the city — 185,000 people — and these Atlantans were subject to the same tax code as white people. The US Supreme Court's *Plessy v. Ferguson* decision had established the separate but equal doctrine. While Walter had no access to statistics on tax spending on public schools,* he did not need them to know that public schools could not be "equal" when white public high schools existed and Black ones did not. The situation seemed, as Walter put it, "hopeless."

One of his colleagues, a man named Harry Pace, made a suggestion: they should write to the National Association for the Advancement of Colored People, known as the NAACP.

At the time, the NAACP was a nascent organization headquartered in New York City, a metropolis a thousand miles away that, for Walter and his friends, might have existed on the moon. The only reason Walter and his group probably knew of the NAACP was because W.E.B. Du Bois, the famous writer and educator, edited the association's magazine, *The Crisis*. Du Bois was the first Black American to earn a PhD at Harvard. He was the author of the landmark 1903 book *The Souls of Black Folk*. And he was also a former faculty member at Atlanta University.

On February 3, 1917, Walter sent an application for an NAACP branch, along with a cover letter. "There are so many things that need correction here in Atlanta that it is hard to decide just what to fight first," he wrote. "But this quandary was settled for us by word that has come to us that the city board of education is planning to take away the seventh grade from the colored public schools." Walter and his friends were ready for a fight. "If this is done," he wrote, "they will have to do so, figuratively speaking, 'over the bodies' of the Atlanta branch of the NAACP."

Within days the NAACP national office responded with a promise to send a representative to help. The association also suggested that the At-

---

* According to a 1967 report by Professor Edgar A. Toppin of Virginia State University, counties in Georgia in 1910 where African Americans constituted 75 percent or more of the population spent an average of $19.23 per white student and $1.61 per Black student. According to this same report, during 1917, the year Walter White took up the fight for Atlanta's seventh grade, white teachers in Georgia earned an average of $69.78 per month, compared with Black teachers' $32.42.

lanta activists form an emergency committee to take on the school board, which they did. Walter was not invited because he was considered "too young and too hot-headed," as he recalled. On February 17, 1917, the committee went before the school board and presented a case to save the seventh grade. The hearing turned into a dramatic debate between a city councilman, who was against abolishing seventh grade for Black students ("I want to plead guilty . . . every word spoken by these men is true . . . we have not given them a square deal"), and Atlanta's mayor, who was *for* abolishing seventh grade ("I do not wish to plead guilty. Let us not give way to hysteria, but look at this matter in a sane manner").

The school board decided to save seventh grade for the time being. Walter was so excited that he wrote to NAACP headquarters: "If the NAACP does no more, it has earned its right for existence."

ROUGHLY A MONTH LATER, in March 1917, in an auditorium inside the Odd Fellows Building on Auburn Avenue, the skeleton crew of what was soon to be Atlanta's pioneering NAACP branch held its first rally. Walter was the force and energy behind the meeting. He remembered the place being "so packed with eager-faced Negroes and even a few whites that we had difficulty wedging the platform party [the speakers] through the crowd to enter the auditorium."

Onto the stage walked the night's main attraction: James Weldon Johnson, standing tall and erect in an immaculate suit. For Walter, it was like witnessing a mythical figure appear in the flesh. Walter would have first heard James Weldon Johnson's name as a child, as Johnson and his brother, J. Rosamond Johnson, had written "Lift Every Voice and Sing," the song that had become known as the "Negro national anthem," in 1900. Johnson was second only to W.E.B. Du Bois among the small number of Black intellectuals with a national presence. He was an editor and writer at a major Black newspaper, the *New York Age*. He had written the influential novel *The Autobiography of an Ex-Colored Man*. He was a renowned poet, a former diplomat, an educator — and the NAACP's field secretary, whose job it was to help groups open new branches and recruit members.

When Johnson stood onstage that night, against a backdrop of advertisements for local Black-owned businesses (the Gate City Drug Store, the Standard Life Insurance Company of Atlanta), he held his audience captive. In the crowd, amidst lawyers, doctors, college professors, bankers, and public school teachers, Walter sat next to Dr. John Hope, the president of Morehouse College — a Black men's liberal arts college in Atlanta. Because Walter was the organizing force behind this rally, he was called upon to say a few words. Turning to Dr. Hope, he nervously asked what he should say.

"Tell them about the NAACP," Dr. Hope answered.

Walter walked onto the stage and launched into an impromptu speech. "We have got to show these white people that we aren't going to stand being pushed around any longer," he shouted, and because most in the crowd knew him, few saw the irony of a man who appeared Caucasian sharing such a sentiment. "As Patrick Henry said, so must we say, 'Give me liberty, or give me death!'"

Walter was shocked by the blaze of applause. He found that he liked the sound of it.

Before leaving Atlanta, Johnson came to Walter's home and met his parents, George and Madeline White. He stayed to sample Madeline's cooking, and throughout the dinner, his eyes kept turning to Walter. Later, after leaving Atlanta, Johnson recorded his thoughts.

"From the whole group," he remembered, "a very young man who acted as secretary of the conference became singled out in my mind. I saw him several times and was impressed with the degree of mental and physical energy he seemed to be able to bring into play and center on the job in hand. I did not need to guess that the representative conference and the extraordinary mass meeting were largely results of his efforts. I left Atlanta having made a strong mental note of him."

THE ATLANTA BRANCH of the NAACP was born in April 1917, and Walter was a charter member. It was a springtime dominated by news of war in Europe. The Germans, Russians, French, British, and Austro-Hungarians were fighting to the death, employing new methods of killing, such as armed flying machines, submarines, bombing dirigibles, and poison gases. However, in the United States, a new domestic war was in the making, one that would never be declared in any official sense but would nonetheless make the bloodiest mark on the country since 1865.

In Washington, DC, Woodrow Wilson's administration was in the process of segregating the machinery of federal government. Separate bathrooms, separate cafeterias, separate drinking fountains. When Wilson — who came from the former slave state of Virginia — was campaigning for the presidency in 1912, he had promised the "colored people" that "they may count upon me for absolute fair dealing." Upon his election, he fired most of the small number of African American federal employees who had been hired under Theodore Roosevelt. Years earlier, when Wilson was a Princeton University academic, he had written a book called *Division and Reunion, 1829–1889,* and in it he had predicted the "inevitable ascendancy of the whites." Now that movement was happening, and he himself was a progenitor.

In 1915, Wilson became the first president to watch a movie in the White House, and that movie was about to light a racial firestorm. *The Birth of a Nation* made its debut on February 8, 1915, in Los Angeles, to a packed house. Directed by D. W. Griffith, the film was based on the hugely popular Thomas Dixon novel *The Clansman,* and told a tale of the Civil War and Reconstruction, portraying Black men as animal-like creatures incapable of controlling their lust for white women. The Ku Klux Klan — a group that originally formed at the end of the Civil War but had since faded away — was depicted as a vigilante group that saves the day and brings order to the white South in the face of racially charged chaos.

The Birth of a Nation became the first ever movie blockbuster; it was hugely influential in shaping a new image of the Ku Klux Klan for millions of white Americans. When Wilson saw the movie in the White House's East Room, he was awed. He would be quoted countless times saying, "It is like writing history with lightning, and my only regret is that it is all so terribly true," although biographers have challenged the veracity of the quote. Atlanta turned out in force for *The Birth of a Nation.* A preacher named William J. Simmons took a particular liking to it. On Thanksgiving night in 1915, not long after seeing *The Birth of a Nation,* Simmons organized a white supremacist pilgrimage to the top of Stone Mountain, an eight-hundred-foot rock dome northeast of downtown Atlanta. Dressed in the white robes and hoods of the original KKK, Simmons and his followers declared themselves the founders of a new Ku Klux Klan.

Atop Stone Mountain, they burned a cross under the moonlight in a scene that might have come right out of *The Birth of a Nation*. The *Atlanta Constitution* reported, "The exercises were held by fifteen klansmen who gathered at the behest of their chieftain, W. J. Simmons, and marked the foundation of the invisible empire, Knights of the Ku Klux Klan."

News of the new KKK spread, and the secret society's influence began to creep across the white South, into its rural communities, its churches, police departments, and boards of education. By the time Walter and his friends were fighting to save the seventh grade in Atlanta, the new KKK had become a rising social force.

A month after the Atlanta NAACP branch formed in 1917, a race massacre in East Saint Louis, Illinois, shocked the country. Rioting over the course of weeks left dozens of Black Americans dead in the streets. The exact number killed has never been known. In response, James Weldon Johnson organized a historic protest in New York that came to be known as the Silent Parade. It was a tour de force of visual power: some ten thousand Black people marching in perfect rows, the women and children dressed in white, the men in black suits — all perfectly silent as they marched. Children held signs reading MOTHER, DO LYNCHERS GO TO HEAVEN? Men held signs reading, TREAT US THAT WE MAY LOVE OUR COUNTRY. The Silent Parade planted the NAACP's seed in the American consciousness. It was the first time the crusading organization made national news.

Two cultural forces were organizing and crystalizing their power at the same time, destined to become ruthless rivals: the NAACP versus the KKK.

On April 2, 1917, the same month that the Atlanta branch of the NAACP formed, Woodrow Wilson asked Congress for a declaration of war against Germany. It would be, he said in his famous speech, "a war to make the world safe for Democracy." Walter was rejected by the draft board after his physical; later he came to believe that the rejection was because he identified as African American, and thus the army did not want him. He would not see the Great War in Europe firsthand, but his life was about to take an unexpected turn nevertheless. On October 7, 1917, he received a letter from James Weldon Johnson, written in elegant longhand on plain monogrammed stationery.

"My dear Mr. White," it began. "I want to know if I might use your name as a candidate for a responsible, executive position with the association. The position would necessitate your living in New York City. The salary would, I am confident, be adequate. I hope you will give this favorable consideration; for I feel that it is something that would give any young man of the race an unsurpassable opportunity for good work and a bright future. Sincerely yours, James W. Johnson."

WALTER WAS TWENTY-FOUR AND AT A CROSSROADS. He had recently been promoted to cashier at Standard Life, a good job at an excellent company, with the promise of a future and a salary that could support a young family. He feared the cost of living in New York City. He wrote to Johnson on October 10, 1917.

"You realize my position here and my chances for advancement," Walter wrote. He had a lot of questions about the job and the finances.

Johnson lobbied hard. "I made some inquiries about the cost of living," he responded a few days later. "You can get a room with a very nice family and your board, which in New York means breakfast and dinner, for thirty-five dollars a month. . . . Thirty-five dollars for board and lodging in New York is very, very reasonable." The job title would be assistant secretary. "In the absence of the Secretary," Johnson wrote, "he [the assistant secretary] will be in charge of the main office. The Board of Directors have directed me to offer you this position at a salary of twelve hundred dollars a year."

Walter would have to take a pay cut to move to Manhattan. In discussions at the family table on Houston Street, his mother was adamant that he reject the offer, that he should never live in that "Sodom and Gomorrah" up north. Walter had been raised in a home where alcohol was not permitted, nor tobacco, nor books that were not at least twenty-five-years old. In New York, Madeline White was sure, lecherous characters and evil temptations lurked in every alley.

When Walter sought his father's advice, George White suggested they go on a horse-and-buggy ride together. As the horse clip-clopped through Atlanta, Walter could sense his father's ambivalence. Clearly George knew his son was no normal young man, that Walter was ambitious, inordinately intelligent, and, just possibly, capable of great things. For George, God's omnipotence was unquestioned, and surely he thought that the Lord's will was in play.

"Your mother and I have given you the best education we can afford," George said, "and a good Christian home training. Fortunately, it is better than most colored children have had. Now it is your duty to pass on what you have been given by helping others less fortunate to get a chance in life. I don't want to see you go away. I'll miss you. But remember, God will be using your heart and brains to do His will. You'll be misunderstood and criticized when you fight so difficult a battle as that created by the race problem. But decide, with the help of God, what's right and don't falter or turn back."

Walter wrote his acceptance letter to Johnson on January 31, 1918. Soon he was on a swaying train out of Atlanta, the only home he had ever known, headed for New York City.

3

It was written I should be loyal to the nightmare of my choice.
—Joseph Conrad, *Heart of Darkness*

WALTER ARRIVED ON MANHATTAN ISLAND on a bone-chilling February day in 1918. Nothing could prepare him for his first sight of Harlem. James Weldon Johnson, forty-six years old at the time (nearly twice Walter's age), was by his side.

"Indeed," Johnson said in describing Harlem, "it is Mecca for the sightseer, the pleasure-seeker, the curious, the adventurous, the enterprising, the ambitious, and the talented of the Negro world." It was "a black city located in the heart of white Manhattan, and containing more Negroes to the square mile than any other spot on earth. It strikes the uninformed observer as a phenomenon, a miracle straight out of the skies."

Not only was Harlem so dark-complexioned, but it had never been so crowded. Walter was part of what would later be called the Great Migration — masses of predominantly Black Americans leaving the South for industrial northern cities and the jobs they offered. Starting in roughly 1916, hundreds of thousands of African Americans departed their homes in Georgia, Alabama, Mississippi, and Louisiana, landing in Detroit (home of the colossal auto industry), Pittsburgh (steel), Chicago (stockyards and slaughterhouses), Cleveland (steel), Akron, Ohio (tire factories), Saint Louis (brick mills), and most of all, New York (anything goes). For some it was because of money. Others were fleeing Jim Crow.

Walter was one of roughly 235,000 Black Americans who arrived from the South in New York City between 1910 and 1930. He was the only one, however, to have the lucky fortune to move to Harlem as the protégé of James Weldon Johnson, who broke the ice by insisting that Walter call him Jim.

On that first day, Johnson escorted Walter to the boardinghouse that would be his new home. The landlady was instantly inviting, and a master at the stove. She was a retired caterer and could make ninety-two different soups; Walter would never decide which he liked most. The next morning, Johnson ushered him into the NAACP offices for the first time. Headquarters was located many blocks south of Harlem, at 70 Fifth Avenue, just north of Fourteenth Street, at the northern edge of Greenwich Village.

Upon entering, Walter found the space not so different from where he had worked at Standard Life in Atlanta. Jingling telephones, typewriter keys hammering, the smell of stale tobacco smoke. But the more he looked around, the more he realized this office was no ordinary place at all. On the wall was a map of the United States like one that might be found in any office or classroom, only this one had a pin marking every spot where a person had been lynched in recent years.

Walter shook the hand of John Shillady, the new executive secretary (the term the NAACP used for CEO). Shillady — a white Irish American, handsome and slightly portly — had a background in social work and had recently joined the staff, having come from the Charities Department of Westchester County. He had gray eyes, graying hair, and an air of tragedy about him. He and his wife had recently lost two of their children. Shillady was so haunted by this loss that he never spoke of it, and nowhere is it recorded how his children met their demise. He was a man preordained for tragedy, unaware of another terrible fate that would meet him in just one year's time.

Walter and his mentor, James Weldon Johnson, struck up a routine of lunching most days at the nearby Horn & Hardart automat, a self-service lunch counter that was essentially a giant vending machine. No Whites Only signs here; everyone sat shoulder to shoulder eating cheap fare with hot coffee. After, Johnson and Walter browsed at nearby Brentano's bookstore in Greenwich Village. "All the sales clerks knew and admired Jim," Walter remembered. "Thus began for me a liberal education in contemporary literature, as Jim either purchased for me or recommended my buying books of fiction, poetry, and history and discussion of social problems which he thought would be of permanent value."

Johnson also liked to talk to his new protégé about leadership. He was full of maxims that sounded almost biblical, such as, "Of the real leader the people some day become aware, and say: This man serves well, let us follow him." Johnson believed that leadership was best imagined as two forces pulling against each other: radicalism that motivated people with fresh ideas, and conservatism, to balance the radicalism with rational decision making.

Meanwhile, Walter tried to settle into the rhythm of the teeming metropolis. For the unaccustomed, New York threw the nervous system into a state of agitation, all the senses alive to the overload of input. As the poet Edna St. Vincent Millay wrote around this time, "In New York you can *see* the noise!" Everywhere Walter's eyes turned, they focused on something he had never seen before: rows of concrete skyscrapers, elevated subway trains, newspaper balls blowing like tumbleweeds over frozen pavement. Motorcar traffic, New York cops on horseback. So many languages and skin colors. In some sections of the city, every vertical surface screamed out some consumer product that could be had for a low, low price: Stroh's beer, Chesterfield cigarettes, Hohner harmonicas, shirt collars, boot polishes, frankfurters, live shows of all kinds. There was a feeling on these streets like at any moment anything could happen: assignation, fisticuffs, the apocalypse.

In the office Walter set himself to work at his desk, tapping out correspondence and filling ashtrays. In the days before email, when long-distance phone calls racked up heady bills and most NAACP branches had no phones anyway, the typewriter was the singular weapon in organizing a national movement. One had to stay focused and type fast. Walter was beginning ambitiously, learning what this new organization was about, how it functioned, and how he could begin to climb its ranks.

• • •

THE ASSOCIATION WAS NINE YEARS OLD when Walter arrived. John Shillady and James Weldon Johnson ran the office, and the entire paid staff consisted of four others, not including Walter — a stenographer named Richetta Randolph, bookkeeper Frank Turner, and two clerical workers. From a neighboring office, W.E.B. Du Bois edited the magazine, *The Crisis,* independent from the rest. Caustic and well aware of his monumental status, Du Bois was more than a little intimidating. The board of directors was a guiding group that met monthly. Though the entirety of the NAACP numbered so few, it was a constellation of brilliant, larger-than-life crusaders.

While the association was technically founded in 1909, its genesis harkened back four years earlier to a 1905 conference near Niagara Falls, organized by Du Bois. The so-called Niagara Movement was created to chart a new course for Black America, away from Booker T. Washington's leadership and his Atlanta Compromise. While Washington advocated for education, vocation, and submission to the white elite, Du Bois wanted equality and power — everything that was promised to all Americans in the nation's founding documents.

The Declaration of Independence declared that "all men are created equal." The Constitution and the Bill of Rights promised due process of law, equal voting rights, and equal opportunity for all Americans. The Niagara Movement attempted to put a spotlight on America as it had been imagined by the Founding Fathers and in the founding documents and the reality of the America that actually existed — and then to destroy the chasm that lay between.

From the Niagara Movement sprang a series of meetings and resolutions that led to the founding of the National Association for the Advancement of Colored People, in New York City. None of the founders liked the name — even the acronym felt too long. But no one could think of a better one.

The NAACP's board of directors was entirely white. There was Moorfield Storey, the towering legal mastermind of Boston, who served as president of the board. And New York *Evening Post* publisher Oswald Garrison Villard, the grandson of William Lloyd Garrison, a prominent

Civil War–era abolitionist. "We were a group of primarily white people," recorded a founding board member, Mary White Ovington, "who felt that while the Negro would aid in the [group's] work, whites who were largely responsible for conditions and who controlled the bulk of the nation's wealth ought to finance the movement."

From the start, the founders knew they were attempting to do something that had never been done. Du Bois explained in a letter to a friend: "No organization like ours ever succeeded in America; either it became a group of white philanthropists 'helping' the Negro like the Anti-Slavery societies; or it became a group of colored folk freezing out their white coworkers by insolence and distrust. Everything tends to break along the color line. . . .

"How can this be changed?" Du Bois continued. "By changing it. By trusting black men with power."

One thing was missing: money. "We were desperately poor," Ovington recorded.

In November 1910 Du Bois launched the NAACP's "organ" — its magazine. Issue number one of *The Crisis* spelled out its mission on its editorial page: "The object of this publication is to set forth those facts and arguments which show the danger of race prejudice, particularly as manifested today toward colored people. It takes its aim from the fact that the editors believe that this is a critical time in the history of the advancement of men."

By the time Walter White arrived early in 1918, the NAACP consisted of seventy-six branches spread out mostly on the East Coast, with 8,490 members, and it had moved into its current headquarters on the sixth floor at 70 Fifth Avenue. When Walter was introduced to the board members, two stood out. Mary White Ovington was "the Fighting Saint," as Walter would come to call her. Born into a wealthy family in Brooklyn, Ovington was a fifty-two-year-old suffragist who had been fighting for civil rights ever since she heard Frederick Douglass speak in a church before Walter was born. A journalist and book author, she had never married. Activism was her spouse.

Then there was Joel Spingarn, forty-three, who was tremendously combative for a man with so slight a build. Spingarn had spent his early career as the Jewish wunderkind of Columbia University's comparative literature department, and later as its chair. A tireless explorer of the intellectual fringe, his work crossed into horticulture, progressive politics, and verse writing. He was forced out of Columbia in 1910 because of his quick temper. Soon after, he began to devote his time to the NAACP. Like Ovington, Spingarn was a born activist. "Virtue is never solitary," he wrote. "It takes part in the conflicts of the world."

For a team of race crusaders, the NAACP's inner circle was decidedly bookish. The white board members were almost all accomplished literary figures. Du Bois and Johnson were the two most heralded writers of their race. It remained to be seen if Walter would find a home in this ferociously ambitious crowd. All were eager to find out.

ON THE MORNING of February 13, 1918 — Walter's thirteenth day in New York — he was riding a bus with Johnson to the office, a routine the two now shared. They came across a newspaper story about the murder of a Black man in a place called Estill Springs, Tennessee. "A mob of more than 1,500 people burned Jim McIlherron, a negro, at the stake there tonight," the *New York Times* reported that morning. The story got more appalling. The *Times* reported that McIlherron was believed to have shot and killed two white men, and that "hot irons were applied to his body for about ten minutes in an effort to get him to make a confession." His slaying had occurred the day before, on Abraham Lincoln's birthday.

In the office, Walter sat discussing the McIlherron case with Johnson and Shillady. They set in motion the usual NAACP machinery when lynchings occurred. Shillady telegrammed Tennessee governor T. C. Rye in Nashville: THOUSANDS OF COLORED MEN IN YOUR STATE AND THE NATION NOW SERVING THEIR COUNTRY IN THE BATTLE FOR DEMOCRACY AWAIT TENNESSEE'S ANSWER TO THE APPEAL FOR JUSTICE AT HOME.

Shillady telegrammed President Wilson in the White House:
SPEAKING IN BEHALF OF MILLIONS OF AMERICANS, WE RESPECTFULLY CALL YOUR ATTENTION TO THE HORRIBLE CRIME AT ESTILL

SPRINGS, TENN. . . . YOU HAVE SPOKEN OUT SO NOBLY AGAINST
GERMAN CRIMES IN BELGIUM AND ON THE HIGH SEAS THAT WE
BEG OF YOU TO BREAK YOUR SILENCE AND DENOUNCE PROPERLY
THESE TERRIBLE MOB ACTS WHICH COVER US WITH SHAME AND
HUMILIATION.

This telegram never made it to Wilson's office. However, US assistant
attorney general William C. Fitts responded to Shillady: "Under the decisions of the Supreme Court of the United States, the Federal Government
has absolutely no jurisdiction over matters of this kind." Governor Rye
of Tennessee wrote Shillady to say that he could take no action "without
being requested so to do by the local officers or court officers."

The only law enforcement in Estill Springs lay in the hands of the local
officers — and them alone. As far as Johnson and Shillady could remember, they could never recall a single instance in which anyone was indicted for these kinds of crimes.

Walter had an idea. What if he were to visit this town? What if he were
to pose as a white man and personally dig out the facts? "I asked permission to go to the scene to make a first-hand investigation," he remembered.

The NAACP had tried something like this before. After a lynching in
Coatesville, Pennsylvania, a few years earlier, the association had hired
the Burns Detective Agency to obtain the facts. But the plot did not go as
planned. As Ovington remembered, two undercover detectives, "heavy-
jowled and strikingly stupid looking, opened a restaurant in Coatesville
hoping to secure evidence from the talk of their patrons." They came up
with nothing but a large bill for their services.

Walter, however, was on the NAACP's staff. There would be no bill.
His ability to "pass" offered special benefits. Not only could he travel posing as a white man, but he was from the South. He knew the customs,
the dialects, of both white and Black communities, and could penetrate
both. The danger in white communities would be high. If his identity was
discovered, he would almost certainly face torture and a violent death.
But Walter was game; he was the NAACP's new kid, and this was a way
he could prove himself. Johnson opposed the plan, fearing for Walter's

safety. "Eventually, however, he gave reluctant consent," Walter remembered, "and thus I started a phase of work for the Association which neither it nor I had contemplated when I was employed."

Soon Walter was on a train barreling out of Grand Central Terminal. "My self-confidence steadily declined and my fear rose on the train ride," he recalled. "It was my first planned attempt to pass."

AS THE TRAIN CAR SWAYED AND THE TRACKS RATTLED, Walter used the long hours to dream up his undercover persona while passengers around him read the latest war news in the papers. The Germans had sunk eight ships in the Strait of Dover, close to British shores. American troops were heavily engaged on the western front, where casualties were high. When Walter's train reached the Mason-Dixon Line, Black passengers had to move to segregated Jim Crow train cars; Walter almost certainly did not.

On the evening of February 17, 1918, he pulled into Chattanooga's Union Depot on the Tennessee River and carried his small suitcase to the nearby Hotel Patten, where he passed as a white man and checked in. Staying at the Patten surely stretched his wallet, as it was called "the finest hotel in the south" and the "Million Dollar Hotel" when it had opened ten years earlier. Walter was back on a train at 5:30 the next morning.

When he arrived at the depot in Estill Springs, he carried his suitcase into town, which was nothing more than a row of storefronts lining a single side of a main unpaved street three blocks long, the buildings leaning shoulder to shoulder as if holding one another up. Only two hundred people lived in Estill Springs, and the town was surrounded by rivers. This place was a far ride from anywhere, and a telephone or a newspaper would be hard to find. It was cut off from the outside world.

Walter walked the main drag, making mental notes: "There is one bank, the Bank of Estill Springs, purely local in nature; a barber shop, a drug store and five general merchandise stores of the type indigenous to small rural communities in the South." Six churches stood downtown, four for white congregants, two for Black. The locals seemed to have more appetite for God than for food; the only butcher shop was closed, out of business. In the windows of many homes, residents had placed the logo of the National Food Conservation Commission, an organization formed to help get food overseas to keep American soldiers fed. Perhaps it was nerves, but Walter sensed an energy in the air, what he described as "very great excitement."

The only hotel, the Goddard House, was across the street from the train depot. Walter walked under the weather-beaten sign and through the door, where he found a lanky white hotel clerk behind a desk. His skin appeared to be strangely discolored. Walter checked into a room, left his suitcase behind, and headed back outside to begin his investigation. His first stop was a country store on the main drag. He opened the door and found a small group of white men lounging inside. When they asked who he was, he told them that he was a traveling salesman with the Exelento Medicine Company. He was selling a hair-straightening product but was all out at the moment. So he had plenty of time to kill.

These men reminded Walter of people he had met while traveling through rural Georgia selling insurance policies. They were "leisurely of manner and slow of speech and comprehension," he recalled. When he brought up the recent troubles, they were more than happy to talk. They had no reason to fear any consequences for their statements or actions in this small community. "Even when they boasted and began to reveal far more than they realized as to the actual participants [of the killing]," Walter remembered, "I deliberately intimated that I had known of much more exciting lynchings than that of McIlherron."

Walter realized that he had walked into a hornet's nest. He believed he was now among the killers themselves. This was his first undercover investigation, and he learned a lesson that would prove its worth time and again over the years: "Nothing contributes so much to the continued life of an investigator of lynchings and his tranquil possession of all his limbs as the obtuseness of the lynchers themselves. Like most boastful people who practice direct action when it involves no personal risk, they just can't help talk about their deeds to any person who manifests even the slightest interest in them."

4

Lynch (v): To punish (a person) without legal process or authority, especially by hanging, for a perceived offense or as an act of bigotry.
—*American Heritage Dictionary*

ON FRIDAY, February 8, ten days before Walter arrived in Estill Springs, an African American man known locally as Jim McIlherron walked into a store and purchased fifteen cents' worth of candy. McIlherron lived in this town with his parents and several siblings, and the family had a reputation. The McIlherrons were landowners and had become relatively wealthy by local standards — wealthier than some of their white neighbors, which did not make them popular. Jim McIlherron in particular was known as a proud figure who did not take kindly to Jim Crow customs, to being treated as a second-class citizen. He was "known to be a fighter and the possessor of an automatic revolver," according to Walter's subsequent reporting. He was "a dangerous man to bother with."

At roughly 5 p.m., in front of Tate & Dickens's store on Estill Springs' main strip, McIlherron encountered three white men: Pierce Rogers, Frank Tigert, and Jesse Tigert. Rogers and the Tigert brothers yelled an insult, and McIlherron, still holding his candy, stopped in his tracks. "At this point," according to Walter's reporting, "the Negro turned and asked if they were talking about him." One of the white men ran into Tate & Dickens's store, and McIlherron, believing there was about to be a fight, drew his revolver.

Six shots later, two white men were dead and a third wounded. McIlherron was gone.

When news of the shootings spread, a group of local white men set out with bloodhounds. On a tip, the posse ended up at the home of a Black preacher named Lych, believing that Lych had aided McIlherron in his getaway. Two men from the posse stepped forward and confronted the preacher, demanding information on McIlherron's whereabouts. Lych wasn't talking. "One of them pointed his gun at the preacher and pulled the trigger," according to Walter's reporting. The gun did not go off. The preacher jumped forward and grabbed for the gun. A fight to the death lasted just seconds, as one of the mob wrestled the gun clear and fired a shot through the preacher's chest, killing him instantly.

It took three days for the bloodhounds to locate McIlherron, who was hiding in a barn near the Collins River in McMinnville, forty miles northeast of Estill Springs. The posse — a hundred strong at this point — surrounded the barn and opened fire. McIlherron fired back but was overwhelmed by a storm of bullets. He took one in his eyeball and two in his body. The posse penetrated the barn, took the wounded man, and carried him to the local station, boarding train number 5 back to Estill Springs, where they arrived at 6:30 p.m. on February 12.

By this time, some fifteen hundred to two thousand people had poured into this town of two hundred inhabitants, in autos, buggies, on horseback, and by foot. The crowd was a testament to how well organized this event was, to get all those people out there from the surrounding areas, given how few telephones existed in rural Tennessee at this time. The sister of one of the men slain by McIlherron in front of Tate & Dickens's store became "frantic," according to Walter's reporting, pleading with the mob "to let her kill the Negro." McIlherron — still conscious — found himself chained to a hickory tree and bleeding from his wounds.

In the presence of local police officers, McIlherron gave a tortured confession. "A wide iron bar, red-hot, was placed on the right side of his neck," Walter wrote. "When McIlherron drew his head away, another bar was placed on the left side." After McIlherron confessed, members of the mob unsexed him. Then the fire was lit, a few feet from the victim.

The higher the flames reached, the more frenzied the crowd grew. Some from the back of the crowd squeezed through to the front for a better view, as members of the mob pushed the fire closer to McIlherron, until it was at his feet. Mothers with their children, men and women, old and young — they watched McIlherron slowly roast. "The statements of onlookers are to the effect that throughout the whole burning Jim McIlherron never cringed and never once begged for mercy," Walter wrote. Some were quiet while others spit and shouted epithets at the victim, until one of the mob came forward and doused him with fuel, igniting him completely.

All of this information Walter managed to gather in a single day of sleuthing. Exhausted, he returned to his room at the Goddard House that night and, on hotel stationery, wrote a letter to John Shillady.

"I got all the information I needed," he wrote. "By the way, I am a salesman for the Exelento Medicine Company of Atlanta selling hair straightener." He promised to deliver his full report soon, and to return to New York as fast as he could.

A FEW DAYS AFTER THE IMMOLATION of Jim McIlherron, James Weldon Johnson stepped through the door of the Oval Office, becoming the first NAACP official to visit the president of the United States in the White House. Johnson arrived with three other African American activists from Harlem. President Wilson had met with few members of the Black community during his administration, and Johnson knew he had one shot to make this meeting count. He had come on a specific mission.

A year earlier, a fight between members of the all-Black Twenty-Fourth Infantry Regiment and members of the Houston Police Department at Camp Logan in Texas had resulted in the mutiny of dozens of soldiers. Rioting left fifteen white civilians, five white police officers, and four of the Black soldiers dead. The army had sentenced thirteen mutineers — all Black men — to the gallows and had hung them in predawn darkness without any official review of their cases. Five others had been sentenced to death and were awaiting their hangings. Johnson came with a petition carrying twelve thousand signatures, requesting that these five lives be spared. The president sat in a chair in front of his desk, while Johnson and his fellow crusaders formed a semicircle around him. Johnson stood when he spoke.

"We come as a delegation from the New York branch of the National Association for the Advancement of Colored People, representing twelve thousand signers to this petition which we have the honor to lay before you," Johnson began. He asked for "executive clemency," claiming that the "bravery and loyalty of our Negro soldiery in every crisis of the nation give us the right to make this request."

Johnson believed that the condemned men deserved a trial, that to hang them without one was a violation of their rights. "The hanging of thirteen men without the opportunity of appeal to the Secretary of War or to their Commander-in-Chief, the President of the United States," Johnson argued, "was punishment so drastic and so unusual in the history of the nation that the execution of additional members of the Twenty-Fourth Infantry would to the colored people of the country savor of vengeance rather than justice."

Johnson finished and took his seat. He asked the president if he had heard about the story of James McIlherron. "We were surprised that he had not heard of the burning at Estill Springs," Johnson remembered. "He asked us to give him the facts about it; and declared that it was hard for him to think that such a thing could have taken place in the United States." Johnson pleaded with the president to make a statement against mob lynching, and while Wilson demurred, saying he did not believe any such statement would do any good, he promised to "seek an opportunity."

THE CRISIS published Walter's report on the McIlherron case in the May 1918 issue under the title "The Burning of Jim McIlherron: An N.A.A.C.P. Investigation." The story made its way through the mail to NAACP branches in cities and rural backwaters. Governor Rye of Tennessee made no public statement condemning the killers. But the outcry could be heard in small-town newspaper editorials and in the fighting words of branch members and organizers. "The facts I uncovered created a modest sensation," Walter later wrote. The anger was moving people to organize. The energy could be felt in the mail arriving at 70 Fifth Avenue.

"Your organization is a fighting as well as an enlightening force," wrote Henry Mims, chairman of the Houston branch. "The Negro down here to whom you must tie to is the Negro who is willing to fight for his rights. I mean fight in the courts, in the press, in the pulpit, in vigorous protest and in every conceivable way to bring about results."

"I want you to know that I will devote some time in getting the local association on its feet," wrote Oscar W. Baker, an attorney out of Bay City, Michigan. "I want to help as much as I can in the great work with which you are connected. . . . There is nothing [that] beats organization." This writer prophetically added, "I think the time has now arrived."

Walter's role at the NAACP was expanding beyond what anyone had planned. Hired to be an assistant in the New York headquarters, he was spending almost all his time on the road in the South — speaking in lecture halls, organizing branches, moving from town to town. Due to the publicity of his McIlherron report, his lectures drew teeming crowds. Local branches flooded their towns with flyers announcing his arrival: "Mass Meeting . . . N.A.A.C.P. . . . Hear Mr. Walter F. White of New York City . . . You are invited . . . Bring a friend . . ."

He spoke to a capacity crowd in James Weldon Johnson's hometown of Jacksonville, Florida. "Splendid meeting [in Jacksonville] Sunday," he wrote Shillady afterward. Days later he crossed into Louisiana, where he made "the best speech I have made," he reported, even though he was ill with food poisoning. "In New Orleans I had one of the best meetings I ever had," he wrote Johnson. "The meeting was held in the Pythian Temple Theater, which is said to hold 1,200 people and not a seat was vacant." In anticipation of Walter's swing through North Carolina, Johnson wrote the branch secretary in Raleigh: "Mr. Walter F. White, Assistant Secretary of the Association, is making a trip through the south . . . I am writing to ask that the officers and the executive committee get together and arrange for a large meeting. . . . The work which is taking Mr. White south is one of great importance."

Having learned a few things from his mentor, Walter found he could command an audience. He spoke with rhythm and cadence, and his message was militant. America was at war, he told his audiences. Some four hundred thousand Black Americans were in uniform, serving their country, in some cases giving their lives for the cause of justice and democracy abroad. Now was the time to demand justice and democracy at home. If a Black man could be drafted, if he could be made to die for his country, should he not be allowed to sit next to a white person on a bus?

Timing was of the essence, Walter urged his crowds. "The Negro race is today in possession of the greatest opportunity that he has ever known since emancipation."

As Walter traveled, a devastating influenza pandemic spread, and he found he had to cancel some meetings. Hospitals were full, and entire communities felt the grip of fear tightening around them. Reports of breakouts were filing into New York headquarters. "We have been deprived of holding any meeting for three weeks on account of the Spanish influenza," reported one branch in Beaumont, Texas. It was "raging in our city," reported branch leadership in Charleston, West Virginia, while branches in the District of Columbia and Montgomery, Alabama, reported difficulty recruiting because people could not congregate for rallies.

People were afraid to gather, afraid to travel, afraid of strangers. Walter pushed on.

MAY OF 1918 SAW WALTER ON A TRAIN roaring into the South, to go undercover as a white man again. This time he was headed to his home state of Georgia. Already he had investigated a number of racial murders, but none resembled anything like what he would find in Lowndes and Brooks Counties, near the Florida border. This was to be the story of Mary Turner, a story that Walter would tell again and again. Like the Atlanta riot of 1906, it would become part of his mythology.

According to the newspapers, the violence was initially sparked by the killing of a white farmer named Hampton Smith. Apparently Smith had made a habit of beating the Black farmhands that he employed, and failing to pay their wages. One farmhand, a Black man named Sidney

Johnson, had decided he was not going to work until he received his promised pay. The white farmer, Smith, bloodied Johnson savagely, and in a fit of vengeance Johnson snuck up to the farmer's home, aimed a rifle through a window, and killed Smith with a bull's-eye shot. He then shot and killed the farmer's wife.

When news spread through rural Brooks and Lowndes Counties that a Black man had killed his white employer, townspeople organized a mob. By the time Walter read about the situation in the newspapers, the reporters were claiming a half dozen vigilante slayings. Walter was about to find that the situation was more depraved than he could yet imagine. "I reached the scene shortly after the butchery," he recorded after arriving by train in the town of Valdosta, Georgia, "and while excitement yet ran high."

Valdosta was a prosperous community. "The stores were well stocked," he noted. "The white inhabitants belonged to the class of Georgia crackers — lanky, slow of movement and of speech, long-necked, with small eyes set close together and skin tanned by the hot sun to a reddish-yellow hue." On the morning of Walter's arrival he walked into a general store and struck up a conversation with the merchant working there, about the weather and the war. The merchant offered a box to sit on and a Coca-Cola. Walter brought up the recent troubles, and the merchant flinched. Walter later remembered the conversation:

"You'll pardon me, Mister," said the shopkeeper, "for seeming suspicious but we have to be careful. In ordinary times we wouldn't have anything to worry about, but with the war there's been some talk of the Federal government looking into lynchings. It seems there's some sort of law during wartime making it treason to lower the man power of the country."

"In that case I don't blame you for being careful," Walter said. "But couldn't the Federal government do something if it wanted to when a lynching takes place, even if no war is going on at the moment?"

"Naw. There's no such law, in spite of all the agitation by a lot of fools who don't know the niggers as we do. States' rights won't permit Congress to meddle in lynching in peace time."

"But what about your State government — your Governor, your sheriff, your police officers?"

"Humph! Them? We elected them to office, didn't we? And the niggers, we've got them disfranchised, ain't we? Sheriffs and police and Governors and prosecuting attorneys have got too much sense to mix in lynching-bees. If they do they know they might as well give up all idea of running for office any more — if something worse don't happen to them."

The merchant had seized, in Walter's mind, on the very power structure that enabled lynchings to occur in these rural places. In the close-knit white communities, nobody believed it was in their best interest to indict or prosecute anyone for such crimes, and because African Americans could not vote, because they were not represented in local government or law enforcement, because they were largely poor and uneducated in this, only the second or third generation since the slave era, they were helpless to do anything about it.

That is where Walter hoped that the NAACP could make a difference.

He kept the conversation with the merchant simmering. "Little by little," Walter recalled, "he revealed the whole story." By the end, the merchant was slapping his thigh and cackling as he detailed one specific murder, calling it "the best show, Mister, I ever did see."

WALTER SPENT FOUR DAYS in southern Georgia, impersonating a reporter with the New York *Evening Post*. His star witness became a figure named George Spratling, a Black man who worked for one of the ringleaders of the lynch mob and was forced to attend some of the killings. In a secret meeting in a doctor's office in the village of Quitman, Georgia, Spratling confirmed to Walter the names of the killers he witnessed in the act. In Walter's signed account of this meeting, he wrote, "[Spratling] declares that none of the mob wore masks and that he positively identified all of the men." Walter was able to subsequently interview figures who freely admitted to participating in the torturing and killing.

His investigation revealed more murder victims than the papers had reported. The first, Sidney Johnson, who had killed the white farmer

Hampton Smith, was shot dead. A rope was tied around his neck. "The other end was tied to the back of an automobile," according to Walter's reporting, "and the body dragged in open daylight down Patterson Street, one of Valdosta's business thoroughfares." The mob had taken the lives of two other farmhands, Will Head and Will Thompson, who apparently had had nothing to do with the killing of Hampton Smith. Walter wrote, "Members of the mob stated to the investigator [Walter himself] that over seven hundred bullets were fired into the bodies" of these two victims.

Another Black farmhand, Chime Riley, was tied up with weights and thrown into the Little River in Brooks County. Another, named Simon Schuman, who was rumored to have conspired in the shooting of Hampton Smith, was kidnapped. A mob destroyed his home. Schuman was never seen again, and his fate has never been known. There were others, too.

Ultimately the investigation led Walter to a murder scene near Folsom's Bridge, which ran over southern Georgia's muddy Little River along a dirt road, miles outside of any town. There stood a small oak tree, its branches hanging over the road. The tree showed the scarring from dozens of gunshots. Here a Black woman named Mary Turner was murdered by the vigilante mob. Her apparent offense: vowing to avenge the death of her husband, Hayes Turner, killed by the same mob. Her murderers shot her countless times, then hung her upside down by her ankles from a tree branch and set her ablaze. She was eight months pregnant at the time.

About ten feet from the bullet-riddled hanging tree, Walter found the grave that held her and the unborn child. It was marked by a whiskey bottle with a half-smoked cigar sticking out from the neck. Walter stood over the grave site, examining it. Judging from his subsequent actions, his emotions moved from heartbreak to disbelief to rage. He was going to do all he could to make sure Mary Turner's name and the facts of her death would be remembered.

Before leaving the area, he visited the merchant who had been so friendly earlier on. Only this time the man was not so warm. The merchant confronted Walter.

"You're a government man, ain't you?"

"Who said so?" Walter asked.

"Never mind who told me; I know one when I see him."

Walter considered for a moment. As he later recalled the dialogue, he said, "Don't you tell anyone I am a government man; if I am one, you're the only one in the town who knows it."

The sun was setting. Walter headed for his hotel room when a Black stranger approached "with an air of great mystery," Walter remembered. The stranger said he had just overheard some white men talking and that, if Walter stuck around, "something would happen."

Walter steadied himself and said, "You go back to the ones who sent you and tell them this: that I have a damned good automatic" — almost certainly a lie — "and I know how to use it. If anybody attempts to molest me tonight or any other time, somebody is going to get hurt."

AFTER FOUR DAYS OF INVESTIGATING, Walter reached Atlanta exhausted. He typed out a letter to Shillady from the offices at the Standard Life Insurance Company, where he had worked not even a year earlier. How much had changed in that short time.

"I reached Atlanta this morning," Walter wrote, "and plan [on] being here for three days. I have had a very successful trip so far and the investigation in Valdosta was the most successful of any I have had. Instead of six persons being lynched as the press reports gave to us, I secured the names of eight who were killed together with three persons who were found in the river unidentified."

The following day, Walter visited Georgia's statehouse, where, once again posing as a reporter for the New York *Evening Post,* he demanded a meeting with Governor Hugh M. Dorsey. The governor must have been surprised by the audacity of the twenty-five-year-old. Dorsey was even more shocked when Walter handed over a six-page report detailing the murder spree in Brooks and Lowndes Counties. It was dated July 18, 1918, and it began: "Below are given some of the facts discovered during a recent visit to Brooks and Lowndes Counties, with reference to the lynchings in these two counties."

Walter catalogued thirteen members of the mob by name, with their professions and in some cases their addresses: a clerk in a post office, an employee of the Griffin Furniture Company, an agent for the Standard Oil Company, numerous farmers. Walter left out none of the gory details, including the story of Mary Turner and the specifics of what her killers had done to her.

Walter demanded justice, and Governor Dorsey surely sensed that Walter's report was a bombshell. From association headquarters in New York, Shillady sent a summation of it to newspapers across the nation. New York's most widely talked-about paper — Joseph Pulitzer's *World,* a birthplace of muckraking journalism — printed the summation verbatim, causing an explosion of publicity. Shillady also sent Walter's report to the president of the United States, Woodrow Wilson.

"We are enclosing for your examination," Shillady wrote in his cover letter, "a copy of the report of a special investigator who, on July 10, presented to Governor Hugh M. Dorsey of Georgia the results of his investigation, showing that ten and probably eleven persons have been lynched as the result of a single episode."

Officers at the NAACP had heard rumors that President Wilson was going to make a statement on race violence and the war effort, and indeed, the very day Wilson received Walter's report (July 26, 1918), the president released his statement.

"I allude to the mob spirit," Wilson told the country. "There have been many lynchings and every one of them has been a blow at the heart of ordered law and human justice. . . . Every American who takes part in the action of a mob or gives it any sort of countenance is no true son of this great Democracy, but its betrayer." Wilson implored every state and police official to cooperate in the effort to stamp out lynching, "not passively merely, but actively and watchfully — to make an end of this disgraceful evil."

ONCE AGAIN, a Walter White investigation sparked more publicity than the NAACP had seen before. "The governor of the state of Georgia must do something," stated the nation's most powerful Black newspaper, the *Chicago Defender.* The *San Antonio Express* offered a reward of $1,000 for information leading to any convictions.

A lawyer named C. P. Dam out of Washington, DC, wrote Walter directly after reading his article in *The Crisis* on the killing of Mary Turner, entitled "The Work of a Mob." "The details of the murder of the colored woman, Mrs. Turner, and her unborn infant, are so horrible that it is almost impossible for an American to believe that such a damnable crime could be committed in an American community and by men supposed to be American citizens," Dam wrote. "That the perpetrators of these murders should be allowed to go free and unpunished is unthinkable."

Still, no arrests were made in Brooks and Lowndes Counties. None of the thirteen individuals fingered in Walter's report were ever forced to testify or to give depositions. Governor Dorsey of Georgia did respond to the NAACP, some six weeks after Walter handed him his report. "So far as I am able to ascertain," Dorsey wrote, "no definite results have been obtained in the effort to apprehend the guilty parties. I shall take pleasure in advising you in the event any developments take place." The coroner's office ruled that the victims in Brooks and Lowndes Counties were killed at the hands of persons unknown.

5

The task is Power! Power! That is the thing. It is a new thing to
us. . . . We are not a weak people. There are twelve million of us. . . .
A right is not a thing issued on a silver tray . . . not a thing you can
put in your pocket like a gold piece. You have to fight to keep it.
That is the mission of this organization.
—James Weldon Johnson, NAACP rally, 1919

IN ITS RELATIVELY SHORT LIFE on the global stage, New York City had
seen its share of historical events. But never had New Yorkers seen anything like what they saw on February 17, 1919 — the day the Harlem Hellfighters marched.

A little before noon that morning — barely three months after the Central powers surrendered in Europe, ending the Great War — the United
States Army's 369th Infantry Regiment gathered at Twenty-Third Street
and Fifth Avenue. Wearing tan uniforms with the regiment's insignia — a
coiled rattlesnake — the regiment began to march, some three-thousand
soldiers beating out a rhythm with their boots on the black pavement.
Leading the group was Colonel William Hayward, still limping from a
battle wound. This was the first Black American army regiment to fight
overseas in World War I, the most famous Black fighting unit of all, and
the first regiment of any kind to return from battle and parade on Manhattan Island.

At the beginning of the conflict, the 369th had been recruited from
the streets — one battalion from Manhattan, one from Brooklyn, and

one from the suburbs. These soldiers had trained in a dance hall. They had gone south to a camp in South Carolina, where white soldiers refused to march beside them. They had gone to Europe to fight. Fearing racial strife among the troops, American commanders placed the 369th Regiment with the French forces. Now they had come home victors, at least what was left of them — eight hundred remained in Europe, in their graves.

These soldiers had fought longer in the trenches than any other US regiment — 191 straight days. The Harlem Hellfighters had even brought along their own soundtrack — a sixty-piece band commanded by the now legendary leader Captain James Reese Europe. A $10,000 charitable donation paid for the musicians to carry their instruments through France and Belgium. When not on the front lines, the band blew away crowds with syncopated rhythms and trumpets that could talk. Now in New York, Captain Europe marched with the rest of the regiment, the band silently carrying their gear.

At Thirtieth Street they moved past an official viewing stand where New York's new governor Alfred E. Smith sat beside the newspaper tycoon William Randolph Hearst and Mrs. Vincent Astor. Cigarettes and chocolates rained on the troops, along with ticker tape from office building windows. James Weldon Johnson was in the crowd that day; as he described this event in his column in the *New York Age:* The Harlem Hellfighters "furnished the first sight that New York has had of seasoned soldiers in marching order. There was no militia smartness about their appearance; their 'tin hats' were battered and rusty and the shiny newness worn off their bayonets, but they were men who had gone through the terrible hell of war and come back."

Upon reaching Harlem, after marching about a hundred long city blocks, Captain Europe's band burst into song. "For the final mile or more of our parade," remembered the 369th's Major Arthur Little, "about every fourth soldier of the ranks had a girl upon his arm — and we marched through Harlem singing and laughing."

The pride was tangible. Some 400,000 African Americans had served in the military during the war, a higher percentage per capita on active duty than white Americans. The highest military leaders had sung the praises of these soldiers. Secretary of War Newton Baker wrote in February 1918, after visiting the troops in Europe: "The great test of the quality of America is being met by the colored people of the country." The Harlem Hellfighters were, Baker wrote in a letter to Du Bois, "a credit to their organizations. . . . I have come back with an increased pride in these units."

Now that the war was over, the Hellfighters represented—as far as Walter White and all his colleagues at the NAACP were concerned—all of Black America. They had proved their patriotism, earned their place as civilians. Fearing that revisionary historians would wipe away their accomplishments, the NAACP's board of directors sent W.E.B. Du Bois to Europe to gather documentation and research for an article about the contributions of African American soldiers. In the May issue of *The Crisis,* Du Bois's report "Documents of the War" appeared.

But it was his now famous prose poem in that same issue of the magazine—tucked amidst advertisements for $8.95 "stylish perfect-fitting suits" and "Madam C. J. Walker's Wonderful Hair Grower"—that hit readers with more impact. The prose poem was titled "Returning Soldiers."

This is the country to which we Soldiers of Democracy return. This is the fatherland for which we fought! But it is *our* fatherland. It was right for us to fight. The faults of *our* country are *our* faults. . . . But by the God of Heaven, we are cowards and jackasses if now that that war is over, we do not marshal every ounce of our brain and brawn to fight a sterner, longer, more unbending battle against the forces of hell in our own land.

We return.

We return from fighting.

We return fighting.

Make way for Democracy! We saved it in France, and by the Great Jehovah, we will save it in the United States of America, or know the reason why.

Never had African Americans sensed such a turning point. They would demand the rights of citizenship, and the NAACP was poised to lead the charge.

Association officials were not naïve; they knew that white supremacy and race prejudice would not now simply disappear, and that a terrifying chapter in America's story was about to begin. The association's chairman of the board, Moorfield Storey, wrote to Shillady soon after the Harlem Hellfighters marched. "The negroes will come back feeling like men," Storey wrote, "and not disposed to accept the treatment to which they have been subjected."

Storey concluded: "I foresee a crisis."

ON MARCH 10, 1919, the association held its first board of directors meeting after the Hellfighters march, in conference room 621 at 70 Fifth Avenue. Taking his seat, Walter sensed the excitement in the room. The NAACP was growing so fast, he felt himself part of a rising wave of power. Mary White Ovington (who was present) put the moment in perspective: "Our organization was like a boy who has been growing from babyhood through childhood to youth, but is gawky, loose-limbed. Then suddenly, almost overnight, the youth becomes a man. . . . Now we were to become a firmly knit, well-appointed national organization."

Du Bois, then fifty years old, sat in his seat, his golden-brown face framed by a winged moustache, bald head, and a pointed goatee. Commented Ovington: "His head [looked] like Shakespeare's done in bronze." Called upon to report on *The Crisis*, Du Bois told the group that every one of the most recent issue (February 1919) had sold out, some 85,000 copies. Johnson reported on national outreach. In just a month's time since the last board meeting, new branches were formed in Albany, Georgia; Wharton, Texas; Birmingham, Alabama; and four locales in Kentucky: Henderson, Hopkinsville, Owensboro, and Lexington. The association had published a study called *Thirty Years of Lynching in the United States, 1889–1919*, documenting the murders of 3,224 African Americans. The booklet sparked extraordinary publicity. The *New Republic* magazine's reaction to it: "We are a nation disgraced; and the disgrace deepens year by year."

Change was afoot. Moorfield Storey was retiring, and the group voted to make Mary White Ovington chair of the board. John Shillady turned the conversation to the most exciting news: plans for the NAACP's first national conference on lynching. "Arrangements are well underway," Shillady reported. The attorney general of the United States, A. Mitchell Palmer, had agreed to be one of the speakers. It was going to be the most noteworthy rally in the NAACP's short history.

On Monday, May 5, 1919, at New York's Carnegie Hall on Fifty-Seventh Street, an eclectic mix of major figures filled the auditorium to kick off the conference — Zionist rabbi Stephen S. Wise, former Supreme Court justice Charles Evans Hughes, Brigadier General John H. Sherburne. The goal of the NAACP's first National Conference on Lynching was to open the eyes of Americans who did not know of this phenomenon. The two-day event ended with a climactic keynote speech by James Weldon Johnson. Walter sat in the front row as his boss rose amidst roaring applause. Johnson recalled, "The famous auditorium was packed to capacity. . . . When I rose, every nerve in my brain and body was quickened by the intensity of feeling that came across the footlights from the audience to me."

Johnson spoke of the day he watched the Harlem Hellfighters leave New York for the war in Europe, earlier in 1917, and the feeling that came over him when a mighty chorus belted out "The Star-Spangled Banner" and the Black soldiers going off to war saluted their flag. That very American flag that those soldiers carried into battle, Johnson told the crowd, held "the stains of Disenfranchisement, of Jim-Crowism, of mob violence, and of lynching."

"The record of black men on the fields of France," Johnson said, "gives us the greater right to point to that flag and say to the nation: Those stains are still upon it; they dim its stars and soil its stripes. Wash them out! Wash them out!" He then spoke the most noteworthy words ever attributed to him: "The race problem in the United States has resolved itself into a question of saving black men's bodies and white men's souls."

In his seat, Walter looked around and saw shock on the faces of white and Black people alike. Johnson's statement had laid bare a truth so raw, it hit its audience almost like a physical blow.

When the crowds spilled out of Carnegie Hall that night, a spring rain was falling. Walter stood on the sidewalk of Fifty-Seventh Street almost overcome with optimism. He had been with the association not yet a year and a half, and that night felt like a coming-out party, onto the national stage. But the events of the next four months were about to change everything.

The Red Summer of 1919 was about to begin. As Du Bois later wrote, "The facts concerning the year 1919 are almost unbelievable as one looks back upon them."

THE YEAR 1919 would be remembered for many things. This was the year that Congress passed the Volstead Act, ushering in the era of Prohibition. This was the year that Congress passed the Nineteenth Amendment, aiming to give women the right to vote (but not necessarily Black women). It was the second year of the Spanish flu pandemic, and the year that domestic terrorists sent mail bombs to American officials including US attorney general A. Mitchell Palmer and US senator Thomas W. Hardwick — bombs that brought on the "First Red Scare."

In the New York offices of the NAACP late that spring, officials began to notice a startling uptick in lynching reports. *The Crisis* kept a tally of them, publishing lists of the murders of Black men, women, and children along with the towns where they occurred and the crimes for which the victims were accused.

May 2, Warrenton, Georgia: Benny Richards, burned alive, accused of murder.
May 5, Plano, Texas: Tom Embrey, shot, accused of attempted murder.
May 9, Pickens, Mississippi: a soldier and a woman, accused of the "crime" of writing an insulting note to a white woman.
May 15, Dublin, Georgia: Jim Walters, accused of attempt to rape.
May 22, Eldorado, Arkansas: Frank Livingston, soldier, burned alive, accused of murder.

In June a Black man named John Hartfield was accused of raping a white woman in the town of Ellisville, Mississippi. When he was captured, newspapers as far off as New Orleans and New York reported the time and place of his lynching, before it happened. Mississippi's *Jackson Daily News* ran the headline on June 26: JOHN HARTFIELD WILL BE LYNCHED BY ELLISVILLE MOB AT 5 O'CLOCK THIS AFTERNOON. Governor Theodore Bilbo of Mississippi declared himself "powerless to prevent it." Ten thousand people — a crowd larger than those at some major-league baseball games — turned out for the event.

In July full-scale racial rioting broke out in the nation's capital, brought on by salacious and unfounded newspaper headlines about a Black serial rapist attacking white women. "Before the very gates of the White House," one eyewitness recorded, "Negroes were dragged from streetcars and beaten up while crowds of soldiers, sailors and marines dashed down Pennsylvania, the principal thoroughfare of the downtown section, in pursuit of fleeing Negroes. In one instance a restaurant, crowded with men and women diners, was invaded by a crowd of uniformed soldiers and sailors in search of Negro waiters." More than a dozen Washingtonians were killed — white, Black, even police officers.

Days later Chicago fell to the same fate. Rioting broke out after a fight on a segregated Lake Michigan beach. The NAACP dispatched its investigator, Walter White, who traveled to America's second-largest city to go undercover. When Walter arrived on August 6, the worst of the violence was over, but still, he found Chicago in a state of apocalyptic siege. He checked in at the NAACP branch and learned of rumors that more violence was pending the following morning. The city had been shut down. But now Black workers, some three thousand of them, were scheduled to return to work in the stockyards. So the next morning Walter put on old clothes and went to the scene.

"I spent three hours there," he wrote Ovington that day, "and the only thing that prevented serious clashes was the presence of thousands of police and state troops. There was considerable hooting and muttering and the tension was very great, but the presence of the troops with rifles and also several machine guns mounted on automobiles held the mobs in check."

At one point Walter was walking south on State Street — one of the city's major public thoroughfares — around sunset, on his way to an appointment at the Binga bank, Chicago's first Black-owned bank for Black customers, when he saw a suspicious African American man in the shadows. The man was hiding behind a tree. Walter watched him take a bead with a rifle and, apparently believing Walter was a white man, fired off a shot. "I ducked as a bullet whanged into the side of the building exactly where my head had been a fraction of a second before," he recalled.

The weeklong Chicago riot of 1919 left a reported twenty-three African Americans and fifteen whites dead. More than a thousand homes burned to the ground, a majority of them in the city's Black neighborhoods. Walter's Chicago investigation led him to a short list of names, white mob leaders who he claimed had led the charge. He delivered his memorandum to Chicago's mayor and Illinois's attorney general, then left for Atlanta, where he wrote Ovington on July 30 about three more undercover investigations he was completing: the lynching of Bud Johnson in Florida, of an unreported lynching that had apparently occurred in Wrightsville, Georgia, and the killing of a dining car waiter in Picayune, Mississippi. "All three of these I expect to finish this week," he wrote.

Throughout his travels in the South, he had noticed the growing presence of the KKK. As he put it at the time: "It is not possible to write of race relations in the South today without giving due prominence to the revival of that sinister organization, the Ku Klux Klan. There is hardly a town or community to be found which does not have its branch. Certain it is that wherever one goes in the South one hears of the 'Klucks' and what that order is going to do to maintain 'white supremacy.'"

In Atlanta, where the new Klan was born, its influence was overwhelming. Walter arrived in his home city right after he investigated the Chicago riot, and wrote to Ovington of "an unusual tenseness in the air among both races such as has never been seen before."

"It seems that there is an air of expectancy," he wrote, "of something which is about to happen — no one knows what — with the result that everybody is afraid to talk. This feeling has been greatly aggravated by the wide publicity given in Southern papers to the Washington and Chicago riots, and the feeling seems to be that something similar is liable to break out at any moment in the South. Never before have I seen or felt such a wide-spread feeling of unrest."

Every pawnshop and hardware store was crowded with white people buying every gun they could, he reported. "Frankly, I don't know what it will end in."

6

There have been times I have felt with a sweep of fear that the patience of the colored man is close to its end.

— Walter White, *A Man Called White*

WHILE WALTER WAS IN ATLANTA, John Shillady and Mary White Ovington remained in New York headquarters facing yet another crisis in the Red Summer of 1919. The NAACP had recruited more new members in Texas, of recent, than in any other state. However, the association had received a letter from the acting attorney general in Austin, the state's capital, accusing the NAACP branches of operating illegally. He claimed that the NAACP had incorporated in New York, not in Texas. So the branches had no right to conduct business there.

The argument, both Ovington and Shillady believed, was a sham, but in Texas, politicians could simply bully the branch leaders until they shut down. Talking it over at headquarters, Ovington and Shillady decided that if Shillady visited Austin personally, he could smooth out the situation.

"Do you think there is any danger?" Shillady asked.

Ovington remembered: "I recall how we stood in his office talking the matter over. . . . I looked at him as he stood there, a gentleman, not only in speech and manner, but in instinct, and I pictured him as meeting other gentlemen, officers of the state."

"There might be danger to someone else," she said to Shillady, "but not to you."

Shillady reached Austin on a humid July day and met with leaders of the NAACP branch there, to get their side of the story. Then he arrived at the Texas capitol, a magnificent domed building that stood taller than the US Capitol in Washington. Shillady was led into an office where he met Texas's acting attorney general and acting adjutant general. They informed him of rumors that Black citizens were buying rifles and were planning an "armed uprising." They told Shillady of the "evil effects" of certain publications in "inciting" the Black population to violence, clearly referring to *The Crisis.*

According to the NAACP's official report of what happened next, Shillady "remarked that he felt certain the branches had had nothing to do with that and that the association's sole reliance was on legal and constitutional methods for gaining its ends." He explained that the NAACP sought change only through peaceful means, and then quoted the association's 1918 annual report: "Its fight is of the brain and the soul and to the brain and the soul of America. . . . It seeks to reach the conscience of America."

The Texas officials complained that the NAACP was demanding "social equality," and that it was "stirring up the niggers." Shillady responded by handing over the NAACP's report *Thirty Years of Lynching in the United States, 1889–1919.* He then left but was soon confronted outside the statehouse by a constable named Charles Hamby, who subpoenaed him. Shillady found himself in a court of inquiry, in front of a judge named Dave Pickle, who mocked the NAACP man for being white and supporting African Americans.

Shillady was asked, "If you're a 'nigger' lover, why don't you go and stay in a 'nigger' hotel?"

The NAACP's chief executive was told to leave the building. The next morning he walked out of his hotel and was standing on the sidewalk when he heard a car motor up behind him. Out stepped the constable Charles Hamby, who had subpoenaed him the day before, and Judge Dave Pickle. The men accused Shillady of inciting Black Texans to rise up.

"You don't see my point of view," Shillady said.

"I'll fix you so you can't see," Hamby answered.

Without warning, they attacked Shillady—men in suits throwing punches, landing audible blows to Shillady's face. Shillady felt his body hit the ground and nearly lost consciousness as he begged for mercy. The assailants got back into their car and left him lying on the pavement, bleeding heavily.

In shock, Shillady sought out a doctor; he required stitches in his face. He called the mayor of Austin and demanded protection so that he could safely get to the train station. That afternoon Mary White Ovington and others at NAACP headquarters saw a press report that Shillady had suffered a beating. Ovington immediately telegrammed Texas governor W. P. Hobby, and he responded: "Shillady was the only offender in connection with the matter referred to in your telegram and he was punished before your inquiry came. Your organization can contribute more to the advancement of both races by keeping your representatives and their propaganda out of this state than in any other way."

AS THE RED SUMMER WORE ON, two Americas were galvanizing, opposing forces, proving once again Newton's third law of motion: For every action or force in nature, there is an equal and opposite reaction. Much of white America blamed the Red Summer on Black protest, and on organizations such as the NAACP and its leaders. Black America blamed violent racists for the bloodletting. Both were sure of their point of view with immaculate conviction.

A few days after Shillady returned to New York from Austin, Texas governor Hobby said in a speech: "I believe in Texas for Texans only, and just as strongly do I believe that Texans should say how the affairs of the state should be conducted and I believe in sending any narrow-brained, double-chinned reformer who comes here with the end in view of stirring up racial discontent back to the North where he came from, with a broken jaw if necessary."

In Washington, on August 25, 1919, James F. Byrnes—a future United States secretary of state and Supreme Court justice but at the time a thirty-seven-year-old congressman from South Carolina—gave a rousing speech on the floor of the House of Representatives blaming the Red

Summer on Black protesters, a speech that shocked NAACP leaders due to what they saw as blatant misinformation.

"These radical leaders of the negro race are urging their followers to resort to violence in order to obtain privileges they believe themselves entitled to," Byrnes pronounced. He singled out W.E.B. Du Bois and *The Crisis* magazine and even read Du Bois's prose poem "Returning Soldiers" in its entirety into the *Congressional Record*, intoning Du Bois's words with a heavy South Carolina drawl ("Make way for Democracy! We saved it in France, and by the Great Jehovah, we will save it in the United States of America . . ."). Byrnes castigated Black soldiers who had fought for the Allies in the Great War because they had fought under the French flag — where they were placed by American military leaders.

"No intelligent American negro," Byrnes said, "is willing to lay down his life for the United States as it now exists. Intelligent negroes have all reached the point where their loyalty to the country is conditional. . . . No greater service can be rendered to the Negroes today than to have them know that this government will not tolerate, on the part of their leaders, action which tends to array them against the government under which they live, and under which the negro race has made greater progress than it has under any other government on earth."

Meanwhile, the lynchings continued.

At one point Walter traveled undercover as a white man to the rural backwater of Shubuta, Mississippi, where he investigated the murders of four young Black Americans. All four, he concluded, were entirely innocent of the crime for which they were accused — the murder of a white dentist. The facts of the case seemed so shocking to Walter, and so easy to obtain with just a little sleuthing, it seemed impossible to believe that local authorities would turn a blind eye. But they did.

Walter's investigation led him to a hanging bridge, a rusting metal pathway over the chocolate-brown Chickasawhay River. Here the four victims met their fate. All four were between the ages of fifteen and twenty. One of them, a young woman named Maggie Howze, fought so fiercely for her life, she kept catching herself, and the mob had to throw her off the bridge three times. Standing on this bridge in the middle of nowhere, Walter could hear nothing but the peaceful rambling river, perhaps the rustling of leaves in the trees from wind. He could only imagine the sounds that filled the murderers' ears that terrible night.

In his scathing internal NAACP report, "An Example of Democracy in Mississippi," he juxtaposed the patriotic fight for democracy overseas with the lack of it in Shubuta. When his report landed on the desk of Mississippi's governor, Theodore Bilbo, the press asked the governor if he would comment. Bilbo answered, "No, not tonight, but I might give you a little advance information to the effect that I will tell them, in effect, to go to hell."

Every instance of injustice, every story of murder with impunity, hardened the will of Walter White to fight back — and that of his colleagues too. As James Weldon Johnson put it, the Red Summer marked "the turning point in the psychology of the whole nation regarding the Negro problem. . . . There developed a spirit of defiance born of desperation. Radicalism in Harlem, which had declined as the war approached, burst out anew."

Nobody voiced this new radicalism better than a young black poet named Claude McKay, who was in Washington, DC, huddling terrified in a doorway during the Red Summer rioting in the nation's capital. His poem "If We Must Die" appeared in the July issue of a magazine called *The Liberator*.

If we must die, let it not be like hogs
Hunted and penned in an inglorious spot,
While round us bark the mad and hungry dogs,
Making their mock at our accursèd lot.
. . . .
Like men we'll face the murderous, cowardly pack,
Pressed to the wall, dying, but fighting back!

IN OCTOBER 1919, Walter read of yet another murderous spree, this time in Phillips County, Arkansas. This was to be the climactic convulsion of the Red Summer. The story broke in New York on the morning of October 3.

The *New York Times* reported on page 6: "Scattered clashes today between troops, white posse men, and negros who have taken refuge in the cane-break country in southern Phillips County, Arkansas, swelled the known death toll to sixteen on the second day of the race riots which started yesterday morning at Elaine, Ark."

Walter approached John Shillady, who was showing clear signs of a full nervous breakdown following his beating in Texas two months earlier. "[I am] exceedingly anxious to make the investigation personally," Walter said, "and I . . . am assuming complete responsibility for any personal consequences which may . . . arise." Shillady's beating had no effect on Walter. The abject terror experienced by victims in the cases in which he investigated also seemed to have no effect. He was driven to penetrate the mind of the lyncher, to understand the compulsion to torture and kill — and to exact revenge through legal means.

He finagled credentials from the *Chicago Daily News* and went undercover as a reporter, arriving in Arkansas's capital city, Little Rock, a few days after the rioting had ended. His first move was to lie his way into the office of Arkansas governor Charles H. Brough, where Walter used his skin color to put the governor at ease. "I purposely led him to believe," Walter recalled, "that I had little knowledge of the Negro question and was open-minded to whatever facts he, as chief executive of the state, cared to give me."

Walter laid on the charm. He recalled Governor Brough responding, "I am delighted that a Northern newspaper has sent so able and experienced a reporter to answer the foul lies the *Chicago Defender* [the nation's most influential Black newspaper] and that infamous National Association for the Advancement of Colored People have been telling about the good white people of Arkansas." The governor complained about Black agitators in Phillips County, adding that the white people who lived there had shown great restraint. Walter recalled, "The cause of the Phillips County trouble, according to Governor Charles H. Brough, was the circulation of what he considers incendiary Negro publications like *The Crisis.*"

For Walter, the facts already did not add up. Phillips County's population was 78.6 percent African American. The newspapers, however, had reported some twenty-five African Americans killed compared with five Caucasians. If the Black population was to blame, why was the death toll so one-sided?

Walter aimed to find the facts. He convinced the governor to give him a letter of introduction he could use to present to officials and others. In this letter, Governor Brough called Walter (as Walter himself later recalled) one of the most brilliant newspapermen he had ever met, and asked that the officials of Arkansas take Walter White seriously. Walter then traveled into the epicenter of the violence. When he reached the town of Elaine—a tiny rural village a couple of miles from the Mississippi River—he was singled out for suspicion. "As I stepped from the train at Elaine," he recalled, "the county seat, I was closely watched by a crowd of men. Within half an hour of my arrival I had been asked by two shopkeepers, a restaurant waiter, and a ticket agent why I had come."

Not surprisingly, the reality he discovered in Phillips County was very different from the one he had read about in the newspapers.

USING GOVERNOR BROUGH'S LETTER AS AN ENTRÉE, Walter began to infiltrate the rural communities of the Arkansas delta of the Mississippi River. All around the towns of Elaine and Helena—the two epicenters of the massacre—were cotton fields. The little balls colored the landscape white as far as the eye could see. Cottonseed was the wellspring of the economy for miles in all directions. Cottonseed was also the root of the Phillips County massacre's story, Walter quickly learned.

On the night of September 30, 1919, a group of Black sharecroppers gathered inside a church in Hoop Spur, a town that was little more than a crossroads, two miles outside of Elaine. At some point a car pulled up and a special agent for the Missouri Pacific Railroad named Adkins stepped out into the darkness, in company with a local deputy sheriff named Charles Pratt. Both men were in plain clothes, and they had arrived in an unmarked car. The two officers were white; everyone in the church was Black.

"According to Pratt," Walter later reported, "persons in the church fired without cause on the party, killing Adkins and wounding Pratt. According to testimony of persons in the church, however, Adkins and Pratt fired into the church, apparently to frighten the Negroes gathered. The fire was returned with the casualties noted. Whatever the facts may be, this incident started four days of rioting."

Walter interviewed sharecroppers, landowners, and cotton agents. The story they told illuminated how the economy in the region functioned, and why the killing began. According to the decades-old tradition of sharecropping, wealthy white landowners rented out farmland to Black sharecroppers, who were largely uneducated and vastly poor. The sharecroppers farmed the cotton and gave it to the landowners, and then the profit was split.

It was simple math, except when it wasn't. The sharecroppers had to buy all their seed and equipment from the landowners and pay the farm rent. Additionally, the landowners who sold the cotton could claim whatever profit they chose, and pay out as little as they wanted. Thus the sharecroppers remained poor and indebted. Sharecropping had been created in cotton-growing regions after the Civil War by white plantation owners to maintain the system of cheap farm labor. (As explained by the historian Sven Beckert, "Plantation owners . . . sought to restore a plantation world as close to slavery as possible.")

Walter gathered court records full of financial data, which he believed proved blatant financial misdeeds on the part of the landowners. One sharecropper told him how he had confronted his landowner over profit share, only to be told, "Get the hell out of here. You have taken up all that's coming to you, and I don't make settlements with niggers anyhow."

Ultimately, the local sharecroppers decided to blaze a new trail. They formed a union — the Progressive Farmers and Household Union of America. Walter was able to obtain the union's literature. The organization's purpose was "advancing the intellectual, material, moral, spiritual, and financial interest of the Negro race." Potential members had to answer questions on an application, to make sure they were upstanding citizens: "Do you believe in God?" "Do you attend church?" "Do you believe in courts?" "Will you defend this Government and her Constitution at all times?"

When the union amassed enough funds in donations, they hired an attorney named Ulysses Bratton out of Little Rock. That is when the local white landowners got angry. That, Walter believed, was when they began to spread misinformation — that the sharecroppers' union was no union at all but rather a Black mob planning a violent insurrection. According to a legal brief later filed in the Phillips County massacre court case, the white locals of Elaine and Helena accused the union members of "a plot to massacre whites." "A large number of white men armed themselves," the brief went on, "and rushed to the scene of the trouble and to adjacent regions and began the indiscriminate hunting, shooting and killing of Negroes."

To stop the violence, Governor Brough ordered five hundred soldiers from nearby Camp Pike to the scene. According to the local newspaper, the *Arkansas Democrat,* the troops were "under order to shoot to kill any Negro who refused to surrender immediately." The ruthlessness of the violence shocked even Walter. In one instance, an Arkansan named Leroy Johnston, who had just spent nine months in the hospital recovering from wounds received while fighting for his country in France, was pulled from a train and murdered beside three of his brothers.

"I was never able to fix definitely the number of Negroes who were killed," Walter reported, "but did gather evidence establishing a total in excess of 200. Every colored man, woman, and child who could do so fled the county, many of them by foot through the swamps and woods under cover of darkness during several days and nights of slaughter."

At one point before Walter left Phillips County, he walked down West Cherry Street, a main road through Helena, on his way to the jailhouse, where dozens of Black men had been imprisoned after the rioting and were awaiting trial. He got a tip that there was a plot to take his life, that his identity had somehow been revealed. Surely in this moment he confronted what might happen to him, what it would be like to burn to death at the stake or to be hanged in front of a crowd. He hurried to the train station, sweating in the Arkansas heat. Only two trains rolled through Helena daily, and he told the ticket agent he wanted to get on the next one.

"Why, Mister," said the ticket agent, "you're leaving just when the fun is going to start! There's a damned yaller nigger down here passing for white and the boys are going to have some fun with him."

Walter asked what kind of fun these "boys" had in mind.

"Wal, when they get through with him," said the ticket agent, "he won't pass for white no more."

WALTER'S REPORT RAN NATIONWIDE with an ironic title—"'Massacring Whites' in Arkansas"—in the December 6, 1919, issue of *The Nation.* The title and the story pointed to a macabre irony. The massacre in Phillips County had begun, the white communities claimed, because they feared a murderous uprising among the Blacks. But Walter found no evidence of any such uprising planned, only union organizing. In the end, sixty-seven Black men and zero white men were formally charged with crimes.

In court the trial lasted roughly one hour; an all-white jury deliberated for seven minutes, finding all sixty-seven guilty. Twelve were sentenced to death and the rest to prison terms ranging from one year to life. Walter later described his impression of the trial: "The court room was thronged with an armed mob threatening death to any juror voting for acquittal. A lawyer was appointed by the court to defend the Negroes; that lawyer did not consult his clients before going to trial, produced no witnesses in their behalf, and did not even place the defendants on the stand to testify."

In *The Crisis,* Du Bois commented, "There is not a civilized country in the world that would for a moment allow this kind of justice to stand." The NAACP's Joel Spingarn wrote Governor Brough: "You have it in your power to perform a national service at this crisis, and I feel sure that you will not shrink from it." Spingarn's letter was never answered. A Black attorney named Scipio A. Jones in Little Rock took on the case and reached out to NAACP headquarters, asking for money to defend the Phillips County prisoners.

In a desperate letter to Walter White, Jones wrote, "I don't know where I can get the money. This is a life and death struggle with us. . . . These men should not and must not go to the electric chair, if it can be prevented — and it can! I know that we are engaged in a just cause, a right-eous fight and we must win."

Thus far Walter's investigations had led to explosive publicity — but zero convictions. A new strategy was needed. It was one thing to fight with activism and publicity. It was another to fight with attorneys, in a court of law, and so the NAACP began a campaign to raise money for legal expenses. Walter cranked out letters asking for money. Donations began to trickle in: $5.50 from the Columbus, Ohio, NAACP branch, $5 from the Lexington, Kentucky, branch, $10 from the Mothers Charity Club of Oakland, California.

Before the watchful eyes of the American people and the world, the Constitution of the United States itself would go on trial, in Arkansas. The fate of the sixty-seven prisoners — a dozen of them on death row — hung in the balance.

7

But, ah! Manhattan's lights and sounds, her smells,
Her crowds, her throbbing force, the thrill that comes
From being of her a part, her subtle spells.
Her shining towers, her avenues, her slums —
O God! The stark, unutterable pity,
To be dead, and never again behold my city!
— James Weldon Johnson, "My City"

IN 1920, NAACP officials collectively traveled enough miles to circumnavigate the globe three times — Walter with the most, some 23,000 miles. Still, "these years were not all devoted to work and tragedies," he recalled. Among the many things that Walter and his mentor, James Weldon Johnson, had in common was a taste for nightlife, which New York supplied endlessly.

"Frequently, [the Johnsons'] apartment was the gathering place of writers, poets, singers, and men and women of the theater," Walter recalled. "Many an evening we talked until long after midnight. The color line was never drawn at Jim's. It was there that many who were later to do much in wiping out the color line learned to know each other as fellow human beings and fellow artists without consciousness of race."

Walter was on the scene, cigarette in his lips, always impeccably dressed when he was in New York. He spoke like a wind-up doll that didn't stop until the motor ran out. "I am an all-or-nothing man," one friend remembered him saying. "I don't believe that half a loaf is better than none — or half a life. Lincoln said a country cannot exist half slave and half free; neither can an individual. I am sick and tired of the 'yes but —' people. I want to shake some guts into them. It's a mixed-up metaphor but that's just what they need. They are for you but they are against you . . . yes . . . no . . . maybe . . . not yet . . ."

Now entering his third year in New York, Walter had come to the city at an opportune time. New York in the immediate postwar years was exploding with energy and newness, with ideas and audacity. The city was emerging as the global capital of just about everything — commerce, literature, art, theater, advertising, architecture. It was home to Wall Street, now becoming the nerve center for global finance. It was the world's biggest publishing center too, with some 270 publications printing in more than twenty languages. The New York tycoons of newspapering — Joseph Pulitzer, William Randolph Hearst, James Gordon Bennett Jr. (who had just passed away) — shaped the way millions of people saw the world.

In 1912, New York had 8.8 telephones per 100 people. By 1920 that number had roughly doubled. In 1920, elevated trains and subways, and electric and steam riverboats, gave 2.5 trillion rides around the boroughs, while at the same time the city brought motorcar traffic congestion into the modern age. All the manifestations of modernity played out before one's eyes. "The whole world revolves around New York," said Duke Ellington, who was on the verge of becoming the city's new hotshot bandleader. "Very little happens anywhere unless someone in New York presses a button."

For Walter White and James Weldon Johnson, New York was a mecca for another reason. Both were baseball fanatics, and New York was home to the Brooklyn Dodgers — who played in the World Series in 1920 — and the New York Yankees — for whom Babe Ruth suited up for the first time that year.

But it wasn't just New York that was ascending. It was Harlem in particular. "It seems rather like a sudden awakening," Johnson put it, "like an instantaneous change." Only fifteen years earlier, the neighborhood had been almost entirely white. Around 1905 a Black real estate investor named Philip A. Payton Jr. took a chance on a building at 133rd Street, offering renters apartments at a relatively affordable cost. Payton's silent partner was James C. Thomas, a former waiter and mortician and the richest Black businessman in New York. Suddenly more investment and more dark-skinned renters appeared. White residents panicked.

"They took fright, they became panic-stricken, they ran amuck," Johnson explained in his book *Black Manhattan*. "Their conduct could be compared to that of a community in the Middle Ages fleeing before an epidemic of the black plague."

Now, in 1920, Harlem's arms opened wide and African Americans from across the country arrived by the day to recreate themselves. From Los Angeles, a young post office worker named Arna Bontemps sent a poem to *The Crisis;* when the magazine published the poem, Bontemps decided to quit his job and move to Harlem, where he would find success as a major writer. Another arrival was Zora Neale Hurston, soon to be one of Harlem's literary stars. As her biographer put it, she planted her feet in Harlem "with one dollar and fifty cents in her purse, no job, no friends, but filled with hope." No place had ever offered so much promise for what W.E.B. Du Bois called the Talented Tenth — intellectually gifted Black Americans who were interested in cultural progress.

The global human phenomenon of the era was the movement of humans from farms to cities. As Oswald Spengler wrote in volume 1 of his vastly influential book *The Decline of the West,* published in German in 1918 and translated into English soon after, "It is a quite certain, but never fully recognized, fact, that all great cultures are city-born. . . . This is the actual criterion of world history, as distinguished from the history of mankind: world history is the history of city men. Nations, governments, politics, and religions — all rest on the basic phenomenon of human existence, the city."

If all great cultures were city born, Black America was now a great culture. If world history was the history of city men, Harlem was now its own city on the world stage. A phrase came into the popular lexicon that embodied this new spirit. It appeared in a headline in the Harlem magazine *The Messenger* in 1920: "The New Negro — What Is He?" Soon the term was spreading across urban centers westward. "The New Negro, unlike the old time Negro, does not fear the face of the day," proclaimed the *Kansas City Call.* "The time for cringing is over."

As an emerging race leader, Walter White was among the influencers defining the New Negro. He had become a big-city man, a Harlemite. "I need the smell of carbon monoxide to do my best work," he liked to say. The city opened a door to a certain freedom that could only be understood by one who walked through it. In Harlem, as opposed to Atlanta, Walter was able not just to be himself but to *create* himself.

When he looked in the mirror, he saw looking back at him a proud Black man with a hunger for fame. He was constructing an iconography around himself, using his double life and his skin color to do so, and he seemed to care nothing what anyone thought about it. As the Black historian David Levering Lewis wrote of him, "Everything White did was done without brakes on, with a nervous single-mindedness that would have been abrasive but for a touch of style. . . . Walter Francis White was cocky. Harlem loved him for it, even if some folks wondered why he said he was Afro-American. Physically, he was not only white, he was . . . one of the whitest white men ever to have an octoroon for a grandfather."

ON AUGUST 1, 1920, a Sunday, Harlemites gathered on sidewalks and watched a parade march down 138th Street to a great ballroom called Liberty Hall. Inside, the hall was festooned with alternating flags — the Stars and Stripes along with the red, black, and green flag of an organization called the United Negro Improvement Association (UNIA). The UNIA's leader, Marcus Garvey — who had built out Liberty Hall as a sort of cathedral for his own spiritual movement — appeared onstage, and when he spoke, his words electrified the crowd, not a white face among them.

Garvey opened the first national convention of his United Negro Improvement Association, which he had founded just a couple of years earlier. The purpose of the convention was to create a Black "bill of rights," and to elect a "world leader and a negro leader of the 12,000,000 people of the United States." By the end of the evening, followers had named Garvey the Provisional President of Africa.

The next night Garvey packed Madison Square Garden with 25,000 followers. "What is good for the white man," Garvey told his audience, "is good for the negro, we believe, and that is freedom, liberty and democracy. . . . 400,000,000 black men are ready to fight the battle of the democracy on the field of Africa. We have no apology and no compromise to offer; the negros of the world shall do no less than strike for freedom. If the English claim England, the French France, and the Italians Italy as their native habitat, then the negroes shall claim Africa as their native habitat and shed their blood to maintain their claim."

Harlem had never seen a figure like Marcus Garvey, nor had anyone in America. He was, in the words of James Weldon Johnson, "one of the most remarkable and picturesque figures that have appeared on the American scene." He had only been in New York a short time and had succeeded in creating a following of such wild enthusiasm, his UNIA was threatening to eclipse the power and the reach of the NAACP. The UNIA flag of red, black, and green stood for spilled blood, Black skin, and what Garvey called "the luxurian vegetation of our motherland" — Africa. When Garvey closed his month-long national convention, he declared red, black, and green the colors of a new "Negro nation." The convention was such a success, one man present later said of it, "As far as I am aware, it was the greatest demonstration of colored solidarity in American history, before or since."

A native of Kingston, Jamaica, Garvey was largely self-educated, the son of a brick and stone mason. He was first drawn to race activism after reading Booker T. Washington's book *Up from Slavery*. As Garvey later explained, "Being a race leader dawned upon me. . . . I asked: 'Where is the black man's Government? Where is his King and his kingdom? Where is his President, his country, and his ambassador, his army, his navy, his men of big affairs?' I could not find them, and then I declared, 'I will help to make them.'"

Still a young man, he traveled through Central America and Europe informally studying human motivations — what made people tick — before returning to Jamaica to found the UNIA. Sensing that this small island was no place to launch a massive international movement, he set his sights on New York. He arrived in Harlem on March 23, 1916, at age twenty-eight.

On the corner of Lenox Avenue and 135th Street, people would gather to hear local political and religious speakers. A man stood out one morning in the spring of 1916 and yelled, "There's a young man here from Jamaica who wants to be presented to this group! He wants to talk about a movement to develop a back-to-Africa sentiment in America!"

On that street corner, Garveyism was born in the United States. "The man spoke," James Weldon Johnson recorded, "and his magnetic personality, torrential eloquence, and intuitive knowledge of crowd psychology were all brought into play. He swept the audience along with him."

In the summer of 1918 Garvey published the first issue of a weekly newspaper, the *Negro World*. Amidst news stories and editorials, he ran advertisements urging readers to send the UNIA money: "Send Us a Dollar: An Appeal to Every Reader of the *Negro World*." The newspaper's readership grew remarkably quickly. Every issue's front page carried an editorial addressed to "Fellowmen of the Negro Race" and signed by "Your obedient observant, Marcus Garvey, President General."

Garvey announced the formation of a steamship company called the Black Star Line, with which he intended to link together the Black peoples of the world in mutually beneficial commerce. Using his newspaper to spread the word, he sold stock in the Black Star Line. The money rolled in. He bought a ship for $165,000, christening it the *Frederick Douglass,* then announced plans to expand his fleet. By selling stock in his shipping company, he promised African Americans the ability to do what so many white Americans did: use their money to make more money, while participating in the building of commerce created for their own benefit.

Garvey's star rose so fast, he made enemies along the way. Harlemites were shocked when, in 1919, an insane follower shot Marcus Garvey with two bullets while the UNIA leader was sitting in his office. Garvey gave chase through the streets of Harlem, blood streaming from his wounds, until the shooter was captured by the NYPD. The would-be killer was apparently disgruntled over a small debt; he committed suicide the next day in a Manhattan jailhouse. The story only brightened the spotlight on Garvey, who recovered and began to appear at his rallies in military tunics with colorful plumes and gold braids. "There were gorgeous uniforms, regalia, decorations, and insignia," recalled Johnson. Garvey spread his message all over the country and in the islands of the Caribbean.

"The world has made being black a crime," he said. "I hope to make it a virtue."

"Garvey was the first Negro in the United States to capture the imagination of the masses," Mary White Ovington wrote of him. "The sweeper in the subway, the elevator boy." Many years later Martin Luther King Jr. called him "the first man on a mass scale and level to give millions of Negroes a sense of dignity and destiny."

In structure, Garvey's UNIA mirrored the NAACP. It had a central national office in New York, with roots sprouting across the country in the form of organized branches. That, however, is where the comparison ended. The NAACP supported the Great War and urged African Americans to participate. Garvey opposed any African American support for the war and openly wept in public the day the Harlem Hellfighters marched on Manhattan. The NAACP sought to destroy the color line, and for full American rights and citizenship. Garvey supported a separate and militant Black nationalism, and a return to the "motherland" of Africa. The NAACP was multiracial. The UNIA did not invite white members.

Garvey contrasted with Walter White in a more profound way. While Walter was, in flesh and bone, a walking symbol of miscegenation, Garvey was of full African descent, with dark brown skin and an ideology that favored people like himself in terms of social status.

Writing in *The Crisis*, Du Bois confronted the mystery surrounding Garvey. "It is a little difficult to characterize the man Garvey. He has been charged with dishonesty and graft, but he seems to me essentially an honest and sincere man with a tremendous vision, a great dynamic force. . . . But also has he very serious defects of temperament and training; he is dictatorial, domineering, inordinately vain and very suspicious."

Walter's first direct communication with Garvey came in the form of a letter in 1920. Garvey had received communication from a prisoner at the Leavenworth federal penitentiary, who needed legal assistance. Garvey forwarded the letter to the NAACP's assistant secretary, explaining that the UNIA "does not deal with such cases." The letter came on UNIA letterhead with the organization's motto across the top: "One God! One aim! One destiny!"

Meanwhile, letters poured into the NAACP's headquarters from concerned citizens who wanted to send their meager savings to Garvey but were nervous about doing so. Some of these missives were written in the scratch of the barely literate. "Is this Marcus Garvey really in earnest about his work?" wrote one man from Cleveland, Ohio, his signature unreadable. "Is it safe to deposit money with him for stock?"

The right answer was anyone's guess.

AS GARVEY'S STAR ROSE, the NAACP faced a series of setbacks in 1920.

John Shillady continued to spiral into a helpless depression. In the office each day, he appeared like a haunted man, as if a tap on his shoulder might cause him to shatter. "John's physical condition from the beating and the deterioration which followed from the crushing blows on his head was pitiful to watch," Walter recalled. An association board member named George Crawford wrote to the other members: "I am of the opinion that for his own good and his good to the work, Mr. Shillady should have at once a vacation for a month to six weeks during which he would be absolutely free from any responsibilities of the office." Shillady, the writer concluded, "seems to need it."

Shillady took this vacation and did not come back. He disappeared altogether, never to be heard from again.

At the same time, while the nation was pulling out of the flu pandemic, a stark economic downturn — the depression of 1920–1921 — brought its own existential threat. The association was "broke," Walter recalled. "We owed sizable debts for printing, rent, and other operating costs."

Walter's report in *The Nation* on the massacre in Phillips County —"'Massacring Whites' in Arkansas" — had earned the association huge amounts of publicity, which brought in donations from members who wanted to help save the dozens of martyrs still in prison. "Our empty treasury began to be replenished by the contributions of white and Negro Americans who were shocked by the story," he recalled. The association's attorney in the Phillips County case, Scipio Africanus Jones, who had been born into slavery, was now, decades later, engaged in the most high-profile case of his career, one that would come to be known as *Moore v. Dempsey*. But the legal fight in Little Rock was costing the NAACP more than it was bringing in.

The board of directors elected James Weldon Johnson the new secretary, to replace Shillady. Johnson became the NAACP's first Black chief executive. However, the timing presented little hope for success. There was no money even for salaries; while the stenographers were paid, both Walter and Johnson went about four months with no paychecks.

Still, the most unnerving news at association headquarters in 1920 was the continued rise of the Ku Klux Klan. Throughout the year, the association's mailbags filled with desperate letters from Black Americans whose livelihoods and homes were being threatened, all over the country but mainly in the South.

A woman named Ruth Crowd wrote asking for help for her father, Frank Crowd, who ran a barbershop in Jacksonville, Florida, and had been threatened by the Klan with violence if he did not leave town. "He is a respectable businessman," she wrote, "and has had this same shop for over 35 years."

A mechanic working at the Princeton Buick Company in Princeton, Indiana, received a note reading, "Nigger, we are here. Move out of the white folks' neighborhood. If we have to again warn you God help you. Ku Klux Klan."

A black pharmacist in Jackson, Mississippi, wrote to the NAACP after receiving a letter that read, "You niggers are getting too much of a foot hold in Jackson and we propose to put a stop to it." The letter threatened murder and was signed, "Ku Klux Klan."

The Greek owners of the Little Savoy Café in Goldsboro, North Carolina, reported being threatened for serving food to Black customers.

The Chicago owner of the MacNeal Publishing Company, A. C. Mac-Neal, wrote Walter directly. "The activities of the Ku Klux Klan here show some rather sinister and deep-seated aspects." He asked Walter to make one of his investigations. "Can you make such an investigation? What is your figure?" MacNeal continued, "If you wire, take care in the use of your words," as Klan spies were everywhere.

All of these writers and so many more wanted the NAACP's help, to save their necks, their homes, their businesses, because they believed the police would not help them. This same year, the KKK's Grand Wizard, William J. Simmons — who had founded the new Klan five years earlier when he led his white pilgrimage to the top of Atlanta's Stone Mountain — issued a philosophy in Klan recruitment literature. "The modern Knights of the Ku Klux Klan is a legally chartered patriotic and fraternal organization," Simmons wrote. "It stands uncompromisingly for enforcement of all laws and stands ready at any and all times to assist if called upon in aiding properly constituted authorities in suppressing outbreaks against law and order. . . . Being strictly an American institution only one hundred percent American citizens are eligible for membership. These must be white, native-born, adhere[ing] to the tenants of the Christian religion."

In the fall of 1920 Walter applied for membership to the secret society that espoused the theory of "America for Americans." He inquired through the KKK's Atlanta national headquarters and was sent an application. It arrived on official stationery, reading across the top, "Imperial Palace . . . Invisible Empire . . . Knights of the Ku Klux Klan (Incorporated) . . . Atlanta Georgia."

"Your inquiry has been received by the Kligrapp of the great Wizard," a cover letter read, "and he is instructed to propound to you the following necessary interrogatories."

Walter answered the questionnaire in his usual elegant handwriting.

- Is the move prompting your inquiry serious? *Yes*
- What is your age? *27*
- What is your occupation? *Journalist*
- Where were you born? *Atlanta, Ga.*
- How long have you resided in your present locality? *Three years*

- Are you married, single or widower? *Single*
- Were your parents born in the United States of America? *Yes*
- Are you a gentile or a Jew? *Gentile*
- Are you of the white race or of a colored race? [left blank]
- Color of eyes? *Blue*. Hair? *Golden*. Weight? *135*. Height? *5 ft. 7 in.*
- Do you believe in the principles of PURE Americanism? *Yes*

Walter signed the form with his Harlem address — 226 West 138th Street, New York City — and dated it September 21, 1920. Nothing came of the application. It was his first attempt to infiltrate the Ku Klux Klan, a goal that was about to turn into an obsession.

8

Through the efforts of the National Association for the Advancement of Colored People, the efforts of the Ku Klux Klan in terrorizing Negroes in the South have been brought into light. . . . Will you help to defeat this organization which seeks to further embitter America against the Negro?

— *The N.A.A.C.P. vs. The K.K.K.,* NAACP pamphlet, written by
   Walter White, 1921

ON THE FIRST TUESDAY OF NOVEMBER in 1920, Republican Warren G. Harding defeated Ohioan James M. Cox to win America's twenty-ninth presidency. The vote indicated a severe dividing line in America, as the Republicans won every state except eleven — all eleven of those in the Deep South. The same party lines that had existed in Abraham Lincoln's time still existed, for the most part, over a half century later: Democrats in the South, Republicans in the North.

Immediately following the election, a series of events conspired to land Walter White in the hot seat, testifying before an angry congressional committee in Washington for what would be the first of many times during his life.

Two days after the election Walter noticed a headline in the *New York Times:* KILL TWO WHITES AND SIX NEGROES IN FLORIDA RIOT. The story told of "an election riot" set off when a Black farmer named Mose Norman attempted to vote in the town of Ocoee, Florida. Refused by election officials, according to the *Times* article, "he returned later, armed with a shotgun; but it was taken from him and he was driven away." Tempers flared. When another Black man named July Perry attempted to vote, a white posse formed and attempted to arrest Perry, who defended himself when he saw the posse outside his home. Gunfire and rioting ensued, and July Perry was killed.

"Several other negroes perished when the buildings in which they sought shelter were burned," the *Times* reported. "Armed whites were reported patrolling the region and closing in on negroes who fled to the woods, the pursuit being accompanied by intermittent firing."

At the same time, a congressman by the name of George H. Tinkham, Republican of Massachusetts, came forth with a startling House resolution. The 1920 census had just been completed, showing that the nation's population had increased 13.7 million since the last census was taken, ten years earlier. One of the first acts of the next Congress would be, by law, to examine representation in Congress according to the new figures. Congressman Tinkham, a northerner, stunned some of his colleagues when he declared that the current system was unconstitutional because disenfranchisement in the South gave too much power to white voters from southern states.

"My resolution," he announced, "proposes that an investigation be made of existing disenfranchisement in several States and that where disenfranchisement is found as a fact, the representation of those States in the House of Representatives shall be reduced in accordance with the Constitution. The issue is purely one of law and order, Constitutional enforcement, and political equality."

Tinkham's argument, at its root, was simple: By law, the number of voting congressmen in the House of Representatives per state was based on the state's population. But if a state did not allow some of its citizens to vote — such as Black citizens in many southern states — then the white voters of that state had a disproportionate amount of power. Disenfranchising Black voters in the South also gave an advantage to the Democratic Party (because those Black voters would almost certainly vote Republican, if they were permitted to vote). Tinkham argued that House representation should not reflect the population of a state but the population of a state that was *allowed to vote.*

He bolstered his argument with statistics. For example, both Florida and Colorado had four representatives in the House of Representatives. However, voting statistics showed that 208,855 people voted in Colorado in 1920, and only 31,613 in Florida. Why? For one reason, Black Americans, who formed a huge population in Florida, were not allowed to vote. Why, Tinkham argued, should 31,613 Floridians have as much power in the House of Representatives as 208,855 Coloradans?

South Carolina had seven representatives in Congress, while Nebraska had six. In South Carolina, where a large population of Black Americans lived and were not allowed to vote, 25,433 people went to the polls in 1920. In Nebraska, where Black Americans *were* allowed to vote, 216,014 cast ballots. So why should South Carolina get more representation in Congress, given that the state had less than one eighth the number of voters that Nebraska had?

Congressman Tinkham demanded a full-scale investigation into the 1920 election, to prove clearly that disenfranchisement of Black voters violated the Fourteenth and Fifteenth Amendments. And if disenfranchisement were permitted to exist, then Congress had a duty by the Constitution to lessen the number of House members (and thus lessen the voting power) representing the states where disenfranchisement was practiced.

Tinkham needed witnesses to testify before the Census Committee in Washington. He found officials of the NAACP more than willing. Walter, meanwhile, realized that if he could put together a speedy investigation of the voting riot in Florida that he read about in the *New York Times,* he could appear before Congress with a hell of a story — a violent story, the guns still smoking. When he reached out to the congressman from Massachusetts, he found in Tinkham a worthy partner.

"There is no question of course for a moment in any one's mind," Tinkham wrote Walter, that "extensive unconstitutional disenfranchisement exists in most of the Southern states either by laws or with terrorism and intimidation."

Walter responded to say that the NAACP was at the ready, with all its 354 branches and its 100,000 members, "to bring all pressure possible to bear on Congress." Then he packed his suitcase. His plan: to assume the identity of a white northern real estate agent, hunting for a piece of orange-grove property in Orange County, Florida.

ON DECEMBER 29, 1920, in the nation's capital, a delegation of officials from the NAACP appeared before Congress's Census Committee — James Weldon Johnson, Walter White, the association's brilliant field secretary, William Pickens, and the head of the Washington, DC, branch, Archibald H. Grimké, a white-haired African American who had been born into slavery in South Carolina and had gone on to graduate from Harvard Law School. Walter had only recently returned from Florida, and he was prepared to reveal what he had learned there. Congressman Tinkham opened the discussion with fighting words:

"This committee must inquire under the Constitution as to the existence of this disenfranchisement, and if it finds disenfranchisement, reduce the Representatives of that State or those States which maintain a system which disenfranchises."

Congressman Carlos Bee of Texas said, "Is that a threat or a promise?"

Tinkham: "It is a statement of fact."

From the beginning it was clear the proceedings were going to be brutal. The NAACP officials faced off against a Census Committee heavily represented by old guard, white politicians from states where Jim Crow thrived. Pickens testified first, explaining how his research clearly showed that Black voters were refused by the voting registrars of South Carolina and Virginia. Congressman William Larsen of Georgia took the floor and called Pickens a liar, setting the tone and the strategy for his colleagues from the South. They would refuse to admit to disenfranchisement in their states, while attempting to intimidate the witnesses with bluster and condescension.

"Mr. Chairman," Larsen said after Pickens spoke, "I would like to know if the members of this committee have to sit here and hear a commonwealth insulted by the witness. If so, I do not care to remain."

Congressman Loren Wheeler of Illinois spoke: "Then, according to your statement, in the South, the Negro is permitted to vote with the same freedom that he is in the North?"

Larsen answered, "Absolutely, and any statement to the contrary is unfounded." This was a statement that everyone in the room knew to be a lie.

For hours on December 29 and 30 the NAACP men gave testimony, and when it was Walter's turn, he told the story of what he had discovered during his investigation into the voting race riot of Ocoee, Florida, a story he would subsequently recount in articles in both *The Crisis* and *The New Republic*.

How an upstanding Black man in his community, an owner of an orange grove named Mose Norman, had attempted to vote. Norman was not only refused the ballot, he was severely assaulted.

How thousands of African Americans had organized themselves to vote, how they had lined up and stood all day on November 2, only to be refused the ballot. (Walter had pictures of this.)

How a white mob had burned down buildings in the Black neighborhood of Ocoee during the voting race riot and had sprayed gunfire into the people fleeing from those burning buildings.

How a KKK rally had been held in Orlando right before Election Day, specifically to intimidate would-be Black voters.

Walter had gathered numerous signed affidavits swearing all this to be true, including one from a white lawyer named Alexander Akerman of Orlando, who was a former United States district attorney. (Specifically, Akerman's affidavit read, "In Orlando, a like band of KKK paraded the streets October 30, 5000 strong. . . . They paraded through the entire Negro section and around the Negro churches to intimidate and frighten the Negro voters.")

Congressman Frank Clark, Democrat of Florida, refused to believe Walter's story of what had occurred in his own home state. "In my county," he said, "we have got Negro farmers who drive by my house on Saturday in automobiles. Negroes who are amply able to pay their way here and come before this committee and if they have any complaint to make, they can make it for themselves and they do not need these Negroes from New York to come here and represent them."

James Peter Glynn, a Republican representative from Connecticut, spoke up: "Mr. White is not Negro."

For a moment a confused Congressman Clark examined Walter's face. "If he is not," Clark said, "I never saw one in my life, and if he is not, I have less respect for him."

Ultimately Walter's testimony devolved into an angry debate with Congressman Carlos Bee of Texas. "You state upon your authority," Bee asked Walter, "as an officer of this organization that the majority of the people of the Southern States are lawless or law violators?"

"In many of the communities, that is so."

"I asked you if your statement was that the majority of the people of the South were lawless and law violators."

"I say that in many communities of the South, the majority of them are lawless."

"In what community of the South are they lawless?"

Walter answered without hesitation: "In answer to your question, I will mention Phillips County, Arkansas."

WALTER AND HIS COLLEAGUES returned to New York thrilled by the excitement of their testimony yet dubious that Congressman Tinkham's call for an investigation into the 1920 presidential election would get anywhere. Walter wrote to the NAACP's recently retired chairman of the board, Moorfield Storey: "I suppose you have seen by the newspapers, the accounts of our exciting time before the Census Committee. Inspite [*sic*] of the very vicious methods of three southern representatives, I believe that a great deal of valuable work was done."

To Walter's surprise, the Imperial Wizard of the KKK personally responded to the NAACP's testimony, after the Census Committee hearings.

We are told that the Ku Klux Klan is stirring up race prejudice [William Simmons told a reporter]. What then, may we ask, is stirred up when the National Association for the Advancement

of Colored People feels its power so strongly that, alone and un-
aided, it openly and brazenly goes before Congress with the
demand that representation of the South be cut down as punishment because of "discrimination against the Negro at the ballot
box"? We presume that there was no possibility of stirring up race
prejudice when this association willfully and deliberately uttered
the falsehood that members of this organization paraded the
night before the recent presidential election for the purpose of
terrifying Negro voters and that on election day members of this
organization beat and killed Negroes because they sought to vote.

Facts were a peculiar thing, Walter understood. They depended not
always on the truth but on who was speaking and what that speaker's audience wanted to hear. Walter was infuriated — and impatient. He wanted
results.

On January 10, 1921, less than two weeks after his testimony in Washington, at the monthly Board of Directors meeting at 70 Fifth Avenue,
Walter formally asked that he be allowed to attempt his most dangerous
undercover investigation yet. The meeting minutes: "The Chairman
[Mary White Ovington] requested the Assistant Secretary to present to
the Board his request that he be allowed to investigate the Ku Klux Klan."

"Considerable discussion" followed, according to the minutes, after
which the board refused White permission. It was too dangerous, and the
recent fate of John Shillady felt too raw.

But Walter could not give it up. Through a friend, he finagled an invitation to formally join the Klan. He received a letter that began, "As a leading citizen of your community, and having confidence in your patriotism,
I take the liberty of bringing to your attention a matter which cannot fail
to appeal to every real American. The story of the Ku Klux Klan, of the
reconstruction days, and its valiant services in behalf of white supremacy,
insures it a place in the heart of every true American. . . . A branch of the
reorganized Klan of today . . . should be in every community in the Nation." The letter was signed by Edward Young Clarke, who was just at that
time taking over as the new acting Imperial Wizard of the KKK.

Walter responded to Clarke directly. "I wrote the Klan on plain stationery," Walter recalled, "saying that as a native Georgian, although now living in New York, I was greatly interested in the reorganization of the Klan and would like information regarding memberships." Several congenial and probing letters went back and forth between Atlanta and New York, as Walter fished for evidence of fraud or any other admittance of lawbreaking. Suddenly, he recalled, the congenial letters were replaced by "letters threatening my life if I ever revealed any of the information about the Klan which I had gained in my correspondence with Clarke."

Walter's next move was to create a pamphlet called *The N.A.A.C.P. vs. The K.K.K.,* which broke down all the strategies the association was undertaking to destroy the Klan. How the NAACP had testified before Congress, how "monster mass meetings" were being held, how the association had aroused through all its members "to stamp out attempts to form branches of the Klan." The pamphlet was published and sent out to association branches nationwide.

Hoping to engage law enforcement in the fight, Walter turned over his files on the Klan to state, local, and federal agencies. He wrote to friends saying he was going to be "fighting fire with fire," that the Klan would be "met by armed resistance," even how he intended to "laugh the Klan out of existence" by mocking its pillow-and-bedsheet costumes and bizarre lingo (its klorans, kuklos, klarogos, and kilgrapps). He was good at making friends and had put that skill to work while he was in Washington testifying; now he got a dozen senators and congressmen to issue statements excoriating the Klan.

One day in the summer of 1921 a reporter from Joseph Pulitzer's New York *World* named Rowland Thomas came into the NAACP offices to discuss the idea of publishing an exposé on the KKK. Walter turned over all his information, and the *World* ran a series of articles—co-promoted by the NAACP—that detailed four alleged Klan murders, forty-one alleged Klan assaults, and numerous instances of tarring and feathering. The first article appeared on the paper's front page on September 6 with the headline, "Secrets of the Ku Klux Klan Exposed by the World." The exposé made the KKK the talk of New York. The articles were also published in nearly twenty other newspapers, in Boston, Saint Louis, Pittsburgh, New Orleans, Seattle, Milwaukee, Minneapolis, and throughout the state of Texas. The *New York Times* followed up the *World* exposé with its own report.

"That the Ku Klux problem has assumed nation-wide proportions cannot longer be denied," the *Times* stated. The KKK was now "threatening control of the political machinery of our political parties."

For Walter the fight was personal, and he was determined to win. Then early one Sunday morning he was awakened to find a hulking Irish American New York City Police Department Bomb Squad officer at his apartment door. The officer told Walter that detectives were being assigned to protect him and his family, as they had evidence that Klan members were after a "Negro named Walter White." All morning Walter's telephone rang and rang. Volunteers in Atlanta vowed to look after his parents. NYPD officers remained in his Harlem apartment. One said, "No Kluxer will ever put a hand on you or your family."

That remained to be seen.

9

85 WHITES AND NEGROES DIE IN TULSA RIOTS AS 3,000
ARMED MEN BATTLE IN STREETS; 30 BLOCKS BURNED,
MILITARY RULE IN CITY
— *New York Times* front page, June 2, 1921

THE TULSA RACE MASSACRE — a forty-eight-hour frenzy of violence on the last weekend of May in 1921 — would come to be called "the single worst incident of racial violence in American history." But at the time, May 30 of that year started out as any ordinary day.

At roughly 4 p.m. a nineteen-year-old African American shoe shiner named Dick Rowland entered an office building at 319 South Main Street in Tulsa, Oklahoma, looking to use a bathroom. Rowland took the elevator to the fourth floor, where he found a restroom with a sign out front: Colored Only. Minutes later, Rowland called for the elevator so he could return to the street. When the elevator doors opened, he saw that a white woman was operating it. Elevators were the only mode of transportation not segregated in Tulsa and communities like it all over the South. It was too expensive and logistically difficult to build extra elevators in buildings, so these little moving boxes were the only place where white and Black Americans might find themselves alone, in public. When Rowland went to step on board, the seventeen-year-old white female elevator operator started the car plunging downward while he was halfway inside. He said he lost his balance and stepped on her foot.

She cried rape.

Authorities jailed the youth, and the *Tulsa Tribune* ran a story with the headline "Nab Negro for Attacking Girl in Elevator." A Tulsan named William Danforth Williams recalled of that time, "It depends on where you were, your version of the riot. All of us agree that it started because of the threat through the *Tribune* paper that they were going to lynch a Negro tonight."

TULSA WAS A BOOMING OIL TOWN IN 1921 — "the Oil Capital of the World." So much money and so many people had poured into the city over the previous decade, Main Street looked as prosperous as any in the country. The community was also a growing hub for the Ku Klux Klan. One Tulsa engineer, named W. R. Holway, later remembered, "They ran the whole county and state. The schools. Juries. Everything."

By daybreak after Dick Rowland's elevator episode, a mob of hundreds of white men had gathered outside the jailhouse that now housed him. At the same time several Black men from the nearby Greenwood neighborhood of Tulsa had also gathered, because they had heard rumors that a lynch mob was out for Rowland. They wanted to protect him. A local official announced that there would be no lynching. The sheriff had disabled the elevator in the jailhouse to keep Rowland safe, and an armed guard stood at the top of the stairs. William Danforth Williams remembered: "So they all started away, and I guess about a block away somebody fired a shot. Whoever it was, black or white. And then right down there all hell cut loose. And they fought all night."

Greenwood was called "Black Wall Street," because it was prosperous and African American, with a thriving business district. This became the battleground. The Tulsa police deputized white citizens and armed them with guns. Men motored through Greenwood in swarms of cars, firing weapons. A mob torched buildings, turning Black Wall Street into a sprawling, hellish inferno. Churches, businesses, apartment buildings — towering columns of flames engulfed all of them.

Eyewitness accounts told of airplanes flying over Greenwood with guns blazing. One account described "a dozen or more" aircraft circling, dropping firebombs — "burning turpentine balls." Thousands of National

Guard troops rushed in to restore peace, and soon they were parading
Black men, women, and children at gunpoint into internment camps and
rounding them up into the backs of trucks. About forty urban blocks
were reduced to smoldering ash. Another eyewitness account:

> After twenty-four hours of one of the most disastrous race wars
> ever visited upon an American city . . . the negro quarter of Tulsa,
> comprising upwards of thirty densely populated blocks, was
> wiped out by fire. . . . The entire "black belt" of Tulsa is now only
> a smoldering heap of blackened ruins. Hardly a negro shanty
> is standing throughout an area that housed upward of 15,000
> blacks. Domestic animals wandering among the wreckage give
> the only token of life over a desolate territory.

"I arrived in Tulsa while the excitement was at its peak," Walter White
remembered. Posing as a reporter for a northern newspaper, Walter met a
local commercial photographer. "From him I learned that special deputy
sheriffs were being sworn in to guard the town from a rumored counter-
attack by the Negroes."

Using this photographer as a contact, Walter found his way that night
inside Tulsa's City Hall, a regal stone building at the corner of East Fourth
Street and South Cincinnati that was lined out front by parked cars. Local
authorities asked Walter three questions: his name, age, and address. "I
might have been a thug, a murderer, an escaped convict, a member of the
mob itself which had laid waste a large area of the city," he remembered
eight years later, in 1929. "None of these mattered; my skin was apparently
white, and that was enough." In a speedy ceremony, as he later reported,
he was among roughly fifty men sworn in to uphold the laws of Oklahoma and the US Constitution. He was one of the "white" citizens deputized by Tulsa police. After this ceremony, the man standing next to him
turned and said, "Now you can go out and shoot any nigger you see and
the law'll be behind you."

Some US Constitution, Walter surely thought to himself.

A man wearing a US Army uniform stood nearby looking at Walter,

as if he knew him from somewhere, which made Walter exceedingly nervous. If his identity was learned, he would almost certainly die that night.
The man approached, with four others closely behind him. Walter recalled the dialogue:

"You say that your name is White?"

Walter answered affirmatively.

"You say you're a newspaper man?"

Yes again. "Would you care to see my credentials?"

"No, but I want to tell you something. There's an organization in the
South that doesn't love niggers. It has branches everywhere. You needn't
ask me the name — I can't tell you. But it has come back into existence
to fight this damned nigger Advancement Association. We watch every
movement of the officers of this nigger society and we're out to get them for
putting notions of equality into the heads of our niggers down South here."

Walter reached for a cigarette, trying to keep his hand from shaking.
The man in the army uniform stood with his nose just inches from Walter's own.

"All of this is very interesting," Walter said, "but what, if anything, has
it to do with the story of the race riot here which I've come to get?"

Finally the man backed off. "Oh, nothing," he said. "Except I wanted
you to know what's back of the trouble here."

THROUGHOUT THE NIGHT Walter remained embedded, patrolling Tulsa
in a car with these same men, eyeing the apocalyptic imagery that would
later stun the nation as the photographs appeared in the newspapers. In
his mind he was already piecing together the facts and the scene setting
for his report. Tulsa looked like the images of bombed-out villages in
Europe from the Great War. Some two thousand of the newly homeless
Black Tulsans were huddled in the city's baseball park, guarded by militia
patrols bearing machine guns.

"Detachments of guardsmen," recalled one eyewitness, "were scattered throughout the city prepared to meet all emergencies." Walter was
undercover, as one of those guardsmen.

When the calm finally returned, Tulsans were left to take stock of their city. A local lawyer named Buck Colbert Franklin was one of the thousands of Black Tulsans arrested during the rampage. When he was released, he returned to find his office "in ashes. . . . As far as one could see, not a Negro dwelling-house or place of business stood."

Another account published in *Tulsa Daily World* described Black citizens of Greenwood sitting in the smoked ruins amidst the broken glass and wreckage: "The look in their eyes was one of dejection and supplication. Judging from their attitude, it was not of material consequence to them whether they lived or died. Harmless themselves, they apparently could not conceive the brutality and fiendishness of men who would deliberately set fire to the homes of their friends and neighbors and just as deliberately shoot them down in their tracks."

The governor of Oklahoma ordered an inquiry into the sheriff of Tulsa County's role in the rioting and killing. Former president of the United States William Howard Taft published an essay in the *Washington Post*: "No matter whether it was a negro or a white man who began the initial fight, one can not escape the conclusion that the awful character of this cruel massacre was largely due to the outrageous malevolence and cruelty of the whites who took part in the conflict. This is clearly indicated by the number of the negro dead as compared with the dead whites, by the wholesale destruction and looting of the negro settlement and business quarter."

Three days after it ended, the new president, Warren G. Harding, delivered a speech at Lincoln University in Pennsylvania and addressed the tragedy head-on. "Despite the demagogues, the idea of our oneness as Americans has risen superior to every appeal to mere class and group," the president said. "And so, I wish it might be in this matter of our national problem of races." Speaking directly about Tulsa, he said, "God grant that, in the soberness, the fairness, and the justice of this country, we never see another spectacle like it."

The nineteen-year-old boy accused of rape in the elevator at 319 South Main Street—Dick Rowland—was released, after the young woman whose foot he stepped on dropped all charges. The number killed in the Tulsa massacre has never been officially determined, but Walter estimated that it cost the lives of some 50 white Tulsans and between 150 and 200 Black Tulsans. The thousands who lost their homes and their businesses had no recourse—no help from the law or the courts, no hope at all.

Walter White's report was published in *The Nation* that summer. He wrote:

> There is a lesson in the Tulsa affair for every American who fatu-ously believes that Negroes will always be the meek and submis-sive creatures that circumstances have forced them to be during the past three hundred years. Dick Rowland was only an ordi-nary bootblack with no standing in the community. But when his life was threatened by a mob of whites, every one of the 15,000 Negroes in Tulsa . . . was willing to die to protect Dick Rowland. Perhaps America is waiting for a nationwide Tulsa to wake her.

Walter's article, "The Eruption of Tulsa," took on a life of its own, and the publicity revealed his identity as an African American and an officer of the NAACP. "More than a hundred anonymous letters threatening my life came to me," he later recalled.

Tulsa's police chief was ultimately found guilty of two crimes, but he never served a day in prison. Only one person, a Black man, ended up doing time.* But the shock value of the event started a movement in Washington, DC, to create a federal anti-lynching bill. If local authorities refused to enforce laws in their communities, could the federal govern-ment intercede?

THREE YEARS BEFORE THE TULSA MASSACRE, a congressman named Leonidas Dyer of Missouri had introduced a federal anti-lynching bill,

---

* The Tulsa massacre of 1921 made front-page news in 2020, when President Donald Trump was criticized for holding a political rally there during protests over the police killing of a Black man, George Floyd. As late as June 2021, anthropologists and archaeologists were still finding unmarked mass graves believed—but not yet proven—from the 1921 massacre.

the so-called Dyer bill, which sought to give the federal government jurisdiction in lynching cases, if states did not enforce their own laws themselves. Dyer came to the lynching cause through a heartbreaking experience. He had started his career as a lawyer in Saint Louis and represented that district of Missouri in Washington. Following the East Saint Louis race massacre of 1917 (the incident that provoked James Weldon Johnson to create the Silent Parade in Manhattan, back when Walter was still living in Atlanta), Dyer had interviewed witnesses about the atrocities, the killing of innocent Black people, and these interviews turned him into a civil rights crusader.

Walter's involvement in the federal anti-lynching bill dated back to his first months with the NAACP, in 1918, when he visited Congressman Dyer in his office in Washington. Dyer moved Walter so much that Walter wrote him after that visit. "It is . . . our desire to launch a campaign," Walter wrote, "national in its scope in support of your bill." The NAACP would generate "tremendous public sentiment."

So began Walter's lifelong journey in Washington, fighting for a federal anti-lynch law.

Opposition to the Dyer bill seemed inexplicable to Walter, yet it was strong. The constitutionality of the bill was questionable — whether or not the federal government could claim jurisdiction to enforce laws within states. This constitutional question was at the heart of the Civil War (could the federal government force the states to outlaw slavery?), and so it touched a nerve for southerners. But from Walter's early days of involvement, he understood there were more sinister forces at work. As Congressman Merrill Moores of Indiana — a coauthor of the Dyer bill — wrote to Walter in 1918, "The real trouble with this legislation is that there is a very bitter prejudice against the negro existing in many of the members of Congress and if the bill is made too obviously for the protection of the negro, the prejudice will certainly defeat its enactment." Moores told Walter, "If my bill will stop one lynching and save one man's life, it will not be in vain."

The bill had been knocked around the halls of Congress for years. But after the Tulsa massacre, support for the federal anti-lynching bill burst anew. Walter and his boss, James Weldon Johnson, began commuting to Washington to lobby for it. Johnson recalled, "The entire machinery of the Association, its full organized strength and all the collateral force it could marshal, were thrown behind this measure."

Johnson wrote President Harding demanding that he back the Dyer bill. Harding's secretary wrote back: "I am directed to say that the President still has [this request] in mind and that the failure to take definite action thus far in no wise indicates a loss of interest. There has, however, been so great a pressure of public duties that it has been impossible for him to give this subject the attention necessary before he takes action."

In January 1922, eight months after the attack in Tulsa, the bill finally came up for debate on the House floor. "There was intense excitement," Johnson recalled. "The news that the Anti-lynching Bill was being debated jammed the galleries . . . the majority of the crowd being Negroes."

Charging out to defend states' rights against federal encroachment was Representative Hatton Sumners of Texas. "Mr. Chairman," he said on the House floor. "I am opposed to mob violence . . . I am opposed to lynching." But the Dyer bill, he said, was unconstitutional. "Today the Constitution of the United States stands at the door, guarding the governmental integrity of the States."

And then there was the matter of race. "Only a short time ago," Sumners said, "their [African Americans'] ancestors roamed the jungles of Africa in absolute savagery. . . . Now we have them here. . . . You do not know where the beast is among them. Somewhere in that black mass of people is the man who would outrage your wife or your child, and every man who lives out in the country knows it." Of lynching, he said: "When men respond to the call, they respond to a law that is higher than the law of self-preservation. It is the call to the preservation of the race. When that call comes every man who is not a racial degenerate has to answer it."

Behind the scenes, James Weldon Johnson lobbied congressmen to get behind the Dyer bill. "I am pouring into them as much of our dope as they will hold," Johnson told Walter. Daily newspaper editorials fanned the flames on both sides. The *Macon Daily News* of Georgia called the Dyer bill a "monstrous attempt to federalize the police powers of the

State" and the NAACP a group of "sociological imbeciles [who] derive their knowledge of the negro from hearing jazz orchestras recruited from the West Indies in the rancid cafes of Paris."

At one point, on the floor of the Capitol during the congressional debate, a statement by a representative offended the crowd in the galleries, causing an eruption of booing. A voice from the floor yelled, "Sit down, you niggers!"

A voice came back, "You're a liar! We're not niggers!"

Walter and Johnson were almost certainly in the gallery when Congressman Thomas Sisson of Mississippi launched into a speech defending lynching. In the process, Sisson revealed in spite of himself a naked truth — that countless Americans, particularly in the South, had formed their image of the Black race based on the portrait in the 1915 movie blockbuster, *The Birth of a Nation.*

"You who are supporting this bill are traitors to the white race," Sisson declared, in a rant that went on for many thousands of words and held his colleagues spellbound. "You who vote for this bill are destroying white civilization. . . . We are going to protect our girls and womenfolk from these black brutes. When these black fiends keep their hands off the throats of the women of the South then lynching will stop, and it is never going to stop until that crime stops. . . . Before God and high heaven this is the sacred truth. I would rather the whole black race of this world were lynched than for one of the fair daughters of the South to be ravished and torn by one of these black brutes. Now, if this be treason, make the most of it."

The room erupted in applause and boos simultaneously. Congressman Henry Allen Cooper of Wisconsin spoke up: "Mr. Chairman, if I had a minute I would like to answer that. . . . It is the first time that I have heard mob law openly advocated in the Congress of the United States."

Applause erupted on the floor and in the gallery.

Sisson: "I never advocated mob law. Does the gentleman advocate rape?"

Congressman William Fields of Kentucky, referring to the African Americans in the gallery: "Mr. Chairman, I make the point of order that the gallery is out of order."

Sisson: "I want to know if the gentleman advocates rape."

Cooper: "Oh, that is simply silly. . . ."

Sisson: "The gentleman is just as idiotic as any man I know."

Cooper: "The gentleman has openly advocated mob law right here in the Congress of the United States —"

Chairman: "All gentlemen will be seated."

Sisson: "Let the Chairman get that black crowd in the galleries in order, and the gentleman from Wisconsin who began this in order, and I will be in order and not until then."

Two days after Congressman Sisson's speech on the House floor, on January 27, 1922, at 3 p.m., the Dyer bill went to a vote in the House of Representatives. When it passed by 230 to 119, "a wave of thanksgiving and jubilation swept the colored people of the country," Johnson recalled. Now the fight would move to its ultimate stage: a vote in the Senate. President Harding released a statement: "If the Senate of the United States passes the Dyer anti-lynching bill, it won't be in the White House three minutes before I'll sign it and, having signed it, enforce it."

ACROSS THE COUNTRY IN 1922, debate about the Dyer bill cleaved Americans into camps — those for it, those against it. The bill's legacy would go so far beyond anything that its creators could have imagined. Ever since the Great War, the race issue radicalized Americans on both sides. The Red Summer, the Tulsa massacre, the Dyer bill — each of these episodes strengthened the resolve of those who supported the NAACP and those who supported the KKK. Both sides used the Dyer bill to recruit members and raise funds. Now, as the Dyer bill neared a climactic vote in the Senate, Walter White and his colleagues felt in their bones the chilling rise of KKK radicalism.

In Atlanta on May 8, 1922, after the House had passed the Dyer bill but before the Senate vote, leaders of the Klan met for its first national congress — a "Klanvocation" — on the seventh anniversary of the founding of the modern KKK. That same day an investigation in California broke news that the Klan was alive in Los Angeles, Oakland, Bakersfield, Fresno, and Sacramento; "scores of officials of the various municipalities, and hundreds of members of state, county, and city police forces are also members of the Klan," reported the *Christian Science Monitor*. The *Wilmington Advocate* in Delaware reported on July 1, 1922: "Ku Klux Growing by Leaps and Bounds in Delaware." Four days later, a burning cross was spotted on a hilltop in Paterson, New Jersey.

On November 22, 1922, thirty-three Klan women in white robes marched in Atlanta. "We are in politics from the word go," said a Klan spokeswoman. "Our principles are of the rock-ribbed 100 percent brand for which the Ku Klux Klan stands, and we are ready to defend those principles, even at the risk of our lives."

Meanwhile, the Senate prepared to vote. "We must use every effort," Walter wrote to his friend Bishop John Hurst in Georgia, "not only because of the integrity of the Association, but because of the destinies of all of our people." As Moorfield Storey wrote to another of the Dyer bill's supporters in Congress, Frederick Dallinger, Republican of Massachusetts, "I hope your act will . . . become a law, for I feel very sure that unless lynching of colored people is stopped we are drifting into what may well become civil war." (Congressman Dallinger read this letter aloud while testifying as a witness in favor of the Dyer bill.) In June 1922 organizers of major organizations put together a march through Midtown Manhattan in support of the federal anti-lynching law. Among them was the UNIA, with Marcus Garvey in the flesh, along with the NAACP. It was a rare moment when the two organizations came together.

On the Senate floor the Dyer bill never had a chance, literally. Democrats from the South conducted what one journalist reporting on the procedures called "one of the most efficiently conducted filibusters in the history of the Senate." The rules dictated that any senator could speak on an issue for as long as he wanted, and so southern Democrats led the group of ninety-six lawmakers into verbal gridlock. The Senate could not conduct any business until the filibuster ended. And so, on December 3, 1922, the Senate abandoned the Dyer bill — without any vote. The *New York Times*'s front-page headline: FILIBUSTER KILLS ANTI-LYNCHING BILL.

In protest, the NAACP and the American Fund for Public Service paid for an advertisement, a full page, to run in nine newspapers, total-ing a readership of two million people. Under the heading "The Shame of America," it read: "Do you know that the United States is the Only Land on Earth where human beings are BURNED AT THE STAKE?" ("The ad is great," Johnson told Walter. "It has made a sensation here among our people.")

On December 13 the association sent out an open letter to every sena-tor of the United States. It began, "From December 4, the day the United States Senate abandoned the Dyer Anti-Lynching Bill, to December 12, there have been four lynchings in this country, one for each two days, one of the victims being publicly tortured and burned at the stake. The outbreak of barbarism, anarchy and degenerate bestiality and the blood of the victims rests upon the heads of those Southern senators who have obstructed even discussion of the measure designed to remedy this very condition."

Walter White was already at work creating the next chapter in the fight for a federal anti-lynching law, while taking solace in the deceased Dyer bill's having at least opened the eyes of many Americans to the evil among them. "The campaign for federal legislation publicized the facts about lynching," Walter later wrote. "Americans were astounded (some of them still are) to hear that fellow Americans have been put to death by mobs for such 'crimes' as 'being too prosperous for a Negro,' talking back to a white man, and for refusing to turn out of the road to let a white boy pass."

10

I got the world in a jug, the stopper's in my hand.
—Bessie Smith, "Down Hearted Blues"

ONE DAY Walter White was at the Abyssinian Baptist Church on 138th Street in Harlem with a writer named Konrad Bercovici, attending a service, which was rare for the assistant secretary. "The NAACP is religion enough for me," he once said. The church was full of African American Harlemites, but Bercovici spotted a boy with Caucasian skin and blond hair, handing out literature.

"Surely," he whispered to Walter, "this young boy is not colored?"

"He is," Walter answered. "Only one drop of colored blood makes a white man a negro, but nine-tenths of white blood in a colored man does not make him a white man. It has been so decreed. See how white he is," Walter said, nodding to the boy. "Should he live among white people and should they find out he is of negro ancestry, they would draw away from him as if he were the worst kind of criminal."

Herein lay the simplest and most direct definition of race Walter White would ever utter, and in those few sentences he encapsulated the story of his own whiteness and Blackness. One drop of blood made the difference. He was of the first generation in his family not born into slavery. The race of his family could be defined in an equation: white slave master plus Black slave equals Black child, no matter how white the skin. That is why Walter's parents had raised him the way they did; they had always been considered "Afro-American" in their community. This was all they knew.

Walter and his brothers and sisters were the first generation of his family with the option to choose. He knew countless light-skinned men and women who were "colored," by his definition, who lived their lives as white people. "There are few Negroes of my acquaintance who do not know of at least one ex-Negro," he wrote around this time. "I know personally at least half a hundred, among them some of my own relatives." Why? What was the reason for passing? "There are naïve whites who believe that light-skinned Negroes cross the color line solely because they believe there is some miraculous virtue and happiness simply in being white. . . . Nearly all of the 'passing' with which I am familiar finds its inception solely in the desire for improving one's lot and enlarging one's opportunity."

Anyone who had ever suffered the ignominy of being turned away at a restaurant, or who got paid less to do the same job, could understand the impulse to pass, he explained.

But Walter's own story of passing was unique. He passed as a white man, but not for the reasons that others did. He crossed over to become an agent of change, a crime fighter. In 1922 he wrote an article in the New York *Evening Post* about his undercover life, titled "Exploits of a Colored Investigator of Lynchings."

"What sort of a looking man is a lyncher?" the article began. "How does he differ from the man you met on Broadway or Michigan Avenue or Boston Common? How do you make an investigation? Do you use a disguise? How do you get away with it? Isn't there danger in it if you should be discovered?" All of those questions he answered through anecdotes from his own story, of weaponizing his skin color to become a force of justice.

Another newspaper story in 1923 ran with the headline "'It's a Cinch to Pass for White,'" with a photo of twenty-nine-year-old Walter, blond hair mid-parted and slicked, moustache well trimmed. That same year he told a friend, "I have personally investigated thirty-six lynchings and eight race riots. Because of the peculiar advantage I possess of being able to go either as a white man or a colored man I have talked on terms of intimacy with hundreds of white men *as one of them* and to hundreds, nay thousands, of Negroes *as one of them.*" (Italics are his own.)

His double life was making him famous, and he was becoming something of a public attraction in Harlem. What fascinated people most was his threshold for danger and his desire to keep his foot firmly planted on the proverbial gas pedal. He was living like a man destined to die young. He rarely slept and was up to three packs of smokes a day. "I have to have something to do with my hands," he said. He worked endless days in the office. "With Walter," one confidant explained, "it was almost a fetish to be immediately available to anyone who needed him. In the office he made it a rule that all his calls should be given directly to him. No secretary intervened."

Although he worked fanatically, he seemed allergic to money. "Walter was just an impossibly generous person," remembered Joel Spingarn. "You were afraid to tell Walter that perhaps you didn't have a certain book. He was always broke, but if you didn't have that book, the next day he'd go down and buy it and send it to you. I remember we had a dinner with a man who gave us [the NAACP] $10,000 — one of the richest men in the country, and Walter insisted on paying for the dinner. He always did. He was just incurably generous and always broke."

In 1922 Walter married an NAACP stenographer named Gladys Powell. Born in Mexico City, raised in Philadelphia, she was the daughter of a concert baritone and had ambitions for a life on the stage. Like Walter, she was of mixed race — part white, part Black, and part Native American. As a *New Yorker* writer later put it in a profile of Walter, his wife was "considered by many of her acquaintances the most beautiful woman they ever saw." The two moved into an apartment at 90 Edgecombe Avenue at 139th Street, and had their first child, a daughter they named Jane.

Meanwhile, work at the association was so brutally busy, Walter's boss was beginning to show signs of extreme exhaustion. James Weldon Johnson was fifty-two in 1923; his face was thinning out, and his eyes carried heavy bags under them. At one point he was told by board members to take a rest or else. Walter wrote to former board chairman Moorfield Storey, "Mr. Johnson intimated to me your feeling of apprehension regarding his health. Entreaties having failed, we here are now using sterner methods and we are barring Mr. Johnson from the office for two weeks, sending him away on an ocean trip of some sort."

Like Walter, Johnson was incapable of taking a break. As his protégé, Walter was next in line. He was riding a wave of success, and he knew that if he wanted it, leadership of the NAACP was within his grasp. It was just a matter of time.

BECOMING A FATHER had no effect on Walter's workaholism, or his partying. By 1923, his fifth year in New York, Harlem was being hailed as the "Nightclub Capital of the World," and the bartenders knew Walter by first name. The term "Jazz Age" was coined by F. Scott Fitzgerald in 1922. This was an ethos as much as a style of music, and it grew its deepest roots in the pavement of Harlem. "Nowhere in the city except in the Harlem or in the Brooklyn negro sections does one hear so much frank laughter," the writer Konrad Bercovici wrote at the time. "Four hundred thousand negroes in New York! There has never been such a number of negroes in any one place."

At all hours the music reached out from Harlem clubs onto the sidewalks, as if grabbing passersby by the collar. Johnson remembered, "Grace and I entertained occasionally at our home in Harlem. And so did Walter White and his wife at their home. . . . More than once we closed the evening, or began the morning, by all going to one of the Harlem cabarets to dance."

There was the Bamville Club, Connor's, the Clam House, and Tillie's Inn. At some late-night joints a white man would risk his life by walking through the door. At others, the bartenders were happy to serve anyone who had a nickel (often the cost of a drink). To pry open the door of Pod's and Jerry's after midnight was to come face-to-face with the likes of Jimmy Walker, New York's "Nightclub Mayor" and master of the wisecrack. In 1923 the Club Deluxe — the favorite hangout of former heavyweight champ Jack Johnson — changed its name to the Cotton Club, opened its doors, and the Duesenbergs lined up out front. The Cotton Club became a whites-only club (except for the entertainers and staff) and Harlem's gaudiest by far.

Harlem's pool of musical talent was unprecedented: Florence Mills, Josephine Baker, Duke Ellington. One writer remembered seeing Fats Waller play in a nightclub: "Although his fingers looked like bundles of knockwurst, they raced over the keys of the organ as lightly as any safecracker's." At Edmond's on Fifth Avenue at 130th Street, Ethel Waters belted out "Shake That Thing." The Garden of Joy between 138th and 139th Streets was a favorite for a new crowd of 1920s gender benders. As one Harlemite described it: "Night after night there would arise the mingled strains of blues and spirituals, those peculiarly Negro forms of song, the one secular and the other religious, but both born of wretchedness in travail, both with their soarings of exultation and sinkings of despair."

The American economy was suddenly booming, and for the first time, Black America had a taste — nowhere more than Harlem. "You had rights that could not be denied you," the young Black writer Rudolph Fisher recorded in his first published short story, "The City of Refuge." "You had privileges, protected by law. And you had money. Everybody in Harlem had money. . . . It is a meteoric phenomenon. . . . Negro stock is going up, and everybody's buying."

The parties at Walter White's home were legendary. The guest list was often a who's who of Black Harlem and white Greenwich Village: Heywood Broun (newspaper columnist); Claude McKay (poet); Paul Robeson and Jules Bledsoe (concert singers); Carl Van Vechten (novelist, *Vanity Fair* writer); Newman Levy (lawyer, fiction writer, poet); Carl Van Doren (writer and literary critic); Edna St. Vincent Millay (poet); Sinclair Lewis (novelist); George Gershwin (hit jazz and orchestral composer); Willa Cather (novelist); Blanche and Alfred Knopf (avant-garde publishers). Walter held court weaving stories, often telling the heartbreaking tale of the lynching of Mary Turner in Georgia back in 1918, a story that left his audiences with jaws agape.

Walter was "one of the best-known figures in Harlem," wrote Bercovici. "Welcomed everywhere, known everywhere, a fluent talker and fiery orator, as ready with tears in his eyes as he is with a smile on his lips. . . . He has investigated almost every riot and lynching for the last ten years; and should one want a nightmare without going to the trouble of eating Welsh rarebit, he can have it if he meets and listens to Walter White."

For Walter, Harlem presented a diametric reality to the one he experienced when he crossed the Smith & Wesson Line into the South. Here he lived as a Black man, and there he was white. Here he was married, there single. Here he was becoming famous, and there he was always a stranger. Who was the real Walter White? He embodied the Cole Porter lyric: "Black's white today . . . Anything goes!"

ON JANUARY 13, 1922, federal agents appeared at the apartment building at 129 West 130th Street in Harlem, the home of Marcus Garvey, and arrested the leader of the United Negro Improvement Association. Garvey no doubt had seen it coming. The charge: using the federal mail system to defraud stockholders of the Black Star Line. The man who called himself the Provisional President of Africa was handcuffed and taken into custody.

His followers were stunned and angry. Outwardly, Garvey's UNIA had seen growth and wealth. He had sent his first mission to Liberia to begin negotiations whereby the UNIA could establish its colony and ultimately a place to serve as ground zero for Black Zion. Garvey's rallies had become increasingly ornate and ritualistic. Newspapers called him "the Black Moses" or "the Negro Moses." "The movement became more than a movement," wrote James Weldon Johnson. "It became a religion, its members became zealots."

Garvey had created within the UNIA a hierarchy of sycophants — commanders of what he called "the Sublime Order of the Nile" and a division of female "Black Cross nurses." Rallies at his Liberty Hall took on an air of sect-style ritualism. He had succeeded in exalting himself to a place no race leader had ever been. But behind the scenes, the Black Star Line was sinking, literally and figuratively. One of its ships was found taking on water about a hundred miles outside of New York Harbor and had to be rescued by coast guard. Another had its cargo seized by government officials.

The truth was, Garvey had no idea how to run a shipping company, and the men he hired proved mostly incompetents. "I gave everybody a chance," Garvey said privately. "And the story is that nearly everyone that I placed in a responsible position fleeced the Black Star Line."

Meanwhile, federal attorney general A. Mitchell Palmer had begun monitoring the activities of "foreign radicals," with a young upstart named J. Edgar Hoover as his assistant. Palmer had assigned an African American special agent to watch Garvey and his UNIA, which ultimately led to Garvey's arrest.

In February 1923, while Garvey was out on bail, a breaking news story sent a shock wave through Harlem. The new head of the Ku Klux Klan, Edward Young Clarke, testified before a federal grand jury in New York, asserting that he had held a secret meeting in Atlanta with the most controversial race leader in the world — Marcus Garvey.

Walter and his fellow NAACP officials were stunned. Du Bois vowed, "This open ally of the Ku Klux Klan should be locked up or sent home [to Jamaica]," calling Garvey "a lunatic or a traitor."

It all seemed so far-fetched. What could the KKK have to do with Marcus Garvey's back-to-Africa movement? Forced to comment, Garvey addressed a crowd of his followers in Harlem. "Knowing the power and influence and intention of the Klan," he said on July 9, 1922, "I interviewed the executive for the purpose of getting them, if possible, to adopt a different attitude toward the race I represent, and thus prevent a repetition in many ways of what happened during the days of Reconstruction."

If Garvey was being truthful, Walter and his colleagues argued, then why had the meeting taken place in secret? To employ a conceit popular at the time: something smelled fishy. Walter explained in a letter to a friend what he believed to be the truth: "The sense of this interview was an agreement whereby Garvey was to be allowed to come into the South to sell stock to Negroes in his various enterprises, particularly the Black Star Line with the protection and sanction of the Ku Klux Klan while in return Garvey was to seek to break up organizations among Negroes opposed to the Klan, and particularly the National Association for the Advancement of Colored People."

By this time, Garvey's newspaper had grown increasingly crowded with ads pleading with readers to send money. "Universal Negro Improvement Association borrowing $2,000,000 From Its Members To Start Building a Nation for the Negro Peoples of the World," read one ad. "Read About It and Help with a Loan." "You Work Hard For Your Money," read another. "Why Not Make It Work for You? Give Your Money a Job at the Black Star Line by Buying as Many Shares as You Can."

News of Garvey's KKK meeting fueled a "Garvey Must Go" campaign — led by W.E.B. Du Bois, who wrote attack pieces in *The Crisis* and elsewhere. The NAACP versus UNIA rivalry became increasingly bitter and public. Du Bois called on Garvey to release financial data, for if Garvey's Black Star Line went bankrupt, it could take with it the savings of Black Americans who had purchased hundreds of thousands of dollars' worth of stock.

"This would be a calamity," Du Bois wrote in *The Crisis*. "Garvey is the beloved leader of tens of thousands of poor and bewildered people who have been cheated all their lives. His failure would mean a blow to their faith, and a loss of their little savings, which it would take generations to undo." In another opinion piece, Du Bois wrote, "Marcus Garvey is, without doubt, the most dangerous enemy of the Negro race in America and in the world."

These blows to Garvey's reputation were the latest in a yearlong downward spiral. Soon after Garvey was arrested, a Black leader named A. Philip Randolph attacked the UNIA leader in an article published in *The Messenger* magazine. Randolph received a package in the mail holding a severed human hand, along with a note reportedly signed by the KKK: "Be careful, or we may have to send your hand to someone else." Garvey was rumored — though never proven — to be behind the incident. Soon after, a former Garvey disciple named James Eason, a preacher from Philadelphia, went to New Orleans to deliver a speech to an anti-Garvey group. Afterward, he was ambushed and shot dead on a public street. Two Garvey supporters were arrested, both Jamaicans, and found guilty; Garvey himself was never implicated.

Garvey attempted to lay blame for all his ills on the NAACP. In an editorial in the *Negro World*, he wrote, "All the troubles we have had on our ships have been caused because men were paid to make this trouble by certain organizations calling themselves Negro Advancement Associations." The further he sank, the more threatening his attacks became. "Let me tell you somebody is going to be smashed in New York between the 1st and 31st of August," he wrote in the *Negro World* in 1922. "Any Negro individual or Negro organization . . . that thinks it can fight and intimidate the Universal Negro Improvement Association — let you be the National Association for the Advancement of Colored People — let you be Negro socialists — let me tell you, you are preparing for your Waterloo."

By the spring of 1923, Garvey's legal and financial troubles had gotten the best of him. On June 21 he was sentenced to five years in prison for mail fraud. US marshals led him through the doors of the sketchiest prison in New York, the Tombs. He was later sent off to prison in Atlanta. The Black Star Line dissolved. Even then, a majority of his UNIA followers believed Garvey to be a martyr.

"Within ten years of reaching New York," James Weldon Johnson wrote, "Marcus Garvey had risen and fallen. . . . Within that brief period a black West Indian, here in the United States, in the twentieth century, had actually played an imperial role as such as Eugene O'Neill never imagined in his *Emperor Jones*." While money troubles led to Garvey's downfall, Johnson believed the culprit lay in Garvey's conception of Black Zion itself. "The central idea of Garvey's scheme was absolute abdication and the recognition . . . that this is a white man's country, a country in which the Negro has no place, no right, no chance, no future. To that idea the overwhelming majority of thoughtful American Negroes will not subscribe."

"Collapse of the Garvey bubble had at least one virtue," Walter later wrote. "It made clear that this vision of escape for the Negro from his problems in the United States was pure illusion." Fighting for rights in America — that was Walter White and the NAACP's mission.*

• • •

---

*Garvey was released from prison in 1928 and deported to Jamaica. Generations later, Garvey's Black nationalism became influential again among a new generation of leaders, among them Malcolm X, whose father, Earl Little, was a Garveyite.

ONE NIGHT AT WALTER'S HOME ON EDGECOMBE AVENUE some guests came for what Walter promised would be a special party. The centerpiece of the Whites' apartment was a piano, which seemed odd to some because neither Walter nor his wife, Gladys, played particularly well. But the piano was there for a reason, as the guests were about to learn.

At about 9 p.m. Walter introduced Jules Bledsoe, a twenty-six-year-old Black Columbia University medical student with a face as round as a dinner plate and a demeanor so shy, his smile seemed to sneak out of the corner of his mouth only to duck back inside. When Bledsoe sat down at the piano keys, however, he became a different person. His voice entranced Walter's party guests for four hours.

"He has a gorgeous baritone and extraordinary range, his high notes being almost those of a tenor and taken with a smooth, vibrant clarity," Walter wrote a friend afterward. "His middle register is rounded and lovely while his lower notes are like those of a cello."

Walter introduced Bledsoe to New York, tirelessly promoting him. Bledsoe wrote to Walter that in the future, if he became famous, he "would always be able to look back on these days of sympathy and encouragement such as you and Mrs. White have given."

Within a year, Bledsoe had become one of the first "New Negro" stars of Broadway.

On another night Walter invited the newspaper columnist Heywood Broun over to hear another singer: Paul Robeson, a Harlemite. Walter thought Robeson was a genius, and he wanted Broun to help spread the word. In the coming months, Walter's typewriter thundered as he cranked out letter after letter urging friends and theatrical impresarios to listen. Robeson started getting gigs. When he went off to perform in London, he sent Walter newspaper clippings of the reviews. Walter wrote to him, "Gladys and I sat up late Friday night and read every word of each of the clippings. It is another milestone passed and I greet you at the threshold of a great career. I couldn't be a bit happier — perhaps not as happy — if it had been my own success."

Robeson quickly became one of the most popular singers of New York. Around 1922, Walter read some verse written by a young poet still in his teenage years, Countee Cullen, the adopted son of a Harlem preacher. Walter wrote to Cullen, who was then a New York University student. "I want to have a talk with you sometime soon. I want to look over some of your poetry that you like best. Something worth while may come of it because of a statement made to me last night by a certain publisher."

Walter helped Cullen get his first book of poems published, *Color.* Within a year of meeting Walter, Countee Cullen became the best-known new poet of Harlem.

Walter promoted the Black singer Roland Hayes, and when Hayes went off to perform in Europe, he wrote, "Walter, I am really doing my best! Nothing matters to me but *our goal,* and I shall give every ounce of energy, strength, and whatever other powers I possess towards the end progress — not only for our race, but also for the white race, too."

What did "our goal" signify? Walter believed — as he had learned from James Weldon Johnson — that success in the arts was its own form of race activism. Walter's two great passions were art and activism, and from his point of view, nothing benefited the one more than the other.

But what really thrilled him was the written word. Johnson had lectured him on the importance of literature to a race, how words could be more effective than fists in the fight for justice and equality. "Although there is no single recipe to be followed for making a race great," Johnson once wrote, "there is a single standard by which the greatness of a race can be measured. The greatness of a race may be measured by the literature it has produced."

By 1923, Harlem had begun to explode with raw literary talent. In June 1921, *The Crisis* published Langston Hughes's first poem to appear in print: "The Negro Speaks of Rivers." Walter became a friend and promoter of Hughes's work. A year later the poet Claude McKay published *Harlem Shadows,* which established him as a major new writer on the scene. Walter became a friend and promoter of McKay's (often lending him money too). A year after that, Jean Toomer's novel *Cane* hit, blowing the doors off the offices of literary critics who had never read anything like it. To capture the essence of the Black American experience, Toomer invented an experimental narrative structure, and his lyrical rhapsodies mesmerized.

"It dances," one critic wrote of *Cane*. The famed white novelist Sherwood Anderson called it "the first negro work I have seen that strikes me as really new." Walter became a friend and promoter of Toomer's as well.

Harlem was becoming a beacon for literary talent. Walter's own first attempt was a play he wrote in 1922 that he sent to H. L. Mencken, the literary king of sarcasm, whom Walter had met through Johnson. Mencken was then editing *The Smart Set: A Magazine of Cleverness*. Mencken read Walter's play and wrote him, "This play looks to me to be hopeless. The long speeches in the first episode would drive an audience out of the theatre and the climax at the end of the last episode would make it laugh. . . . Moreover, I doubt that the fundamental idea is plausible."

As a consolation, Mencken sent Walter a new novel called *Birthright* by the white writer T. S. Stribling. Walter read it and responded in a lengthy missive pointing out how white writers lacked the race consciousness to bring real Black characters to life. "I said that Stribling's depiction of Negro servants was not too bad," Walter later recalled, "but that he fell down badly in his portrayal of what educated Negroes feel and think."

Mencken replied, "Why don't you do the right kind of novel? You could do it, and it would create a sensation."

A sensation? The challenge was irresistible — to write a kind of novel that had never been done, a novel about the New Negro of the 1920s, written by a member of the race. Nobody had yet brought to life in popular fiction an educated, morally upstanding, patriotic Black American character. A doctor, perhaps, or a lawyer, or an artist. Arguably, the most elemental portrait of the African American in literature remained Uncle Tom — the subservient if affable slave character in *Uncle Tom's Cabin*, a book published some seventy years earlier.

In the office, Walter talked over the idea with Johnson and Mary White Ovington, and Ovington offered to have Walter sojourn at her secluded cottage, Riverbank, in the Berkshire Mountains of Massachusetts. On February 15, 1923, Walter and Gladys packed some clothes, a typewriter, paper and pencils, some cloth diapers for their baby, Jane, and little else — not even the plot for a novel — and headed for Grand Central Terminal.

At Riverbank, "I started to write," Walter remembered, "and found that many of the characters seemed to rise up begging to be described, and creating their own story. I wrote feverishly and incessantly for twelve days and parts of twelve nights, stopping only when complete fatigue made it physically and mentally impossible to write another word. On the twelfth day the novel was finished and I dropped on a near-by couch and slept for hours." As he wrote in a letter to the novelist Claude McKay: "The accumulation of experience and the intimate knowledge of what a colored man undergoes in a southern community poured out of me like a veritable flood."

Back on a train, headed south for Harlem, Walter now held in his suitcase a manuscript. He was going to Manhattan like countless others before him in the great American literary tradition, novel in hand, hoping to find someone in the publishing capital to make him immortal.

||

Kenneth Harper gazed slowly around his office. A smile of satisfac-
tion wreathed his face, reflecting his inward contentment.
— Walter White, opening sentences of *The Fire in the Flint*

IT HAS BEEN SAID that anyone who completes writing a novel has to be
at least a little manic. To complete a novel in twelve days? That was Walter White at age twenty-nine. He submitted the work to a major publisher
called Doran.

"Now," he explained in a cover letter to editor Eugene Saxton, "here is
what I tried to accomplish. I took a town in South Georgia which seemed
to me typical — a town in which I have spent many months. I mentally put
there Kenneth Harper . . ."

Walter's main character, Kenneth, is a Black doctor and war veteran
who, after getting his medical degree at a northern university, returns
to the small southern town in Georgia where he was born to practice
medicine. There Kenneth begins to understand the degree to which the
rural Black sharecroppers living there are essentially enslaved. They are
peons. He attempts to organize them in a cooperative society. But the
KKK strikes back. Kenneth finds himself fighting a battle he cannot win,
against white power that controls justice, and just about everything else.
He is overwhelmed with despair. When Kenneth's Black sister is raped by
a white man, the good doctor is driven psychopathic and commits murder. On the final page, he is lynched.

The manuscript was a thin veil of fiction laid over the real American South that Walter had personally experienced as an undercover investigator. For a publisher, he wanted "as conservative and respectable a white firm" as he could find, he wrote H. L. Mencken. In other words, a publisher of books that *white* people read. He hoped to shock readers who still believed "the ex-Confederates are right when they use every means, fair or foul, 'to keep the nigger in his place.' I need not say that such are legion — I meet them every day of my life."

Doran immediately expressed interest. Then, without warning, Walter received two pieces of news: one, in an about-face, Doran decided not to publish his novel; and two, a young Black writer named Jessie Redmon Fauset, who happened to be Du Bois's literary editor at *The Crisis,* sold a novel called *There Is Confusion* to the publisher Boni & Liveright. Her book, like Walter's, was an attempt to depict the New Negro in fiction.

Walter wrote a pleading letter to the editor at Doran to reconsider. "Boni and Liveright will bring out in the spring a novel by Miss Jessie Fauset," he wrote. "The first novel in the field giving the reactions of the educated Negro is going to have a tremendous advantage. That is why I want Doran to publish the novel prior to any other of its kind."

Saxton sent a surprising response. The problem with the manuscript, Saxton wrote, was that it presented the Black side of the story and not enough of the white, and that the whole thing was too inflammatory. "We have gone over the whole question very carefully and I had a talk with Mr. Doran about it this morning," Saxton wrote. "The verdict, I am sorry to say, is against the book."

More to the point, Saxton wrote: "It seems to us that the race question is so vital and enters so penetratingly into most of our communities that the publication of a partial statement — especially a statement which tends to inflame one section against the other — would only result in putting off further a decent settlement such as we all desire. . . . Practically speaking, there is nobody in court but the attorney for the prosecution."

Walter was furious. The rejection was aimed not at his work as an artist. It was a rejection of his work as an activist. Saxton's letter rejected the idea that a Black point of view on the subject of lynching, distilled into a novel, was worth publishing. Walter responded with a furious note: "The principal reason *we have a race problem and out of it a problem of intolerance of alarming proportions is because we have not had the courage to face the bitter facts underlying these problems.*" (his italics)

Months later Walter found his publisher in Blanche and Alfred Knopf, whom he knew personally from the literary parties he frequented. Jessie Fauset's novel, *There Is Confusion,* would beat Walter's to bookstores. Still, he could never have imagined what was in store for him once his novel was in print.

ON JUNE 25, 1923, the United States Supreme Court issued its ruling on *Moore v. Dempsey,* the case against the African American defendants sentenced to death following the Phillips County massacre in Arkansas. In a historic decision, the court ruled that these men did not receive a fair trial, and that the Phillips County riot's death row inmates were to be freed. The mob spirit in the courtroom, the speed of the jury's deliberations, there having been no witnesses called — the Supreme Court saw the criminal case as a sham, and found that the defendants' Fourteenth Amendment rights had been violated.

The Black attorney Scipio Jones had won this case with hard facts, plus funds and legal assistance provided by the NAACP. Justice Oliver Wendell Holmes wrote the court's majority opinion, which read in part, "If in fact a trial is dominated by a mob so that there is an actual interference with the course of justice, there is a departure from due process of the law."

Walter got the news via a telegram in his office. He immediately wrote to Louis Marshall, the famed attorney. "I am writing within five minutes of receiving the telegram to inform you of the wonderful victory we have just won in the Arkansas cases," he wrote. "This ends the most important case of its kind in the history of America. . . . A great victory for justice has been won."

All week news of *Moore v. Dempsey* played out in the newspapers.

ELAINE RIOTERS FREED, the *Pittsburgh Courier,* one of the most widely read national Black weekly newspapers, announced in a front-page headline. The whole story of *Moore v. Dempsey* began with a Walter White undercover investigation. Outside of the attorney Scipio Africanus Jones, Walter received a lion's share of the credit.

The association rode the wave of excitement into the biggest rally in its history, in Kansas City, chosen because Missouri was a border state along the Mason-Dixon Line. Most of Kansas City was fully segregated, and Black schools were underfunded — several of the Black grammar schools had outhouses and no indoor plumbing. When the NAACP came to town, Kansas City came alive. One young reporter attending the conference, Roy Wilkins, remembered the emotion: "It was my first chance to see the leaders of the NAACP — James Weldon Johnson, the poet, playwright, diplomat and gentleman; Walter White, a light-skinned Negro who had investigated some of the most revolting lynchings in the South; Du Bois; and Williams Pickens, the droll field organizer."

Delegates from twenty-nine states led a silent parade to the city's Convention Hall for the opening rally. Inside, ten thousand men and women stood on their feet. Johnson spoke. Walter spoke. Missouri's governor sent an official to represent him at the convention, and when this emissary spoke to the crowd, he used the word *darky.* The audience exploded with boos and stamping feet, the cacophony so loud, Convention Hall felt like it was lifting off its foundation. Johnson smashed his hand on a table, and the giant room felt instantly silent.

"Look around you, sir," Johnson said, while glaring at the governor's emissary, "at these thousands who by thrift and industry, by study and by devotion to church, have made themselves worthy to enjoy the rights of American citizens. But, sir, do they enjoy them?" Then: "We are here to serve notice that we are in a fight to the death for the rights guaranteed us as American citizens by the Constitution."

The young Kansas City reporter Roy Wilkins — who would in the distant future become chief executive of the NAACP — recalled this moment: "Ten thousand black people rose to their feet. They cheered and clapped until their voices were hoarse and their hands stinging with pain. As they cheered, the soft sunlight streamed down around James Weldon Johnson, and I knew I had seen a great leader — and found my own cause."

ON MARCH 21, 1924, at the Civic Club in Manhattan, white and Black intellectuals gathered for a party that would be remembered as the birthing evening for the Harlem Renaissance. The fete was in honor of Jessie Redmon Fauset and her book, *There Is Confusion*. The Civic Club — located on Twelfth Street, a five-minute walk from NAACP headquarters — was a favorite hangout for Walter and his friends, the only elite evening spot in New York that drew no color line. Booze was plentiful, even during Prohibition, and the Belgian chef served what Mary White Ovington called "as good meals as any club in New York."

Johnson spoke that night, as did Du Bois. Walter gave a speech about the literary outlook and how exciting the future was going to be for Black poets and novelists. Hosting the evening was Charles Spurgeon Johnson, editor of *Opportunity* magazine; he would later call this party "one of the most significant and dramatic of the announcements of the Renaissance. It marked the first public appearance of young creative writers in the company of the greatest of the nation's creative writers and philosophers."

Walter sat next to Horace Liveright, whose publishing house, Boni & Liveright, was among the most respected in New York. Liveright had brought out Jean Toomer's experimental novel *Cane* and now Fauset's *There Is Confusion*. Biggest among the literary hitters that night was Carl Van Doren, whose 1921 book *The American Novel* had dug Herman Melville's *Moby-Dick* out of the dusty stacks and declared it to be what it remains today: the benchmark for "the great American novel." Van Doren's speech that night — "The Younger Generation of Negro Writers" — was the key to the ignition that set a whole movement into motion: white intelligentsia's new passion for all things African and artistic.

"What American literature decidedly needs at this moment is color," Van Doren told his audience. "Music, gusto, the free expression of gay or desperate moods. If the Negroes are not in a position to contribute these items, I do not know what Americans are."

When Jessie Fauset rose to speak, she explained how her novel was rejected by the first editor she gave it to because the editor thought that no buying public would stand for a novel by a Black woman about a refined and cultured Black main character, that book audiences were expecting more Uncle Tom. She then thanked her publisher, Horace Liveright, for taking a chance on her and her book. The applause was so loud, some in the crowd heard her call Liveright "the most sporting editor in New York," others "the most sparing editor." Nevertheless, sitting next to Liveright, Walter looked on through plumes of cigarette smoke, exceedingly jealous but playing the good sport, knowing it could have been him up on that stage that night.

Another six months passed before his novel, *The Fire in the Flint,* appeared. Walter took the title from the saying "The fire in the flint never shows until it is struck." The feeling of anticipation — to hold that first copy in his hand — was like nothing he had experienced. Exhilarating. Terrifying. The novel was 63,350 words long (he had counted). Handing the book over to the critics felt like ushering 63,350 beloved kittens across Broadway. What would happen if the critics crushed the book? Perhaps worse: Would it be ignored? What would Johnson and Du Bois think of it? Ovington and Spingarn? One writes a book — especially a novel — in an emotional vacuum. How strange it feels to then invite the world inside.

When the book hit in October 1924, it launched Walter to a new realm of fame. The *International Book Review* called *The Fire in the Flint* "the greatest novel yet written by a negro in this nation." Freda Kirchwey, the political radical and editor at *The Nation,* went further. "It manages to make civilization live. Walter F. White, Georgian and negro by birth, investigator and writer by profession, has put upon paper a problem that is in his own bone and fiber. . . . [He] has written a book that lives and breathes by the terrible truth and reality of its substance." The *Pittsburgh Courier* created renderings of all of Walter's characters, making them look like the cast of a Broadway drama. The *Courier* called Walter "one of the foremost novelists of the century."

Even more satisfying was the correspondence Walter received from some of America's living literary icons. Sinclair Lewis, author of the novels *Main Street* and *Babbitt* (and a future Nobel Prize winner), called the novel "splendidly courageous, rather terrifying and of the highest significance." Lewis wrote Joel Spingarn that "*The Fire in the Flint* and [E. M. Forster's] *A Passage to India* will prove much the most important books of this autumn." Walter received a personal letter from Eugene O'Neill, the most famous playwright of the 1920s. "'The Fire in the Flint' held me in its tense grasp from first page to last," O'Neill wrote.

Curious was the reaction from reviewers in the South, of which the book was a clear indictment. One reviewer in Virginia's *New Journal and Guide,* an African American publication, called Walter "one of the younger writers of the race who went to sleep unknown and woke up famous as Lord Byron did upon the publication of Childe Harold." The book was "a great novel, and so acclaimed by the best literary critics of the country." At the same time, the white press in the South spit the kind of venom Walter expected and desired; he wanted to rile up the Ku Klux Klan and the race baiters. The *Savannah Press* called *The Fire in the Flint* "unfair, unjust, and thoroughly reprehensible." A judge from Walter's home state of Georgia named Blanton Fortson commented on the novel: "To those who are intelligently working towards a solution of the race problem with open minds it must appear as but another proof of the belief that to give the Negro an education along other than industrial lines, is frequently worse than useless."

"I am glad to say," Walter wrote to Moorfield Storey, "I am getting reactions from the South and am being violently denounced by various Georgia newspapers. The first edition has already been exhausted. It looks like the novel is going to have a wide sale."

Walter's biggest dream was to see his book dramatized onstage or on a movie screen. He imagined the financial freedom that could bring, and the joy of seeing the world he imagined in three dimensions, his characters in real flesh and bone. He suggested the idea to Eugene O'Neill, whose plays *Beyond the Horizon* and *The Emperor Jones* had both enjoyed successful recent Broadway runs. O'Neill responded, "Your idea of dramatizing your book sounds darned interesting. There is certainly a fine play in it and it should come right out of the novel without much trouble." Walter reached out to the film impresario Cecil B. DeMille and all but begged him for interest.

He had made literary success look easy, and he set to work on dreaming up his next novel. As one friend of his wrote about him at the time, perhaps jealously, "The acid test which proves whether or not a writer is a novelist, as critics assert, is that writer's second book. . . . I confess I am both hopeful and apprehensive for him."

AT THE SAME TIME WALTER RELEASED HIS FIRST BOOK, the country was speeding into the highly combative election season of 1924. When the Democrats arrived in New York by the trainload in June, all eyes turned to Madison Square Garden. The 1924 Democratic National Convention would be called "the wildest in U.S. history."

The party had openly split into two factions, one led by William McAdoo, who hailed from Georgia and was the candidate of the Ku Klux Klan, and the other helmed by Governor Al Smith of New York, who was opposed to the Klan. The southern Democrats were split from the northerners in a tug-of-war over the soul of the party, the KKK being the rope. This would be the longest running national political convention in history, because neither side could gather the two-thirds vote to get their candidate on the 1924 ticket. Not a single Black delegate was present.

Heavily perspiring crowds shouted opposing chants: "Mac! Mac! McAdoo!" versus "Ku! Ku! McAdoo!" With its fistfights and shoving matches, oratorical gymnastics, and Confederate flags, the convention came to be known as "the Klanbake." Over sixteen days, delegates voted 103 times until finally a third, neutral candidate walked away with the nomination — little-known John W. Davis of West Virginia.

When Republican delegates arrived in Cleveland that same month for their national convention — the "Party of Lincoln" being unanimously favored among African Americans — Black delegates arrived to find that a segregated seating section had been assigned to them, marked off by chicken wire.

Black Americans had nowhere to turn in 1924; they were ignored by both parties. Meanwhile, as powerful as the KKK had grown among the Democratic Party, the NAACP had ample evidence to show that the Klan was infiltrating Republican-controlled communities in the Midwest — most important, in Indiana and Ohio, both potentially swing states.

The association's bylaws dictated that it would remain apolitical and nonpartisan. From here on out, however, the NAACP would make it a point to support any candidate who denounced the KKK, and to fight against any candidate who supported it. "The Klan has a large following both in Ohio and Indiana, where, it is indicated, the colored people will center their fight," the association stated in a press release. The election of 1924 marked the beginning — a toe dipped in the water — of the association's political action.

On the first Tuesday of November 1924, once again the election's result drew a color line across the country that looked like the Mason-Dixon Line. The Solid South of the Democratic Party, where African Americans were disenfranchised and Jim Crow ruled, went to little-known John W. Davis, as expected, with massive majorities in Alabama, Georgia, Texas, South Carolina, Louisiana, and Mississippi. Every other state but one (Wisconsin, which voted for its homegrown third-party candidate Robert La Follette) voted for Coolidge, the Republican. So it was during Abraham Lincoln's era, so it was in 1924, sixty years later.

Soon after the election, on August 8, 1925, the Ku Klux Klan held the biggest rally in its history, in a symbolic city: Washington, DC. A parade of Klansmen and women gathered at 3 p.m. and marched down Pennsylvania Avenue right past the White House. Police estimated from 35,000 to 45,000 members of the not-so-secret society; at this rally, KKK members wore no masks, only their flowing white robes. Wizards and dragons and Kleagles, banners reading 100 PERCENT AMERICAN, bands thumping out "The Star-Spangled Banner" — all of it was led by a white-robed Klansman on horseback bearing a colossal American flag.

"As far as the eye could see Pennsylvania Avenue looked like a gigantic snow bank," said one eyewitness, describing the scene. "That this was the greatest demonstration ever staged by the Ku Klux Klan was admitted tonight, even by the enemies of the order." The *New York Times* ran a front-page headline: SIGHT ASTONISHES CAPITAL [*sic*].

ONE DAY soon after the Klan Konvocation in Washington, a physician named Ossian Sweet arrived at his new home with his family, ready to move into a sturdy brick house at 2905 Garland Avenue in Detroit, Michigan. Dr. Sweet pulled up to the home in a motorcar filled with family members — his wife, their fourteen-month-old baby girl, two of his brothers, and a friend who was a federal narcotics officer. The vehicle was driven by a chauffeur. The federal officer was along for the ride, likely, because the financially successful Sweet family was Black and was moving into a white neighborhood. There had already been threats.

That first night in their home, the Sweets began to notice something unnerving: a crowd gathering out front. As Mrs. Sweet cooked a celebratory dinner in her new kitchen — roast pork, baked sweet potatoes, mustard greens, and cake — Dr. Sweet kept his eye out his window. The crowd kept getting bigger, every face Caucasian. He decided to call the police. When the officers arrived, they simply joined the crowd. After the sun set, the mob continued to grow steadily. Eyewitnesses that night put the number anywhere from twenty-five people to five thousand out in front of the Sweets' home — and the extraordinary discrepancy in those two numbers would become part of this story.

At one point two Black men walked by the edge of the mob. They were set upon and beaten while the police officers stood by. When the Sweets started hearing chanting — "Get the damn niggers" — they shut off all the lights in the home. Members of the mob began throwing rocks at the house. Windows shattered. Inside, Dr. Sweet feared that he would not be able to protect his wife and his baby daughter from danger.

Suddenly, a gunshot rang out, then another. It remained unclear whether shots were fired from both sides and, if they were, which had fired first. Nevertheless, a white man lay dead in the street, and another was wounded. The police stormed the house and arrested all the occupants, separating the baby girl from her parents.

The next morning a tiny item appeared in the New York *World*. "Homicide warrants were recommended today against ten Negroes arrested last night following a riot at the home of Dr. O. H. Sweet, a Negro," the newspaper reported. On this day, James Weldon Johnson was in New Jersey playing a round of golf. He was interrupted and called into the clubhouse for a telephone call. He never returned to the game. At NAACP headquarters, Johnson huddled with Walter that afternoon. They sent off a telegram to the Detroit NAACP branch asking for the FULLEST INFORMATION POSSIBLE. The next day the Detroit branch sent its report. The mob outside Dr. Sweet's home the night before, the telegram said, was made up of 5,000 INFURIATED PEOPLE . . . PROTESTING AGAINST HIS LIVING IN A WHITE COMMUNITY.

SUGGESTIONS APPRECIATED, the telegram concluded. MAY NEED WALTER.

The Detroit branch then followed up with another memo explaining that the police were refusing to release any information, nor would they release the Sweet family on bail. "It will be necessary to have an experienced investigator to secure evidence to aid in defense of this case, Mr. White being the logical man," W. Hayes McKinney of the Detroit branch wrote. "We are therefore urgently requesting that Mr. White be sent to Detroit immediately."

12

The eyes of America are on Detroit and the fight that the citizens
of Detroit are putting up for Doctor Sweet and his codefendants
is a fight for every one of the eleven million Negroes in the United
States. The National Office is behind the fight and we will do everything we can to secure full justice for the eleven martyrs.
— Walter White, September 19, 1925

ON SEPTEMBER 15, 1925, Walter arrived in Detroit on the Wolverine, a
train that traveled overnight from New York to the Motor City. His next
two months would prove so exhausting, they would test the limits of his
physical and mental stability. Even before he arrived, he had written his
friend Claude McKay, the Black writer, "I have been almost forced to give
up even sleep."

The Statler Hotel bustled that morning as Walter met for breakfast
with Judge Ira W. Jayne, a friend of a friend and also one of the closest
advisors to Detroit's mayor John W. Smith. Already, the Sweet narrative
was moving at alarming speed. Walter arrived in Detroit on a Tuesday,
and the preliminary court hearing was set for Wednesday. Surely this case
touched a nerve for Walter, bringing back memories of when he was thirteen, that night of the 1906 Atlanta race riot when a threatening mob had
gathered outside his own home. He was uniquely qualified to empathize
with the Sweet family.

At their breakfast meeting, Judge Jayne tried to paint a picture of
Detroit for Walter, what this city had become in recent times. Over the

previous ten years, the Great Migration had lured some 75,000 Black Americans into Detroit from the South to work in the auto factories. The housing infrastructure could not keep up, and overcrowded ghettos resulted. It was inevitable that families such as the Sweets would go hunting for a more comfortable place to raise their baby girl. Meanwhile, racial clashes had become routine in the city.

"Judge Jayne tells me that the Commissioner of Police, Crowell, has tried to stop this," Walter documented, "but his hands have been tied by the fact that the police department is honeycombed with Klansmen. One lieutenant of police resigned when censured for failure to protect the home of a colored man, declaring that he would get out rather than 'protect niggers.'"

After meeting with Judge Jayne, Walter met with the two Black lawyers whom the Sweets had brought in to represent them. Walter did not come away with a good impression. He thought it would be essential, to sway an all-white jury in this city, to have a white lawyer with a sparkling reputation join the team. When he raised the idea, the two Black lawyers threatened to quit.

"I pointed out that this cast no reflections of the colored lawyers," Walter recorded, "but that it was a question bigger than Detroit or Michigan . . . for it was the dramatic climax of the nationwide fight to enforce residential segregation." This case, Walter argued, could have huge national consequences. If a Black family moved into a neighborhood that was considered white, did that then mean whites could assault them or their property with impunity? If Black families paid taxes that were used to fund police departments, should they not then expect law enforcement to do the same job for them as they would for white families?

Walter's next stop was city hall, where he asked the mayor's office for a "police card" that he could use so strangers would know he was not an outside agitator. Judge Jayne smoothed it out, and the mayor's office produced a letter on Detroit Police Department letterhead signed by police deputy superintendent James Sprott. It read, "The bearer of this letter, Mr. Walter White, is a personal friend of the writer, and any courtesy extended to him will be very much appreciated."

Walter then scoured the city to collect facts. CONFERENCES ALL DAY, he wrote in a telegram to Johnson on his first day in Detroit. SITUATION SERIOUS.

BY THE TIME WALTER GOT TO WRITING a full memorandum of his first day in Detroit, he had gathered so much information, it took four single-spaced pages to download it all. "Here is the story of the trouble here to date," he wrote Johnson.

Dr. Ossian Sweet, his wife, Gladys, and nine others who were in the Sweet residence the night of the shooting were imprisoned, charged with murder, and denied bail. Dr. Sweet had given a statement on September 12 as to what had happened. Originally the Sweets were scheduled to move into their new home on August 1, but the family had been threatened for attempting to move into a white neighborhood. At a meeting of Detroit's Water Works Improvement Association, a real estate agent had said, "We'll throw no stones, we'll fire no guns, but we'll load this nigger's goods on the same van that brings them out and send them back to where they came from." The Sweets delayed their arrival until September 8 — at which point they were determined to live in the home that they had purchased.

The night they moved in, a crowd began to gather in front of their house between 6 and 8 p.m., Sweet explained in his statement. The crowd remained on the opposite side of the street from the house. Despite police presence, stones started hitting the house at 8 p.m. "About 2000 whites around house at that time," Sweet said in his statement. "Threw stones all way up steps of house. [sic] Yard and porch covered with missiles. . . . About fifteen minutes later there was a crash above as window breaking. . . . Several shots fired from outside."

Dr. Sweet maintained that shots came from outside before any firing came from inside. He did not reveal who from inside had fired any weapon. Still, his word meant little within the eyes of the law. What were the chances that the Sweets could receive a fair trial anyway?

Walter believed there would be ample evidence when it was all laid out that the Sweets acted in self-defense, that they had every right to be in their home on Garland Avenue, to protect their home, and to protect themselves. He also believed that the KKK was firmly planted in Detroit and was behind the protest in front of the Sweets' home. Already members of the mob were trying to lie their way out of guilt, Walter explained. In order to prove self-defense the Sweets would have to show that a riotous assemblage had gathered to threaten them. "Under Michigan statutes," Walter wrote his boss, "a riotous assemblage consists of twelve or more men armed with clubs or other dangerous weapons, or thirty or more unarmed persons."

Original newspaper accounts stated the mob consisted of as many as five thousand. Dr. Sweet's statement had put the number at two thousand. Now reports were claiming twenty-five unarmed people — *beneath* the threshold to qualify as a dangerous mob, according to the law. How could five thousand people, or two thousand people, have been mistaken when twenty-five were present? It was impossible, Walter believed. But there were no photos.

On the positive side, Dr. Sweet was an exemplary character, "from one of Detroit's oldest and most respected colored families," Walter reported. The doctor "has been practicing medicine here for four years and is very highly respected as a law abiding citizen." Walter felt sure the Black community of Detroit would pull together and fight. "The people are very much stirred," he wrote.

Johnson wrote back, "Splendid work on your part. Sending out [press] release. Continue to handle the delicate points in the situation with all the tact and diplomacy possible."

THE NEXT DAY Walter attended the preliminary hearing. The courtroom was jammed so tightly with spectators, Black and white, the lawyers had trouble taking their seats. The Sweets and their fellow defendants appeared nervous and worn. The prosecutor, Lester S. Moll, stepped out in front of the judge and said, "The evidence shows no act of violence or provocation on the part of the victims or any other persons, and the crime must be called premeditated murder. . . . As we are unable to say who fired the fatal shots we must charge them all [the eleven defendants] equally with the crime." The judge denied any motion for bail, and then hammered his gavel.

In protest, the Detroit NAACP branch held a rally in a church. These people were angry. From his jail cell, Dr. Sweet gave another statement. He had no intention of backing down. "For a good cause and the dignity of my people," he declared, "I am willing to stay indefinitely in the cell and be punished. I feel sure by the demonstration made by my people that they have confidence in me as a law abiding citizen. I denounce the theory of Ku Kluxism and uphold the theory of manhood with a wife and tiny baby to protect." Mrs. Sweet added from her own cell: "Though I suffer and am torn loose from my 14 months old baby, I feel it is my duty to the womanhood of my race." Mrs. Sweet bravely continued, "If I am freed I shall return and live at my home on Garland Avenue."

Walter drew some conclusions from the preliminary hearing. The prosecutor Moll was brilliant, "one of the best trial men I have ever heard," he wrote Johnson. "The case is not going to be easy. . . . But we've got to see it through for the Klan and the segregationists are hot after convictions."

The Sweets' attorneys, however, were not going to be able to match up. Walter felt adamant: to sway an all-white jury in Detroit, these two lawyers were not going to get the job done. "I am convinced more than ever," he wrote, "that we must have the best white lawyer we can get."

But who?

Due to an NAACP publicity campaign, the nation had its eyes on this case. The Sweets' story had become front-page news, coast to coast. Who could not understand the impulse of a man under attack, wanting to protect the home that he had paid for, wanting to protect his wife and baby, when the police refused to help? "No case of this kind has ever attracted such attention and sympathy as this one," Walter wrote at the time. In another letter, he wrote to his friend Fay Lewis that if Dr. Sweet had not acted, he would be either "without a roof over his head or . . . in his grave if that mob had gotten hold of him. I am, of course, opposed to war and physical violence — except when absolutely necessary. The Negro has been so patient that his patience has been construed as cowardice and that is why mobs have been attacking him with impunity."

Walter prepared a list of the finest lawyers in Michigan and set about consulting them, but each had some reason why he could or would not take the case. He recalled, "Several other lawyers, somewhat less frank, demanded fees so huge that it was utterly impossible to pay them." He returned to New York from Detroit "to make a very depressing report."

Whether it was Walter's idea or Johnson's is not known, but ultimately the association officials made a decision: now was the time to make a statement, to do something that would be remembered. They would go after the man they believed to be the greatest criminal lawyer in the world.

IN NEW YORK, in whatever hours he could find, Walter was writing desperately quickly, as he had promised a new novel to Knopf and was behind schedule. He was also broke again. His salary had climbed to $4,000 a year — a decent lot in 1925, but clearly not enough. On October 8, one month after the shooting at the Sweet home in Detroit, he wrote Blanche Knopf asking for an advance on royalties for his new book, which he was calling *Flight*.

"I have got to go to Detroit tomorrow (Friday) but I will be back Sunday or Monday," he wrote. "This unexpected trip may make me a day or two late getting the revised MS. [manuscript] in but I promise to by the latter part of the week. . . . I should like very much to have the check before I go to Detroit tomorrow afternoon."

Back in Michigan, Walter met with Dr. Sweet and the other defendants in Ward 5 of the Wayne County jailhouse. He found himself waiting in a detention pen for what felt like an eternity, smelling that peculiar jailhouse odor of sweat and anger and fear. When Dr. Sweet appeared along with his wife and the nine other defendants, Walter made eye contact. The physician looked aged well beyond his thirty-one years; he was two years younger than Walter and, like him, a young father. Mrs. Sweet was distraught over her baby. When Walter identified himself as an official from the NAACP, one of the defendants, on the edge of tears, exclaimed, "Thank God! We can now rest easy and get some sleep!"

Walter talked about the gravity of the case. As he later put it, "The importance of the case to the Negro cause was obvious. If the Sweets were not given adequate legal defense, if the ancient Anglo-Saxon principle that 'a man's home was his castle' were not made applicable to Negroes as well as to others, we knew that other and even more determined attacks would be made upon the homes of Negroes throughout the country." Walter convinced Dr. Sweet and the others to fire their lawyers and to trust the association to take control of their fate. On September 25, Dr. Sweet and the other defendants signed a letter, committing themselves to the plan.

The defendants signed their statement in Ward 5 of the Wayne County jail: "It is our separate and collective wish that the National Association for the Advancement of Colored People take full and complete charge of the case of the Defense at once."

At the same time, Walter wrote a telegraph to the office of Clarence Darrow, the Chicago attorney who had become globally renowned recently for his defense work in two of the most controversial trials in American history. A year earlier Darrow had defended Leopold and Loeb, the two University of Chicago students who had kidnapped and murdered fourteen-year-old Bobby Franks. Believing they were intellectually superior enough that they could commit what they called "the perfect crime" and get away with it, Nathan Freudenthal Leopold Jr. and Richard Albert Loeb were caught and tried for what was called "the crime of the century." The defendants confessed, and Darrow argued to spare their lives on the grounds that capital punishment was morally wrong; his summation speech lasted twelve hours and was considered one of the most magnificent orations in the history of American jurisprudence. Leopold and Loeb both escaped the gallows and were sentenced to life plus ninety-nine years each.

Then, four months before Dr. Sweet and the others were arrested for murder, Darrow had defended the schoolteacher and football coach John T. Scopes in the so-called Scopes Monkey Trial. Scopes was arrested for violating Tennessee's Butler Act, which made it illegal to teach evolution in a publicly funded school. The three-time presidential candidate William Jennings Bryan represented the state, arguing that the Word of God as expressed in the Bible took priority over all human knowledge, while

Darrow represented the teacher, arguing that modern science should be taught in schools.

The case riveted the country. Thousands of miles of telegraph wires were hung specifically to allow the more than two hundred reporters covering the proceedings to send out telegraphs with news of the case's twists and turns. In support of the teacher, pro-science advocates had trained chimpanzees to perform on the courthouse lawn, in an attempt to lend weight to the theory of evolution, while preachers holding Bibles led street-corner services all around the overwhelmed town of Dayton, Tennessee.

Ultimately, a jury found Scopes guilty and the judge charged him a $100 fine. The case made Darrow an international figure — a philosopher of the courts and a target for would-be assassins who believed his argument for teaching science in schools made him the devil incarnate.

When Walter reached out to Darrow's office, Darrow's secretary said that the lawyer was traveling to New York and that he could be reached through another attorney: Arthur Garfield Hays, who was himself a nationally known figure. Hays had assisted Darrow in the Scopes Monkey Trial and was a cofounder of the American Civil Liberties Union. At Hays's New York home, Walter came face-to-face with both attorneys. The Ohio-born Darrow was sixty-eight years old, his facial features severe and birdlike. He emanated such intellectual intensity, it was impossible to relax in his presence. Hays appeared more legal powerhouse out of central casting.

Walter had come to the meeting with Arthur Spingarn, Joel Spingarn's attorney brother, plus another white lawyer on the NAACP's board. Spingarn gave Darrow the story of the Sweet case. As Walter recalled, Darrow "listened with deep sympathy and when Arthur had finished, he said softly, 'I understand. I know the suffering your people have endured.'"

An awkward silence followed. Spingarn realized that Darrow had been told ahead of time that one of the NAACP officials visiting him was African American, and he had mistaken Spingarn for that man. Spingarn corrected Darrow — he was Caucasian. Darrow turned to the other white lawyer who was part of the NAACP group.

"I mean *your* race," he said.

The second lawyer corrected Darrow, who offered a look of confusion. "But they told me one of you was a Negro," Darrow said. He turned to Walter. "And surely, it can't be *you*."

DARROW HAD TO LEAVE NEW YORK for Chicago the following day, so Walter followed him, determined to get him to commit to the Sweet case. Meanwhile Walter informed Dr. Sweet, in a telegram to the Detroit jailhouse: NATIONAL OFFICE OF NAACP CONDUCTING VERY IMPORTANT NEGOTIATIONS WITH ONE OF THE MOST EMINENT CRIMINAL LAWYERS IN THE COUNTRY FOR DEFENSE. OUTLOOK VERY FAVORABLE.

On October 14, 1925, Walter met Darrow again in the lawyer's office in the Windy City. Darrow asked, "Did the defendants shoot into that mob?"

Walter feared Darrow would refuse the case, so he sidestepped the question.

"Don't try to hedge," said Darrow. "I know you were not there. But do you *believe* the defendants fired?"

"I believe they did fire," Walter said. "And —" He was about to add that he thought the Sweets were justified in shooting. But Darrow interrupted.

"Then I'll take the case. If they had not the courage to shoot back in defense of their lives, I wouldn't think they were worth defending."

The trial was set to begin in two days, on October 16. The day before, the association made the announcement: Clarence Darrow would defend the Sweet party, and Arthur Garfield Hays would serve as secondary council for free. The announcement included a statement from Darrow: "I am going to get $5,000 to fight this case. I would do it for nothing if I could afford it because there is principle involved. These colored people are entitled to a fair shake. It will cost me more than $5,000 to try this case. I do not want the public to think that I am defending these Negroes because of an exorbitant fee."

On the following day Darrow appeared in the Detroit courtroom of Judge Frank Murphy, who okayed a delay to give the attorney time to prepare his case. Turning to the jury, Judge Murphy made clear that his courtroom would not tolerate mob spirit or prejudice. Walter would remember Murphy's words for the rest of his life.

Dr. Sweet [Judge Murphy said] has the same right under the law to purchase and occupy the dwelling house on Garland Avenue as any other man. Under the law, a man's house is his castle. It is his castle, whether he is white or black. And no man has the right to assail or invade it. The Negro is now by the Constitution of the United States given full citizenship with the white man and all the rights and privileges of citizenship attend him wherever he goes.

Back in New York, Walter worked over the final draft of his new book, *Flight;* he was late on his deadline and the Knopfs were not happy. On October 29 he mailed Blanche Knopf the manuscript with a note. "Here at last is 'Flight.' I have done all that I can to it." He then left immediately on a speaking tour in support of the Sweets: Cleveland on November 1, Toledo the next night, Chicago the next, then Saint Paul, Minnesota. Suffering an energy-sapping cold, he was on the brink of collapse.

The trial was set to start. Soon the fate of the Sweets would be in a jury's hands.

FROM THE BEGINNING of the Sweet trial, Walter was present in the courtroom making a meal of his fingernails. There was trouble from the start: How could the defense agree upon a jury that could be relied upon to be free of race prejudice? As a reporter with the nation's most influential Black newspaper, the *Chicago Defender,* put it: "The city of Detroit prosecutor has been unable to date to find 12 of its citizens free enough of race hatred to give a woman and [ten] men a sporting chance in a death trial."

Walter heard secondhand that one of the prospective jurors had announced, "I don't give a God damn what the facts are. A nigger has killed a white man and I'll be burned in hell before I ever vote to acquit a nigger who has killed a white man!"

When the day arrived for the opening arguments, the courtroom and the warrens outside filled with crowds. Arthur Garfield Hays made the opening statement for the defendants. "We are not ashamed of our clients and we shall not apologize for them," Hays said. "We are American citizens." He turned to the all-white, all-male jury. "You men of the jury are

American citizens." He turned to Dr. and Mrs. Sweet. "They are American citizens."

And with that, from Walter's point of view, a spectacle of profound hypocrisy got under way.

The prosecution tried to prove that there was no mob in front of the Sweets' new home, that there was no cause for provocation. Clarence Darrow skewered his witnesses in cross-examinations. He had a way of staring out a courtroom window calmly asking his questions, then turning to the witness with a thundering voice that straightened every spine in the room. When Detroit police lieutenant Paul Shellenberger testified that there was no mob, Darrow pointed out that the officer had already testified in preliminary proceedings that he believed between 150 to 200 people had gathered in front of the Sweets' home that night.

"Well, I hadn't counted accurately," said the officer.

"It wasn't that," Darrow retorted. "You were more interested then in telling the truth."

Witness by witness, Darrow tore down the prosecution as Dr. Sweet and Mrs. Sweet watched from the defendants' table, along with the other nine defendants. Then it was time for the Sweets themselves to take the stand. When asked about his state of mind at the time of the shooting, Dr. Sweet spoke in a slow voice, emphasizing each word: "When I opened the door I saw the mob and I realized . . . I was facing that same mob that has hounded my people throughout its entire history. . . . I was filled with a fear that only one could experience who knows the history and the sufferings of my race."

Meanwhile, the press turned to Walter White for background on the case. Harlem's biggest paper, the *New York Amsterdam News,* reported on its front page: "In connections with the disorders Mr. White reports the following facts: 1) Mayor Smith charges the disorders were due directly to instigation by the Ku Klux Klan. 2) The Detroit police [was] honeycombed with Klansmen." Walter published an essay in *The Nation* called "Negro Segregation Comes North," on how cities like Detroit, now swelled with southern whites and Blacks due to the Great Migration, faced a housing crisis that created segregated slums. "Are Negroes to be forced to resort to threats and bloodshed in order to secure decent places to live and rear their children?" Walter asked his readers.

The age-old race war of the South was going to explode in new urban battlegrounds of the North, Walter believed, citing the Sweet case as proof.

"At last all the testimony was in," Walter remembered. "Every available space in the courtroom was jammed with those eager to hear the great lawyer in summation to the jury." These people were expecting something special from Clarence Darrow, and he didn't disappoint. "A deep silence fell over the crowded noisy courtroom," wrote the attorney David Lilienthal, who was there covering the trial for *The Nation*. "The old man with the unutterably sad face and the great stooped shoulders seemed no mere lawyer pleading for hire. He seemed, instead, a patriarch out of another age. . . . His voice was a low rumble, in it resounded all the misery his tired eyes had seen."

Jury deliberations began the day before Thanksgiving, 1925. At 2 a.m. Judge Murphy sent everyone home. The next day, jury members ate sandwiches for Thanksgiving dinner while continuing to deliberate. Walter believed that the jury would be hung and a mistrial would be declared — and he was right. The jury could not, or would not, agree on a verdict. The NAACP spent $21,897.67 on the case, and the court would have to start the process from scratch, with a new jury. Mrs. Sweet was permitted to leave on bail to be with her child, but Dr. Sweet stayed in lockup.

DURING THE DELAY BETWEEN TRIALS, the NAACP organized a mammoth rally in Harlem, where Darrow would appear. A mass mailer went out: "Clarence Darrow, the greatest criminal lawyer in America, and speaker of international reputation, and a lover of humanity, will speak on the Sweet Case at Salem M.E. Church, (Seventh Avenue and 129th Street), Sunday afternoon, December 13th at 3 o'clock sharp." As a warm-up speaker, Walter would talk on Darrow's work "from the point of view of a Negro and of an observer of the legal battle which Mr. Darrow has declared is one of the most thrilling in which he has ever been a participant."

On the day of the event, the scene outside the Harlem church resembled a funeral service for a Black president. Men and women in their Sunday clothes formed huge crowds by the church door, snaking down the block in either direction and around the corners. Rev. F. A. Cullen, father of the young Harlem poet Countee Cullen, gave the invocation. James Weldon Johnson's brother, the Broadway song arranger Rosamond, sang "Lift Every Voice and Sing," the "Negro National Anthem." Walter spoke, not that this crowd needed any warming up. Then Darrow climbed to the podium. The crowd came alive, but he quickly hushed them, and began to speak in brutally honest words.

"The sooner you people find that you can't depend on David and the Lord," Darrow said, "but get busy yourselves, the better off you will be. If the Lord was going to do anything for you, he would've done it already."

Darrow then spoke the words that were to change the course of Walter White's life. He urged African Americans to stop voting in a block for the Party of Lincoln. What were the Republicans doing for the Black man and woman in America? Why vote blindly for them, just because of what Abraham Lincoln had done sixty years earlier? "The only weapon the Negro in the North has is the ballot and you have thrown that away," Darrow said. "There are several states in the North where the Negro holds the balance of power. I want you to be absolutely independent in your voting. I want you to keep the white politicians guessing."

Some in the church were most certainly offended — that a white man would come into their place of worship, question the worth of their faith in God, and tell them how they should vote. But Walter heard in these words an epiphany, one that was about to change the entire trajectory of the NAACP. He was thinking: Black America could fight with activism and get nowhere. As the Sweet trial proved, not even the courts could be relied upon for justice. The ballot box was the ultimate source of power in America. If the NAACP was going to effect change, it had to become a national *political* force.

Before Darrow was done, he moved the crowd to such a frenzy that church windows were accidentally broken and eleven chairs too. So many people had turned out, Darrow had to give his speech a second time, to an overflow crowd in the church basement.

Not until April 1926 did the Sweets' second trial begin. Darrow and Hays once again argued the case, once again to an all-white jury. This time, after three hours and twenty-seven minutes of deliberation, the jury brought a verdict of not guilty. The second trial threatened to bankrupt the NAACP, costing $37,849.

The Sweets were free, and a precedent set. But the tragedy of the Sweet family was not over. Dr. Sweet did eventually move back into his home on Garland Avenue, but the house was to become far quieter than he imagined it would be. Gladys Sweet came down with tuberculosis, which she believed she contracted in the Wayne County jail, and she communicated the disease to her baby daughter. The child, Iva, died two months after her second birthday in 1926, and Gladys died soon after. Dr. Sweet lived on to old age but never fully recovered mentally. He died by suicide, in 1960, at age sixty-four.

13

It is the duty of the younger Negro artist, if he accepts any duties at all from outsiders, to change through the force of his art that old whispering "I want to be white," hidden in the aspirations of his people, to "Why should I want to be white? I am a Negro — and beautiful."

. . . We younger Negro artists who create now intend to express our individual dark-skinned selves without fear or shame. If white people are pleased we are glad. If they are not, it doesn't matter.
— Langston Hughes, "The Negro Artist and the Racial
Mountain," 1926

THE SWEET TRIAL — like the victory in *Moore v. Dempsey* before it, the freeing of the Phillips County death row defendants — spread the gospel of the NAACP. Soon after the verdict, chairwoman Mary White Ovington took a trip to California and was surprised by her experiences. "I did not find a town with fifty colored voters that did not have a branch," she remembered. She spoke to classes at the University of California, to church groups and women's clubs. Everywhere there were crowds applauding, joining, asking what they could do to help, giving money. "It was roses, roses, all the way," she recalled.

In 1918 when Walter joined the staff, the NAACP had 43,994 members in 165 branches, with little reach west of the Mississippi or north of Chicago. Now, in the winter of 1925–26, membership had well more than doubled since that time, with 372 branches. Michigan had a dozen branches. Even Montana had three.

Inequality in education had been the launching pad for Walter White's activism. In 1925, eight years after the fight to save the seventh grade in Atlanta, Howard University's commencement catalogue listed 52 African American bachelor of arts graduates, 43 bachelor of science graduates, 72 doctors of medicine, 26 bachelor of law graduates, 26 doctors of dentistry, 11 pharmaceutical chemists. "Negro illiteracy had fallen below 20 percent," recalled the Kansas City writer and activist Roy Wilkins. "The death rates were dropping, the net worth of Negroes had risen from zero to more than $2 billion, the era of one-room shacks for schools was giving way to universities and long lines of honors graduates."

For the first time in history, parents of African American kids could buy them dolls that had brown skin, made by the Harlem-based toy company Berry & Ross. The first Black labor union was launched the same year as the first Sweet trial — the Brotherhood of Sleeping Car Porters — headed by A. Philip Randolph, a brilliant Black leader emerging as a force on the national scene. Even in the pages of white newspapers of the South, progress could be seen in editorials taking an unqualified stand against lynching: the *Atlanta Constitution,* the *Columbia Record* and the Charleston *News and Courier* of South Carolina, the *Greensboro Daily News* of North Carolina, the *Birmingham News* of Alabama, the *Chattanooga Times* of Tennessee, and the *San Antonio Express* of Texas, among others.

"This new phase of things is delicate," the Black writer Alain Locke, who was head of Howard University's philosophy department, wrote in 1925. "It will call for less charity but more justice; less help, but infinitely closer understanding. This is indeed a critical stage of race relationships because of the likelihood, if the new temper is not understood, of engendering sharp group antagonism and a second crop of more calculated prejudice."

That winter of 1925–26, Harlem celebrated another milestone. In December, Walter and Gladys White turned out for an evening affair at Harlem's oddly named Hotel Men on West 135th Street. The crowd was a who's who of "the Talented Tenth." While most of the conversation that night was as ephemeral as the smoke twirling off of Du Bois's Benson & Hedges, the party was celebrating a landmark new book — *The New Negro,* a collection of the best Black literary voices all in one place, edited by Alain Locke, who declared on the first page of his foreword:

> This volume aims to document the New Negro culturally and so-
> cially — to register the transformations of the inner and outer life
> of the Negro in America that have so significantly taken place
> in the last few years. . . . Of all the voluminous literature on the
> Negro, so much is mere external view and commentary that we
> may warrantably say that nine-tenths of it is *about* the Negro
> rather than of him. . . . So far as he is culturally articulate, we shall
> let the Negro speak for himself.

The New Negro was the most powerful statement yet of the philosophy voiced by James Weldon Johnson: "The real pride of a people is not in its men of wealth but in its men of letters." The collection featured fiction by Jean Toomer, Rudolph Fisher, Zora Neale Hurston, and Bruce Nugent; poetry by Countee Cullen, Anne Spencer, Arna Bontemps, Claude McKay, and James Weldon Johnson; essays by Du Bois and Charles Johnson. James Weldon Johnson celebrated one of his favorite topics in his essay "Harlem: The Culture Capital." Walter appeared with an essay called "The Paradox of Color."

Almost all of those figures were there that night. The most exciting new voice came from the typewriter of an unlikely young man: Langston Hughes, who was also in the crowd. Though just twenty-three, Hughes had led a life so adventurous, he was instantly a subject of fascination. He had studied at Columbia University, had worked as a cook, a launderer, and a busboy. He had traveled to Africa and Europe as a seaman and then moved to Washington, DC, where he started writing poetry. The title poem of his upcoming debut book, "The Weary Blues," appeared in *The New Negro* collection and accomplished something that had yet to be done in poetry: to infuse verse with the syncopated rhythm of a jazz piece, making the flavor unmistakably Black. (Knopf was set to publish the book a few months after this party, in 1926.)

As Walter had done with singers Jules Bledsoe and Paul Robeson and poet Countee Cullen, he took Langston Hughes under his wing, making introductions to such influential critics as the Van Dorens, H. L. Mencken, and John Farrar (later a cofounder of the publisher Farrar, Straus and Giroux).

The New Negro drew sparkling reviews. "It is a book of surprises," Dorothy Scarborough concluded in the *New York Times Book Review.* Irita Van Doren — wife of Carl Van Doren and book editor of the *New York Herald Tribune* — attended *The New Negro* party at the Hotel Men's restaurant. One week later, her newspaper made the declaration that — by most accounts — gave the Harlem Renaissance its name: America was "on the edge, if not already in the midst, of what might not improperly be called a Negro renaissance."*

"Things are certainly moving with rapidity now so far as the Negro artist is concerned," Walter wrote to the Black novelist Claude McKay, who was traveling in Paris. "Countee Cullen has had a book of verse accepted by Harper to be published in September and just a day or two ago, Knopf accepted a volume by Langston Hughes. Rudolph Fisher of Baltimore has had two excellent short stories in the *Atlantic Monthly* (February and May) and he is, I think, by far the most promising short story writer we have. James Weldon is at work on a book on Negro spirituals and the field of creative writers seems to be growing daily."

All of this set the stage for Walter to publish his second novel, *Flight,* in spring 1926. *Flight* would make its landing among talented and youthful competition. Perhaps Walter knew he was in trouble when his friend — the novelist Sinclair Lewis, who had come out so feverishly for Walter's

---

* Although this quote in the *Herald Tribune* is generally given credit for naming the Harlem Renaissance, W.E.B. Du Bois wrote an essay six months before that article was published, called "A Negro Art Renaissance." It appeared in the *Los Angeles Times* on June 14, 1925.

previous book and who would win the Pulitzer Prize in 1926 for his novel *Arrowsmith* — declined to write a blurb of enthusiasm to be printed on the back of *Flight*. Lewis refused to say why. Blanche Knopf wrote Walter ominously, "The Sinclair Lewis business is serious."

FLIGHT was published in April 1926. Walter received large brown envelopes at his office from a newspaper clippings service, filled with reviews. He recalled the sensation of opening those envelopes with trembling hands.

"I slit them open eagerly and my eye runs briskly down each clipping," he wrote, "picking out all the most favorable phrases and skipping as far as possible the intimations that the reviewer found spots in my book which were slightly less than perfect."

Flight told the story of Mimi Daquin, a light-skinned African American woman from New Orleans who moves to Atlanta and decides to pass as white. Things do not go as planned, and she returns to her original racial identity. The novel was an attempt to make white readers understand the experience of racial discrimination and the struggles of identity. The reviewers weren't buying it, nor were enough readers. The novel was "less important and persuasive" than Walter's first, the *New York Times Book Review* concluded. "'Flight' is not perfect," the *Pittsburgh Courier's* critic found. "Mr. White has a very plain style. He lays little claim to literary art."

Flight's only glowing review in a major outlet came from Carl Van Vechten, who wrote in the *New York Herald Tribune:* "It is a pleasure to be able to state that Mr. White's second novel is much better than his first." But those who knew Walter knew to take this one with a grain of salt. Walter and Carl Van Vechten — the Caucasian *Vanity Fair* writer and novelist whom Walter affectionately called Carlo — were famously friendly drinking buddies often found sharing an ashtray in Harlem nightclubs.

"Reactions to criticisms are funny experiences," Walter wrote of *Flight's* reception. By funny, he was being sarcastic. Bad reviews hit him like existential low blows. His trajectory up to now had been fueled by indestructible self-confidence; for the first time, he felt racked by failure. He read his own book anew and felt strangely puzzled by the words on the pages, as if someone else had written them.

"I can imagine no job which has quite so much discouragement and so many periods of depression as that of writing novels," he wrote his friend Ethel Bodient Gilbert. "This depression comes when one reads a book after it is in print and realizes the huge margin between the picture one had in one's mind when writing and the one which was actually caught in the words." To another friend, John Haynes Holmes, he wrote, "I am too new at the game of writing to be impervious to adverse criticism. . . . I just couldn't see how the story as I felt and wrote it could be as bad as some critics said it was. . . . Some of the critics have revealed that they think me somewhat unbalanced mentally when I do a picture of a person with Negro blood who can 'go white' but who instead chooses voluntarily and not through forces of circumstance to go back to being colored."

What stunned Walter most was how closely *Flight*'s main character, Mimi, resembled a female version of himself, and how her struggles illuminated his own in ways he did not even realize when he created her. "In telling of Mimi," he wrote two weeks after the book came out, "I revealed, I now realize, a great deal more of myself than I knew at the time."

The timing for *Flight* did not help its cause. Within the previous year, book buyers had been deluged with extraordinary works of fiction. Ernest Hemingway's first major book, *In Our Time,* F. Scott Fitzgerald's *The Great Gatsby,* Sinclair Lewis's *Arrowsmith,* Willa Cather's *The Professor's House,* and John Dos Passos's *Manhattan Transfer* all came out in 1925, right before *Flight.* Hemingway's *The Sun Also Rises* appeared in 1926, as did new novels by Vladimir Nabokov, Colette, H. P. Lovecraft, and Agatha Christie. Walter's wife was particularly smitten with Theodore Dreiser's new novel *An American Tragedy,* which might have pleased Walter none too much.

The most sensational novel of 1926, however, came from Walter's close friend Carl Van Vechten — *Nigger Heaven,* published by Knopf. Here was a novel that read like a white man's guide to Harlem in the guise of a roman à clef, something that had not been done. Among Black intellectuals, it was a ghastly affront, not just because of the title, or because the story felt exploitive, but because even during Harlem's literary renaissance, it was a white man telling his version of it to the masses. In the opening line of his review, Du Bois called *Nigger Heaven* a "blow to the face" and said he needed to take a shower after reading it. Langston Hughes, James Weldon Johnson, and Walter White all defended it. Walter in particular had to answer for it to some of his friends because Walter had been Van Vechten's go-to guide to Harlem after dark, and everyone in Harlem knew it. Nevertheless, *Nigger Heaven* eclipsed *Flight* entirely.

Walter believed the only saving of this novel would be if he could sell it as a movie. Film studios such as Fox Film Corporation, Paramount, and Metro-Goldwyn-Mayer were emerging as juggernauts in American entertainment, and the famous HOLLYWOODLAND sign had gone up in the Los Angeles hills in 1923, like a birth announcement for the new West Coast film colony (the last four letters were later removed, and the sign, of course, still stands). Walter had reason to believe he had a shot.

"We have been in communication with Universal Pictures Corporation re: *Flight*," Blanche Knopf's assistant wrote Walter. "This picture is now in work, and they have decided to call it The American Eagle." At the same time, Walter heard rumors that the film impresario Cecil B. DeMille, who would produce four feature films in 1926, was going to make a movie about race in America, and that he wanted Walter's friend Paul Robeson to play the lead. According to the rumor mill, DeMille wanted Walter to concoct the story.

"By the way, do you know Cecil DeMille?" Walter wrote a friend in Los Angeles, Jim Tully, two weeks after *Flight* was published. "Some days ago, there appeared a story that DeMille is going to do a film of Negro life. . . . Dudley Murphy, who did the Ballet Mecanique, approached me the other day and said that he was in touch with DeMille and wanted me to do the story." A month later Walter wrote Tully again: "Evidently, things have been moving without my knowing it." Walter had heard that "DeMille had abandoned all of the persons who had been considered to do this story with the exception of myself and that DeMille was anxious to have me do the story. As a matter of fact, he thought I had already signed a contract."

During the summer of 1926, however, all of those dreams evaporated. DeMille never made any movie about race. Universal Pictures never put *Flight* into production. White was left despondent and unsure of his next move. Then in October came news of another violent episode — a racially charged murder case, as grim as they came. Walter was already a ball of nerves when he got the call. He was asked to shed his African American identity and to go undercover again.

14

When I am discouraged or disheartened, I have this to fall back on:
if there is a principle of right in the world, which finally prevails,
and I believe that there is; if there is a merciful but justice-loving
God in heaven, and I believe that there is, we shall win; for we have
right on our side.
— James Weldon Johnson

ON THE MORNING OF APRIL 25, 1925, Mrs. Annie Lowman, fifty-five, and
her daughter Bertha, twenty-seven, were in the backyard at their rural
farmhouse thirteen miles outside of Aiken, South Carolina. The elder
Lowman woman was making soap in a pot, and her daughter was sweeping leaves. They were enjoying a spring sun, warm on their brown faces.
Suddenly there appeared four strangers — white males whom they did not
recognize — in their yard.

The patriarch of this family, Sam Lowman, was away, at a mill having
meal ground. Two other Lowmans — Demon, twenty-one, and Clarence,
fourteen — were working in a field near the farmhouse, as the Lowmans
were sharecroppers. Upon seeing these white strangers converging, Bertha and Annie retreated toward the house.

When the strangers drew revolvers, the Lowman women panicked.
Bertha Lowman reached the back porch at the same time as one of the
white men did. He bloodied her mouth with a pistol, and she screamed.
Annie Lowman grabbed an axe to protect her daughter. One of the white
men emptied his gun into her, killing her instantly. The two Lowmans

working in the field — Demon and Clarence — heard the screams and gunshots and came sprinting. They entered the house, grabbed weapons, and unleashed a crackle of bullets. When it was over, one of the white men lay dead, another lay bleeding, and the three surviving Lowmans — Demon and Clarence and Bertha — were all wounded with gunshots.

The dead white man turned out to be Aiken County sheriff H. H. Howard. These white strangers were all police officers. When the law took Bertha, Clarence, and Demon Lowman away that day, Annie Lowman remained, dead on the ground.

Twenty-four hours after the shooting, locals from Aiken packed a funeral service for Sheriff Howard, among them some two hundred Klansmen. The day after that, officers went to the Lowman home and charged Sam Lowman with bootlegging, claiming they'd found two jugs of whiskey on the property. (This was during Prohibition.)

On May 12 the Lowmans entered a courtroom in Aiken, where they sat at the defendants' table facing a white judge named Rice and an all-white, all-male jury. During the proceedings, the judge eulogized the fallen sheriff, in a speech that would have been cause for a mistrial, had this been a fair courtroom. He asked the jury members of this small community not to hold a grudge against the public defenders who had to represent the Lowmans. They were just doing their jobs, Judge Rice told the jury. With little in the way of testimony, the judge sentenced Bertha Lowman to life in prison, Sam Lowman to two years on a chain gang for bootlegging, and the two boys, Clarence and Demon, to the electric chair.

None of this news made the press, outside of local newspapers. However, the Lowmans' story now became highly unusual. A Black attorney named N. J. Frederick was so outraged by the sham trial that he took it upon himself, free of charge, to appeal the case, and in October 1926, over a year after the shooting took place, a new trial began. Frederick argued that the white policemen who had showed up at the Lowmans' home had never identified themselves as law enforcement, that they were dressed in plain clothes and never showed any law enforcement insignia. The Lowmans had every right to protect themselves and their home, Frederick argued.

The case reached South Carolina's Supreme Court. Sheriff H. H. Howard did have a warrant to search the Lowman home when he showed up there on the day he died. But, the state supreme court ruled, "This charge excluded the right of the defendants to protect themselves against search if they did not know the parties making the search were officers."

It now appeared that the Lowmans would be freed.

On the night of October 8, 1926, at about 3:45 a.m., a masked mob of roughly 150 men appeared outside of the Aiken jailhouse, where the Lowmans were still being held. According to testimony from others in the jailhouse that night, Bertha Lowman began screaming uncontrollably, as she knew what was about to happen to her. Sam Lowman was in another jail at the time. The jailers, according to testimony, handed the keys over to the mob. The victims were pushed into cars, and drivers began motoring out of Aiken.

At the scene of the execution were five hundred parked cars and some two thousand spectators. The three prisoners were let loose and told to run. They did not make it far before they were cut down by gunfire. As the lynching historian Mark Robert Schneider later wrote, "If not for the NAACP, that would have been the last anyone would have heard of Bertha, Demon, or Clarence Lowman."

SHORTLY AFTER THE LOWMAN LYNCHINGS, some of the most extraordinary letters Walter White would ever see landed on his desk at NAACP headquarters. Some were signed. Others, anonymous. Perhaps the most surprising was from a white newspaperman named James L. Quinby, a small-town journalist from Graniteville, South Carolina, who had written an editorial blasting Aiken's law enforcement for its handling of the killings.

Quinby had already received a death threat. "Now this is no idle threat," he wrote to NAACP headquarters, his letter dated October 12, 1926, "as I live within six miles of Aiken, the scene of the crime, and a large delegation of murderers are from this town. But this is a small matter, as I am entirely in the hands of God."

He then launched into a series of paragraphs beginning with the words "Did you know."

Walter F. White's graduating class from Atlanta University, circa 1916. Walter is standing at far right. Two years later, he was plucked from obscurity and brought to New York City to work for the fledgling NAACP. *Rose M. Palmer*

The Silent Parade was held to protest the East Saint Louis race massacre of 1917. Ten thousand people marched through Manhattan in total silence, and in the process, put the NAACP in the national spotlight for the first time. *Underwood Archives / Getty Images*

The modern Ku Klux Klan formed at an Atlanta cross burning in 1915. The group's power spread nationally into state houses, police departments, and even school boards. Pictured here is a KKK rally in Washington, DC, in 1925 that drew roughly forty thousand Klansmen and women. *Bettmann / Getty Images*

Walter in the 1920s, the decade in which he conducted over forty undercover race murder investigations. This photo appeared in *American Mercury* with a Walter-penned article titled, "I Investigate Lynchings." *Schomburg Center, New York Public Library*

James Weldon Johnson, Walter's mentor and one of the most influential race leaders of the twentieth century. Acclaimed novelist, educator, former diplomat, song lyricist, poet, newspaperman — Johnson was a Black Renaissance man. *Library of Congress / Corbis / Getty Images*

W.E.B. Du Bois in his office at *The Crisis,* the NAACP's magazine. The first Black Harvard PhD, Du Bois was the most influential African American intellectual of his era. He was a mentor, and later a nemesis, of Walter's. *Schomburg Center, New York Public Library*

The Red Summer of 1919 saw an explosion of race violence in the US. As Du Bois put it, "The facts concerning the year 1919 are almost unbelievable as one looks back upon them." Pictured here is a scene from the Chicago race riot, which Walter personally investigated. *Chicago History Museum / Getty Images*

On May 31 through June 1, 1921, white mobs attacked the Greenwood neighborhood of Tulsa, Oklahoma, burning about forty blocks to the ground. Walter went undercover as a white man to investigate the Tulsa massacre, which is arguably the most destructive incident of racial violence in American history. *Corbis Historical / Getty Images*

Oklahoma Historical Society

During the 1920s, Walter helped launch the Harlem Renaissance. Pictured here is poet Langston Hughes (far left), famed Black scholar Charles S. Johnson (next to Hughes), and writer Rudolph Fisher (second from right), all of whom were among Walter's close friends. *Schomburg Center, New York Public Library*

During the Jazz Age, Harlem became the "Nightclub Capital of the World." Walter and his mentor James Weldon Johnson were fixtures in Harlem after dark when they were in New York. Pictured here is Duke Ellington and his orchestra in 1929. *JP Jazz Archive / Getty Images*

Marcus Garvey, founder of the United Negro Improvement Association, emerged as the most controversial Black leader of the 1920s, and a rival of the NAACP. "The world has made being black a crime," Garvey famously said. "I hope to make it a virtue." *Bettman / Getty Images*

In 1931, Walter (center) took over as chief executive of the NAACP, which by this time had become the most powerful civil rights organization in the world. His two most important hires of the 1930s were Roy Wilkins (left), a future NAACP chief executive, and young attorney Thurgood Marshall (right), later to become America's first Black Supreme Court justice.
Library of Congress / Corbis / Getty Images

Clarence Darrow, the most famous lawyer of the 1920s. Walter recruited Darrow to represent Dr. Ossian Sweet during the Sweet cases of 1925–26, which riveted the nation. Darrow became the inspiration for Walter's trajectory into national politics. *Chicago History Museum / Getty Images*

Walter's friendship with First Lady Eleanor Roosevelt was a catalyst for a historic shift of Black voters from the Party of Lincoln to the modern Democratic Party during the Great Depression. Here she passes out Christmas gifts to Black students. *Bettman / Getty Images*

Walter with his wife Gladys and their two children, Walter Carl Darrow White and Jane White, in their Harlem apartment in the 1930s, which was sometimes called the "White House of Negro America." *Rose M. Palmer*

For years, Walter hid the secret of his white paramour, Poppy Cannon. As the most powerful African American political and social leader of his time, he knew that this mixed-race, adulterous relationship would destroy him if news of it were leaked. *Bettman / Getty Images*

During the war years, race riots swept the nation. The night of the Harlem riot of 1943, pictured above, Walter watched the violence unfolding with New York mayor Fiorello La Guardia from the back of a squad car.
Bettman / Getty Images

The Detroit race riot of 1943 was the deadliest US riot of the war years. A scathing investigation by Walter and Thurgood Marshall found numerous killings of Black Detroiters by white police officers.   *Bettman / Getty Images*

Isaac Woodard (center), decorated US Army veteran, was blinded during an altercation with a white police officer in South Carolina in 1946. At left is former heavyweight champion Joe Louis. Spurred on by Walter and the movie star Orson Welles, Woodard's story became a national cause célèbre.
New York Daily News Archive / Getty Images

Walter, Eleanor Roosevelt, and President Harry Truman on June 29, 1947, the day Truman became the first American president to address the NAACP. It was a climactic moment in Walter's life and cemented a lifelong friendship with Truman.

Abbie Rowe, National Park Service.

Harry S. Truman Library

"We must make the federal government a friendly, vigilant defender of the rights and equalities of all Americans," Truman said in his now-iconic NAACP speech. "And again, I mean all Americans." Some historians regard this speech as the launching point for the modern civil rights movement.

National Archives / Getty Images

Did you know that the Judge who sat upon the bench in this case was a member of the Ku Klux Klan?

Did you know that the sheriff and his deputies belonged to the Klan, that the sheriff who was killed belonged to the Klan, and that this whole murder was under Klan management . . . ?

Did you know that as soon as the news got out about the murder, that certain people involved in this murder, in order to muddy the waters, and cover up their guilt, tried to precipitate a race riot, and went about frightening the white people, telling them that the Negroes were armed, and were going to rise at night and kill us all?

Quinby ended his letter with a PS: "If I should happen to be killed, you have my full permission to publish this letter."

Other missives came into national headquarters from South Carolinians pleading for help. James Weldon Johnson received one from an agent with the Southern Railway Company named A. H. Johnson, dated October 12. "The guilty parties that pulled the awful murder at Aiken five miles from here, and my county seat on October 8th, could be caught if you care to investigate; let your man see me at Warrenville depot and I can give him some pointers quietly."

Perhaps most important, Johnson got a letter from the Black lawyer who had defended the Lowmans in their second trial, N. J. Frederick. "As you perhaps know, I am the colored attorney that took up this case after the conviction of these unfortunate people last year in Circuit Court," he wrote. "As I knew the whole case from the beginning up to the lynching, I have been wondering if in any way I could be used in an effort to focus the attention of the country on the evil of this thing and aid in the building up of sentiment for the passage of a Federal Anti-lynching law. If anything can be done while this horror is fresh, I would be glad to give any assistance possible."

South Carolina's governor, Thomas G. McLeod, had given a statement to the press about the killings, promising that "everything possible will be done to bring to justice the members of the Aiken mob. I am giving the matter my constant attention, and will make a thorough investigation. I feel assured that something can be done and is going to be done." However, Governor McLeod appeared to be doing nothing. A grand jury investigation had found no reason to bring any indictments, due to lack of any evidence, even though the killings took place in front of some two thousand spectators.

No one would speak up. So as it stood, the matter was over.

At the time these letters appeared at NAACP headquarters, Walter was suffering burnout, and he had quietly sought out the assistance of friends to write him recommendations, as he was applying for a grant from the Guggenheim Foundation. He was hoping to become the first African American to get a Guggenheim grant, and he was planning to either take a leave of absence from the NAACP or to quit his job and devote himself to writing. But now duty called. The Lowman lynching case was in addition to four others that occurred in the month of August 1926 — one each in Arkansas, Georgia, Virginia, and Florida. One of the cases even involved the lynching of a white man.

From what Walter was reading about Aiken, there seemed to be an opportunity to bust a case wide open and make national news. He also believed this could be the case to revive the federal anti-lynching bill, which had stalled years earlier due to a Senate filibuster.

Walter reached out to the New York *World,* Joseph Pulitzer's hugely read newspaper, and quickly heard back. Assistant managing editor W. P. Beazell wrote to Walter, "We should be glad indeed to have you let us know what you find out as a result of an inquiry into the situation."

That was enough for Walter. He left New York on October 22, two weeks after the Lowman murders. "I am leaving New York this afternoon (Friday) for South Carolina," he wrote his friend Bishop John Hurst, who lived there. "My mission you can easily guess."

WALTER ARRIVED IN AIKEN on the morning of October 23 and found the small city quiet and even quaint. It was located a few miles from the Georgia border. Northern tycoons from the Vanderbilt, Astor, Whitney, and Harriman families wintered here. There was no particular history of race violence in Aiken. However, South Carolina had given rise to some of the most notoriously racist politicians in American history, men such as "Pitchfork" Ben Tillman, the one-eyed former South Carolina governor, and Cole Blease, who had been governor when Walter was a teenager and openly justified lynch mobs.

"Whenever the Constitution comes between me and the virtue of the white women of South Carolina," Blease famously said, "then I say, 'To Hell with the Constitution!'"

Walter had lined up appointments with men who had written letters to NAACP headquarters about the killings—first and foremost, the lawyer who had defended the Lowmans in their second trial. Arriving at N. J. Frederick's office, Walter immediately felt pity for this brave figure. "I don't recall any man so isolated by his community as was the lawyer who had defended the Negroes," Walter later wrote. "He told me freely and frankly the names of the ringleaders and, in particular, the name of an individual who lived in a nearby cotton mill town who could give me additional information."

This individual happened to be James L. Quinby of Graniteville, the same man who had written the "Did you know" letter to national headquarters less than two weeks earlier. Walter asked Frederick for a ride to this nearby cotton town on the outskirts of Aiken. Frederick turned and looked out his office window. He answered anxiously, "I will go with you if you will promise to get back to town before sundown."

Why so much caution? "Surely no one would dare harm so well-known and respected a person as yourself," Walter said.

"Those mill hands and Kluxers would harm anybody," Frederick said.

As a Black lawyer who had defended the Lowmans for their killing of a white police officer, Frederick had plenty to fear. Walter realized that snooping around in the rural areas outside of Aiken might be more dangerous than he thought. "If the Klan would molest him," he thought, "it did not take much imagination to figure out what they would do to a stranger."

Frederick drove Walter out into the countryside, to a house on the side of a hill in Graniteville. Gray-haired James Quinby opened the door, looked at the pair, and asked what they wanted. Walter told him: facts about the Lowman lynchings. Quinby invited them inside. They talked, and at one point Quinby excused himself and left the room. Moments later there appeared something of an apparition: a man in full white KKK regalia, hood over his head.

Walter nearly panicked. Had he walked into a trap? Quinby then removed his hood. He said, "I show you this so that you will realize I know what I am talking about."

QUINBY EXPLAINED that he had been one of the founding members of Aiken's Kleagle, because he thought the group could fight corrupt local politicians and support law enforcement. That had always been part of the KKK's proposed mission, Quinby said. To help police departments.

But that was not all that the Klan was about, Quinby learned, and so he quit the group. Ever since, he feared for his life. He led Walter to an adjoining room and showed him an impressive collection of guns and ammunition, which he had amassed should he need it to protect himself and his family. Quinby told Walter everything he knew about the Lowman case, from the point of view of an insider in this small community where people kept their mouths shut to outsiders. According to Quinby's account, some white spectators had actually been driven to the lynchings by Black chauffeurs. Quinby's information opened a window for Walter into a terrifying rural underworld of corrupt officials, a "very extensive business of distilling of liquor," as Walter later put it, and a "reign of lawlessness and barbarity."

Among the people Walter interviewed was a local who stopped him in the middle of their discussion. "Mr. White," this man said while putting his hand on Walter's shoulder, "work into your story the fact that you were sent by God. For seven weeks a group of white people has met in my house here every night and prayed that some men from out of the state be sent to open up this mass of corruption and to publish to the world the terrible state of affairs prevailing here. You are the answer to that prayer."

At 9 a.m. on October 25 Walter met with A. H. Johnson at the train depot in Warrenville, a village just west of Aiken. Johnson had been the one who had written the letter to association headquarters: "Let your man see me at Warrenville depot and I can give him some pointers quietly." Walter was nervous, as he feared this meeting was a trap. But it was no setup. A. H. Johnson was a man of the community. He knew people. He gave Walter a list of twenty-one men who he claimed were leaders of the Aiken mob that killed the three Lowmans. He named two police officers — including one named Robinson, who had been present at the Lowmans' farm eighteen months earlier at the gun battle that had started the whole affair. It was Robinson, Johnson said, who had shot dead fifty-five-year-old Annie Lowman, and it was Robinson who had handed over the three other Lowmans to the lynch mob.

At one point Walter came face-to-face with one of the killers, who told the story firsthand of how the mob had murdered the Lowmans in a hail of bullets. He said of Bertha Lowman, "We had to waste fifty bullets on the wench before one of them stopped her howling."

Walter put all the pieces together, and on October 26, he sent a typed letter, six pages single spaced, to South Carolina's governor, Thomas G. McLeod. It was a veritable time bomb set to explode in forty-eight hours.

"My dear Gov. McLeod," Walter's letter began. "I have just left Aiken, which I visited along with other cities in South Carolina as a representative of The New York World." Walter quoted McLeod in the letter, how the governor had said on numerous occasions that he would pursue justice in the Lowman case. The governor had said as much nearly half a dozen times, to reporters at local newspapers. But nothing had been done. Now Walter claimed to have all the facts.

"I am now en route to New York," he wrote, "and I shall place all of this material in the hands of my paper upon arrival there. This will give some forty eight hours for action before any of the material I have gathered will be published. Here are the facts which I have secured."

Walter laid out the story of the "cold-blooded, carefully planned and premeditated murder of the three Lowmans." How a group of white men gathered in the office of an Aiken attorney named Stansfield the night of the lynchings, to organize the mob. How two men named Sheppard (a police officer) and Anderson (who worked for Carolina Light & Power) used wire cutters to cut off electricity to the jail—lights out. How a police officer ordered people to move their cars away from the jailhouse so that the lynching party would have a place to park when they arrived. How at 3 a.m. on October 8 three police officers (Walter listed their names) went to the jail cell of Bertha Lowman and told her to put on her street clothes as she was wanted downstairs. How she refused because she feared for her life, and how they dragged her kicking and screaming from her cell, down a flight of stairs, to the jailhouse's front door.

The Aiken jailhouse was four years old and well constructed, with two outer doors made of steel. The keys to the cells were kept in a steel vault behind a steel door two inches thick. Yet there was no sign of any dynamite blast or anything else that might have been used to get the keys to the Lowmans' jail cells. According to Walter's report, police officers (Walter named them) handed the three Lowmans over to the lynch mob. The Lowmans were placed in cars (Walter named the drivers). He continued:

> On the way from the jail Clarence Lowman, 14 years of age at
> the time Sheriff Howard was killed and 15 years old when he was
> lynched, jumped from the car which was taking him from the jail
> to the scene of his death. Clarence was shot and recaptured. I am
> informed that to keep blood from getting in the car, a rope was
> tied to Clarence and to the car and his body was dragged in this
> manner to the scene of his execution. The mob went out York
> Street on the Dixie Highway to a point about 1-1/2 to 2 miles from
> Aiken near a Tourist camp. I am informed that Bertha Lowman
> begged so piteously for her life that members of the mob had a
> hard time killing her.

For his climax, Walter listed the full names of those he believed to be members of the lynch mob, with their addresses and occupations. Some of those names must have shocked Governor McLeod to the bottoms of his feet.

The list included two Aiken deputy sheriffs named McElheny and Sheppard, an Aiken blacksmith named Howard, a man named Hart "who is a Special State Constable for Your Honor the Governor of South Carolina," Walter wrote. There was a man named Anderson, also a "Special Constable for the Governor." An Aiken policeman named Woodward "who wore his uniform to the lynching." The Aiken attorney Stansfield whose office was used to organize the mob before the event. A man named Buckingham who was "Master of Ceremonies at the lynching," and who had served three terms as a South Carolina legislator. An Aiken traffic officer named Salley. An Aiken butcher named Somers. A man named Taylor who was a guard at the Aiken jail. Walter even listed a farmer and merchant from the village of Ellenton who was a "member of the Grand Jury which investigated the lynching" and recommended no charges be filed.

This was a shocker — that a member of the lynch mob had actually investigated, as part of a grand jury, his own crime, and had helped to clear himself and other perpetrators of wrongdoing.

Walter listed the full names of the three men he called "the chief executioners" — one of whom was an Aiken police officer. He also listed witnesses to the killings, among them three of Governor McLeod's own cousins.

At the root of Walter's investigation was an underbelly of vicious criminality and intimidation that pulsed through this southern town. "A number of white men as well as Negroes have been flogged and killed and the more law abiding and respectable element is living in constant terror," Walter wrote. "In all my experiences, I have never before seen such a reign of lawlessness as exists in and near Aiken." The entire Lowman affair, he wrote the governor, had largely been organized by the Ku Klux Klan.

"If you care to do so," Walter finished, "you may communicate with me in the care of Herbert Bayard Swope, Executive Editor of the *New York World*, Pulitzer Building, New York."

IN SOUTH CAROLINA, Governor McLeod had the public relations problem of a lifetime. As promised, Walter released all his information to the *World*, and he himself issued a press release telling his whole story, so even before the *World* got to it, newspapers nationwide were on to the scoop. The *World* sent star reporter Oliver H. P. Garrett to South Carolina, and for the next thirty days the story of the Aiken lynchings made the front page. Governor McLeod's term was ending, and it appeared he would slip away quietly into retirement and let his successor clean up the mess. In his article for *The Crisis* Walter singled him out. Walter called McLeod a "pussyfooter" who "will do nothing."

"My God, I wish this was over," McLeod was heard to say with a groan.

A new governor took over and ordered a grand jury investigation, but the grand jury (all white men) again found insufficient evidence to proceed with indictments, even though the New York *World* had confirmed many of Walter's findings. It appeared that everyone in Aiken knew who the lynchers were. But no one would speak up; perhaps even if they wanted to, they feared for their lives if they did.

The Afro-American called Walter's Aiken probe the "most daring of his investigations." His friend Bishop John Hurst (who was really like an uncle to Walter) wrote him, "Mrs. Hurst was not joking when she showed herself anxious over your visit to Aiken. These atrocities down there had a terrible effect on her. She became nervous any time she attempted to discuss the tragedy. I knew myself the full value of the attempt you were making. It was a man, as I saw it, taking his life in his hands. Well, Walter, we have got to fight it out to the end. No matter what it costs, we have got to fight it out."

With all the publicity, many in Aiken now realized that the "white" man who had come from the north to investigate the Lowman lynchings was Walter White — NAACP man. A Black man. One of the Aiken contacts that Walter had met, an elderly white attorney known locally as Colonel Claude E. Sawyer, wrote Walter. "Is that true?" he asked. "I had on amber colored glasses and did not take the trouble to scrutinize your color but I really did take you for a white man and, according to the laws of South Carolina, you may be."

Walter responded:

So far as I can remember, your letter of November 23d comes very close to being the most interesting one I have ever re-

ceived. . . . While I was in South Carolina, I neither told anybody I was white nor did I tell them I was colored. According to
the laws of the State of South Carolina as given by you, I suppose
I am legally a white man inasmuch as that law states that when
a person has one-eighth or less of Negro blood he is white. On
the other hand, I do know that I have Negro blood though it has
never seemed to me important to ascertain the precise amount in
my veins. . . . When I talked with some of the lynchers and others in Aiken, if I had to choose between being a Negro with all
the disabilities which the Negro suffers in America, and being of
the class of South Carolina white to which I refer, I would always
choose being the former.

ACCORDING TO THE STATE OF SOUTH CAROLINA, the three Lowmans met
their death at the hands of persons unknown. No charges were ever filed.
No police officer was fired. However, as Walter and James Johnson had
hoped, the case did initiate a new movement in Congress to pass a federal
anti-lynch law. In Washington, Congressman Dyer resurrected the Dyer
bill, and once again Walter was given the credit due to one of his now
famous undercover investigations. "The result of this dramatic achieve-
ment," the *Afro-American* — an influential newspaper out of Baltimore —
stated, "has been to revive the issue of lynching throughout the United
States, church bodies, newspapers and many individual citizens voicing a
renewed demand for federal action to stamp out this crime."

On March 27, 1927, the NAACP held a mass rally at Gibson's New
Standard Theatre in Philadelphia. An ad promised special music and a
special guest speaker. That night every seat was filled as twelve hundred
packed the place. Onto the stage walked Sam Lowman. He had spent seventeen months on a chain gang for possessing liquor, a Prohibition-era
crime he may or may not have committed. Walter introduced Sam Lowman to the crowd.

"This is the man the crackers said was a desperado," Walter said, "a
moonshiner, a menace to the community. Can you look at him and see
any of those criminal traits?"

Lowman appeared elderly and so tired, it was as if he needed the crowd applause to hold him up. His entire family had been lynched. He attempted to speak but could only utter what one present remembered as "a few rather incoherent words." He returned to his seat, but the crowd kept thundering. It was not a lot of solace for a man who had lost everything.

15

The civilized world today and the world half-civilized and uncivi-
lized are desperately afraid. The Shape of Fear looms over them.
Germany fears the Jew, England fears the Indian; America fears the
Negro, the Christian fears the Moslem, Europe fears Asia, Protes-
tant fears Catholic, Religion fears Science. Above all, Wealth fears
Democracy. These fears and others are ancient or at least long-
standing. But they are renewed and revivified today because the
world has at present a severe case of nerves.
— W.E.B. Du Bois, "The Shape of Fear," 1926

IN NEW YORK Walter White was becoming legitimately famous. One day
he was on a subway platform and when the train pulled up, in the shuffle
of bodies, he accidentally stepped on a stranger's toe.

The stranger — a Black man — turned to Walter with eyes aflame.

"Why don't you look where you're going?" he said. "You white folks are
always trampling on colored people." Then the look in his eyes changed.
He scrutinized Walter's face and said with a hint of awe, "Are you Walter
White of the NAACP? I'm sorry I spoke to you that way. I thought you
were white."

Walter was used to being perceived as Caucasian. But he was not used
to being recognized and addressed respectfully by strangers on the street
because they knew who he was and what he had done for them.

Fate was a force in Walter's life. He had come of age at the same time
as Jim Crow. He had joined the NAACP right when it was poised to burst

upon the national scene, and at a nation-defining moment in terms of racial identity — the end of the Great War and the beginning of the Red Summer. He had moved to Harlem right when its cultural renaissance began. All of it had lifted him into this trajectory — to where, he did not yet know.

Fame always has its consequences. While Walter's career had taken off as he never could have imagined, by 1926 his home life was starting to show signs of disrepair. He was always either on the road or in the office. When he was at home, it seemed to be always about him. Gladys White had dreams of her own. She had wanted a career on the stage, and in 1926 she debuted in a new Broadway play called *Deep River* — a jazzy opera sprung from the African American spiritual of the same name. The show, starring Jules Bledsoe, opened in September 1926 at the Imperial Theatre. The whole White family reveled in the excitement and hope that *Deep River* would launch Gladys's career. Pre-show buzz was high; one theater writer noted it was going to be "the most elaborate production ever staged which featured Negroes."

The play flopped and proved a financial disaster for its producers. Soon after, Gladys became pregnant with the Whites' second child. Her career on the stage looked to be at an end, while her husband's public persona continued to blossom. From here on out, she would remain almost entirely out of the public eye, leaving barely a trace of herself behind.

Walter was awaiting news from the Guggenheim Foundation about his fellowship application. If he got the fellowship, he planned to take a year in Europe writing. He requested letters of recommendation from a lineup of heavy literary hitters, and he got them from Carl Van Vechten, Carl Van Doren, and Sinclair Lewis. Among them, Lewis's was a piece of such obvious hagiography that Walter wrote him in response: "Good Lord, man. . . . After reading your report to the Guggenheim Foundation, I don't know how I shall ever be able to notice ordinary mortals again."

On March 12, 1927, Walter heard from the foundation. "I got it!" he wrote Joel Spingarn on that day. "I have just received official notification of being chosen by the Guggenheim Foundation for one year beginning April 1 'for creative writing in France; stipend @2,500.'"

Walter was the first African American to win a Guggenheim fellowship. When Spingarn heard of Walter's plan to disappear to Europe for a year, he was alarmed. "I am much disturbed to hear of your decision to give up what I had thought was to be your life-work," Spingarn wrote. "Before you come to a final decision I wish that I might have a talk with you."

Two days later the NAACP board of directors held its monthly meeting. Into the conference room walked Johnson, Joel Spingarn and his brother Arthur, Ovington, and Walter himself, among a handful of others. As usual, Walter reported on a bunch of cases he was working on. He expressed considerable concern about reports he was getting from Detroit, that the city was on the verge of something terrifying. He talked about preparations for the annual NAACP national conference that was coming up, in Indianapolis. "Mr. Darrow has tentatively accepted an invitation to speak," Walter said.

Finally the board arrived at his request for a year's leave of absence. Walter had written a long letter to Ovington, the chair of the board, and she read it aloud to the group.

> This fellowship [Ovington said, reading White's words] brings
> with it a certain amount of regret in that its acceptance would
> mean at least temporary severance of my connection with
> the Association on leave of absence should it be granted. The
> NAACP and the cause it represents is very close to me — perhaps
> not an overstatement to say that it is almost a religion. For over
> nine years I have sought to give to it whatever energy and ability I
> possess. . . . I came to the Association, as some have expressed it,
> as a boy and all of my mature life has been spent in it. The knowl-
> edge and experience that I have gained through traveling around
> 175,000 miles . . . the invaluable experience gained in the inves-
> tigation of some forty-one lynchings and eight race riots and of
> handling the details of such cases as the Arkansas riots, the Sweet

Cases, and others, has given me a chance to develop mentally and spiritually as I could have done in no other field.

When Ovington finished, the room fell awkwardly silent. The board voted, and not only did the group approve Walter's request, he was sent off with three months of full association pay. He was to leave his position on July 15, 1927.

The next four months passed in a dizzying montage of historic events. Charles "Lucky" Lindbergh took off in his *Spirit of St. Louis* and made the first ever solo flight across the Atlantic. The accused anarchists Nicola Sacco and Bartolomeo Vanzetti were convicted of murder (they were defended by Walter's friend Arthur Garfield Hays) and sentenced to death by electric chair. In June Walter traveled to Mississippi to investigate a flood disaster zone along the Mississippi River. In a chilling article in *The Nation* called "The Negro and the Flood," he reported on harrowing conditions in which federal aid, sent to a devastated stretch of American farmland, ended up almost entirely in the hands of white people despite the huge population of African Americans living and farming there. The report was highly critical of those in charge of the flood relief — namely, Secretary of Commerce Herbert Hoover.

Hoover was infuriated. One of his staffers commented, "White is literally the nigger in the woodpile, and if anything can be done to placate or squelch him I think there will be no more trouble."

Just days after returning from Mississippi, Walter and Gladys checked into the hospital where she was to give birth to their second child. They spent hours on the night of June 12, a Sunday, reading poetry together — "God Give to Men" and "A Black Man Talks of Reaping" by Arna Bontemps; "Mulatto" and "Brass Spittoons" by Langston Hughes. Two days later Walter Carl Darrow White was born. The Whites named their son after Walter himself, Clarence Darrow, and Walter's friend Carl Van Vechten, the controversial white author of *Nigger Heaven*. Some of Walter's friends found it odd that he should name his son after two white men. Nevertheless, once Gladys had recuperated, the White family boarded the

Cunard line's RMS *Carmania,* bound for France. The ship set off on July 23. Walter was hoping to revive his literary career, and he was armed with a gift from the NAACP office — a new dictionary to put on his writing desk.

He had a five-week-old son and a four-year-old daughter. He had a marriage in need of repair — which was no secret to the family. (As his sister Helen would put it to him in a letter years later, "We have known for years . . . that you and Gladys didn't get along. . . . She loves you in her own cold way.") Walter was hoping a year in France — away from the rigor of association work and constant travel — might fix his family, and he had a book idea he hoped would fly like an arrow, bull's-eye into the conscience of America. Watching the Manhattan skyline disappear, he might have thought of his mentor James Weldon Johnson. Earlier in Johnson's life, he too had traveled to France in hopes of finding an artistic awakening. "From the day I set foot in France," Johnson later wrote, "I became aware of the working of a miracle in me." Walter was hoping for the same.

ON THEIR FIRST DAY IN PARIS, the Whites ate what Walter called "the most delicious luncheon of our lives," at a restaurant in the neighborhood of the Bois de Boulogne. This was the Paris of the Roaring Twenties, the Paris of the Lost Generation, the city that just a year earlier Hemingway had brought to life in the pages of his first fully imagined novel, *The Sun Also Rises.* "If you are lucky enough to have lived in Paris as a young man," Hemingway wrote, looking back on those days, "then wherever you go for the rest of your life it stays with you, for Paris is a moveable feast."

For the Whites it was a different story. They had two small children, in a foreign city full of loud noises and speeding automobiles. They stayed just two days in the City of Light — spending one night in the apartment of the author and literary agent William Aspenwall Bradley, where they played Paul Robeson's first phonograph record and watched the famed dancer Isadora Duncan give an impromptu performance. Then they departed for Villefranche-sur-Mer, a village outside of Nice on the Côte d'Azur. They had picked this Mediterranean beach town upon the advice of the writer Rebecca West, who told them at a New York party, "It's the one place worth living in which British and American tourists haven't invaded, and it's the most beautiful place in southern France."

For the first week they hunted for a home to rent, as the prices were predictably higher than what they had been told. They eventually found one on the avenue Victor Emmanuel III. On August 16, 1927, Walter wrote to Johnson: "We found just the villa we had dreamed of and hoped for! It is a charming little place of white stone (there are no wooden houses here) with two tiny front balconies on the second floor, a wide terrace, with electric lights and hot and cold water and a lovely bathroom. It is perched high on a sloping hill. In front of us lies the Mediterranean whose beauty justifies all the lavish praise which has been heaped upon it."

The woman who owned the villa rented it to them for the equivalent of $50 a month, in francs. She knew just a few words in English, and Walter thought it ironic that she had named the villa Sweet Home. How different it was from Dr. Ossian Sweet's house on Garland Avenue in Detroit. "Imagine coming four or five thousand miles to live in a place with such a name," Walter wrote Johnson, who quickly wrote back, "I will always be glad to do anything for you on this end that I can."

The Whites found that food was expensive in their little village, but they could take a short train ride to Nice to do their shopping. A hired cook cost just four hundred francs, the equivalent of less than sixteen dollars a month. So they hired one. Her name was Victoria, and while Walter thought she looked like a gargoyle, "she could cook like an angel." A bottle of Pommard 1915 cost eighty cents, a quart of Black & White scotch two dollars, and a liter of beer just eight cents. And, alcohol was legal! Altogether, it felt like paradise, but Walter also felt homesick. "Lovely as this place is I miss the office and the folks there," he wrote Johnson. "I miss our lunches together and the rides home and our talks and association. I want to know how everything is moving along so please keep me informed."

Walter's idea for his first book of nonfiction was — to use a metaphor he might've used given his passion for baseball — a fastball down the middle. The obvious choice. People always said: Write about what you know. Historians told stories of wars, peoples, and nations. Biographers wrote of history's great heroes and villains. Theologists tackled God and the metaphysical. Who better than Walter White to write the story of lynching in America?

Why did humans burn other humans at the stake, or hang them from trees?

What was it about Black men that white men so desperately feared?

And why was this a uniquely *American* phenomenon?

With the Mediterranean sprawling out his window, Walter set to work.

16

The loosening of murderous passions always ends in the glorifica-
tion of the most proficient killer.

— Walter White, *Rope and Faggot*

IN THE BEGINNING, there was Judge Charles Lynch. Born in 1736 in what
later became Lynchburg, Virginia, Judge Lynch was a prominent Quaker
and member of Virginia's House of Burgesses. America at the time had
yet to be born. The land remained vastly unpopulated and, although still
ruled by the British, mostly ungoverned — a sort of Hobbesian state of nature. In a place where the nearest official court was a long distance away,
Judge Lynch formed an extralegal court of his own to administer justice and named himself chief magistrate. Criminal cases were heard, witnesses called. Lynch's extralegal justice system spread across the frontier
and became known as lynch law.

Lynch law used fear of punishment, real justice for real crimes, to
maintain order on the frontier. But it took on new and different meanings
after the Civil War, when slaves were freed, when Black men and women
were given constitutional rights and the entire socioeconomic structure
of the South was suddenly turned on its head. Lynch law became, as Walter called it, "the lynching industry."

The first thing to understand about the phenomenon, Walter wrote in
chapter 1 of his book, was "the mind of the lyncher." Killing with impunity
could only occur in a community in which such practices were accepted

by that community. The phenomenon took root in places "where leaders of the mob are exalted as men of courage and action," Walter wrote. Killing necessitated absolute power of one individual over another, and once that power, Walter theorized, was ordained in a community by the statehouse, the jailhouse, and the pulpit, the lynching industry began to thrive.

Walter began with the statehouse. During the post–Civil War Reconstruction, a new breed of white supremacist politician took charge in the former Confederacy. Fueled by revenge over having lost the war and a desire to maintain what had been the racial status quo before the war (slavery), these politicians created a loosely knit paramilitary arm of the fiercely anti-Lincoln Democratic Party. Most noteworthy, perhaps, was "Pitchfork" Ben Tillman, the one-eyed South Carolina senator (1895–1918) and governor (1890–1894). Tillman is quoted in the United States *Congressional Record* having bragged about his policies toward Black people: "We took the government away. We stuffed ballot boxes. We shot them. We are not ashamed of it." There remained in Walter's time politicians who had inherited the mantle of white supremacy and openly advocated for it, such as Cole Blease (US senator and former governor of South Carolina), Theodore Bilbo (a former governor and future US senator from Mississippi), and Eugene Talmadge (an attorney and future three-term governor of Georgia.

It could not be coincidence, Walter argued, that lynchings occurred with the most regularity by far in the same states where these Democratic politicians all but ruled. According to NAACP statistics, Walter wrote, the states that saw the most kills were Mississippi (561 between 1882 and 1927), followed by Georgia (549), then Texas (534), Louisiana (409), and Alabama (356) — all states in the heart of the former Confederacy, the Democrats' Solid South. "The lyncher and the legislator," Walter wrote, "the latter through disenfranchisement laws, joined hands to eliminate the Negro from politics and thus prevent the possibility of the Negro's holding the balance of power. This was the death-blow to the hope of salutary political life in the South."

Walter's writing on the church would stir fury in the South when his book was published. He gathered statistics that illustrated how the states that had the highest number of lynchings all had a high percentage of people who considered themselves Christian churchgoers. In Mississippi, 87.5 percent were Baptists or Methodists. In Georgia, 89.8 percent. Common were statements such as this one from the senator from South Carolina Cole Blease: "In the South we believe that white supremacy is a part of the Christian religion."

Walter could speak of the religiosity of the lynch industry firsthand, from his own experiences seeing church services in action. "No person," he wrote, "who is familiar with the Bible-beating, acrobatic, fanatical preachers of hell-fire in the South, and who has seen the orgies of emotion created by them, can doubt for a moment that dangerous passions are released which contribute to emotional instability and play a part in lynching." It was no accident, Walter argued, that the founder of the modern KKK, William Joseph Simmons, was a Methodist lay preacher.

All of this explained why lynchings often took on the eerie ritualism that Walter uncovered during his investigations, and why they so often occurred on Sundays.

Only when the politician and the pulpit accepted the theory of racial superiority could the act of extralegal killing be sanctioned. Lynching was tacitly approved — at times, even encouraged — by people who held power. "Until very recent times," Walter wrote, "and in most of the south, even today, no lyncher has ever needed to feel the slightest apprehension regarding punishment or even the annoyance of an investigation."

That is why Walter's forty-one undercover investigations had resulted in zero murder convictions. According to Walter, "mobbism has inevitably degenerated to the point where an uncomfortably large percentage of American citizens can read in their newspapers of the slow roasting alive of a human being in Mississippi and turn, promptly with little thought, to the comic strip or sporting page. Thus has lynching become an almost integral part of our national folkways."

While his work in progress thus far explained *how* the lynching phenomenon had taken root, it still did not explain the *why*. This tangled conundrum Walter began to unweave in chapter 4 of his book, titled "Sex and Lynching."

"FOR TWO AND A HALF CENTURIES OF SLAVERY slave women had no control over or defense of their bodies," Walter wrote. "As chattels, their bodies were their own only in so far as their owners were men of moral integrity." On the one end were moral men and families who owned and cared for enslaved people as their own family members. On the other were men who "deliberately used slave women as breeders of half-white slaves — combining, as it were, pleasure with business."

The social, familial, and gender dynamic, over time, created a pathological anxiety inside the white man's consciousness, Walter concluded. "For more than two hundred years this moral deterioration has affected the Southern states," Walter wrote, "and from that decay arises the most terrifying of all the aspects of the race problem to the white man." For if tradition would have it that white men and Black slaves should be intimate, what law of nature could assure that love and lust might not be born, of white women with Black men?

By far the most common defense of the lynch mob was that it was protecting the safety and purity of white women, and thus, not only was the act of killing justified, it was to be lauded. This notion, Walter argued, only added to the hypocrisy of it all, since accusations of rape, statistically, accounted for a small percentage of lynch mob murders. (Here Walter was clearly basing his argument on the work of pioneering female anti-lynching activist Ida B. Wells-Barnett, who as early as the 1890s became the first person to tackle the hyper-controversial topic of sex, rape, and race, in newspaper columns she wrote for the *New York Age* and other publications. "Nobody . . . believes the old thread-bare lie that Negro men assault white women," Wells wrote in 1892.)

Ultimately, Walter concluded, the most important reason that lynching had taken root as a cultural phenomenon — and as an inherently American one — was economics. "Lynching has always been the means for protection, not of white women, but of profits," Walter wrote. The states where lynchings most often occurred were all agrarian. The biggest crop was cotton, a crop that had to be picked by hand. Before the machine age, the whole farming industry and thus the entire economy of the South was built upon a foundation of cheap labor. That is why slavery existed for the most part, in the first place, and why it disappeared from northern states that became less agrarian and more industrial. When slavery was outlawed in the time of Abraham Lincoln, wrote Walter, "it was at this point that the lyncher entered upon the scene as a stalwart defender of the slave owners' profits."

Lynching was a means to keep African Americans "in their place" through intimidation, Walter argued. They were to be uneducated. They were to be beholden to the farms. Those strategies were used not only to keep wealthy white men in power, Walter reasoned, but also to keep poor white men empowered over Black men. Or as H. L. Mencken put it: "Ku Kluxery is the Southern poor white's answer to the progress of the emerging Negro."

Until, that is, 1918. That year, Black Americans proved their patriotism on the battlefields of Europe, earning (they believed) their rights as American citizens. That year, the Great Migration brought thousands of African Americans out of the South and into the North where they could vote and find non-agrarian jobs. That year, the NAACP was doing its work to organize the race. That was the year that the South saw its way of life threatened anew, and why the number of lynchings began to skyrocket, notably during the Red Summer of 1919, White argued.

Behind all of this, Walter postulated, was fear. Fear of the loss of profits. Fear of the loss of mythical white supremacy. Fear of having to compete with the Black race for simple resources such as food and jobs. Fear, ultimately, of losing control. Walter was surely influenced by W.E.B. Du Bois on this point. Du Bois's essay "The Shape of Fear" had been published the year before Walter left for France. Du Bois wrote:

> Before the wide eyes of the mob is ever the Shape of Fear. Back
> of the writhing, yelling, cruel-eyed demons who break, destroy,
> maim and lynch and burn at the stake is a knot, large or small, of

normal human beings and these human beings at heart are desperately afraid of something. Of what? Of many things but usu-
ally losing their jobs, of being declassed, degraded or actually
disgraced; of losing their hopes, their savings, their plans for their
children; of the actual pangs of hunger; of dirt, of crime. And of
all of this, most ubiquitous in modern industrial society is that
fear of unemployment.

In the end, Walter's many ideas boiled down to an equation. If you
take that fear, place behind it the power of politicians and the pulpit, add
in the modern inventions of cars and telephones and newspapers that
could be used to organize lynch mobs and large crowds of spectators, you
end up with ritualistic and deeply symbolic orgies of torture and violence,
rendered before white men, women, and children who considered themselves Christians, patriotic Americans, and upstanding figures in their
communities.

WALTER FINISHED HIS MANUSCRIPT around Christmastime in 1927, and
he named the book *Rope and Faggot: A Biography of Judge Lynch.* The
title came from a euphemism for lynching at the time (the rope being
the noose, the faggot being a tree branch), and the subtitle was clever but
misleading, as little in this book was about Judge Lynch himself. Walter
sent the manuscript to James Weldon Johnson for his comments. Johnson
wrote back, "I think you have done a big job, and done it mighty well. It is,
by far, the best thing on the subject." Walter sent the book to the Knopfs,
and they agreed to publish it upon Walter's return to the United States, in
1929. It was as controversial as all hell, and he looked forward to the explosion of publicity it would cause — good and bad.

But first, it was time for a break.

The White family had never spent a Christmas holiday outside of New
York. It would be different in France. "The terrace of our villa is covered with roses and the gardens are filled with flowers," Walter wrote to
Richetta Randolph, an assistant at the NAACP. "The weather is so warm
that Jane [now five years old] is unable to get much of the Christmas spirit

and seems wholly indifferent to the coming of 'Pere Noel' which is French for Santa Claus." Walter and Gladys had taken to calling their baby boy "le petit pigeon," or simply Pidge — a nickname that would stick for the rest of the boy's youth.

Villefranche-sur-Mer was a few miles from the Italian border. Benito Mussolini had taken power just a few years earlier, and Walter learned that his cook, Victoria, was housing refugees who were fleeing the new fascist government under the cover of darkness. Walter met some of them, and their stories haunted him. Although he could not know it at the time, these refugees were a harbinger of a world war to come.

Now, in the tourist season, vacationers flooded the beachy villages along la Côte d'Azur. "With painful frequence," Walter recorded, "the noisiest, most drunken, and most unpleasant tourists were Americans." The Whites decided to move to Avignon, a city on the Rhône River in southeast France where the living was quieter and cheaper. Avignon was significantly smaller than Paris but had much of the charm. The weight of history was palpable when one walked the Saint-Bénézet Bridge over the Rhône. Avignon had been home to the papacy during the fourteenth century; in the glow of moonlight, the Palais des Papes (Palace of Popes) appeared almost mystical and otherworldly.

Walter kept company with other expatriate writers in Avignon — Somerset Maugham and Ford Madox Ford — and he was planning to write a novel before the end of his fellowship, about a prizefighter. But a letter arrived, dated February 21, 1928, from Charles H. Studin in New York, the prominent white attorney (he was Arthur Spingarn's law partner). Walter knew Studin well because Studin threw some of the best parties in Greenwich Village. But this letter was no party invitation.

"Although I have thought of you frequently since you left here," Studin wrote, "with my accustomed lack of energy I have failed to write to you until now."

Studin was interested in the political future of New York's governor Al Smith. The governor was going to run for president in 1928. "I have been consulted by some of the powers that be as to the best method of promoting his [Al Smith's] interests with the colored voters throughout the country," Studin wrote, "and have come to the conclusion that the most advisable method of handling the situation would be through placing a colored man on the firing line."

The words *firing line* piqued Walter's interest, and Studin had certainly placed them there on purpose, knowing Walter's taste for dangerous endeavors. Studin wanted an African American to sell Al Smith to Afro-America. That man, argued Studin, should be Walter White.

17

When I was a boy I was told that anybody could become president.
I'm beginning to believe it.
— Clarence Darrow

WALTER WAS IN A BIND. He had four more months of his fellowship left, and he had begun writing a new novel and a series of articles for the *Paris Review*. He had just signed a lease on an Avignon apartment at 700 francs per month. But Charles Studin wanted him in New York *now*. Walter wrote to his friend Bishop John Hurst.

"I have been asked by certain persons very close to Gov. Smith to take charge of the entire campaign for among colored people," Walter explained. The main reason against taking the job, he explained, was obviously Black America's firm opposition to the Democratic Party. Ever since the Civil War, Black Americans who could vote voted Republican — for the party of Abraham Lincoln, who had led the charge to end slavery. Of the nearly two-dozen Black men voted into the House of Representatives in the post–Civil War years, every one of them belonged to the Republican Party.

Al Smith was virulently anti-KKK and an agent of change against the old-school Solid South. But still, he was a Democrat. That put him in the same political party as Theodore Bilbo of Mississippi, of Cole Blease of South Carolina — the most outspoken of the white supremacist politicians. Could Walter really go out and campaign for the Democrats?

But there was also good reason to support Al Smith. What had the Republicans done for the African American race recently? From Walter's point of view: nothing. "The Negro is being kicked out of the Republican Party," Walter wrote Bishop Hurst. Herbert Hoover was likely to be the Republican candidate. "The Hoover forces have quite obviously made up their minds to throw the Negro overboard in their efforts to Republicanize the South."

Surely Walter was thinking of the speech Clarence Darrow gave in that packed Harlem church, during the Sweet trials two years earlier. *"The only weapon the Negro in the North has is the ballot and you have thrown that away. There are several states in the North where the Negro holds the balance of power. I want you to be absolutely independent in your voting. I want you to keep the white politicians guessing."*

"The Republicans believe that they own us," Walter wrote Bishop Hurst, "body and soul, and will keep on believing that until we ourselves do something about it."

There was also another reason to support Al Smith. The New York governor wanted to end the Noble Experiment — Prohibition.

Walter decided to go for the job. He booked a ticket to set sail from Le Havre on April 4 on the SS *Île de France*. Gladys would take the kids to Paris and stay through the summer. Walter wrote of his philosophy at the time to a confidant: "I firmly believe that if ever the Negro once demonstrates that he can be independent of the Republican Party, that never again will they start campaigns as now counting the Negro vote theirs without an effort — they will know that they must make concessions of importance to the race if they are to get that vote. A man doesn't scramble for a thing which is already his. Today the Negro vote holds the balance of power in not less than ten states and in eleven others his vote is considerable enough to be of real importance in a close race."

In typical Walter fashion, he threw himself maniacally into the project. His idea was to create a National Negro Smith for President Association, with support from all the powerful people he could gather. On the boat across the Atlantic, he strategized and jotted notes on what he would need: "Establish office in New York, secure tables, desks, typewriters, stationery, telephone, stenographers, etc." He created a list of all the Black newspapers and their editors. He created a statistical report called

"Analysis of Possible Effect of Negro Vote in the 1928 Election," listing the states where "the Negro vote unquestionably holds the balance of power" — if he could get people to come out and vote: Delaware (three electoral votes), Maryland (eight), Kentucky (thirteen), Tennessee (twelve), Missouri (eighteen). That alone totaled fifty-four electoral votes.

What he envisioned was nothing short of a historic, tectonic shift in Black political identity. In a letter to the retired NAACP chairman Moorfield Storey, written on July 22, 1928, Walter shared a vision of the true future of the American political party system.

"Eventually it appears to me that we are going to have an entirely new political alignment — the Republicans will absorb the anti-Negro south and become, through the compromises necessary to gain that end, the relatively anti-Negro party, while the Negro will find refuge in the democratic party controlled by the north. . . . Such an arrangement will not, I know, take place immediately but from present indications will occur before many decades have passed."

All of it depended on a total commitment from Al Smith himself. As Walter wrote in his personal notes: the entire plan "is dependent for success upon a definite statement from Gov. Smith . . . upon which an appeal can be made to Negro voters to support his candidacy."

The program's success also depended on victory by Smith. If Walter backed Smith and threw himself into a campaign to engineer a historical political shift of Black political power, and then *lost* — would his career as a Black race leader be destroyed? Would he be able to even support his family? As he wrote Bishop Hurst, "If Gladys and I had no children we could weather any storm which might arise. But, have I the right to jeopardize the future of Jane and Walter [Jr.]?"

On the other hand? By Walter's reasoning, "If Smith is elected, the NAACP will be the power behind the throne."

ON APRIL 11 Walter rushed down the gangplank of the *Île de France,* placing his feet home again on the concrete of Manhattan Island. Charles Studin was there to meet him. Studin whisked Walter off to the apartment of Belle Moskowitz, the wealthy Jewish philanthropist who was also a founding member of the NAACP. Vivacious and full of influence, Moskowitz had masterminded Al Smith's two victorious campaigns for New York governor and had been working with him for ten years. She was going to serve as campaign manager for Smith's national run.

Walter was on board, he explained. But only on one condition, he told Moskowitz: that Al Smith promise to make a statement that he would fight for the causes of Black Americans. Walter was not prepared to go out on a limb for Al Smith alone. He wanted Al Smith out there with him.

After meeting with Moskowitz, Walter headed to Albany to meet Smith himself, in the governor's mansion. Smith had grown up poor in Brooklyn, and was twenty years Walter's senior. The governor spoke in that inflection common among Irish American New Yorkers at the time — *woik, youse people*. He had gathered strength as a pro–law-enforcement politician during the Prohibition-era gang wars, which saw the rise of Meyer Lansky and Al Capone. Walter said he would join Smith's campaign — if Smith promised he would (in Walter's words) "be president of all the people" and would not be "ruled by the anti-Negro South" that formed a powerful coalition of his own Democratic Party.

Smith agreed and asked Walter to draft a statement. The governor told Walter exactly what the NAACP man wanted to hear: "I know Negroes distrust the Democratic Party, and I can't blame them. But I want to show them that the old Democratic Party, ruled entirely by the South, is on its way out, and that we Northern Democrats have a totally different approach to the Negro."

Back in Manhattan, Walter drafted the statement for Smith and sent it to the governor's mansion. He waited for a response. And waited. It never came. Walter inquired with Belle Moskowitz, who sheepishly explained that Smith's running mate, Senator Joseph Taylor Robinson, was from Arkansas. He and several other strategists advised the governor against making any statement to court the Black vote. By courting the Black vote in the North, these strategists believed, they would lose even more white votes in the South.

Moskowitz pleaded with Walter to join the Smith campaign anyway. "Can't you — won't you take the Governor on faith as we have?"

Walter refused. What if he campaigned for Smith, and Smith did not then support the African American cause? Just as Woodrow Wilson had done years earlier? Walter would be humiliated and ruined.

Still, he had his first taste of national politics, and it grabbed him firmly. He was determined to join the national political conversation. While he was in France, the Supreme Court had landed a stiff blow to the Solid South, in the case of *Nixon v. Herndon.* Fought with the backing of the NAACP, the case struck down a law forbidding African Americans from voting in the Texas Democratic primary. Since the Republican Party was barely active in this southern state, the Democratic primary decided who would win Senate, House, and gubernatorial races. The Supreme Court ruling was the first of its kind, and Walter believed that, in time, it was going to revolutionize the political status of African Americans in many states.

If Walter wanted to join the national political conversation, now was a good time to do it.

FOR MANY IN THE UNITED STATES, particularly in New York, the summer and fall of 1928 were all about excitement and futurism. Radio had become the new entertainment pastime; NBC was founded in 1926 and quickly dominated the new acoustic playground. The creation of the television machine seemed fantastical, like a thing out of science fiction. When Herbert Hoover appeared on a television screen in New York while he stood with his feet planted in Washington, DC, the newspapers boldly reported that "time and space were eliminated." Perhaps most exciting was the introduction of sound to cinema and air conditioning to the theaters. For many New Yorkers, movie theaters were the place to go for cool air in summer, and Al Jolson's voice in *The Jazz Singer* (1927) introduced the world to the "talkie" film.

Electric refrigerators, hotels with private bathtubs, radios — new luxuries and gizmos lured Americans into a frenzy of consumerism. On December 2, 1927, Ford unveiled the successor to the Model T — the Model A. Americans went hysterical for the new car; riot police had to fill the streets outside Ford showrooms in Chicago, Detroit, Cleveland, and New York to keep people calm.

Everywhere the eye turned in New York were signs of unparalleled prosperity. Between 1910 and 1930 the city's population had doubled. Within two years of Walter's return to Manhattan from France, five skyscrapers would be erected: the Bank of Manhattan building, the Chrysler Building, the Chanin Building, the Daily News Building, and the Empire State Building. Wealth was like a new religion, and Wall Street was its altar. The idea that money could beget money in the stock market, like financial immaculate conception, drove Americans wild.

"Everyone was a broker, more or less," remembered John Steinbeck of the late 1920s. "At lunch hour, store clerks and stenographers munched sandwiches while they watched the stock boards and calculated their pyramiding fortunes. Their eyes had the look you see around the roulette table."

Though Prohibition was still in effect, drinking had become something of a sport in America. "It was impossible to get a drink in Detroit," one newspaperman famously quipped, "unless you walked at least ten feet and told the busy bartender what you wanted in a voice loud enough for him to hear you above the roar." Analyzing the 1920s, historian Ann Douglas noted in her landmark book, *Terrible Honesty: Mongrel Manhattan in the 1920s,* that almost every famous writer, artist, and musician of the day was alcoholic: F. Scott Fitzgerald, Eugene O'Neill, Dorothy Parker, Hart Crane, Sinclair Lewis, Ernest Hemingway, Louise Brooks, Wallace Thurman, Fats Waller, Bessie Smith, Charles Gilpin, Bert Williams, Jean Toomer, Heywood Broun, Damon Runyon, Ring Lardner, Elinor Wylie, Louise Bogan, Edna St. Vincent Millay, Edmund Wilson, Thomas Wolfe, Harold Stearns, Robert Ripley, William Faulkner, Horace Liveright, Charles MacArthur, John Barrymore, Laurette Taylor, Lorenz Hart, Robert Benchley, and William Seabrook.

"Alcohol played a part in the death of all these people," Douglas points out, "save possibly Bessie Smith," who died following a car accident.

The biggest story of the fall of 1928 was the election of Republican

Herbert Hoover to the White House. Hoover clobbered the Democrat Al Smith, winning 444 electoral votes to Smith's 87. Americans called Hoover "Wonder Boy" and "the Great Engineer," because he had come to wealth and power as an engineer and mining genius. Upon his inauguration, the *New York Times* journalist Anne O'Hare McCormick (who was the first woman to win a Pulitzer Prize) put into words the nation's excitement for the incoming administration: "We turned over to that mind all the complications and difficulties no other had been able to settle. Almost with the air of giving genius its chance, we waited for the performance to begin."

UPON THEIR RETURN FROM FRANCE, the Whites moved into a new apartment, #8-I, at 409 Edgecombe Avenue. Standing on a promontory called Sugar Hill, 409 Edgecombe was home to James Weldon Johnson, Jules Bledsoe, and Harlem's favorite gangster, Stephanie St. Clair, who ran the neighborhood's gambling rackets and was known in town as Queenie and Madam Queen. (She was highly respected because she was a civil rights activist and, for a gangster, a walking emblem of Black gravitas.)

Walter was thrilled with his new place, as the windows offered a view of both the Polo Grounds in Upper Manhattan, where the New York Giants played, and the new Yankee Stadium in the South Bronx. Gladys surely loved it too, as it was the most desired address in Harlem. In those days, one had to write a letter to the New York Telephone Company to request a phone. Walter requested a French model telephone rather than the upright kind.

He returned to the bustling offices on Fifth Avenue, to the smiling faces of Mary White Ovington, Joel Spingarn, William Pickens, and Johnson. Walter threw himself back into the crusade. The NAACP was fighting the Harlem Hospital, because it did not hire Black physicians. (That would soon change.) The association was fighting for equal pay for Black teachers, who earned far less than white teachers for doing the same jobs. (That would soon change too.)

As everyone in the Whites' social circles knew, Walter's friend Charles Studin threw the best literary parties in New York, fetes that placed the most diverse individuals in intimate conversation. One might have found archbishop of New York Patrick Joseph Hayes chatting with a contender for the heavyweight crown. At one party Studin pulled Walter into his kitchen, where a sprightly woman of twenty-four was making sandwiches. Her name was Poppy Cannon, and she was a South Africa–born, Pennsylvania-bred white woman, of great social and career ambition. She herself remembered this moment from the perspective of years later:

> I had no idea who he [Walter] was. . . . More vividly than Walter himself, I can repicture his wife, Gladys, and her twin sister, Madrenne, from Mexico City. All eyes were on them. They were the most beautiful women I had ever seen — identical twins with glorious deep bronze complexions and both of them wearing white satin evening dresses. . . . They were breathtaking. It was impossible to look at anyone else. I did not in any way connect them with the young man at my side. . . . Presently I gathered that he was a writer, that he had recently returned from a Guggenheim fellowship year in France.

Walter had a gift for engaging strangers in probing conversations. The two talked about France, about books and people. Then they fell on the subject of food; both he and Cannon had a passion for eclectic ingredients and wine. All the while, she recalled, she had no idea he identified as Black.

He told her a story of how the writer and satirist H. L. Mencken of Baltimore had sworn by terrapin soup, a recipe native to Maryland. Walter had told Mencken that this could not possibly be anything worth eating, that it was "nothing more than a gizzard stew." Mencken had challenged Walter to come to Maryland to experience it. So Walter was ready to go.

"You must tell me how it all comes out," she said. "Call me up after you get back. Tell me exactly what you have to eat and all about the wine. I do hope it's Madeira or an old Bual!"

When she told Walter she had been born in South Africa, he threw back his head in laughter. She was African and *white*. "Do you know," he said, "that you are the first real — native — African American I've ever met?"

A FEW DAYS LATER Walter returned from Baltimore to report on the terrapin soup. He had his first lunch with Poppy Cannon and learned some key details about her. She was married to a librarian at the New York Public Library named Carl, and she was working in New York's advertising industry, which was experiencing a fantastic boom on the heels of the skyrocketing Dow Jones.

There were more lunches. Always they planned culinary excursions with the excuse that each was the only one the other could talk to about the alchemy of cooking. Ultimately, the pair landed on an idea to do a book together on the traditions of the African American kitchen. Walter contacted the Knopfs, who went for the idea, and soon they signed a publishing contract. Walter sent Cannon on a trip south with a detailed itinerary. He sent out letters to friends asking for recipes and made introductions for Cannon in states she had never imagined she would visit. She even went to Atlanta and met his parents, his sisters, his nieces and nephews, "all of whom," she recalled, "were immensely proud of their Uncle Walter."

When Cannon's husband was transferred to the Yale University Library in Connecticut, Walter took his wife there for boozy social visits. "Let me add a word of warning," he wrote Cannon before one weekend trip, "that any efforts to induce me to do any such horrible things as swimming, horseback riding and the like will be completely wasted. I intend to hoist my feet up to the front porch railing and take them down only at meal time." The two couples got along nicely, and seemingly, from Gladys White's point of view, there did not seem to be anything out of the ordinary. Although both couples had children, it is unclear if the kids got to know one another at this point.

Walter must have seen it all differently, however. He had feelings for Cannon, who was married like he was. And she was *white*. Even rumors of such a romance could harm his career. But there always seemed to be a good reason to see Poppy Cannon again.

18

I wish likewise to acknowledge my gratitude to many lynchers with whom I have talked and who have expressed themselves freely, unaware of my racial identity.

— Walter White, *Rope and Faggot*

ROPE AND FAGGOT: A BIOGRAPHY OF JUDGE LYNCH appeared in bookstores in the spring of 1929, and the firestorm Walter hoped and expected did indeed ignite. Hate mail. Death threats. Walter's phone jingled constantly with news of both praise and loathing. The book seemed to inspire hate or righteousness, with nothing in between. Libraries in Boston banned the book. Clarence Darrow said of it, "This book should be read by every citizen of the United States." Walter dedicated it to the man who had plucked him from obscurity in 1918, James Weldon Johnson.

The *New York Times* began its review: "It is with a distinct jolt to one's Americanism that one reads at the very beginning of Walter White's book and again and again through its pages that lynching has become 'an almost integral part of our national folkways.'" The writer J. A. Rogers called Walter's book "the most thorough exposition of this peculiar American pastime" and questioned how "incredible and monstrous [it is] that the Congress of the United States should permit this evil to go on, even going so far as to register its approval by refusing to pass a law against it."

When *Time* magazine ran a lengthy and favorable review, furious letters from the Deep South came in by the bagful. Eldon O. Haldane of Atlanta wrote, "The well-balanced Southerner hopes that lynching of Negroes will increase rather than decrease, that Cracker fiendishness and cruelty . . . will never diminish, that persecution, prosecution, of and fury against the Negro will prevail until their numbers are eliminated or substantially reduced and preferably exterminated."

Another figure, aptly named Robert E. Lee, from Greenville, South Carolina, wrote *Time* magazine, "If anyone ever needed a coat of tar and feathers it's the author of 'Judge Lynch.'" Walter responded personally to this one, asking that the tar and feathering wait for warmer weather, "tar being so sticky and messy."

On May 15 the Women's Committee of the NAACP threw Walter a book party that drew the best artists and writers of the Harlem Renaissance to the Walker Studio on West 136th Street. Claude McKay, Nella Larsen, and Wallace Thurman (whose important novel *The Blacker the Berry* had just come out) attended, as did Jessie Redmon Fauset and Dr. Robert Moton, head of the Tuskegee Institute. Joel Spingarn and James Weldon Johnson hosted the party together.

Soon after the event, Walter's life took yet another unexpected turn. The NAACP held its annual national conference in 1929 in Cleveland, Ohio. Association officials noticed that James Weldon Johnson appeared unwell and struggling to maintain his stamina. Running the organization was enough to destroy anyone's health, and in 1929, Johnson had been in the top job for a decade. Joel Spingarn noticed Johnson's complexion and was "disturbed by the fatigue and the strain." He wrote to the board of directors urging that Johnson take a rest. Johnson decided to heed the advice, and he informed Walter that he intended to take a leave of absence to join a delegation to the Institute of Pacific Relations in Japan. In October 1929 the board made Walter the acting secretary of the NAACP.

It was an awesome responsibility, and Walter had to protect himself and the association from any untoward publicity. Without any communication, he ended his friendship with Poppy Cannon, which had never passed the platonic stage but meant more to him than that. He could not bring himself to have the face-to-face conversation, so he simply became too busy to speak to her. He no longer took her calls, and soon the calls stopped coming. The book they were to write together never happened.

He knew that socially their paths were tangled, and that one day he would see her again. He could only surmise as to when, and what words would come from his mouth when that day came.

Walter was now the acting chief executive of the most powerful and militant civil rights organization on earth. He was thirty-six years old. It was an exciting time; Walter's ascension occurred in the same year that Oscar De Priest of Illinois was elected to the House, becoming the first Black congressman of the twentieth century. "I blithely accepted the responsibility of acting secretary," Walter remembered, "wholly unaware of the difficult days immediately ahead. The stock market was climbing to dizzier heights than ever before in history. The unemployment and apprehension of the early twenties were disappearing, even for Negroes, as millions of Americans dreamed of becoming millionaires by stock market speculation, and the psychology of unending and unlimited prosperity and peace created by a fool's paradise."

As the new boss, Walter decided to begin his term as only he would. He was going to throw the loudest party the NAACP had ever seen. What could possibly go wrong?

FUELED BY MONEY, MONEY, AND MORE MONEY, Harlem nightlife reached its zenith at the end of the twenties. Marijuana parlors on 140th Street were doing a booming business. The rotund and sexually ambiguous Gladys Bentley pounded piano keys at the Clam House on 133rd Street, before huge fawning crowds. There was always something more to see, always a reason to stay out for one more drink.

Thanks to Carl Van Vechten's novel *Nigger Heaven,* the scene now drew so many white partiers from downtown, its whole complexion had changed. The Black writer Rudolph Fisher left Harlem for five years and returned toward the end of the 1920s. When he went out to some clubs, he was startled by what he saw. "Presently I grew puzzled and began to stare," he recorded. "Then I gaped—and gasped. I found myself wondering if this was the right place—if, indeed, this was Harlem at all. I suddenly became aware that, except for the waiters and members of the orchestra, I was the only Negro in the place." Even the former governor Al Smith had a favorite Harlem watering hole: Pod's and Jerry's, where Willie "the Lion" Smith performed his signature piano slide.

At the same time, the jazz scene was invading Broadway, where musicals drew crowds in record numbers. While Harlem's nightlife was becoming more white, Broadway was becoming more Black. African American productions drew long lines at the box office; there was *Africana,* starring Ethel Waters, at Daly's 63rd Street Theater, and *Rang Tang* at the Majestic, a musical comedy by the smashingly successful comic duo Miller and Lyles. There was *Blackbirds,* a show that James Weldon Johnson called "a sort of New York institution."

Upon taking over the NAACP, Walter had the idea of throwing a benefit to raise money for the association by gathering the most talent he could from both of these worlds, Harlem and Broadway, and putting together a showcase of his own. It would be an unprecedented musical revue. In October 1929 he wrote to theater impresario Bill "Bojangles" Robinson, "The idea is this: We want to give [the] most distinctive and biggest benefit that Broadway has ever known. . . . The [NAACP] Board has appointed me as Acting Secretary during [Johnson's] absence and I am very anxious to make good."

Walter reached out to his friends Jules Bledsoe and Paul Robeson, to Groucho Marx and Fanny Brice. He hand-drew advertisements for the "NAACP All-Star Concert" to be professionally typeset for ads in the New York papers. On October 22 he wrote Florenz Ziegfeld: "Will you be good enough to advise me if the Ziegfeld Theater can be rented for a Benefit for the National Association for the Advancement of Colored People, for the evening of Sunday, December 8?"

Two days after Walter wrote this letter, however, the unthinkable happened. Wall Street crashed. In a single day of trading, October 24, $5 billion evaporated from the stock market, sending a shock wave of anxiety across the country and the globe. President Hoover attempted to calm nerves the following morning. "The fundamental business of the country, that is the production and distribution of commodities, is on a sound and prosperous basis," he told America. Days after that unfortunate statement, Wall Street panicked and the Great Depression began.

For Walter, the show had to go on. He locked in on the popular columnist Heywood Broun to be the emcee and, for the venue, Broadway's Forrest Theatre, on West 49th Street. He had Harlem's premier artist, Aaron Douglas, draw the art for the program, which included advertisements for Black-owned businesses and an essay from Walter called, "What I Think of the NAACP."

On the night of the show there was not a whiff of any financial crisis. Master of ceremonies Heywood Broun greeted the crowd, telling them it was his "night off" and that there was nowhere else he would rather be. "A mixed audience [Black and white] packed the balcony and mezzanine of the theater," remembered one in the crowd.

Duke Ellington stormed the stage and set his Cotton Club Orchestra in motion. George Gershwin appeared to roaring applause. Helen Morgan of the Ziegfeld Theater's *Show Boat* sang "Why Was I Born?" and "Can't Help Lovin' That Man." Edith Wilson of the singing Hot Chocolates did her specialty, "Black and Blue." In the crowd sat (or stood) New York's lieutenant governor, Herbert Lehman, the publishing magnates Alfred Harcourt and the Knopfs, the Spingarns and the Johnsons. New York had never seen anything quite like it.

When it was all over, Walter was left doing the math. He had spent roughly $2,000 on the theater and promotional material and had brought in about $3,500. It was a small success financially, and a big one for morale. One newspaper columnist summed up the event: "[It] certainly was a gala occasion. And what could have been more fitting than that the greatest talent of the race should make offering to the greatest work on our behalf by the greatest organization of the country."

In the weeks following, an existential darkness crept over the country as millions rushed the banks in hopes of pulling out their savings and others saw their stock market wealth disappear. On March 22, 1930, however, Walter picked up the morning newspapers and found a story that piqued his interest, one that made him push all thoughts of the declining economy out of his head, at least for the time being. He had been longing for an opportunity to throw himself into national politics. Now, it appeared, he had found it.

19

Through the agency of this Association [the NAACP], America was made to realize that, after a long lapse following the Reconstruction, the Negro again had become a powerful and an important figure in national politics. The dramatic occasion for that demonstration was the battle in the United States Senate against the confirmation of Judge John J. Parker.

— William Hastie, first African American US federal judge

ON MARCH 22, 1930, newspapers all over the country — the *New York Times, Washington Post, Chicago Daily Tribune, LA Times, Hartford Courant, Atlanta Constitution, Christian Science Monitor* in Boston — all reported the news that President Hoover had appointed a North Carolina Fourth Circuit federal judge named John J. Parker to the United States Supreme Court. Judge Parker was to fill a seat vacated by the recently deceased justice Edward Terry Sanford. According to all that reporting, there was not a hint of opinion that Judge Parker would not be confirmed by Congress.

"Confirmation was inevitable," Walter recalled.

Still, he sensed that something was off. He reached out to NAACP branches in Parker's home state, fishing for news, and his suspicions were quickly confirmed. Two days after the announcement of Parker's appointment, Walter received a communiqué from an NAACP member in North Carolina named Dr. A. M. Rivera. It included a clipping from the *Greensboro Daily News,* quoting Judge Parker from a decade earlier, in April 1920:

The Republican Party in North Carolina has accepted the amendment (of 1901, designed to keep the Negro from exercising his right to the ballot) in the spirit in which it was passed and the Negro has so accepted it. . . . The Negro as a class does not desire to enter politics. The Republican Party of North Carolina does not desire him to do so. We recognize the fact that he has not yet reached that stage in his development when he can share the burdens and responsibilities of Government. . . . the participation of the Negro in politics is a source of evil and danger to both races and is not desired by the wise man in either race or by the Republican Party of North Carolina.

Walter sent the quote to Judge Parker in North Carolina, via a Western Union telegram, asking if it was accurate. "A few hours later," Walter recalled, "Western Union advised us that the telegram had been delivered to and signed for by Judge Parker."

The judge never responded. Walter took this as a personal insult and realized that the Parker matter could be a litmus test. If the NAACP protested, what would happen? If Walter decided to contest the confirmation with all the fight he could muster, he might find out just how much power he and the NAACP wielded.

At 4 p.m. on April 14, in the NAACP's conference room, the board members arrived for their monthly meeting. As acting secretary, Walter began the meeting with his monthly report, which he had submitted to the board ahead of time. Then he asked to supplement his report with an additional matter. He wanted to lead a nationwide battle against the confirmation of Judge John J. Parker, he explained.

No activist organization had ever blocked a president's choice for a Supreme Court seat. Walter believed it could be done, and he had already begun the fight.

JUDGE PARKER was a Republican from a swing state. For years North Carolina had been part of the Democratic Solid South, voting Democrat in every presidential election since 1876. However, Republicans in the state had made huge strides of recent, surprising the national electorate by turning red in the 1928 election cycle and putting the state in Hoover's column. Judge Parker had run for governor on the GOP ticket in 1920, and while he had lost, he showed unexpected strength at the ballot box. The judge had been a force for the Republican Party in North Carolina ever since, and took a lot of credit for turning North Carolina Republican in 1928.

Traditionally, African Americans aligned with the Republican Party, so Judge Parker's denunciation of would-be Black voters spotlighted just how completely both major political parties had abandoned any interest in the Black vote. Now, in 1930, Hoover's Republican administration wanted to reward Judge Parker with the appointment to the highest court in the land. In Judge Parker the president saw an aggressive chess piece unafraid to push into the Democrats' Solid South.

The stakes were greater than they seemed on the surface. The federal Supreme Court was the place where, as Walter put it in an article in *Harper's Magazine* called "The Negro and the Supreme Court," the Black voter "stands his best chance of obtaining justice" in the future. "In that court six notable decisions have been won within the last fifteen years, each of them of far reaching effect on the Negro's Constitutional rights." The most important of those Supreme Court decisions had to do with voting rights. Additionally, numerous Supreme Court rulings of recent times had been decided with 5–4 decisions. Adding Parker to the court with a lifetime appointment could set the fight for voting rights in the South back an entire generation.

As Senator Henry F. Ashurst of Arizona said at the time, with regard to Judge Parker: "The Constitution is what the judges say it is. Past judges made the current Constitution and current judges will make the future Constitution, and this is the standard by which Parker or any nominee should be judged."

WALTER'S FIRST MOVE was to send an affidavit to North Carolina citizens that they could sign saying that they had heard the judge making statements or seen such statements attributed to him that were "inimical to the political rights and prerogatives of qualified Negro electorates." He received fifty-one signed affidavits back and sent them to President Hoover and to numerous senators on the Senate Judiciary Committee. Walter sent letters to 177 NAACP branches in twenty-six states asking members to write their congressmen to protest the confirmation of Judge Parker. "At first a trickle," Walter recalled, "the telegrams, letters, petitions, long distance telephone calls, and personal visits to senators in Washington grew to an avalanche."

He launched a speaking tour against Parker. "The attempt to put Judge Parker on the bench is a slap in the face of all citizens not white, and one which is bitterly resented," Walter told a crowd of thousands in Chicago. "Never before have the forces been so united on any issue. . . . This is a grim, relentless struggle and advices from Washington indicate that the administration is working harder on this one issue than on any other which has arisen since President Hoover took office."

"It was a thrilling battle," recalled Ovington. "Walter White's driving force, his abiding belief in victory, brought him many influential allies who at first were half indifferent, half amused. . . . The enemy varied their tactics. They denied the validity of the statement imputed to Parker. Within twenty-four hours, photostatic copies of the ten-year-old clipping were in the hands of the senators and the President."

Black activist Roy Wilkins, editor of the *Kansas City Call* newspaper, remembered receiving a telegram from Walter urging him to join the fight and delivering an ominous warning. Not only would the NAACP fight the Parker confirmation, it would fight against the reelection of any senator who voted for it: NEGRO VOTERS WILL HOLD THEIR SENATORS ACCOUNTABLE FOR THEIR VOTES ON THE PARKER CONFIRMATION.

Wilkins ran a front-page story in the *Call* with a banner headline: COUNTRYWIDE FIGHT ON PARKER. It showed a photo of the judge with a quote next to it, another from Judge Parker's 1920 gubernatorial campaign: "If I should be elected Governor of North Carolina and find that my election was due to one Negro vote, I would immediately resign my office."

"To me," Wilkins recalled, "the most intriguing aspect of the affair was the way the NAACP had taken to slugging under Walter's direction."

The protest against Parker split the Republicans wide open — for and against — and the president of the United States dug in, standing by his choice for the seat. Working behind the scenes, Hoover lobbied members of his party to support Parker. The president was "taking a most active part in the drive," reported the *Atlanta Constitution*'s Washington correspondent, Francis Stephenson.

Senate hearings began on April 5, 1930, with the two sides battling and the national press packing the hearing rooms. The proceedings began with the usual testimonials, including one from the governor of North Carolina, O. Max Gardner, whose statement was read by Senator Lee Overman from the same state: "There is not, in my judgment, as I have already suggested, the slightest basis of reality, for the fear expressed by one group of our citizens that [Judge Parker] would not, as a judge of the Supreme Court, be absolutely fair and impartial in any case or controversy which may arise."

Walter was the very last figure called to testify. After taking the oath, he began. "My name is Walter White," he said. He then told his side of the story, how he had found this statement by Parker, how he had challenged Parker to comment, and how Parker had refused. Walter told the Judiciary Committee that Parker's statements "flouted" the Fourteenth and Fifteenth Amendments. He went on:

> The National Association for the Advancement of Colored People is convinced that no man who entertains such ideas of utter disregard of integral parts of the Federal Constitution is fitted to occupy a place on the bench of the United States Supreme Court. . . . If Judge Parker, for political advantage, can flout two amendments to the Federal Constitution to pander to base race prejudice, we respectfully submit that he is not of the caliber which loyal, intelligent Americans have the right to expect of justices of the nation's highest court.

Senator Overman, one of the judge's fiercest supporters, went for the jugular, attacking Walter for basing his protest almost exclusively on a single Parker statement. Overman "became incensed," Walter later wrote, "at the temerity of a Negro organization presuming to voice an opinion on a nomination to the Supreme Court."

"Do you know, Mr. White," Senator Overman said, "that most of the intelligent, educated, colored people vote in North Carolina?"

"Some of them can vote in the larger cities of North Carolina," Walter said. "But it is still not a safe matter for negroes, even in North Carolina, Senator Overman, to talk too much about voting in the rural districts."

When the hearings ended, the nation's newspapers engaged in editorial warfare, arguing commonsense victory on both sides. The *Atlanta Constitution* (a white paper) called the NAACP "hell-raising political vampires of New York and Boston who are fighting the Parker nomination, purely on color-line contentions." The *Kansas City American* (Black): "Yes: The negro must have a showdown with President Hoover. Yes: the President wants to pay North Carolina for her electoral vote. What about the electoral vote made possible by the negro in Missouri, Pennsylvania, West Virginia, Ohio, Kentucky, Tennessee, and New York? We have not as yet heard of any reward."

On the day of the vote, May 7, the Senate gallery was packed shoulder to shoulder, and Walter was among the crowd. Fearing there would be a tie among the ninety-six senators, he wrote Vice President Charles Curtis that morning; while the vice president of the United States had few formal duties, voting to break a tie in a Senate vote was one of them. "In the event of a tie vote today on the matter of the confirmation of the Honorable John J. Parker . . . a grave responsibility rests upon you," Walter wrote.

When it was time, one by one, the senators voted *aye* and *nay*. When it was over, the Senate clerk called for the floor. "For confirmation — 39. Against confirmation — 41."

The NAACP had won. Walter would never forget all those handshakes and all those slaps on the back. He would never forget the letters thanking him for his efforts that he received from senators and congressmen who voted against Parker, including such stalwarts as Arthur Vandenberg of Michigan (a Republican, like Judge Parker himself) and Alben Barkley of Kentucky (a Democrat and a future vice president). As a man who relished fame and success, Walter was having a moment.*

Not since 1894 had the Senate rejected a Supreme Court candidate (and it would not happen again until 1968). For days, Walter's name appeared in headlines. WALTER WHITE IS HERO OF JUDGE PARKER'S DEFEAT. NEGRO STAR IN ASCENDANT. It would be said a thousand times that on that day of the Parker vote, "the NAACP had come of age." Walter, meanwhile, had become a political force, overnight. Remembered Roy Wilkins: "The victory made White a national figure, overshadowing [James Weldon] Johnson himself."

---

* Judge Parker's story was not over. He continued his career and proved remarkably fair on cases involving racial issues. Walter later wrote, "In Judge Parker's behalf I should like to add this postscript: Since his rejection, his decisions on both Negro and labor cases which have come before him have been above reproach in their strict adherence not only to the law but to the spirit of the Constitution."

20

Have you ever watched one man die and then another, knowing that your turn was next? Have you ever looked into ten thousand angry faces whose open mouths screamed for your blood? Have you ever felt yourself in the hands of such a mob whose sole purpose was to destroy you?

— James Cameron, survivor of the 1930 Marion lynchings

ON THE NIGHT OF AUGUST 6, 1930, past ten o'clock, a sixteen-year-old Black youth named James Cameron came sprinting to the door of his house on the outskirts of Marion, Indiana. His mother, Vera, had waited up for him and was sewing a patch on a pair of overalls, sitting in a chair with a flickering kerosene light illuminating her face.

"James," she said, "I wish you wouldn't stay out so late at night." She scrutinized his face and saw that he was panting. His chest pounded under his shirt. His mother knew instantly: something was wrong.

"Look at your shirt," she said. "You're wringing wet with sweat!"

He told her that he had been playing football with his friends, but she did not believe him.

"You're lying to me, son. Now tell me what's the matter. Are you in some kind of trouble?"

James Cameron promised his mother that everything was okay, then went upstairs to bed. But in the middle of the night he and his mother were awakened by pounding on the front door, a fist hitting the wood so urgently, the whole house vibrated. James heard his mother move to the door and say, "Who is it?"

"The police! Open up."

Mrs. Cameron opened the door, and a white officer stood in front of her. "Does James Cameron live here?" he asked.

"What's he done?" she responded. She broke into tears and choked out the following words: "What do you want him for? He's a good boy. He's my only son. There must be some mistake!"

Cameron walked down the stairs. "Let's go," the officer told him. "The chief wants to talk with you." The boy would never forget the sound of his mother's voice as the police took him away.

"Lord, Jesus Christ, have mercy . . ."

IN AN INTERROGATION ROOM inside the Grant County jail in downtown Marion, Cameron came face-to-face with Sheriff Jake Campbell and two other men, one in uniform, one plainclothes. The sheriff asked if Cameron knew two men named Thomas Shipp and Abram Smith, and Cameron admitted that he did. Shipp and Smith were friends, and like Cameron, they were African American.

"Tonight," the sheriff said, "just a little while ago, they told me that you shot a white man and raped a white woman. They said they belong to a gang and that you were the ringleader!"

Cameron gave his account of what happened earlier that night. Around sunset, he said, he was pitching horseshoes with Shipp and Smith. When darkness came, they went for a ride in Shipp's 1926 Ford convertible. They motored over the Thirty-Eighth Street Bridge and out into the countryside, all the way to a dirt road people called Lovers' Lane because it led to a quiet spot on the Mississinewa River where couples went to be alone.

According to Cameron's story, Smith pulled out a .38. He said it was his intention for the three of them to rob someone, and he gave Cameron the gun. Cameron had no history of criminal behavior. But he took the gun. They drove on. On the riverside they came across a car with a man and a woman alone in it, and Cameron stepped out into the night, holding the .38. He gave the "stick 'em up" order. He knew what he was doing was wrong, he told the officers.

The car door opened, and out stepped Claude Deeter, twenty-three, and Mary Ball, nineteen — both white. Marion was a small town, and James Cameron worked at the bus station as a shoeshine, so he knew everyone. He recognized Deeter and Ball, and in a panic — according to his side of the story — he dropped the gun and ran.

"I started running away from there as fast as my feet could move me," Cameron told the sheriff. As he ran, he said, he heard gunshots. But he saw nothing. He ran six miles, all the way home, where his mother was awake waiting for him.

Sheriff Campbell explained that the white man, Claude Deeter, had been shot and was clinging to life in a hospital bed. The woman, Mary Ball, claimed she had been raped. She said she knew Cameron from town, and he was the one who did it. Cameron insisted he had nothing to do with it. Upon hearing this, according to Cameron, the police officers then attacked him, punching his face so his teeth loosened from the blows. He was told to sign a confession. He looked down at the paper, then felt another slap across his face. He remembered the plainclothesman in the room say, "The sheriff didn't say read it. He told you to sign it!"

"I had had enough," Cameron recalled. He wrote his name on the paper, and his fate seemed to be sealed.

DURING THE 1920s the Ku Klux Klan had grown in Indiana faster than in any other state, and the so-called secret society thrived openly in Marion. As early as 1922, the *Indianapolis Ledger* reported in a banner headline, KU KLUX KLAN IS SPREADING OVER INDIANA. The historian Cynthia Carr, a native of Marion, wrote in her book *Our Town* that from 1922 to 1925 "the Hoosier State initiated more members than any other.... By 1924 Klansmen were literally running the state. They had taken over the Republican Party and elected the governor, a majority of the state legislature, the mayor of Indianapolis, and numerous other mayors, sheriffs, prosecutors, and school boards." The Indiana Klan even had its own newspaper, the *Fiery Cross*.

The man most responsible for the rise of the KKK in Indiana had been the state's Grand Dragon during the first half of the 1920s, D. C. Stephenson, known as Steve or "the Old Man." Stephenson's Klan leadership made him rich and so influential, at least in his own mind, he had designs to run for president. But in 1925 he was convicted of sexually assaulting a twenty-nine-year-old woman on a train, biting and mauling her all over her body in an alcoholic rage. Her wounds were so severe, she committed suicide. Stephenson was imprisoned for twenty-five years. However, the *Fiery Cross* continued to publish and the Indiana Klan continued to gain power.

In Marion the Klan's lodge was listed in the local phone book. There was nothing secret about it. Locals remembered the date of March 10, 1922, when the Klan staged a parade through town, right past the Grant County Courthouse. Thousands of spectators watched a ceremony whereby Klansmen stood on a makeshift stage built out of two-by-fours, with a massive American flag and a giant burning cross standing behind it. Some seventeen hundred new members were initiated during that one day's ceremony in Marion's Goldthwait Park. It was here on this day that Daisy Douglas Barr, a Grant County native who would go on to become a national KKK leader, uttered what would become her famous phrase: "I believe that if Jesus was on earth today, He would belong to the Ku Klux Klan."

Still, there had never been a lynching in Marion or anywhere near it.

On August 7, the morning after James Cameron signed a confession to the shooting of Claude Deeter and the rape of Mary Ball, he found himself in the "bullpen" in the Marion jailhouse, a room filled with other prisoners. The heat was unbearable and the stench nauseating. A white man with a crooked smile and long blond hair approached him and said, "Hi, there! How ya feeling this morning?"

Cameron burst into tears. "I want my mother!" he responded.

The story of the Lovers' Lane shooting and accusations of rape spread through the jailhouse, and Cameron stood listening as fellow prisoners pointed at him and talked about what was going to happen next. He remembered this dialogue:

"If'n dey don't kill him befo he gits a trial, dey will tell all sorts of lies on him and git him electrocuted!"

"Yeah. If dey don't kill him, dey will keep him in prison until he is an old man."

Some miles from the jailhouse, in a hospital room, Claude Deeter lay dying with his mother sitting by him. Marion's assistant police chief, a man by the name of Roy Collins, interviewed Deeter, who had been shot three times. Deeter could not name the shooter, except to say that he recognized the man. Meanwhile Deeter's mother, according to a story that would be handed down through the family's generations, convinced Claude to forgive whomever it was. For what it is worth, he apparently did. Deeter then died. According to another story that would be verified by numerous sources, Deeter's bloody shirt was hung from the hospital window — a sign for the lynch mob to gather.

From the bullpen on the second floor of the Grant County jailhouse, Cameron remembered looking out the window and seeing a crowd start to gather in the late afternoon. He knew that the other two suspects, Abram Smith and Thomas Shipp, were housed in another part of the building. He recognized in the crowd people he considered his friends, his neighbors, all kinds of Marion locals whose shoes he shined and who tipped him well. He remembered seeing policemen in uniform and Klansmen dressed in plain clothes with their white hoods atop their heads and no face coverings.

"It was indescribable," he later remembered. "It simply left me without hope."

At one point he was called out of the cell, and he was sure his mother had come to see him. He rushed into the sheriff's office hoping to see her face, only to find that the mayor of Marion had come to ask him questions. Later a reporter for the local newspaper came and asked more questions, taking notes for his article, which would run the next day.

"You'll never get out of this," the reporter said to Cameron. "You know that, don't you?"

• • •

IT WAS NOW DARK OUTSIDE, and the crowd had swelled; the mayor would later estimate that fifteen thousand people had come out. From inside the jail, Cameron heard the first telltale sign of his doom: rocks smashing through the jail's windows. Then the rhythmic pounding began: a sledge-hammer on the locked jailhouse door. Finally the mob broke through the door and came upon Sheriff Campbell, who yelled, "Don't shoot! There are women and children out there!"

The mob pulled Thomas Shipp out first. Ringleaders beat him with fists and clubs. One eyewitness remembered a frantic woman using the blade of a high heel shoe to beat the victim's face. Some of this Cameron could see from the window. He would remember the terrific volume of the noise, and how it increased when the crowd laced the noose over Shipp's head, hanging him first from the bars on a jailhouse window. He was then taken down and hanged from a tree branch in front of the jail. Then the ringleaders came back for Smith.

As Cynthia Carr wrote in *Our Town,* "Smith fared no better. Both were killed several times over. Someone rammed a crowbar through Smith's chest, while souvenir hunters cut off Shipp's pants and distributed pieces." The two were left beside each other in the tree, their feet hanging six feet up.

Then the mob came for James Cameron.

The sixteen-year-old stood among his fellow prisoners, who were now screaming and jumping around the room hysterically. One was so terri-fied, he vomited on the floor. The mob ringleaders came upon the bull-pen; they had the keys. One yelled, "James Cameron is in here and we mean to git him! Now where in the hell is he?" Cameron recalled the next few minutes:

> They surged forward in one great lunge, knocking and trampling
> the black prisoners around me. Some of them got their hands on
> me, right away, three on each side, and then the merciless beating
> began. . . . All the way down the corridor outside my cellblock,
> all the way down the stairway, the angry pounding continued. . . .
> Somehow, not because I wanted to, I remained dimly conscious. . . .

I saw the crowd come to life as we emerged from the jail. "Here he comes!" they shouted. . . . I was too weak to fight back anymore. The cruel hands that held me were like vises. . . . Over the thunderous din rose the shout: "Nigger, nigger, nigger!" "I haven't done anything to deserve this!" I heard myself mumbling, weakly. . . . I screamed as loud as I could above the din and the roar of the crowd that I had raped no woman. I had killed nobody!

Cameron tried to summon the image of his mother in his mind for comfort. "I remembered what my mother had told us about sinners facing death, about the thief on the cross with Christ . . . 'Lord,' I mumbled through puffed lips, 'forgive me my sins! Have mercy on me!'"

The mob pulled him to the tree where Shipp and Smith hung, and Cameron felt the rope around his neck. One person in the crowd later recalled the moment: "All I can remember is the look on his face — a man facing death. He had a look of terror on his face."

But then Cameron heard a woman's voice yelling, "Take this boy back! He had nothing to do with any raping or killing!" The ringleaders paused, not knowing what to do next. Someone reached over and pulled the rope off of Cameron's neck. He was barely able to stand. He turned and began to shuffle back toward the jailhouse, and the crowd — quieted now — opened up a path for him.

All night long the bodies of Shipp and Smith hung from the tree, and the crowd remained. At some point someone summoned a local photographer named Lawrence Beitler, who had a studio in downtown Marion. Beitler came with his equipment and staged his camera for a professional photograph. When he snapped his shot, the moment froze in black-and-white film. One man is seen pointing at the dead, staring into the camera's lens with laser-focused eyes. A pregnant woman holds her hands around her belly as she turns toward the camera. A man in a white shirt and thin black tie giggles. An old woman with silver hair stares off as if searching for some truth. Every face in the crowd is white, and the two dangling bodies Black.

Later that night four detectives smuggled Cameron out of the back of

the Grant County jailhouse and brought him to another jail in a neighboring town, for safety. When they arrived an old white man in uniform
was standing out in front of the building. This man ran the Huntington
jail. Cameron got out of the car and stood before him, bloodied and terri-
fied of what was to happen next. The officer looked at Cameron and apologized. He said that for all he knew, his own son might have been among
the lynch mob.

"I am sorry, son," he said. "Sorry to my heart."

WHEN THE SUN CAME UP OVER MARION, a thirty-five-year-old woman
named Katherine "Flossie" Bailey and her husband, Dr. Walter T. Bailey,
came to the square in front of the jailhouse. It was an extraordinary act
of courage, but they had reason to believe they would remain safe. Dr.
Bailey was a physician and Marion's most prominent African American,
and Flossie headed the tiny branch of Marion's NAACP, which had all
of thirty-four members. They looked up and saw Shipp and Smith, still
hanging in the morning sunlight. The crowd refused to disperse, guarding over the bodies to keep the police from cutting them down.

That day the Baileys sent a letter by special delivery to Walter White in
New York, setting a scene of what was happening in Marion. "The night
was one of horrors, thousands milling around down town and running
wild in the streets uttering threats," Flossie Bailey wrote. "Tonight prom-
ises to be another such a one as last night, probably worse. The mob is still
congregating and uttering threats."

Bailey pleaded for assistance. "Mr. White," she wrote, "we are appealing to you for help. Please send us a National representative to help in our
investigation. If we can bring these men to justice or at least make a real
effort it will help us greatly in the future." She included a PS: "A race riot
threatens."

21

The entire country is watching to see if Indiana has courage and honesty enough to effect the punishment of those who took the law into their own hands at Marion, constituted themselves judge, jury, and executioner and flouted not only the law but human decency.

—NAACP press release, September 26, 1930

ALL MORNING ON AUGUST 8, 1930, messengers arrived at the NAACP's national office delivering communiqués from Indiana—from a Marion attorney named R. L. Bailey (a telegram announcing NEGRO SECTION THREATENED WITH FIRE), from the city editor of the *Indianapolis News,* and others. According to these accounts, law enforcement still did not have the situation under control. Locals were driving cars around town firing guns in the air and dragging cans from a rope along the pavement, a threat known as "belling"—a not-so-gentle reminder of the tradition of dragging lynch victims by rope behind vehicles.

At the time, the NAACP's offices were just settling down after the thrilling Parker victory three months earlier. Walter immediately set the association's machinery in gear. He sent a telegram to Governor Harry G. Leslie of Indiana, urging the governor to UTILIZE EVERY POSSIBLE RESOURCE TO PROTECT THE LIVES AND PROPERTY OF INNOCENT NEGRO CITIZENS OF MARION AND THAT EVERY EFFORT BE MADE TO APPREHEND AND PUNISH TO THE FULL EXTENT OF THE LAW THE MURDERERS WHO PARTICIPATED IN LAST NIGHT'S LYNCHING.

He then released that communication to the press and to Flossie Bailey in Marion. As the day wore on, Walter learned more of the story. Even to him, it seemed almost unbelievable. The *New York Times* ran a front-page article that morning with the headline INDIANA MOB OF 10,000 LYNCHES TWO NEGROES; BEATS WRONG MAN AS THIRD ALLEGED KILLER. Flossie Bailey pleaded for help, and for Walter himself to come to Marion. "Mr. White," she wrote, "Marion and Indiana is [*sic*] expecting someone from the headquarters here to help us in this crisis. We are doing the best we can to carry on, but, of course, this is a new experience for all of us and, considering the circumstances we cannot do so much toward investigating as someone with experience."

At 7:13 that evening the Indiana governor responded through his secretary, in a telegram to Walter: STATE TROOPS BEING RUSHED TO RIOTING MARION EVERYTHING BEING DONE. [*sic*] On the ninth, the second day after the murders, an NAACP member named Mrs. Belle Haywood from Muncie, Indiana, telegrammed Walter, also asking for help. None of the undertakers in Marion would take the corpses, she explained, for fear that a mob would break into their buildings and hold some ghoulish event with the dead bodies. So the authorities had brought the remains of Thomas Shipp and Abram Smith to an undertaker in Muncie. The Muncie NAACP branch also wanted Walter's advice and protection.

On August 11 Mrs. Bailey wrote again explaining that while things had calmed down, the photographer Beitler was selling the photo of the hanging bodies from his studio at fifty cents each, and doing a lot of business. She added that she had to go to a neighboring town to send this telegram to Walter, because she and her husband had been threatened. Every time Walter telegrammed her in Marion, she said, everyone in the town knew what that telegram said. There were spies everywhere.

That same day — four days after the killings — Walter booked a ticket on a train called the Spirit of St. Louis, bound west for Indianapolis. He would arrive in Indiana on Friday, August 15, at 7:25 a.m. He asked Mrs. Bailey to make a complete list of everyone he might interview. There was just one more matter.

"In what manner will it be most effective for me to come," he asked, "openly as Acting Secretary of the association, or as a correspondent of a New York newspaper?" In essence, Walter wanted Bailey's advice on whether he should come as a Black man or a white one.

Bailey suggested he come bearing all the power he could leverage, as the acting chief of the most militant race-crusading organization on earth, the NAACP. She recommended he book a room at the Hotel Spencer on Fourth and Adams Streets, the biggest hotel in Marion.

"Even though you are coming as the Acting Secretary for the association," she wrote, "it will be best to keep your racial identity secret, as the hotels do not keep colored people."

BY THE TIME WALTER'S FEET WERE ON THE GROUND in Marion, numerous firsthand accounts of the lynchings had appeared in local newspapers and aired out in an official court of inquiry called by the town's mayor, Jack Edwards. There were so many accounts, it was impossible to believe that no one caught the identities of the ringleaders.

A reporter named Drysdale Brannon from the *Marion Chronicle* described how Shipp lay unconscious. "He was lying there in the street; a young boy came through the crowd, not over sixteen or seventeen years old, yelling, 'Make way for the rope.'" One reporter from the *Wabash Plain Dealer* described a seventeen-year-old girl attacking an already unconscious Smith: "She flew at the prostrate and unconscious Negro and kicked him and spit at him while the crowd thundered all around. The girl worked herself up to such a fury that she fainted."

Walter set up a series of interviews; how he got all these subjects to agree to talk with him is unclear. But they did. He began with the most important one, in the office of Harley Hardin, Grant County prosecutor. Hardin would be the point man in bringing any indictments. Would he even attempt to do so? Walter sat in Hardin's office. The prosecutor was considerably larger than Walter, in every physical dimension. Hardin was president of Grant County's Republican Party committee, and he had a picture of former president William McKinley on his wall. As the two greeted each other, Walter jotted some immediate notes in a pad.

"Hardin about 50," he wrote. "More grey hair — 6 ft — well set. White gold spectacles with bar straight. Full face drooping sharply down at corners."

Hardin said he did not personally know any of the people involved in any of the crimes. Not Shipp, not Smith, not the man shot at Lovers' Lane, Claude Deeter, nor the woman, Mary Ball. "People had been going out to that place for immoral purposes," Hardin said. "Married men with married women, not their wives . . . or with single women." More importantly, Hardin said he did not hear any rumors about the lynching party until after sunset, when, he explained, he got a phone call from Flossie Bailey of the NAACP.

Hardin was at the jailhouse that afternoon and that night. The crowd had started gathering right outside *before* sunset. It seemed everyone in Grant County knew about the lynching by the early *afternoon* of August 7. Locals described traffic jams caused by cars coming in from neighboring towns. It would later be revealed that flyers had been handed out. How prosecutor Hardin — who was at the jailhouse all afternoon and evening — did not know of any lynching plans until 9:30 p.m., as he told Walter, seemed inexplicable. Hardin had to be lying. And if he was lying about this, what else would he lie about?

The prosecutor told Walter how — later that night, once the mob had gathered — he had "mingled in the crowd trying to find the leader." It was "just a howling mob," Hardin said. He estimated between two thousand and three thousand people. "Persons actually participating in lynching," he said, "probably not over 50."

Did Hardin recognize any of them? "Ones I talked with I didn't know," he said, according to Walter's notes. Walter found this "somewhat strange," he later wrote, "in view of the mob, according to other eyewitnesses, being made up in large part of citizens of Marion and Grant County in which Prosecutor Hardin had lived for some forty years."

Walter left Hardin's office disgusted. He found Hardin to be "a timid, blustering official." Hardin was up for reelection in November, in a little more than two months' time. If he brought indictments against white members of this community, he would almost certainly be voted out of office. Walter would have bet anything that Harley Hardin was going to put his personal interests first. He would also later learn that Hardin almost surely knew the identities of at least some of the killers. Hardin had told a prominent member of the Marion community that it would be "impossible to get the witnesses to testify against the names of the lynchers who are known."

MAYOR JACK EDWARDS'S OFFICE was in the Grant County Courthouse, across a small grassy square from the jailhouse. Which meant the lynchings occurred right outside of Edwards's office. He told Walter that, when he first heard news of the murders, he was sitting in a restaurant in Indianapolis eighty miles away. The mayor had lived his whole life in Marion; he was a young man with hair so slicked, it looked like he used motor oil. He had only recently been elected and was new on the job.

Edwards told Walter that the Black community in Marion had never presented any problems. Walter jotted in his notes, "No notorious N [for Negro] criminal experience in Marion within 25 or 30 years." In fact, Mayor Edwards said, the white community had proved more unlawful than the Black community in this town. "Many gruesome white crimes," Walter wrote as the mayor spoke. Edwards then related a surprising story.

In the same jailhouse where Shipp, Smith, and Cameron had been held, on the night of August 7, there was another criminal housed by the name of Boltz. This prisoner had been apprehended for the most ghastly crime anyone in Grant County could remember, up until the night of the lynchings. He had chopped off the head, both arms, and both legs of a man he was living with in a boardinghouse, because he was jealous over the affections of the housekeeper. Mayor Edwards told Walter how Boltz had thrown the body parts in a creek and had then gotten caught. Still, the mob had no use for this murderer, Boltz, who was white. He was unmolested on the night of August 7, though he was in that same jailhouse. The mob was after Shipp, Smith, and Cameron.

Edwards explained that Grant County police had been in charge of everything, that the local Marion police force (twenty-eight officers in total) had never been called in to help. The Marion Police Department had its own armory of machine guns and ammunition that could have been used to stop the mob, perhaps just by threat, without a shot fired. The mayor wanted it known that his city was not culpable, and even signed a statement for Walter that said, "It is my earnest desire to have the people know that the boys were not in our custody, but were taken care of by the County Sheriff, as we do not have a city jail. Our police rendered every assistance that they could but were under orders of the sheriff and our police department and all its resources were at the service of the sheriff and they were not used or asked for."

Though Edwards admitted he was not in Marion on August 7, he believed he knew six to eight men who had taken part in the killing. He gave Walter names. He said that by Indiana law, if a grand jury were called, it would be made up of six men from Grant County. All would be white. And prosecutor Harley Hardin would be in charge. The mayor had no faith anything would be done, he told Walter. Any witness who came forward would be threatened with violence or worse. The only way a case could be brought, he said, was if the state's attorney general, out of Indianapolis, got personally involved.

WHEN WALTER INSPECTED THE FRONT ENTRANCE to the Grant County jailhouse, it told its own story. Walter recounted, "The two most formidable barriers to the jail are two solid steel doors set in steel plates." It had taken the swing of a sledgehammer an hour to knock in the first one, and Walter could only imagine the horror that filled the victims' hearts as that bludgeoning echoed through the jailhouse. That no one did anything to stop the mob for an entire hour while the sledgehammering occurred led Walter to the conclusion that Sheriff Campbell had been grossly negligent.

Equally as puzzling was the existence of a second steel door. That door had no marks on it. When Walter questioned members of the jailhouse staff, an officer named Captain Charles Truex explained that on the night of the lynchings, he had asked the officer in charge of the keys, a man named Tobe Miller, for the key to the second steel door. Turnkey Miller answered (according to Walter's interviews), "Hell only knows when there had been a key to that door." When Walter asked Sheriff Campbell about it, Campbell said he had been sheriff for four years and had never seen any keys to this second door.

While Walter was in Marion, the Beitler photo went — by 1930 standards — viral. It appeared on August 16 in the *Chicago Defender*, in the

Baltimore *Afro-American,* and in the *Pittsburgh Courier,* three of the most widely read Black newspapers, all of which were distributed nationally. Editorials blasted the local law enforcement. The *Indianapolis Times:* "The evidence against the lynchers should be easily obtainable by officials who really have any real desire to get it. It is not possible for a crowd of thousands to witness this open act of barbarism with no one willing to identify those who actually performed the deed." The case was being covered by major newspapers and wire services: the *New York Times, Boston Globe,* Associated Press, *Washington Post, Los Angeles Times.* Never had a lynching drawn such a spotlight as that which was shining on Marion.

Flossie Bailey and her husband were pushing the state's attorney general to make an investigation, but they were increasingly working under the strain of death threats. They received one anonymous letter from someone in Chicago reading: "If so-called Negro leaders would use 1/10 [one tenth] as much energy in teaching negroes to leave white women alone, as they use in protesting against their too terrible death you'd do your own and the white race a favor. When white men consider their women as female beasts to be seized, murdered, or violated by any raving male — then will lynching stop and not before. Your idea of 'Equality' will never exist and 30,000,000 white men will never consent to violation of their women by Negroes."

Meanwhile, Walter built his case. He interviewed Sheriff Jake Campbell and the captain of Marion's city police force, a man named Lindenmuth. He interviewed other witnesses, who gave him names and other clues, such as where the noose had come from, and how members of the mob had gone into the jailhouse garage where the police cars were located and had let the air out of the tires, so officers could not transport Shipp, Smith, or Cameron to another location to keep them safe. Walter had a local attorney draw up a list of state laws that had been broken, not just by the lynching mob but also, potentially, by Sheriff Campbell, who was responsible for at least *trying* to protect the prisoners in his custody. Campbell had learned of the planned lynching before it had occurred. Flossie Bailey herself had called him at six thirty that night and begged him to do something. But the killing happened anyway.

Like many states, Indiana had anti-lynching laws on the books. But what good would that do, Walter figured, if local police refused to enforce them?

The whole town of Marion had come under a spell of fear and anxiety. The Black population feared more violence. Officials such as Harley Hardin and Sheriff Campbell feared losing their jobs and dug in to defend themselves. They were not accustomed to seeing their names in major national newspapers, or their work pilloried in editorials in local ones. The ringleaders in the killings must have increasingly feared they would be arrested and charged.

During Walter's investigation, all kinds of theories arose behind the first shooting out on Lovers' Lane, the killing that had started this whole episode. Nineteen-year-old Mary Ball had a dubious reputation in town. Rumors claimed that she was in on the crime, that she was having an affair with Thomas Shipp and together they had set up Claude Deeter. And that the robbery had gone bad when Deeter fought back and was shot.

Then there was the matter of the third Black teenager — Cameron. Was he telling the truth when he claimed he had run away before the shooting had occurred? Or was he guilty of murder too?

Walter came to the conclusion that Mary Ball was lying, that she had never been assaulted in the first place. Nevertheless, none of that particularly mattered, not to Walter. The kernel of his case was the murder of two men in an orgy of vigilante violence. Whether they were guilty or not, their right to a fair trial, their rights under the Fourteenth and Fifteenth Amendments, had been violated. This much, Walter believed, was indisputable.

ON AUGUST 22, Walter left Marion, bound for Indianapolis. Hustling up the concrete steps of Indiana's colossal statehouse at 200 West Washington Street, he was swallowed up into the ornate columned entrance. In the office of the attorney general James M. Ogden, Walter began his argument. The attorney general had spoken an oath to uphold justice in the state of Indiana. His salary was paid by the taxpayers. And so, Walter argued, the attorney general had a job to do. Walter then told his story, the facts that he had gathered in Marion.

How he had interviewed Mayor Edwards, Sheriff Campbell, and Harley Hardin, among others.

How Sheriff Campbell never called for the assistance of the Marion police.

How he failed to make sure the two front doors to the jailhouse were appropriately locked.

How he never made use of any of the weapons of force at his disposal to protect the prisoners in his custody — a clear violation of Indiana's anti-lynching law. As Walter put it in a report he handed over to Attorney General Ogden, "The Indiana law against lynching, especially as to the duties of the sheriff or other law enforcement officers to protect prisoners, is clear beyond any question . . . We respectfully urge that you, as attorney general of Indiana under the specific authority given you by Section 2534 of the Indiana anti-lynching law, move for the impeachment of Sheriff Campbell and for his removal from office."

Walter continued:

It is our conviction that there is little hope of proper prosecution of the lynchers if the matter is left in the hands of Prosecutor of Grant County, Harley Hardin. . . . In conversation with the Prosecutor, he expressed to me reluctance to proceed vigorously with the arrest and prosecution of the lynchers, basing this reluctance upon the fact that he feared such action would infuriate the mob and stir it to new activity. . . . The opinion is freely expressed in Marion that unless your office takes the initiative, there is little hope of conviction.

Walter then listed the names he had gathered during his investigation, of the men he believed were among the killers. "This information was gathered without great difficulty at Marion," he wrote, "and much more can be secured if an honest and vigorous effort is made. . . . The lynchers are well known and a large part of the lynching mob was composed of citizens of Marion and of Grant County."

At the top of the list: a barber named Bailey, whose shop was at Eighteenth and Meridian. This man had been reportedly bitten on the right arm by Abram Smith while he was tying Smith's hands during the lynching, Walter pointed out, so there would be a scar—clear evidence. Walter named a grocer named Gleason, who operated a shop on Ninth Street between Boots and Gallatin. Two brothers named Lyons, one of whom worked locally for the Whippet Automobile Agency. A man named Hurlock, who was a collector for the Lauber & Spiegel installment furniture house. A man locals called "Thin" Beard, or Bird, who, according to Walter's sleuthing, had bragged that he personally "put the rope around one of the black sons of bitches."

The list went on. Walter sent a copy of this six-page letter also to Governor Leslie. Then he got on a train and headed home to Harlem, to wait and see where the chips would fall.

BACK IN NEW YORK, Walter published his full account of the violence in Marion in an article in the New York *World*. For shock value, the article featured the Beitler photo front and center, but only the bottom of it, so the crowd could be seen, not the brutalized bodies. From Marion, Flossie Bailey sent the names of seven more men who she believed participated in the murders. "They are scared to death," she wrote, "and it would take only a small amount of grilling to make them confess." Walter forwarded the names to Attorney General Ogden. He also wrote to President Hoover, who was now a bitter foe of the NAACP's due to the recent Judge Parker episode.

The Marion case was drawing so much attention, Hoover felt tremendous pressure to make a statement, which he did. "Every decent citizen must condemn the lynching evil as an undermining of the very essence of both justice and democracy," Hoover said.

As predicted, prosecutor Harley Hardin brought no charges against anyone. As Walter had hoped, however, Attorney General Ogden stepped in. Ogden personally drove from Indianapolis to indict eight men (a ninth was subsequently added), and he also filed charges against Sheriff Campbell.

Two brief trials followed, before white judges and all-white juries in

Indiana. No guilty verdicts resulted. Meanwhile, sixteen-year-old James Cameron languished in jail, where he contracted tuberculosis. Prosecutor Hardin personally oversaw the state's case against him. Flossie Bailey appeared in the courtroom for every session of Cameron's trial. Both she and Cameron's lawyers were assigned full-time bodyguards because of death threats.

"There was really no sincere effort made to convict the members of the mob," Mrs. Bailey wrote Walter, "but on the other hand every effort is being made to send this 16-year old boy to the electric chair."

Ultimately the jury believed Cameron's story, that he was not present when Claude Deeter was shot three times. Cameron was convicted of accessory before the fact of voluntary manslaughter, and because he was a minor, sentenced to one year in prison — a term that Flossie Bailey and Walter White both believed to be a victory of sorts.

"Really, Mr. White," she wrote, "I am so tired." Knowing that Walter was not a churchgoer, she added, "I don't know what takes the place of prayer with you, but whatever it is, do that."

THE MARION CASE would continue to haunt everyone involved. The Beitler photo became the most iconic lynching image in history. The singer Billie Holiday later recorded a song inspired by the photo, called "Strange Fruit": "Black bodies swinging in the summer breeze / Strange fruit hanging from the poplar trees." Shipp and Smith were buried in Weaver, Indiana, with no gravestones, for fear that their corpses would be violated or even stolen.

After serving one year in prison, James Cameron was released. He became a writer and an activist. In 1988 he founded America's Black Holocaust Museum in Milwaukee, and was responsible for launching three NAACP branches in the state of Indiana. By many accounts, he is history's only known survivor of a lynching. He died in 2006.

22

Sing a song full of the faith that the dark past has taught us
Sing a song full of the hope that the present has brought us
Facing the rising sun of our new day begun
Let us march on till victory is won.
—James Weldon Johnson and J. Rosamond Johnson,
  "Lift Every Voice and Sing"

JUST DAYS AFTER RETURNING FROM MARION, Walter White walked onto a lighted stage at the Ogden Theatre in Columbus, Ohio. The theater was jammed, and when Walter looked out, he saw that he might have been the only white-skinned person in the place. He began a speech about Judge Parker and the Supreme Court, and how, in the near future, the court would be making decisions that were going to affect every Black American's life with real urgency—decisions about education rights and voting rights. Then Walter brought up a senator who represented these people in Washington—Republican Roscoe McCulloch of Ohio, who had voted to confirm Judge Parker and who was up for reelection in the fall of 1930.

"Senator McCulloch was besought by Negroes of Ohio to vote against confirmation of Judge Parker," Walter told the crowd. "He was faced with a choice between loyalty to the White House and loyalty to the best interest of his Negro constituents. Senator McCulloch chose to be loyal to the administration." Then, with emphasis: "No intelligent unpurchaseable Negro can possibly vote for McCulloch and retain self-respect."

Walter saw the 1930 midterm elections as a key moment to build political stature for himself and the association, in anticipation of a big coming-out party in the 1932 presidential contest. His game plan: to get Black Americans registered to vote in states where they could (such as Ohio) and, specifically, to urge that they vote against any senator who had supported the confirmation of Judge Parker. This was a concrete strategy to demonstrate power on the national stage, and to show politicians — whether Democrat or Republican — that they would be held accountable by a significant portion of the electorate. Ground zero for this battle was the swing state of Ohio, and Walter traveled there for a speaking tour.

Supporters of Senator McCulloch were furious that a "colored" man would come to their state to rally voters against their man. Dirty tricks abounded. At one point Walter got a phone call at a home where he was staying. "The telephone rang and a seductive female voice invited me to come to her house to permit her to tell me the facts about a case in which the NAACP would be interested," he recalled. "When I informed her that I would talk with her only in the presence of witnesses and at a place where I was staying, the conversation abruptly ended."

At another speaking event, Walter arrived to find such a swelling crowd, he had to get out of his car a block away from the theater and push his way through. He hung his coat in an anteroom. After his speech, he went to get his coat with some of his entourage, only to find that someone had planted a bottle of whiskey in one of his coat pockets, which he promptly removed (Prohibition still being in effect). "A number of persons fastened eagle eyes not on us, but on the right-hand pocket of my coat," he remembered. "[They] seemed somewhat disappointed to see nothing there."

On November 3, the day before the 1930 midterm election, Walter got a telegram from an NAACP man with boots on the ground in Columbus, Ohio. Some McCulloch forces were reported to be threatening violence at polling booths, the informant said in a telegram. NEGROES AT FEVER HEAT, the telegram read. VIOLENCE LIKELY TOMORROW. Walter wrote back suggesting that police and the mayor be called upon for PROTECTION AT POLLING BOOTHS WHERE VIOLENCE MAY BE ATTEMPTED BY MCCULLOCH FORCES.

When Election Day arrived, Ohio voters chose the Democrat Robert J. Bulkley over McCulloch by a clear margin, which meant that many Black voters did the unthinkable, upon Walter White's urging: they voted Democrat. McCulloch wasn't the only victim of the anti-Parker forces. There were numerous others, over the next two election cycles. "All the senators who voted for Parker and who could be reached by the colored voters have been defeated," *The Crisis* proudly stated in a December 1934 editorial.

"White politicians, Republican and Democrat, did not like the new situation," Walter later wrote, "but were forced to recognize the Negro voter no longer was gullible, purchasable, or complacent as before and would have to be recognized as an increasingly potent force in the American political scene."

UNLIKE JUDGE PARKER, Walter was quickly confirmed to his next job. James Weldon Johnson announced his retirement and would be accepting a professorship at Fisk University in Nashville. At the NAACP's board meeting on March 9, 1931, the group voted to drop the "acting" from Walter's title. "I was promoted from acting secretary to secretary," he recalled, "and wondered what troubles lay ahead."

Following the announcement, his calendar filled with appointments as reporters requested interviews. The influential Black newspaperman Floyd J. Calvin—who had recently launched the Harlem Renaissance's first radio program—came to Walter's fourth-floor office and found him behind a desk covered in letters, newspaper clippings, magazines, books, and an overflowing ashtray. Also on the desk was a confidential report regarding a breaking story: the arrest of nine Black youths on accusations of attacking two white women in Alabama—what would later be known as the famous Scottsboro Boys case. Walter's desk was like his schedule: no bare space.

The first thing he thought to say to Floyd Calvin was to thank James Weldon Johnson. "I am simply overwhelmed at the great responsibility I have assumed," he told Calvin. "I would not be able to do anything at all had it not been for the good fortune I had to work for 13 years under Mr.

Johnson, the retiring secretary. Since being here I have come to realize more than ever just how great a man Mr. Johnson is."

Calvin's story appeared in the *Pittsburgh Courier* and began with the following assessment of Walter's character:

> The new executive director of the Negro's greatest fighting machine is only 36. He is short, slight, but eager and alert. He smokes numerous cigarettes. He talks rapidly, but with a slight stutter. He is highly nervous, is impatient to be doing something. He admits he fights first and thinks about it afterward. He sits at a big flat-top desk on the fourth floor of the Mercantile Bank building, where 14th Street crosses [5th] Avenue. His day is sometimes (frequently) 18 hours long. He begins work, often, at 6:30 am and closes his official duties as late as 1 am. That is Walter Francis ("Fuzzy") White, the Georgia boy who came to New York and made good. . . . As a "go-getter," Mr. White's record is unparalleled in Negro life.

Around this same time, a photographer came to Walter's home at 409 Edgecombe Avenue and snapped a family portrait. Walter sat in a comfortable chair with an alert foxhound on his lap. His kids, Jane and Walter Jr., were to their father's right, their faces genuinely lit up by the excitement of having their photo taken by a real photographer holding a real camera. Gladys stood behind Walter with her arms folded, staring off, as if dreaming of herself in some other room and some other life. As one historian later wrote of her, "She never was comfortable being Mrs. Walter White." In the photo, only Walter appears Caucasian, his eyes probing through spectacles, his hair prematurely graying.

When the flamboyant Heywood Broun came to profile Walter for his column in *The Nation,* It Seems to Heywood Broun, Broun once again brought up the extraordinary irony of Walter's racial identity. Broun found it "a little ridiculous to refer to Mr. White" as Black. "Mr. White is a Negro largely from choice," Broun wrote. "The community has only his word for the fact that he is Negroid." He asked Walter point-blank, "Why didn't you ever decide to become a white man? It must be hard to remain a Negro when you don't have to."

Walter dove into the story of those two days of his childhood back in 1906, when he witnessed the Atlanta race riot. "I was born in Atlanta," he told Broun. "We had a house right on the edge of the Negro quarter. It was a nice house. One week-end, there were rumors of race trouble." Walter unfolded the story in chilling detail — his version of it, at least. "I was twelve years old [he was actually thirteen] and my father gave me a shotgun and stood me at one of the two front windows on the second floor. He stood at the other window. 'You're not to fire,' he said, 'until they cross the edge of the lawn. When they get that close shoot and go on shooting as long as you can.'"

Broun reported Walter's account of this event in his column verbatim, and while Walter had talked about the episode on numerous occasions, this was the first time that the story of him guarding his family home with a shotgun appeared in public, published in a hugely popular column. Broun also prophetically predicted what was next for Walter White. "He may become one of the most powerful forces in American politics."

Then something strange occurred. Walter often sent important clippings by mail to his family, and when his sister Alice read the Heywood Broun piece, she wrote him, "Many thanks for the articles you sent. Read the one in *Nation* with much amusement. Where did the shot-gun come from?"

Walter's sister — who was there that night in Atlanta in 1906, albeit hidden in another part of the house — did not remember any shotgun, let alone two (one for Walter, one for his father). Walter wrote her back, "Dad did have guns and ammunition in the house."

The story became a private debate among White family members. Walter's sisters, even his mother, remembered no shotguns in the house. In the end, Walter stood by his version, and would spell it out in even more chilling detail in the future, when he would write his autobiography years hence. Still, he had to confront the fact that his family questioned a key part of his story, and not just any story. This story was the foundation for his life's purpose.

Had he invented the shotgun? If he had, what other stories had he invented? How much of Walter White's public persona had he mythologized? How much was a creation of his own imagination? His colleagues, his family, and in the future his enemies—all had an opinion. The one he would hear the most, from this part of his life onward, was that he had mythologized his own race. That he was not really Black at all. That he used the race issue to create his career, even to earn money. These were accusations he would fight against, with unwavering conviction, until the day he died. One thing about him, however, was rarely questioned. As Heywood Broun put it, "His waking hours and perhaps his dreams are given over to the question of race relations."

Once, while traveling in a taxi through Manhattan, Walter stumbled onto the topic of race with a Caucasian driver, who naturally assumed Walter was white like himself. The driver believed that Black people would be better off if they "stayed in their place" and ignored the troublemakers who preached equality and justice. As Walter reached his destination, the taxi driver said, "How would you like your daughter to marry a nigger?"

Walter smiled. Getting out of the car, he said, "She probably will."

WITH JOHNSON'S DEPARTURE, the NAACP needed new blood. While in Kansas City for a speaking engagement, Walter had met the brilliant newspaperman Roy Wilkins, editor of the *Kansas City Call.* Wilkins was a fearless fighter, an attack dog with a typewriter. He possessed all the qualities Walter was looking for: he was a good investigator, reporter, writer, public speaker. And at twenty-nine years of age, he had youth on his side.

On February 26, 1931, Walter dictated a letter to Wilkins. It arrived in Kansas City buried in correspondence and junk mail. The envelope had Walter White's name and NAACP headquarters listed as the return address, and it was marked "Personal and Confidential." Wilkins would remember his hands trembling as he opened it.

"I am writing to you personally and confidentially to ask if you would be interested in an important executive position with the association," Walter wrote. "As you of course know, Mr. Johnson has resigned as Secretary.

We are faced, therefore, with the problem of getting the right man for the position of Assistant Secretary, which I formerly held."

Walter had to plead for his man because there was so little in the bank to pay a new employee, even with the departure of Johnson. Now two years into the Depression, money was painfully short. Walter could offer Wilkins only $2,600 a year, less than he was making editing the *Call*. Wilkins agreed to at least take a train to New York for an interview. "The NAACP was the most militant civil rights organization in the country," he recalled. "These were people who were getting things done."

In early March 1931, one night at the dinner hour, Wilkins appeared at Walter's door. Wilkins had an air of James Weldon Johnson about him —intense dark eyes, square shoulders and jaw, the ability to radiate affability or stone-cold severity with the flick of a mental switch. For hours the two men discussed the job and the nation's current racial discourse while picking at plates of Gladys White's cooking. After dinner Wilkins left and walked alone through Harlem, in his words, "feeling happier than I could remember." The next day in the office Wilkins met Arthur and Joel Spingarn and board chair Mary White Ovington, whom he described as "the NAACP's wealthy maiden aunt." Wilkins took the job, moved to New York with his wife, Aminda Badeau Wilkins, and soon began what would become his life's work for the next forty-six years.

Shortly after, luminaries of the Black and white worlds gathered for a gala send-off party for Johnson at the Hotel Pennsylvania at 401 Seventh Avenue, which, like Pennsylvania Station across the street, was originally built by the Pennsylvania Railroad. Poets, statesmen, clergymen, newspaper columnists, educators, musicians, social workers, artists, men and women of all creative and political professions — dressed in their finest, with quite a few top hats among them — filed into the hotel's Southeast Ballroom. Along one edge of the room was a dais, where the speakers of the evening sat, Walter White among them.

Johnson's brother Rosamond sang "Lift Every Voice and Sing." Heywood Broun spoke. Ovington read Johnson's famous poem "To America." Countee Cullen recited his sonnet "To James Weldon Johnson." Telegrams were read from H. L. Mencken, Senator Arthur Capper, and

The New Yorker's illustrious poet and raconteur, Dorothy Parker, who in her missive called Johnson "a man whose gift, life, and soul, has made me proud to be in the world with him." Everywhere one looked sat one of the era's intellectual powerhouses: Carl Van Vechten, Carl Van Doren, Fannie Hurst, John D. Rockefeller III, publisher of the *New York Post* and *The Nation* Oswald Garrison Villard, the influential book critic Lewis Gannett. It was "one of the most distinguished audiences I have ever seen in New York or elsewhere," noted Walter.

When it was Walter's turn to speak, he told the story of how Johnson had plucked him from obscurity in Atlanta in 1918. "He rescued me from Georgia and brought me here," Walter said, recounting how the two had met in Atlanta, back when they were fighting the city's board of education not to cancel the seventh grade for Black students. This had been thirteen years earlier, but it seemed a lifetime.

When it was Johnson's turn to step up to the podium, he had tears in his eyes. He spoke about how great the country was, where a boy could grow up the son of the head waiter at a Florida hotel and see all the things in life that Johnson had seen, and how much further the country had to go, to be all that it could and should be. In the end, he thanked the person that made it the most worthwhile.

"The luckiest break I got," he said, "was in 1910 when I came 4,000 miles from revolution-stricken Nicaragua [where he was serving as US consul] to marry my wife. For twenty-one years she has gone through the dark as well as the bright days. The thought of how things might have gone without her appalls me." It was classic James Weldon Johnson — powerful and sincere.

Johnson's departure was like a line in the sand for Walter, one that separated the past from the future. Board members and association members waited expectantly to see what Walter would do first.

MONEY WAS TIGHT. "Worry over money," remembered Ovington, "was the first of the many things that our new secretary encountered in his new office. He attacked it valiantly."

The Depression had hit the Black community harder than the white community. As Walter wrote to his field secretary, William Pickens, lawyer fees, printing bills, office and travel expenses, and so much more "have completely exhausted our available resources, and the demands upon us are increasing." As field secretary, Pickens was to travel the country recruiting members and collecting donations. Walter told him to keep his talks "at the appropriate length to get the money. Wherever possible, I wish you would make the appeal and try to get as much cash as possible. . . . We are putting forth desperate efforts here through personal interviews, letters, appeals and the like, to get some money in."

When Walter looked around the NAACP offices, he saw dollar bills flying out the door. Rent cost $1,401.60 a month. Electric bill: $750. Telephone and telegrams: $400. Postage: $1,750. Printing: $2,000. Travel: $1,250. Newspaper clipping service: $300. One of his gravest anxieties was *The Crisis.* The magazine was bleeding green. With NAACP members suffering layoffs nationwide, many Americans did not have money for magazines.

As head of *The Crisis,* Du Bois was the most gifted of all the NAACP founders, but he was terrible with money, and so haughty, he was difficult to engage. (An association lawyer once said to Du Bois, "Look, Doc, your office and mine are side by side and you come in here every morning and you just walk right by." Du Bois coldly answered, "Yeah, that's one of my bad habits," then shut the door behind him.) Walter had to face the reality that the magazine was going to have to fund itself the way others did— through advertising and subscriptions. The association could not afford to keep it afloat for much longer.

"At present time," he wrote to the board, "[there was] no possibility of the association being able to give any further help to *The Crisis* this year."

Du Bois ran the magazine independently—until he needed money. He was also contemptuous of Walter, whom he still remembered as the hungry upstart people called "Fuzzy." As so often happened when money was running out, the office politics were becoming toxic.

ONE DAY shortly into his tenure as chief executive, in May 1931, Walter's phone rang and he learned that his father had been in an accident, in

Atlanta. The story of what happened made Walter instantly nauseated. George White Sr. had been walking down a street holding a lemon meringue pie that one of his daughters had baked for him. He was just a few blocks from his home on Houston Street. When a streetlight turned, he walked into an intersection at Houston and Piedmont; a beat-up roadster sped through, running the red light. The impact was severe. It was broad daylight, with witnesses all around.

Walter's father was nearly as pale-skinned as he was, and George Sr. was taken to a whites-only ward at Grady Hospital on Butler Street. The wounded man had no identification on him, and the doctors had no idea who he was. One of Walter's brothers-in-law was the first to arrive at the hospital. This man had brown skin, and he had heard about the accident through a neighbor who had witnessed it. He found George White Sr. unconscious in a hospital bed. One of the white doctors asked, "Do you know who this man is?"

Walter's brother-in-law answered, "Yes. He is my father-in-law."

"What?" asked one of the doctors. "Have we got a nigger over here on the white side?"

Orderlies scooped up the patient and moved him across the street to a Black ward, which is where Walter found him when he arrived in Atlanta with his wife and children.

As Walter stood over his father's hospital bed, he grew enraged. The hospital was, to Walter's eye, filthy—especially compared with the white ward across the street. "Dinginess, misery, and poverty pressed so hard on one from every side that even a well person could not avoid feeling a little sick in those surroundings," he later wrote. His father had worked for forty-three years without missing a day on the job. He had been the most selfless man Walter had ever known. "On the meagre salary of a postal employee," Walter recalled, "he had educated seven children, all of them attaining a college degree." Now he was dying in a dilapidated hospital ward. When George Sr. regained consciousness, he said, "I feel like a watermelon that has been dropped from a wagon—all squashed up inside."

Sixteen days and nights passed. A young white physician—who was a church missionary—helped care for Walter's father. The missionary was from Alabama, and while there was little he could do to save the dying man, he kept Walter occupied with conversation. "We talked about everything," Walter remembered. "War and peace, and human nature and the race problem, of course." During breaks from the hospital vigil, Walter ventured out and found witnesses of the accident. He interviewed them, gathering the most minute details so he could reconstruct the event in his mind, as if he was conducting one of his murder investigations.

Across from George Sr.'s bed, another patient lay under a canopy, being treated with heat in an attempt to cure a gangrenous leg that gave off a putrid odor. Paint was peeling from the walls, in some places hanging in strips. "The vigil during the day was not too trying because there were diversions to keep one's mind from the inadequacy and sordidness of the hospital," Walter later wrote. "But night was unmitigated horror as Father's life slowly ebbed away. With the dimming of the light and the cessation of movement, the quiet was broken only by the slight stir when a new patient was brought in or when one of those already there died or called out for a nurse."

Cockroaches scuttled about, and Walter remembered seeing an occasional rat. At night he kept his feet off the floor, resting them on the rungs of his chair to avoid the creatures.

"And then," he remembered, "Father died."

WALTER TRAVELED BY TRAIN back to New York, a broken man spiritually. He had put so much time and thought into investigating his father's accident, it was as if he could not get the sound of the impact out of his mind. Gladys and the kids remained in Atlanta for the time being, to be with the White family while Walter returned to work.

Normally, Walter would pose as a white man to get a berth in a Pullman car, where he could lie down for the overnight ride. But there was no room. So he sat all night in an uncomfortable seat in a Jim Crow car. Evidence suggests that during this long ride, he began to come undone. Ever since he had left Atlanta back in 1918, he had worked so hard and traveled so much, he had not seen much of his parents. The guilt must have weighed on him, now that his father was gone. The stress of his job, his wife's unhappiness, it was all too much. One can imagine him staring out a train car window, seeing in his mind's eye the faces of all those lynching victims whose stories he had worked desperately to unearth — Mary Turner and her unborn child, the countless killed during the Red Summer and the Tulsa massacre, the Lowmans, Abram Smith and Thomas Shipp.

Evidence suggests that, somewhere between Atlanta and New York, Walter drank himself into somnolence. At one point he was pickpocketed, and he arrived at Grand Central Terminal in New York with burning red eyes and no wallet. He had enough change in his pocket for a phone call and a subway ride. He slipped a nickel into a pay phone and called his old friend Poppy Cannon. He had not seen her in a couple of years, not since they had planned to write that cookbook that never got written. She was living alone uptown, he had heard, as she had divorced her husband. She was working her way up in New York advertising. When Walter called, she picked up the phone.

"I am at the station," he said. "Could I come to you for a cup of coffee? I just got off the train from Atlanta."

23

But whoso committeth adultery with a woman lacketh understanding; he that doeth it destroyeth his own soul.
— Proverbs 6:32

WALTER STRUGGLED WITH HIS HEAVY SUITCASE as he walked up the stairs
to Poppy Cannon's apartment, looking supremely disheveled. "His face
was so pulled with strain and a kind of horror that I was shocked," she
later recalled. She motioned for him to have a seat at a card table, which
she had covered in a yellow tablecloth. An amber vase filled with daffo-
dils and pussy willows brightened the room but did nothing to erase the
misery on Walter's face. She made coffee, which he drank hot and black,
and toast, which he did not touch. He did not have much time, he said, as
he had to be at the office.

"My father is dead," he told her. "They let him die like a criminal —
like an outcast — like an animal. I wasn't going to talk about it." But he
continued talking. He couldn't help himself. "After forty-three years of
delivering and collecting mail! They gave him a testimonial banquet at
the colored YMCA. A gold watch — for being such a fine public servant
and good citizen! I've always been sorry I couldn't be there, thought it
might have been painful to see him squirm as they praised him. He was a
shy person. I wish I had been there."

She must have wondered why he had shown up at her place that day,
why he had chosen her to be the witness of his breakdown.

"I know all about how it happened," he went on. "You know who was driving that car? It was a doctor from the Henry W. Grady City Hospital. He was scared. He knew what he'd done — trying to beat the light." Then: "Even as he lay dying my father said to us, 'No matter what happens, you must love, not hate.' But I couldn't help myself. I hated all white people. I hated the young white doctor who had been kind to us. I hated the sight of my own white face in the mirror. But then I thought . . ." He paused. "I thought of you . . ."

Many years later, after Walter had died, Poppy Cannon wrote a book about him called *A Gentle Knight,* in which she strongly suggested that their physical affair began on that morning in her apartment. "That day," she wrote, "Walter wept in my arms."

When Walter left and headed for the office, she remained behind and alone. His mood was one of desperation. He had exposed himself to all kinds of dangers in the past, but this was different. How many times during his work at the NAACP had he found himself counseling young interracial couples struggling with their love and the consequences they would face if they made it public — knowing that interracial marriage was illegal in roughly half of the forty-eight states? These were the modern American incarnations of Shakespeare's *Romeo and Juliet.* He had always told them, if there was no doubt in their conviction, "Your way is clear. Be willing to make whatever sacrifices are necessary — but for principle as well as for love."

But now his own situation seemed eminently more complex. He was becoming known at the time as "Mr. NAACP," fighting the forces of segregation that claimed countless times that Black men were after pure white women. If his secret got out, they would claim they were right all along. His critics and his enemies would destroy him. So many people were relying on his work, his integrity, his leadership — his ability to keep himself out of situations exactly like this one.

AT 4 P.M. ON DECEMBER 21, 1931, the NAACP held a special board meeting to address the matter of failing finances. The Depression was worsening.

There was no end in sight, and each day brought with it more uncertainty, more anxiety. When board members and the staff walked into the conference room, Walter drew the meeting to order. The board was to vote, he said, on a new policy reducing everyone's pay. Salaries over $1,300 would be cut by 10 percent, and salaries from $1,000 to $1,300 by 5 percent. Certain clerical staff members would be let go. The board voted, but the outcome was a foregone conclusion. They had no choice.

Then came an even more uncomfortable matter. Walter had engineered a sort of intervention, to confront W.E.B. Du Bois. There was no more money to fund *The Crisis*. Du Bois sat among his peers, his ears pricked. Mary White Ovington was retiring, and though she was present, the new board president, Joel Spingarn, announced that the board was going to create a committee consisting of five board members and two outside experts (who would be convinced, all hoped, to work for free) to "investigate the expenditure of funds by the National Office of the association and *The Crisis*," Spingarn said, as recorded in the meeting minutes.

Du Bois knew this was coming, and he had arrived at the meeting with a bombshell in his pocket. He took out a memorandum he had written that had been signed not just by himself but by four other executives, all of whom were present. Du Bois read the memo aloud. It ruthlessly attacked Walter's spending policies, blaming the financial uncertainty on him.

"The Secretary has absolute dominion of these expenditures and practically reports to nobody," Du Bois said, with Walter sitting just feet away. "Unless Mr. White is going to be more honest and straight-forward with his colleagues, more truthful in his statement of facts, more conscientious in his expenditures of money . . . the chief question before this organization is how long he can remain in his present position and keep the NAACP from disaster. . . . We have all had considerable and varied experiences. But in our several and varied experiences, we have never met a man like Walter White who under an outward and charming manner has succeeded within a short time in alienating and antagonizing every one of his coworkers, including all the clerks in the office."

A gasp sucked the air out of the room. Du Bois's memorandum was for many — especially for Walter — a kick in the gut, four days before Christmas. After the meeting Walter, on the verge of tears, sat with the NAACP's field secretary, William Pickens, talking the matter through. Pickens tried to console him, but it was no good, as Pickens himself had been one of the four executives who had signed Du Bois's memo. The betrayal, Walter believed, was unconscionable.

Over the next few days, however, the real truth came into focus. It appeared that Du Bois convinced the others to sign the memo, and now they all wanted to back out. The NAACP's publicity director, Herbert Seligmann, wrote Walter, "I wish to express my deepest regret that my signature was attached to [Du Bois's memo]; to apologize to you and to Miss Ovington for the substance and manner of the charges made against you; to withdraw every charge and personal innuendo made against you; to authorize you to make whatever use of this letter you see fit; and to offer you my resignation to take effect at whatever time you may determine." A clerk named Jeanette Randolph sent a memo to board members on the same day, disputing Du Bois's position. "I do want you to know that I personally do not subscribe to [Du Bois's] statement."

It became clear that the attack on Walter's leadership and on Walter personally was really coming from one figure alone: Du Bois. Spingarn wrote a scathing memo to Du Bois four days after the Christmas holiday.

"The memorandum which you drafted and which was signed by four other executive officers of the association has now been completely and unreservedly repudiated by these four, and all agree that it was (as one of them put it) 'cruel and indefensible,'" Spingarn wrote. "May I urge you, as your sincere well-wisher, to retract every charge or innuendo against the character, honesty, or motives of the Chairman and the Secretary?"

In another note Spingarn told Du Bois that one board member had said of him, "He's just a badly brought up child who needs a spanking." "It grieves me," Spingarn wrote, "as one of your friends, that you should subject yourself to such a characterization." He requested that Du Bois retract the memorandum.

Du Bois answered with an icy hand-scribbled letter of just twenty-seven words: "Dear Mr. Spingarn: I will not retract or change a single word in the statement I signed and read before the Board. Very sincerely, W.E.B. Du Bois."

When the staff returned to work after the winter holiday, the tension in the office was extreme. "The pall of office politics and intrigue was thicker than the smog in Los Angeles," Wilkins recalled.* "As early as the fall of 1931 it was clear that [Du Bois] and Walter were heading for a terrible collision."

Du Bois had always seen *The Crisis* as the association's primary voice. As the new chief executive, Walter was taking the association in an entirely different direction. In 1931 the national office received thirty-five hundred requests for legal assistance, most of them from Black Americans who believed they were getting railroaded in courts of law. Lawyers cost money, and without money, injustice would stand unopposed. Walter was working eighteen-hour days, and the thrust of his job had become those appeals — which ones to seize on, how to fund them. He was redefining the NAACP's identity and mission, with the main inspiration being Clarence Darrow.

Walter had spent years fighting racial violence and travesties of justice, and what had it earned him? No convictions. Killers walking free. Families decimated, with no justice served. He saw America's racism anew — as institutional. And so he wanted to go after the institutions themselves.

The association's fight would become political and legal, and in the process it would abandon the founding philosophy of social and intellectual activism that Du Bois had created and championed. As Du Bois's biographer David Levering Lewis put it, "If Du Bois was a visionary with a contempt for minutiae, White was a CEO with a policy. If the devil is in the details, White was the devil himself. Reduced to details, White's policy for the NAACP was to be top-down, legalistic, and legislative — in other words, litigation and lobbying."

---

* The reader will excuse Wilkins's use of the anachronism "smog in Los Angeles." Such a thing did not exist in 1931.

• • •

SO BEGAN 1932 — the year of bad news. In March the Lindbergh kidnapping shocked the world. The twenty-month-old son of Charles and Anne Morrow Lindbergh — among the most famous and admired couples in the world — disappeared one night, only to be found weeks later dead in a wooded area of Mercer County, New Jersey. The year 1932 saw Adolf Hitler's Nazi party surge into international prominence. It was the year of the Ford hunger march, a demonstration among desperately hungry and unemployed autoworkers that turned violent, at the front steps of Henry Ford's flagship factory. It was the year that the Dow Jones Industrial Average bottomed out, some 90 percent down from where it had been three years earlier. Though very few in America noticed at the time, Japanese forces completed an invasion of the Chinese province of Manchuria — a skirmish on the Asian mainland that many historians would later call the opening salvo of World War II in the Pacific.

The NAACP spent much of 1932 mired in the Scottsboro Boys case, the landmark criminal and court battle that proved a disaster for Walter. The story began with the arrest of nine Black and three white hobos, from aboard a train in Alabama. At first it seemed a routine incident. But the story took on legs when it was discovered that two of the white hobos — thought to be men — were in fact women. Authorities pressed these two women on whether they had been raped. They maintained that they had not.

Then — in an attempt to avoid criminal charges of vagrancy — one of the women changed her story, and the case exploded in the newspapers.

Nine Scottsboro Boys — all African American, all teenagers — faced trial in Scottsboro, Alabama, on charges of rape, and Walter was on the scene, organizing a legal defense. Driven by sensational race-baiting headlines about the rape of white women, white supremacists showed up in mobs, turning the tiny town of Scottsboro into something of a national convention for their cause. "More than ten thousand whites, many of them making no effort to conceal weapons, jammed the courthouse grounds and the streets of the sleepy little town of fifteen hundred population," Walter recorded. "National Guardsmen with drawn bayonets, tear-gas bombs, and machine guns made the antiquated Jackson County courthouse appear like a fortified position in an advanced battle zone."

The NAACP's dream team of Clarence Darrow and Arthur Garfield Hays agreed to defend the Scottsboro Boys. However, a lawyer with the International Labor Defense (ILD) — the legal arm of the Communist Party USA — came on the scene and convinced the defendants to jettison the NAACP in favor of the ILD. During the Depression, when so many were penniless and hungry, increasing numbers of Americans found hope in the communist ethos, and the Communist Party USA emerged as a political power. The party's legal arm, the ILD, was using the Scottsboro case as a massive publicity campaign to lure African Americans into the fold.

The NAACP had to retreat from what would turn out to be one of the most momentous racial episodes of the 1930s. Eight of the nine Scottsboro Boys were ultimately convicted and sentenced to death, though the case would continue to play out in the courts for years (the defendants would collectively spend more than one hundred years in prison). The episode was seen as a drastic failure of the NAACP even though the association did not defend the Scottsboro Boys. Walter wrote an article published in *Harper's* magazine, "The Negro and the Communists," revealing the ruthless and immoral tactics used by the ILD to wrestle the case out of the hands of the NAACP, noting how the Communists seemed far more interested in recruiting propaganda than they did in actually freeing the Scottsboro Boys (certainly the ILD would not be able to put together the kind of fighting case that Clarence Darrow and Arthur Garfield Hays could). But the article only served to fuel the flames of discontent; White was vilified by the communists on the left, and conservatives on the right who believed the Scottsboro Boys were guilty.

From Walter's office in New York, he refused to allow the Scottsboro tragedy, or the Du Bois mess, to stop him from gunning for his ultimate goal of 1932. It was an election year, one that saw the rise of an exciting new candidate from New York — Franklin Delano Roosevelt, who won the Democratic nomination at the National Convention in Chicago in early July. Ever since 1928, when Walter first got a taste for national politics during the Al Smith affair, he had been carefully constructing the machinery that would help Black America emerge as a national political juggernaut. Now was the time to set it in motion.

Walter recorded: "1932 marked the emergence of the Negro voter, as a force which no political party could longer ignore or flout."

24

So, first of all, let me assert my firm belief that the only thing we
have to fear is fear itself — nameless, unreasoning, unjustified terror
which paralyzes needed efforts to convert retreat into advance.
— Franklin Roosevelt's first inaugural speech, March 4, 1933

THE 1932 PRESIDENTIAL ELECTION was the first of the Depression age. Republicans had controlled Washington for twelve years, through a burst of economic glory. But now the nation was on its knees, and the election was to be a referendum on the way forward. The very idea of democracy was challenged, from the left (the surging Communist Party USA) and the right (as Senator David A. Reed said in 1932, "I do not often envy other countries their governments, but I say that if this country ever needed a Mussolini it needs one now"). In describing the experience of campaigning in 1932, Franklin Roosevelt told a friend, "I have looked into the faces of thousands of Americans. They have the frightened look of lost children."

During the election cycle, Walter White held the NAACP national conference in a symbolic city — the nation's capital, in the shadow of the White House itself. When he gave the keynote speech on the conference's final night, he looked out on a gesticulating mass of thousands in the Washington Auditorium. In what sounded like a future Martin Luther King Jr. speech, Walter told the crowd, "I dream of a world of black, brown, yellow, and white people with no invidious distinctions based upon race." Then: "The general public looks to us now, as never before, to carry on the fight for justice and equal rights."

Walter took to the road on a speaking campaign, as if he himself were running for office. He predicted that 1932 would see Black voters abandon the Republican Party for the first time since the Civil War. It was going to be "the greatest political revolt among Negroes that has ever been known in a national election." In Indiana he said:

> The Negro in America today is literally fighting for his life. He is fighting for a chance to work, to be a full-fledged citizen with all the rights the Constitution guarantees. He is ready to play the game of politics as white men have taught him through long years of bitter education to play it. He can no longer be counted upon as the chattel of any political party. . . . The era of the Negro's new political independence will be plainly established in the coming national election.

On September 16, 1932, the NAACP sent a survey to the two major candidates, Roosevelt and Hoover, calling for a "plain and unequivocal declaration on the subject of race relations." This survey demanded answers from both.

Would they support legislation that would allow Black Americans to vote in Alabama, Georgia, North Carolina, South Carolina, Louisiana, Mississippi, and Texas — states where they had been denied the ballot for decades?

Would they support legislation to end the discrepancy between government spending on Black education and white?

Would they support a federal anti-lynching law?

The climactic question: "Will you in word and deed, so far as in your power lies, procure the recognition and observance of the full citizenship rights of the Negro in the United States?"

Walter then got the New York *World* to reprint the questions and challenge both FDR and Hoover to have the courage to answer them. "The questions are of great interest to all those who have been working for bettered race relations," the *World* stated in a widely read editorial.

From Walter's point of view, institutional racism could only be defeated if the men in charge of the country wanted it defeated. Neither candidate responded to the NAACP's survey. But the questionnaire and the whole NAACP election-season campaign signaled to the candidates that neither would get the Black vote for free, as the GOP had become accustomed. The Black vote was up for grabs and could hold the balance of power in certain key states.

On Tuesday, November 8, some forty million Americans lined up at the polls. In a historic landslide, Roosevelt won forty-two of the forty-eight states (losing almost exclusively in New England). While a majority of African Americans voted for the Republican ticket as usual, for the first time in generations, vast numbers voted against the Party of Lincoln.

Political experts, white and Black, were aghast at what appeared to be the beginning of a sea change in voting power. Right after the election, a friend of Walter's named Isadore Martin wrote him from her home city in Pennsylvania. "Philadelphia has always been a Republican city and for a Negro to say that he was a Democrat meant that he would be considered a kind of outcast and a traitor to his race," she wrote. "But now things have changed and one Baptist minister went so far as to preach a sermon the Sunday before the election against the Republican Party and to give splendid reasons why he was supporting Roosevelt."

The *Pittsburgh Courier,* once a solid Republican African American newspaper, declared, "Go home and turn Lincoln's picture to the wall. The debt has been paid in full." Roy Wilkins remembered the moment: "The seismic shift of Negro voters away from the GOP had been building for more than a decade, and the Parker fight helped push millions of wavering black voters away from the party of Lincoln and into the arms of Franklin D. Roosevelt."

The next day Walter began a relentless campaign to pressure FDR and the Democrats. He released a statement on the day after Roosevelt's victory: "The 1932 election will be a historic one for Negroes. It shows that their political emancipation is well under way. . . . The election also constitutes a great opportunity for the Democrats to convince colored people that they have positive things in the way of citizenship rights, to hope from that party." Then: "It remains to be seen what the new Democratic Administration will do next."

IN THE FALL OF 1933, six months into Roosevelt's first term, a pair of murders once again brought lynching back into the national conversation. On October 18, George Armwood — suspected of assaulting a seventy-one-year-old white woman — was burned to death in front of an audience in Princess Anne, Maryland. No charges were filed.

Five weeks later, in San Jose, California, several thousand watched a mob hang John Holmes and Thomas Thurmond — two white men who had confessed to kidnapping and killing the son of a local shop owner. The governor of California, James Rolph Jr., gave a speech defending the killers, calling the murder "a fine lesson for the whole nation." "They'll learn they can't kidnap in this state," Rolph said. "If any one is arrested for the good job I'll pardon them all." Foes of lynching were so shocked, they created the term "Rolphism" to define the act of defending vigilante murders.

Having read about the Armwood case, James Weldon Johnson wrote to Walter, "That lynching in Maryland was a terrible throwback. But, as paradoxical as it may sound, it is possible that some good may come out of it. . . . It would be a good time to make another try for an anti-lynching Federal law. We came near doing it ten years ago; I believe the chances today are better."

Walter had been looking for a cause that he could use to whip up national outrage while at the same time forcing FDR's hand on the race issue. He could dangle the Black vote in 1936 like a carrot in front of the White House door. Would FDR support a federal anti-lynching law?

In Washington, Walter used his contacts to find senators from FDR's own party, the Democrats, to draft a bill, quickly landing on two — Robert F. Wagner of New York and Edward Costigan of Colorado. Together the three men drafted the Costigan-Wagner federal anti-lynching bill. When hearings began in February 1934 in the Senate Caucus Room of the Capitol, Walter was ringside. The NBC network broadcast the first two days' proceedings, making these the first Senate hearings in history to go live via radio nationwide. With the galleries full, Walter was introduced by Frederick Van Nuys, a freshman senator from Indiana who owed his election, to some degree, to the campaign efforts of Flossie Bailey and the Indiana NAACP. Van Nuys presented Walter saying, "He probably needs no introduction at this time."

Walter began. "I appear today as a representative of the National Association for the Advancement of Colored People," he said, "with national headquarters at 69 Fifth Avenue, and with 378 branches with a total membership of 85,000. Both the membership and the national board of directors of this organization, which celebrated its twenty-fifth anniversary on February 12, 1934, are interracial."

He debunked the myth that Black men were lynched for raping white women, and that the judicial system was inadequate to try these men, if in fact rape accusations were legitimate. "I challenge any reputable and honest person to assert that there is any lack of speed whatsoever in apprehending, indicting, trying, and convicting Negroes charged with crime," he said. He listed the names of state governors who were lynching apologists, told the stories of recent murders that would have outraged the nation had they been committed against white victims, and appealed to the sanity of everyone in the room to give the federal government jurisdiction to try criminal cases if local authorities failed to act.

"'States rights' should not and must not be permitted to deter prompt passage of this bill," he said. "To those who may attempt to use this argument on the floor of either House of Congress I should like to point out that no 'States rights' arguments are ever raised when States seek financial aid for relief, public works, education, and other boons from the Federal government."

Walter knew the whole nation was listening, via radio, and he ended by appealing to the nation's conscience, and its fears. "Lynching is no longer either a sectional or a racial issue," he said. "The United States today stands at a crossroads. If Negroes can be lynched with impunity and without fear of punishment today, white people can be lynched tomorrow. . . . Swift, deep currents of unrest, of bitter resentment against the lynching mob and every other form of proscription surge through the life of those who form one tenth of America's population. . . . I urge prompt and favorable consideration . . . of this sorely needed legislation."

"IT WAS A GREAT OCCASION," Walter wrote Johnson after his testimony in Washington. "You already have seen the list of witnesses who appeared. They represented something like thirty-five million people. . . . The most extraordinary thing of all, however, was the coast-to-coast hook-up. Senator Wagner tells me that this is the first time in history, as far as he knows, where the entire proceedings of a Senate investigation were broadcast."

Walter was certain the bill would pass in the House — and even in the Senate, if it could come to a vote. However, foes would surely launch another filibuster just as they had ten years earlier. A small number of senators could block any vote from occurring, according to the rules of Senate engagement. Walter needed to get Roosevelt on board, to insist on a vote. He wrote FDR's appointments secretary, Marvin McIntyre, on April 14, 1934. "Both Senators Costigan and Wagner have urged me to try to secure an appointment with the President to discuss this matter," he wrote. "Would you be good enough to let me know if you are able to make an appointment for me?"

Roosevelt refused to meet with Walter and would not explain why. But the reasoning was obvious: if the president supported the Costigan-Wagner bill, he would offend a power base of his own party, the Democrats' Solid South. If Roosevelt did *not* support the bill, he would offend Black voters in the North. So he chose to say nothing at all about the Costigan-Wagner bill. Walter was surprised, however, when the First Lady reached out and invited him to the White House. The two met on April 19, and Walter was fascinated to learn that Mrs. Roosevelt supported the bill and agreed to try to sway the president. It was the start of a remarkable friendship that would last until Walter's death.

"I talked with Mrs. Roosevelt at the White House," he wrote Johnson, "and succeeded in convincing her, first, that we had enough votes to insure passage of the bill; second, that the bill would not be brought up unless the President insisted upon the leaders of Congress that a vote be taken."

Debate on the Senate floor continued through the spring of 1934. Walter had prominent Black attorneys Charles Houston and William Hastie preparing briefs and arguments. He recruited Chinese, Haitians, and women to pack the galleries during the debates, in an attempt to demonstrate that Americans of all shades supported the Costigan-Wagner bill. He organized a controversial art exhibition called *An Art Commentary on Lynching* to raise awareness; the show ran at the Arthur U. Newton Galleries in Midtown Manhattan for weeks, with lynch images by George Bellows, Thomas Hart Benton, Isamu Noguchi, and thirty-six other artists. Pearl Buck—whose novel *The Good Earth* had recently won the Pulitzer Prize—spoke at the opening. Crowds jammed the exhibit, and one female attendee found the artwork so shocking, she fainted.

In Washington, white supremacists in the Senate attacked the Costigan-Wagner bill, using their old tactic: the claim that lynching—or at least the threat of it—was necessary to protect white women from the Black rapist. "The virtue of womanhood is a thing which should not be displayed in the courts when the criminal is known and has put himself outside and beyond the pale of the law," Ellison "Cotton Ed" Smith of South Carolina said on the Senate floor. "Nothing to us is more dear than the purity and sanctity of our womanhood and, so help us God, no one shall violate it without paying the just penalty which should be inflicted on the beast who invades the sanctity of our womanhood."

Senator Theodore Bilbo of Mississippi put an exclamation point on the argument: "The underlying motive of the Ethiopian who has inspired this proposed legislation . . . and desires its enactment into law with a zeal and frenzy equal if not paramount to the lust and lasciviousness of the rape fiend in his diabolical effort to despoil the womanhood of the Caucasian race, is to realize the consummation of his dream and ever-abiding hope and most fervent prayer to become social and political equal to the white man."

In this fight the Costigan-Wagner bill received unexpected support from a group called the Association of Southern Women for the Prevention of Lynching, headed up by a reformer named Jessie Daniel Ames, who came from Texas but founded her organization in Walter's home city of Atlanta. While the Senate debate was playing out in Washington, Ames held a national conference, which drew huge publicity. The southern author Lillian Smith famously named Ames's group the "Lady Insurrectionists." Ames collected thirty thousand signatures from white women in the South denouncing lynching.

Still, white men in Washington wielded the power to pass or destroy this law. The vote in Congress was near.

AT THE SAME TIME THAT WALTER WAS IN WASHINGTON lobbying for the Costigan-Wagner bill, the rest of his life was unraveling. He ended his affair with Poppy Cannon but must have known in his heart it was not over. Meanwhile, Du Bois was busy at NAACP headquarters, not so quietly working to destroy him.

In the January 1934 issue of *The Crisis,* Du Bois's "Segregation" — the most surprising and controversial editorial he would ever write — appeared under his byline. "The thinking colored people of the United States must stop being stampeded by the word segregation," Du Bois wrote in the first sentence. He came out in favor of a form of segregation, a world where Black and white could live in the same country but with separate cultures and separate destinies. It "created a furor in Negro life," Walter recalled. The prominent lawyer William Hastie refused to believe Du Bois had written it "until my own eyes convinced me. . . . Oh, Du Bois! How could you?!" Roy Wilkins remembered, "The puzzle was why Dr. Du Bois had adopted the voluntary segregation line. Obviously he had picked up a brick and tossed it through the biggest plate-glass window he could see."

Du Bois was in Atlanta when the issue was published. Walter telegrammed him there. CAN YOU ARRANGE FOR SPACE FIVE HUNDRED TO THOUSAND WORDS IN FEBRUARY CRISIS FOR STATEMENT ON

EDITORIAL ON SEGREGATION JANUARY ISSUE STOP ADVISE DATE
WHEN COPY MUST BE IN YOUR HANDS. WALTER WHITE.

Walter wrote an editorial explaining to readers that the NAACP opposed segregation in all its forms — always had, always would. Du Bois responded to Walter immediately. "I have your article on segregation," Du
Bois wrote. "I will not publish it."

Walter was stunned. Under pressure from the association board, Du
Bois ultimately allowed Walter a one-page rebuttal in the March issue, but
the next month Du Bois's attack on Walter became public and personal.

"If . . . the NAACP has conducted a quarter-century campaign against
segregation, the net result has been a little less than nothing," Du Bois
wrote in the April issue. "We have not made the slightest impress on the
determination of the overwhelming mass of white Americans to treat Negroes as men." Then, in his most electric language, Du Bois went in for
the kill. "Walter White is white. He has made more white companions
and friends than colored. He goes where he will in New York City and
naturally meets no Color Line, for the simple and sufficient reason that
he isn't 'colored.'"

The battle between the two men was now the biggest gossip in Black
America. "For the first time in its twenty-five years history," the *Philadelphia Tribune* noted, "there is open warfare among the official family of
the National Association for the Advancement of Colored People." Taking on Du Bois required extraordinary courage. Du Bois was an unrivaled
Black intellectual powerhouse. "A brilliant student of sociology, a literary
genius, a man of letters," the *Afro-American* wrote in describing Du Bois,
"[he] could grace a chair in any university in the world."

At this point Walter had no choice; in terms of status within the
NAACP, it was kill or be killed. Writing to Johnson, Walter begged for
advice. "I wish you would write me your opinion of the present situation
with regard to Dr. Du Bois. . . . What do you think the Association should
do? And what, if anything, should I personally do?"

Johnson wrote back advising caution. Walter should avoid any public
statements about Du Bois.

Countless phone calls and letters came through to Walter's office expressing bewilderment and anger. Joel Spingarn wrote Walter counseling discretion. "Confidentially," the association board chief wrote, "may I advise you to act carefully when dealing with this whole question, as you are at somewhat a disadvantage? I am not suggesting that you hide your opinions in any way, but that you realize that hundreds of Negroes think you are really a white man."

One of the two protagonists had to go, and the board had to decide. Spingarn and Ovington had reservations about Walter's leadership. He was moving the association into uncharted territory; his vision of the association as a political and legal force was already recasting the NAACP as something vastly different from what it had been when Spingarn and Du Bois and Ovington imagined it in the early years. Would Walter's plan work? Or would the association collapse under the weight of his failure and the Great Depression? As for the choice between Du Bois and Walter, there was little to debate, however.

Du Bois "has been growing increasingly incompetent," Ovington wrote Spingarn. "As a choice between him and Walter White, Walter is worth ten times as much to us."

FOR WALTER, all roads ended at the Oval Office. He lobbied so hard to get himself in front of Roosevelt that his reputation became a matter of debate in the White House.

"Frankly," the president's press secretary, Stephen Early, told the First Lady, "some of his messages to the President have been decidedly insulting." Walter was "one of the worst and most continuous troublemakers," Early said. Eleanor Roosevelt responded, "I think I should have about the same obsession that he has. . . . If you ever talked to him, and knew him, I think you would feel as I do. He really is a very fine person with the sorrows of his people close to his heart."

The Costigan-Wagner bill was at stake, and it could live or die by President Roosevelt's word. "I turned in desperation to Mrs. Roosevelt," Walter recalled. "I explained over long-distance telephone." Eleanor Roosevelt appealed to her husband, and finally FDR caved. He would meet with Walter. The First Lady had discussed the issue at length with the president, she told Walter, and so she coached him on exactly the questions FDR would be asking. The date was set for May 7, 1934.

Arriving on a warm spring afternoon, Walter stepped inside the old house where every American president since John Adams had lived. Ushers led him out onto the South Portico, where Eleanor Roosevelt and the president's mother, Sara Delano Roosevelt, greeted him. It was a dramatic setting — the white pillars, the view of the South Lawn. Walter put his charm to work. "Shortly afterwards, the President arrived in exuberant spirits," he later wrote. "As was his custom when he wished to avoid discussing a subject, he told many gay and amusing anecdotes to postpone an anticipated ordeal." Walter finally brought up the Costigan-Wagner bill.

"But Joe Robinson [Senate majority leader] tells me the bill is unconstitutional," FDR said.

Walter was armed with the opinions of prominent lawyers. It was not, he argued, and he explained why he believed so, most undoubtedly pointing to the Fourteenth Amendment. For every question Roosevelt raised, Walter had an answer.

"Somebody has been priming you," the president said. "Was it my wife?"

Walter smiled and suggested they stick to the conversation. Roosevelt turned to his wife and asked her if she had coached Walter in the questions that would be asked. She too smiled and suggested they stick to the conversation. At which point Roosevelt laughed aloud. Turning to his mother, he said, "Well, at least I know you'll be on my side."

The president's mother shook her head; she agreed on this matter with Walter and the First Lady. Which made Roosevelt laugh harder. But then FDR leveled with Walter and explained his political predicament. He could not challenge the powerful base of the southern Democrats.

"I did not choose the tools with which I must work," he told Walter. "Had I been permitted to choose them I would have selected quite different ones. But I've got to get legislation passed by Congress to save

America. The Southerners by reason of the seniority rule in Congress are chairmen or occupy strategic places on most of the Senate and House Committees. If I come out for the anti-lynching bill now, they will block every bill I ask Congress to pass to keep America from collapsing. I just can't take that risk."

THE NAACP'S CIVIL WAR reached its climax on June 11, 1934. Walter arrived in the association's conference room, greeting Ovington, Joel Spingarn, Wilkins, and Charles Studin, among others. Walter had been commuting back and forth to Washington and had seen little of his family and little sleep. Wilkins wrote in his diary about Walter a few days earlier, "Looks tired and is working much too hard."

Walter gave his monthly report. Then, in a dramatic reading before the group, he read W.E.B. Du Bois's resignation letter — dated June 1 — aloud. Du Bois was absent, but Mrs. Du Bois attended.

"In thirty-five years of public service," Walter said, reading Du Bois's words, "my contribution to the settlement of Negro problems has been mainly candid criticism based on careful effort to know the facts. I have not always been right, but I have been sincere, and I am unwilling at this late date to be limited in the expression of my honest opinions."

Du Bois's NAACP era ended. Roy Wilkins took his job editing *The Crisis*. "I believe we were limping along at slightly less than 10,000 copies a month," Wilkins recalled, "and when I examined the books for the first time, I discovered that our creditors were after us for $1,600 in debts."

If any one person could be credited with founding the NAACP, it would probably be W.E.B. Du Bois. Many saw his departure as the end of the organization. It was up to Walter to prove them wrong.

25

Unless justice is given to the Negro, he may be driven by desperation to the use of force. But we pray God that this may never happen as we know all weapons are in the hands of those who deny us a chance.

—Walter White, July 5, 1935

ON MARCH 19, 1935, a few minutes after 2 p.m., a sixteen-year-old dark-skinned Puerto Rican named Lino Rivera wandered into the Kress five-and-ten store across from the Apollo Theater on West 125th Street in Harlem. Rivera snuck something into his coat pocket—a candy bar by some accounts, a penknife by others—and when he tried to leave the store, an employee nabbed him. The captor threatened to "beat the hell" out of Rivera, and a scuffle broke out. Rivera bit his foe on the hand and ran for it, but he was apprehended by police. A crowd gathered inside and outside the store as an ambulance pulled up out front. When the store owner asked police to let the boy go, an officer led him out the back entrance to avoid the crowd.

Rumors spread through Harlem that a boy had been unjustly beaten —even killed—by police outside the five-and-ten. Someone made leaflets and started passing them out, showing a photo of Rivera and the words "Child Brutally Beaten." Misinformation spread. A brick went sailing through the plate-glass window, and as if a switch had been flipped, madness descended on Harlem. Years of Depression-era angst poured out into the streets.

Businesses known to be white-owned were brutalized. Store owners posted signs in their front windows — COLORED STORE, COLORED HELP EMPLOYED HERE — in hopes that vandals would move on. By nightfall, all available law enforcement — detectives, horse-mounted patrol, emergency squads — were deployed in Harlem as mobs of men carrying clubs and other weapons roamed the streets. Outside the Kress five-and-ten, cops openly battled with three thousand rioters on pavement littered with shattered glass from storefront windows. Police distributed a photo of Lino Rivera, trying to alert people that the "victim" was fine. He had not been beaten, and in fact he was smiling in the photo, seemingly amused by the attention he was getting.

When it was over, three African Americans were dead, dozens more were injured, and Harlem had been all but ransacked. The grim cleanup would take days. Mayor Fiorello La Guardia formed a committee to investigate the causes of the Harlem riot of 1935. The committee's report, issued on May 29, was brutally frank. An excerpt from its introduction:

> This sudden breach of the public order was the result of a highly
> emotional situation among the colored people of Harlem due
> in large part to the nervous strain of years of unemployment
> and insecurity. To this must be added their deep sense of wrong
> through discrimination against their employment in stores which
> live chiefly upon their purchases, discrimination against them
> in the school system and by the police, and all the evils due to
> dreadful overcrowding, unfair rentals and inadequate institu-
> tional care. It is probable that their justifiable pent-up feeling, that
> they were and are victims of gross injustice and prejudice, would
> sooner or later have brought about an explosion.

The riot occurred during the climactic weeks of the fight for the Costigan-Wagner bill, and Walter was likely in Washington at the time. But when he returned and walked the streets, he saw his neighborhood anew. A city was never the same from one day to the next. That was what made it so beautiful to some and so unnerving to others. But for Walter and his friends, the Harlem riot of 1935 signified the end of a dream. The renaissance was dead, its casualties numerous.

The novelist Wallace Thurman — most known for his book *The Blacker the Berry* — had perished at thirty-two after suffering an alcohol-induced internal hemorrhage in front of party guests in his own home. Popular Black singer and actor Charles Gilpin had plunged into alcoholic poverty, dying at fifty-one. Nella Larsen, whose novels *Quicksand* and *Passing* made her a key figure in the Harlem Renaissance, had been accused of plagiarism and had disappeared from the scene, never to publish again.

Langston Hughes despaired over living on white patronage. "[I] could very easily [be] hungry and homeless on a cold floor, anytime Park Avenue got tired of supporting me," he chronicled. The writer George Schuyler, whose *Black No More* was among the best satirical novels about the Harlem Renaissance, eulogized its death: "Gone was the almost European atmosphere . . . the music, laughter, gaiety, jesting and abandon. Instead, one noted the same excited bustle, wild looks and strained faces to be seen in a war time soldier camp. . . . The happy-go-lucky Negro of song and story was gone forever."

The hangover had hit the white artistic world too. Modernist poet Hart Crane had jumped off a cruise ship in the Gulf of Mexico in a panic of alcohol-induced psychosis, his body never found. F. Scott Fitzgerald had caged himself into walls of alcoholism, nursing his mentally ill wife, Zelda, while running out of money and friends. Many of Broadway's once hopping theaters were boarded up. Florenz Ziegfeld — star impresario of the 1920s stage — had died broke.

At NAACP headquarters, hope was drying up along with what was left of the money. Board president Joel Spingarn threatened to resign. When Spingarn took the role of board president five years earlier, he had told his colleagues, "Perhaps few of us realize what an extraordinary Association ours really is. . . . It is one of the few organizations in the world in which men and women . . . have been able to work in harmony, and to serve a single cause, side by side." Now? Not so much. "When I joined the Association," Spingarn wrote to the board, "we had what was a thrilling program, revolutionary for its time, and one that gave us a little hope of solving the whole problem. Now we have only [legal] cases, no program, and no hope."

Spingarn and the others had trouble understanding Walter White's vision. Fighting with lawyers and in politics was all high stakes and long game. The plan, Walter promised, would work in the end. It would take time, but time only existed as long as there was money to pay for it.

Walter begged Spingarn to stay. It would be "a calamity," he told the board, if Spingarn left at this time, that "certain factions" (Du Bois) would spread rumors that the NAACP was on its "last legs." Spingarn agreed to stay on, but for how long, no one could say. And so, as Walter put it, "the dismal decade of the thirties grew more and more dismal."

DAYS AFTER the Harlem riot, the final debate over the Costigan-Wagner bill began in the Capitol. GOOD LUCK, a Chicago NAACP leader named Frances Williams telegrammed Walter in Washington. STEADY NERVES GANGS OF FAITH PLUS COUPLE OF BREAKS [*sic*].

When Senators Costigan and Wagner made their final speeches on the Senate floor, the crowded galleries were "held spellbound," as one person in the room observed. Walter sat in the gallery writing notes. "Crowded galleries laughing derisively at old-fashioned oratory about 'sanctity of our firesides' and 'purity of our womanhood,'" he scribbled. "Chinese, Japanese, Haitian occupants of diplomatic gallery trying to mask their amazement that there should even be debate on such a humane measure. . . . Mrs. Costigan sitting in family gallery every day, all day, watching the fight and showing her deep and sincere interest."

Meanwhile, anticipation of the vote riveted Washington. "Called the political football of many administrations," commented the *Chicago Defender*, "the anti-lynching bill has caused more agitation in the nation than any other single measure during the present century." The NAACP was leveraging all the power it could to push the Roosevelt administration to support it.

At the end of the hearings the Senate filibuster began again. Senators from the South launched into a series of speeches that would not end until the group voted for an adjournment — without a vote on the bill. Those were the rules. According to Walter's tally, fifty-one senators would have voted yes and twenty-one no, with the rest abstaining. But the filibuster prevented a vote, and the Costigan-Wagner bill was declared dead on May 2, 1935, six weeks after the Harlem riot. It was said that the federal anti-lynching bill was once again lynched.

Walter was furious. He had warned the president that if the Senate filibustered the bill, it would give license to lynchers in the future. More people were going to get killed. He wrote Roosevelt a blistering letter.

"My dear Mr. President," it began. "It is my belief that the utterly shameless filibuster could not have withstood the pressure of public opinion had you spoken out against it." Roosevelt had appointed Walter to an advisory council on the Virgin Islands to try to appease him, and now Walter resigned the post. "In justice to the cause I serve," he wrote, "I cannot continue to remain even a small part of your official family."

He then released a statement that would prove surprisingly prophetic: "Does America expect — or dare she demand — fealty and whole-hearted support in the next war from these twelve million [African Americans] when she deliberately refuses to protect them from mob violence in time of peace?"

A COUPLE OF WEEKS LATER, on June 25, 1935, racial tension took on another form, as sixty thousand people jammed Yankee Stadium to see Detroit's Joe Louis, "the Brown Bomber," take on Primo Carnera of Italy, the white heavyweight known as "Mussolini's Man." The Louis-Carnera fight was billed as America versus Europe, and Black versus white. It was "the first significant mixed heavyweight bout that has been staged in New York in modern times, since the turn of the century, if not longer," as the *New York Times* put it.

Among those in Yankee Stadium that night were thirteen hundred police officers and emergency squads with hand grenades and tear gas bombs. Fifteen thousand African Americans had come out to cheer on the Brown Bomber, making this one of the largest mixed-race crowds

New York had ever seen. Officials feared the violence outside of the ring could get bloodier than anything inside the ropes.

Among the boxing greats who saw Louis knock out Carnera in the sixth round were James J. Braddock (the reigning heavyweight champ), Jack Johnson, Jack Dempsey, Jack Sharkey, and Max Baer. When the next day's newspapers listed the celebrities who attended, they mentioned Mayor Fiorello La Guardia, orchestra leader Duke Ellington, and Walter White of the NAACP.

By the second half of the 1930s, Walter began to transcend the NAACP in the national consciousness. Even as the association struggled to stay financially afloat, its chief executive's public persona grew. Throughout his career, Walter had mastered the art of publicity and self-promotion, capitalizing on victories and defeats alike, using the vitriol of his enemies as well as the praise of his fans to thrust himself into the center of conversations. Now tangible fame had swept him up and placed him in the pantheon among Hollywood stars and renowned athletes. As one friend said of him, "Walter White was a man who attracted excitement and activity like a magnet. He lived in a star-studded world."

His alliance with Eleanor Roosevelt moved him closer into FDR's inner circle, and he met with the president in the Oval Office now with some regularity. He met with Albert Einstein. In northern cities his speaking events drew lines around the block, and when he ventured into the South, the KKK turned out in protest. By the 1936 election season, politicians on the national scene could no longer ignore Walter. Instead, many courted him like sycophants.

"Walter White is conducting a Negro campaign along an extended front," the Charleston *News and Courier,* a white South Carolina newspaper, stated in 1936. "The Republican party has always been his ally—no trouble in that direction. Now he has the Northern Democrats on their knees, and he means to see that they give political rights to the Southern Negroes. He is one of them and is entirely sincere; he won't sell out, and most of the office-holding politicians will. Hence he is dangerous—to the white South."

Walter never endorsed FDR. But his relationship with the First Lady communicated volumes. The 1932 election saw the beginning of the defection of the Black vote from the Republicans. Four years later, for the first time in modern history, the majority of Black voters chose the Democratic ticket, helping to launch Roosevelt into his second term. Roughly 70 percent of African Americans voted for Roosevelt in 1936, and many of them had never cast ballots before. Black power was becoming something real, and the white-skinned Walter White was its most dynamic leader. The day after the election, Walter sent a note to Mrs. Roosevelt.

"Isn't it amazing," he wrote, "how overwhelming the President's triumph has been?"

In 1937 Walter found senators willing to introduce another federal anti-lynching bill — the Wagner-Van Nuys-Gavagan bill. When Senator James F. Byrnes of South Carolina spoke out against the bill, he attacked Walter personally in a historic speech on the floor of the Senate, as Walter watched from his seat on the sidelines:

> One Negro, whose name has heretofore been mentioned in the debate, Walter White, secretary of the Association for the Advancement of the Colored People, has ordered this bill to pass. . . . If Walter White, who from day to day sits in the gallery, should consent to have this bill laid aside, the advocates would desert it as quickly as football players unscramble when the whistle of the referee is heard. For years this man White has worked for this bill. Now that he has secured the balance of voting power in so many states he can order its passage. . . . What legislation he will then demand, no man knows.

Twenty years of fighting against lynching had made Walter a public sensation, and lauding him in the press became something of a sport. *Time* magazine put him on the cover in 1938, naming him the Man of the Week. He was "dapper," *Time* said. "Spunky." He was "the most potent leader of his race in the U.S." Langston Hughes wrote a biographical poem about Walter: "Ballad of Walter White." The *Atlanta Daily World* called him an "apostle of human liberty." The *Afro-American:* "The nation owes Walter White, valiant hero of the anti-lynching crusade, a vote of thanks for what he has accomplished, to uphold the good name and honor of the American people in their own eyes and in the eyes of the world. Walter White deserves to go down in history as one of the moral heroes of America."

"In Mr. White we have one who has all the virtues of knighthood," one scribe said of him. "Courage, love, loyalty, and the spirit of adventure. He is our Sir Galahad, in search of the Holy Grail of human kindness." "Modest, genial Walter White is too well known now to investigate lynchings but in the streets of Washington," the DC journalist John Jasper wrote, "he is stopped every block or so by strangers who shake his hand and ask how they can help in the fight his association is waging."

In 1938 Roosevelt finally broke his silence and spoke out in favor of a federal anti-lynching bill, which was once again stuck in a Senate filibuster. Washington correspondent Ralph Matthews spoke for many when he wrote, "Observers are now asking whether President Roosevelt is taking the advice of Walter White." So powerful had Walter become, his apartment was called "the White House of Negro America."

Frustrated by Walter's relentless push for the anti-lynching bill and the success he was seeing in the public sphere, southern senators hired private investigators to snoop on Walter's private life, offering to pay sources for any untoward facts. Whether there were rumors of Walter's infidelity or his enemies were just hunting for dirt is not known.

"My life is an open book," he told the press. "I have nothing to be ashamed of."

26

None of us got where we are solely by pulling ourselves up by our bootstraps. We got here because somebody — a parent, a teacher, an Ivy League crony or a few nuns — bent down and helped us pick up our boots.

— Thurgood Marshall, America's first Black Supreme Court justice

WHEN WHITE JOINED in the winter of 1918, the NAACP consisted of just a handful of staffers; now, at the end of the 1930s, the offices on Fifth Avenue and Fourteenth Street teemed with some seventy employees. "We had a giant banner inscribed with the words 'A Man Was Lynched Today,'"* recalled Roy Wilkins, "and on the days we learned of lynchings we put the flag up outside the window of the office alongside the American flags that flew so cheerfully up and down Fifth Avenue. The owner of our building became so alarmed over the banner that he threatened to cancel our lease. We had to stop flying it, but we had made our point."

Despite the big staff, the association needed new blood. With a little luck and good timing, Walter found it in a thirty-year-old lawyer who officially joined the staff in 1938.

Walter had first met Thurgood Marshall while working on a murder case in 1933. Marshall was in his senior year of law school at the time. Just as Walter had James Weldon Johnson as a mentor, Marshall was the

---

* An image of this flag flying at headquarters is on the cover of this book.

protégé of the Harvard-trained dean of Howard University Law School, Charles Houston, who worked part-time for the NAACP. Walter recalled, "There was a lanky, brash young senior law student who was always present. I used to wonder at his presence and sometimes was amazed at his assertiveness in challenging positions taken by Charlie and the other lawyers. But I soon learned of his great value to the case in doing everything he was asked, from research on obscure legal opinions to foraging for coffee and sandwiches."

When Marshall graduated law school, he opened a small practice in his home city of Baltimore, and desperately on edge financially, he began to piece together cases to fight for education rights for African Americans. In 1935, Marshall won a Black student named Donald Gaines Murray entrance into the University of Maryland's law school. Murray had graduated from Amherst College and was fully qualified but denied due to segregation. In *Murray v. Pearson,* Marshall convinced the Maryland courts that Murray had a constitutional right to attend the University of Maryland Law School, defeating the state's attorney general. The case drew national attention. "What's at stake here is more than the civil rights of my client," Marshall told the press. "It's the moral commitment stated in our country's creed."

Using *Murray v. Pearson* as a precedent, Marshall began to fight for education rights in other states, and in 1938 Walter hired him to head up a new legal arm of the association. "In those days," Wilkins recorded, "Thurgood was lean, hard, and Hollywood-handsome.... He had a neatly trimmed moustache and a way of wrinkling his brow that made him look like a skeptical house detective listening to the alibi of a philandering husband caught in flagrante with a lady of the night."

Walter had an immediate connection with Marshall. Both liked scotch and late nights. Both were marvelous storytellers. Both believed in the inherent truth and justice of integration, that if Black and white could mix freely, live next to one another, work together, and educate together, there would be no color line and no race violence. Both Walter and Marshall were also fearless fighters. Marshall grew up on the tough streets of Baltimore, the son of a railroad porter, who taught him early on: "If somebody calls you a 'Nigger' take it up right then and there. Either win or lose right then and there."

Walter took this young attorney under his wing and gave him the resources to take his education battle national. As Marshall biographer Juan Williams put it, Marshall's "exposure to Walter White had opened his eyes to the idea of civil rights as theater and the power of using dramatic situations to the NAACP's advantage. . . . Walter White also gave Marshall a personal link to high-society white politicians and corporate lawyers. . . . [Marshall] would occasionally go to White's Manhattan apartment for dinner with such prominent political figures as the Republican Wendell Willkie, who ran for president in 1940."

On December 12, 1938, Marshall won a case in the Supreme Court that opened the doors of the University of Missouri Law School to its first Black student, Lloyd Gaines. During the trial, students at the university marched on campus in Columbia, carrying signs reading WHO OBJECTS TO NEGROES AT THE UNIVERSITY OF MISSOURI? WE CERTAINLY DO NOT! Marshall learned how dangerous NAACP work could get. Shortly after the Supreme Court ruled in favor of Gaines and his entry into the University of Missouri Law School, Gaines disappeared. He was never seen again, and the mystery of his disappearance has never been solved.

Around this same time, Marshall took a case defending a man named George Porter in Dallas. Porter, who was Black, reported for jury duty, and when he was told to leave because of his race, he refused. A white man threw him down the front steps of the courthouse. Porter sued, arguing he had every right to serve on a jury. When Marshall announced he would take Porter's case, he was told that he could be killed if he showed his face in Dallas. The Dallas chief of police announced publicly: "Don't lay a hand on him. Don't touch Thurgood Marshall. Because I personally will take him and kick the shit out of him. Personally."

Marshall braved the trip, and while the case did not amount to much, his mission to Dallas put the state's governor on notice that the NAACP had the legal know-how and the political power to fight for the rights of

Black citizens. Weeks later a Black man named W. L. Dickson served on a jury in Texas, with personal police protection assigned by the governor himself.

Walter was particularly excited about Marshall's work in education law — fighting for students and for equal pay for Black teachers. Each of Marshall's education cases was a block in a foundation upon which he and the NAACP were going to challenge the constitutionality of segregation in schools nationwide, and thus, segregation altogether. Walter's activism was first spawned by the battle to save the seventh grade for Black public school students in Atlanta back in 1917. His odyssey had begun with the fight for equal education, and although he did not know it yet, this same fight would be how his story would end.

ONE DAY EARLY IN 1939 Walter was in the Senate gallery in Washington listening to the verbal sparring when a reporter he knew named Mary Johnston came to him. She told him a distressing story. The forty-two-year-old singer Marian Anderson — famous across the United States and Europe and a good friend of Walter's — had a Washington, DC, concert scheduled, but it had been canceled when the venue she was to sing in, Constitution Hall, barred her due to its policy against Black performers. Constitution Hall was owned by a group called the Daughters of the American Revolution. Eleanor Roosevelt was a member, and she was horrified. She quit the group, writing in her newspaper column, "To remain as a member implies approval of that action, and therefore I am resigning."

Humiliated, Marian Anderson's team decided to hold the concert anyway, this time in a local city high school. But the Washington, DC, Board of Education canceled that event for the same reason, even though this high school was a public, tax-supported institution.

When Walter went to see her, he found her in bad shape. "Marian was so heartbroken," he recalled, "that she vowed never to sing again." Walter had an idea. What if she held her concert outdoors? He suggested that she sing at the foot of the Lincoln Memorial, so the giant statue of Lincoln could be watching over her, from twenty feet high. It would be a free concert. The Lincoln Memorial was under the jurisdiction of the Department of the Interior, so Walter went to see the department's second in command, Oscar Chapman. Walter was in a hurry that morning because he had to catch a train to New York. In Chapman's office, he explained Anderson's predicament.

"Oscar," Walter said, "wouldn't it be a ten strike if we could have her sing at the feet of Lincoln, at the Lincoln Memorial?"

Chapman thought for a moment. He said, "You know, Walter, that monument has never been used for a public meeting since it was built, since Harding dedicated it, and it's never been used. That would be a ten strike, and that's the place she ought to sing. And if we're going to do that, let's do it with all the support we can get."

Walter headed for the train, and Chapman headed for the office of his boss, Secretary of the Interior Harold Ickes. Once Ickes was on board, they went to the president and got clearance.

On April 9, 1939, Anderson — wearing a mink coat because of the chill in the air — walked onto a stage and stared out. The crowd sprawled across the National Mall — 75,000 strong, Black and white together. Walter was there with his wife and two kids. "No member of that audience will ever forget the sight of Miss Anderson emerging from a small anteroom beside [the] statue of Lincoln," he recalled. She herself would remember feeling terribly nervous, because the crowd was so big and because the concert had been so heavily publicized. NBC Radio was taking her nationwide. "I could not run away from this situation," she later recalled. "If I had anything to offer, I would have to do so now."

An NBC announcer introduced her: "Marian Anderson is singing this public concert at the Lincoln Memorial because she was unable to get an auditorium to accommodate the tremendous audience that wishes to hear her."

Anderson had only a piano accompaniment. The pianist was white, and she was Black, so the two were like piano keys themselves. She launched into her first song: "My Country, 'tis of Thee," otherwise known as "America." She sang "Gospel Train," and "My Soul Is Anchored in the Lord." "She sang these religious spirituals and I'm telling you, there wasn't a dry eye in the whole audience as I looked around," recalled Oscar Chapman. "Not a dry eye."

At the end of the show the crowd was so stirred that fans rushed forward, wanting to touch Marian Anderson. Walter sprang to the stage and pleaded into the microphone for people to stay calm, fearing that Anderson would be injured. From the stage he caught sight of a young brown-skinned girl in the crowd. She stood as if in a trance, her arms reaching out in the air wanting to touch the singer. "Tears streamed down the girl's dark face," Walter later wrote. "Her hair was askew, but in her eyes flamed hope bordering on ecstasy. . . . If Marian Anderson could do it, the girl's eyes seemed to say, then I can, too."

In hindsight, Anderson's concert would be called "one of the most important musical events of the twentieth century." In the present, Walter knew it was a tremendous success. Few if any statues embodied more symbolism than Lincoln's. It would not be the last time that Walter White would make use of it.

SOME FOUR MONTHS after Anderson's concert at the Lincoln Memorial, on September 1, 1939, the Nazis invaded Poland. Hitler's highly mechanized brand of war, known as blitzkrieg ("lightning war"), was years in the making. This was something the world had never seen — the first ever fully formed air force attacking without restraint, while on the ground below the tanks rolled. Hitler's number two, Hermann Göring, offered a definition of *blitzkrieg* for the newspapers: "aerial attacks, stupendous in their mass effect, surprise, terror, sabotage, assassination from within, the murder of leading men, overwhelming attacks on all weak points in the enemy's defense, sudden attacks, all in the same second, without regard for reserves or losses."

America was divided — whether to join the war against the Nazis or to stay out of it. "Every time you flicked on the radio or opened the newspaper that last year of the thirties," recalled Wilkins, "you heard about defending democracy. For black Americans there was an unmistakable irony behind the headlines: a country that denied democracy to millions of its citizens in the South was suddenly rousing itself to defend democracy thousands of miles away across the Atlantic."

Walter had been attacking Hitler's anti-Semitism in his speeches as early as 1936, comparing the fate of Jews in Nazi Germany to the terror Black people, experienced in some sections of the South. Walter had many Jewish friends and had counted on wealthy Jewish donors over the years. The way he saw it, the war was shaping up to be a clear-cut fight for justice, against hate and racial persecution.

When the Roosevelt administration began to rearm the country, Walter saw an extraordinary opportunity. World War I had given African Americans a chance to prove their patriotism and to demand their rights. If America went to war again, that same opportunity could arise, only now, African Americans could have the power and the organization of all that the NAACP had become. Already, Black men were lining up at military recruiting stations, only to be turned away. There was not a single Black man or woman in the marine corps, nor the tank corps, nor the army air corps. Only four thousand African Americans were serving in the navy, all of them in strictly menial duties. They cooked, washed dishes, and made officers' beds.

Walter approached the White House with a plan to bring a small delegation of leaders to meet with Roosevelt. His goal: to convince the president to desegregate the military and, if the United States was to join the war, to let African Americans fight. Eleanor Roosevelt convinced her husband to take the meeting, and it was set for September 27, 1940.

WALTER ARRIVED AT THE WHITE HOUSE with A. Philip Randolph, the nation's most powerful Black labor union advocate, among a few select others. With the president sat Secretary of the Navy Frank Knox, Secretary of War Henry Stimson, and Assistant Secretary of War Robert Patterson. Roosevelt sat behind his huge desk. The walls around the oval room were covered in paintings of ships. "You would think," one visitor said when describing this room, "you were in the summer residence of the general manager of a steamship company." When pressed about admitting more

Black soldiers into the fighting ranks, Roosevelt told Walter and Randolph to be patient.

"The thing is we've got to work into this," Roosevelt said. "Now, suppose you have a Negro regiment . . . here, and right over here on my right in line, would be a white regiment. . . . Now what happens after a while, in case of war? Those people get shifted from one to the other. The thing gets sort of backed into."

Sitting beside Walter, Philip Randolph asked about integration in the navy. Secretary Knox could not have been more blunt. It was not going to happen, he said. "We have a factor in the Navy that is not so in the Army, and that is that these men live aboard ship. And in our history we don't take Negroes into a ship's company."

Roosevelt added, "If you could have a Northern ship and a Southern ship, it would be different. But you can't *do* that." He suggested putting Black musical bands aboard white ships, to get the sailors used to the idea.

Walter and Randolph made their case to desegregate the military. Nothing could do more to erase the color line in America, they believed, than to have no color line in the country's fighting troops. When they left the White House, both felt they had made some progress. They waited for a response from the president. A week passed. Then the White House press secretary Stephen Early gave out a statement. "The policy of the War Department," it read, "is not to intermingle colored and white enlisted personnel in the same regimental organizations. This policy has been proven satisfactory over a long period of years and to make changes would produce situations destructive to morale and detrimental to the preparation for national defense."

When Early read this statement to the press, he gave a clear signal that Walter White and Philip Randolph had agreed to it. Walter was so angry, he sent the president a furious telegram, which began, WE REPUDIATE [THE] IMPLICATION IN WHITE HOUSE STATEMENT YESTERDAY THAT SEGREGATION POLICY IN [THE] ARMY WAS APPROVED BY MSSRS. RANDOLPH . . . AND MYSELF. WE MOST VIGOROUSLY PRO-

TEST YOUR APPROVAL OF WAR DEPARTMENT POLICY. Walter then gave excerpts of his telegram to the press.

FDR's administration had announced billions of dollars of military spending, which was already resulting in countless new jobs. In 1940 new war factories were going up all over the country, while private companies were receiving huge federal contracts to convert factories over to building military equipment. After a decade of the Depression, Americans were desperate for work, and war plants were refusing to hire Black workers. The general manager of North American Aviation announced, "Negroes will be considered only as janitors. It is the company policy not to employ them as mechanics and aircraft workers." Standard Steel of Kansas City: "We have not had a Negro working in 25 years and do not plan to start now." Vultee Aircraft, out of Los Angeles: "It is not the policy of this company to employ other than of the Caucasian race."

Walter had an idea — to create a new bill in Congress outlawing discrimination in hiring in any factory or at any company that was receiving taxpayer funds. The way the NAACP saw it: if Black Americans had to pay taxes like white Americans, why should Black people be barred from federally funded jobs?

On October 2, 1940, Walter wrote to Thurgood Marshall and attorney William Hastie about "our getting introduced in Congress a bill to prohibit discrimination in employment in contracts financed in whole or in part by the Federal Government. . . . I believe we could whip up a tremendous amount of support." In Washington, Walter recruited a team of senators led by Republican William Warren Barbour of New Jersey, who introduced on the floor of Congress Senate Resolution 75, "to make a full and complete investigation into the participation of Negro citizens in all industrial and other phases of the national-defense program." Walter knew that the First Lady was having an awakening regarding civil rights, and she agreed to testify before Congress in support of the resolution.

Ultimately Walter and Philip Randolph came up with an even more ambitious plan, something they called the March on Washington. They created a committee to organize a march they hoped would bring 100,000 people to the nation's capital. At a Harlem rally of the "National

Negro March-on-Washington Committee" at the Salem Methodist Episcopal Church, Mayor Fiorello La Guardia spoke to a rambunctious crowd
of four thousand, as did Walter and David Sarnoff, the president of the
Radio Corporation of America (RCA was building its first "television machines" at the time). In a letter that went out to branches nationwide, the
NAACP urged all its members to get on board.

"The success of this March on Washington may mean a job for you
and thousands of other colored Americans," the letter said. "The March
on Washington is scheduled for July 1st, and is one of the most militant
actions ever planned by Negroes of this country and should be the largest
mass movement in their history. . . . The time to act is now!"

FDR became so unnerved by the planned demonstration, he grew almost desperate to stop it. Such a display would not look good for his administration, and perhaps he feared a race riot on the streets, right at
the gates of the White House. He called on his friend Aubrey Williams,
head of the National Youth Administration. Williams later recalled the
meeting: "When I got into the President's office, I saw that he was tired
and irritable. I said nothing, waiting for him to speak. . . . He rubbed his
eyes and leaned over towards me and said, 'Aubrey, I want you to go to
New York and get Walter and Randolph to call off the march. . . . Get it
stopped.'"

Walter and Randolph refused to back down. So Roosevelt invited
them back to the Oval Office on June 18, 1941, in an attempt to convince
them. "Mr. President," Randolph said, "we want you to issue an Executive
Order making it mandatory that Negroes be permitted to work in these
plants [federally funded war factories]."

"Well, Phil," the president said. "You know I can't do that." He asked
that the march be called off. "What would happen if Irish and Jewish people were to march on Washington?" Roosevelt asked. "It would create
resentment among the American people because such a march would be
considered as an effort to coerce the government and make it do certain
things."

Walter and Randolph were adamant — their march would not be
called off.

"How many people do you plan to bring?" Roosevelt asked.

"One hundred thousand, Mr. President," Randolph said.

Roosevelt turned to Walter. "Walter," he said, "how many people will really march?"

Walter's eyes did not blink. "One hundred thousand, Mr. President."

Six days later FDR signed Executive Order 8802, "to provide for the full and equitable participation of all workers in defense industries, without discrimination because of race, creed, color or national origin." The order also created a Fair Employment Practices Commission to enforce the order. This was the first time in American history that the federal government issued an action to outlaw discrimination in employment. The *New York Times* called Walter "the author of President Roosevelt's Executive Order." A Black attorney named Earl B. Dickerson, who was appointed a member of the new Fair Employment commission, called the executive order "one of the most significant gains for the Negro people since Abraham Lincoln signed the Emancipation Proclamation."

Here was a high moment in a bleak time. The March on Washington was called off. "Meanwhile," Walter recorded, "Hitler's armies were marching across Europe spreading destruction and devastation."

27

Every single man, woman, and child is a partner in the most
tremendous undertaking of our American history.
— Franklin Roosevelt, December 9, 1941

THE AIRPLANES APPEARED ON THE HORIZON at 7:55 a.m. on December
7, 1941. Aboard the ships of Pearl Harbor, loudspeakers crackled out the
alarm: "Air raid! This is no shit!" When Walter White heard the news —
America was now in a shooting war — he put out a statement from the
NAACP.

> Though 13 million American Negroes have more often than not
> been denied democracy, they are American citizens and will as
> in every war give unqualified support to the protection of their
> country. At the same time we shall not abate one iota our struggle
> for full citizenship rights here in the United States. We will fight
> but we demand the right to fight as equals in every branch of the
> military, naval and aviation services.

During the war years, Walter seemed to be everywhere. An ongoing
speaking tour had him on the road hammering home the message of the
importance of integration to patriotism and victory. One writer who saw
Walter speak at a packed Madison Square Garden concluded, "I have
never seen a livelier or more enthusiastic crowd."

When a labor strike at Ford Motor Company in 1941 turned into a dangerous racial standoff between thousands of Black and white auto-workers, Walter was there keeping the peace. When Hollywood started turning out pro–United States propaganda movies, Walter partnered with the 1940 Republican presidential nominee Wendell Willkie and headed to Los Angeles to help create the interracial Emergency Committee of the Entertainment Industry. Its goal: to convince movie studio executives to change the way minorities were portrayed in film.

When deadly rioting exploded in the streets of Detroit in June 1943, Walter was awoken by a phone call from the city's NAACP branch. "The long expected riot had come," he recorded. "A few hours later I was on a plane." Thirty hours of rioting left thirty-four dead, twenty-five of them African Americans. Thurgood Marshall joined Walter in Detroit, and to-gether they launched an investigation into the Detroit race riot of 1943. With the help of professional investigators, in office space hastily set up in the basement of a YMCA, the team produced a scathing report. Accord-ing to their investigation, white Detroit police officers had killed seven-teen Black men.

Six weeks later — on the night of August 1, 1943 — Walter went to sleep early at home at 409 Edgecombe Avenue. He was so exhausted, he told his wife he did not want to be awoken unless "President Roosevelt or Cleopatra" called. He was asleep just a few minutes when the phone rang. An NAACP staffer was on the line. Gladys White said her husband was asleep and was not to be disturbed.

"But does Mr. White know there is a riot going on in Harlem?" the staffer asked.

Minutes later Walter and Roy Wilkins met in the lobby of the apart-ment building where they both lived and caught a taxi. "Roy Wilkins and I rode down Seventh Avenue Sunday evening on our way to the Twenty-Eighth Precinct where Mayor La Guardia and Police Commissioner Val-entine were marshaling and directing their forces," Walter wrote in a newspaper article days later. "Long before we reached 125th Street, the sound of crashing glass rose in waves."

In a squad car, Walter and Mayor La Guardia drove through Harlem, perspiring in the searing August heat. Walter chronicled a montage of despair: "Wild-eyed men and women, whose poverty was pathetically obvious in their shabbiness, roamed the streets, screaming imprecations. . . . One giant of a man . . . stood on the sidewalk, his clenched fists raised in frenzied anger, and from whose face all semblance of patience had been stripped, leaving bare the fears and bitternesses which his dark skin had brought upon him."

A steady rain of objects came pouring down upon the squad car, hurled by people standing above on tenement rooftops. Looters had taken control. Walter would remember an old woman, ravaged by poverty and hunger, holding the hand of a child as they climbed through a smashed window to fill a pillowcase with food from a grocery store. After sunrise, Walter stood at the front desk of the Twenty-Eighth Precinct with Mayor La Guardia watching arrested men and women getting booked. "I have lived in Harlem since 1918," Walter remembered, "but I had never seen such a concentrated despair as I witnessed that morning."

Never had the country experienced such sweeping shifts of cultural forces, with hundreds of thousands of Americans boarding up their homes and businesses and moving for war-economy jobs often in a different county or state. Never had so many women joined the workforce so quickly. From Walter's point of view, the war exigency forced the workforce to integrate racially as never before. With all of that happening at once on the home front, piled upon years of economic depression, convulsions of hate and violence were inevitable. Many Americans were not prepared to accept Blacks and whites living and working together, nor were they happy to see their ways of life changing, helpless to stop it. One of the most memorable utterances of the World War II home front came from the lips of a Detroit assembly line worker, who said, "I'd rather see Hitler or Hirohito win the war than work beside a nigger on an assembly line."

Even the Red Cross stood by Jim Crow. At a time when American military deaths were routinely listed in newspapers, the Red Cross — which billed itself as the "greatest mother in the world" — refused blood donations from African Americans. The charity changed its position in 1942, but it kept blood segregated. Walter found this policy so insulting, he wrote in a newspaper column that the "spineless" racial policy of the Red Cross was "as Nazi as that of Hitler."

After the Harlem riot, Walter sent out a form letter to NAACP branches, asking for reports on the racial situation. Judging from the response, the country was on the verge of something terrifying. From Atlanta: "There is a definite fear among whites and colored that friction may occur at any moment." Mobile, Alabama: "It should be realized by all of us that the mob psychology has been dangerous here for quite a while, and for it to become further animated could mean only open violence." Washington, DC: "It is our feeling that any untoward act would serve as the spark to the flame."

THE WAR YEARS WERE NOT ALL GLOOM. One night early in 1944, the Grand Ballroom of the Roosevelt Hotel in Midtown Manhattan filled with Walter White's friends and admirers. "Even the balcony was packed with tables," recorded the poet Langston Hughes, who was there. Walter appeared with his wife and children.

The Roosevelt was hosting a dinner to commemorate Walter's twenty-five years with the NAACP (the event had been postponed a year due to the war, so Walter was really celebrating his twenty-sixth anniversary). The years showed in his face and in his waist size. He had come to New York an obscure southern "Black" man, on the brink of destiny, half his life ago. Now he sat on a dais with the night's two principal speakers on either side of him — First Lady Eleanor Roosevelt to Walter's right and the 1940 Republican nominee Wendell Willkie to his left — so he was flanked by powerhouses from both major political parties. This was a carefully orchestrated strategy, as Walter was courting favor within both political parties, leveraging the power of the Black vote.

"White has tenderly cultivated a great variety of glittering acquaintances," a New Yorker writer commented about this night. "A man active in public affairs recently hazarded the guess that Walter calls more Very Important People by their first names than anyone else in the country." By all accounts, there were too many speakers that night. Two figures were sadly missing, the two men who had been Walter's greatest inspirations.

James Weldon Johnson had died in a car crash in Maine, and Clarence Darrow had recently passed away at age eighty.

All the evening's monologues boiled down to a singular point, about the NAACP and about Walter White: "that it is an American organization composed of both Negroes and whites," Langston Hughes wrote in a newspaper column about the event, "and that its real work is sustaining the basic truths of American democracy by clearing away the prejudice and bigotry and anti-democratic debris at the base of the great pillars of our national faith. It is made plain that when democracy for any minority is in danger, then democracy for all is in danger."

At the end of the night the checks poured in — $20,000 worth of donations. Walter was given a leather-bound volume with testimonials written inside from three hundred of his friends: Albert Einstein, FBI chief J. Edgar Hoover,* H. L. Mencken, former heavyweight champion of the world Joe Louis, and civil rights activists Philip Randolph and Mary McLeod Bethune, among them.

Under Walter's leadership, the association was growing impressively, galvanizing the African American community around an ideology: with patriotism and sacrifice comes citizenship rights and an end to Jim Crow. "As the Second World War dragged on," remembered Roy Wilkins, "the NAACP grew stronger and stronger." The Depression was finally ebbing; the association saw over $196,000 in revenue in 1943, its greatest year ever, and 90 percent of that income came from dues of $1, proving the power of grassroots organization. That same year the association launched ninety-three new branches in twenty-seven states. The power and mainstreaming of the NAACP was most pronounced during the war, when Eleanor Roosevelt joined the board of directors.

Walter, meanwhile, had reached the pinnacle of his fame. Around

---

* Given Walter's career publicly attacking law enforcement and criticizing presidents, his having a cordial relationship with the FBI chief J. Edgar Hoover is miraculous and perhaps a testament to the NAACP chief's political acumen. It is this author's conjecture that this relationship could only have occurred if Walter was feeding the FBI director information of some sort.

this time he received a letter from his sister Madeline that put his place in American life in perspective. She was a social worker in Atlanta who spent a lot of time in backwoods Georgia where poor African Americans lived in unpainted shacks. "You have no idea," she wrote her brother, "how many of these homes have your picture, often cut out of a newspaper and tacked to a beam. Or pressed on a little cracked mirror. They depend on you. For many of them you are all they have. You and the NAACP . . . So often to them you are the NAACP."

ONE DAY DURING THE WAR Walter's phone rang and, when he picked up, he recognized a voice from his past. It was Poppy Cannon calling. She was working in advertising, specifically on a symposium about the postwar food market, and wanted to get Walter's thoughts about how this market might be different for Black Americans as opposed to Caucasians. He could tell that she had a valid reason for calling but also that she wanted to hear his voice. It had been ten years since they last spoke.

They met for lunch and talked business. She recalled, "I remember looking at him across the table and finding him still charming but somehow remote and middle-aged. He was wearing steel-rimmed glasses which gave him a professorial look. His hair, which had been blond when I saw him last, was now almost white, and he was pounds heavier than he had been. The extra weight, I thought, made him more attractive."

Walter had big plans, and surely he explained them to her. He was going to apply for a war correspondent accreditation, so he could fly off to faraway war zones to study the conditions of Black soldiers. When the lunch ended, Walter and Poppy parted ways. She recorded her thoughts. "I'm quite free at last," she wrote. "I'm not in love with him any more. I just think he's wonderful. But then everybody thinks he's wonderful!"

Soon after, Walter wrote to request his accreditation. "Dear General [A. D.] Surles, I am taking this means of inquiring if the War Department would favor my going as a war correspondent . . . to visit the areas where Negro troops are stationed or have been stationed."

Walter wanted to see the action firsthand — not so much the fighting but how American democracy was functioning in the military under all the pressures of a world war. He was approved for a press credential to report all over the globe on the state of racial relations in war zones. He received from the War Department permission to travel on navy ships and aircraft; he got a letter of introduction from the president of the United States that he could present to diplomatic and military figures; and he got another letter from J. Edgar Hoover giving permission, as Walter put it in a letter of thanks to the FBI chief, "to go right up to the battlefronts."

Filling out his application for his press card, he checked the "Negro" box as his race, blue for his eyes, gray for his hair, and "light" for his complexion. He listed his height as 5'7½" and his weight as 142 pounds, but when he stepped on a scale, it tipped to 169, so that is how it appeared on his press card.

He began the trip in England, where preparations for the D-day invasion were under way. "No sooner had I been billeted in a small hotel in the outskirts of London," he recalled, "than newspaper correspondents swooped down upon me to ask if it were true that I had come overseas as a special investigator for the White House. . . . It was obvious from the beginning that wherever I went and with whomever I talked, my every movement was closely watched."

WALTER TRAVELED THROUGH NORTH AFRICA, meeting the Black soldiers of the Second Cavalry Division in Oran. Then it was on to the Anzio beachhead in Italy, and to the city of Naples, recently captured from Axis occupation. He spent two days in Cairo with Felix Éboué, the Black governor general of French Equatorial Africa. He met with General Eisenhower and with the US ambassador to Britain, John Winant. He visited officers' clubs where more champagne was spilled than most US privates would sip in their lifetimes, as well as military prison camps. All the while, he transmitted his impressions back to the States in a newspaper column he wrote for the *Chicago Defender*.

At one point, in Britain, Walter had a lunch with Lady Astor, the socialite and Britain's first female Member of Parliament, who showed up a half hour late and greeted him by saying, "You *are* an idiot, calling yourself a Negro when you're whiter than I am, with blue eyes and blond hair!"

Walter traveled to the front lines. "War vehicles of every imaginable description rumble by," he described the scene. "Tanks, half-tracks, ammunition trucks, weapon carriers, jeeps and reconnaissance cars. . . . Notempty ambulances bringing back the dead and wounded."

He delivered reports to the generals documenting incidents in which Black soldiers were court-martialed or imprisoned for offenses while white soldiers in the same camps were let off for similar offenses, and instances of flagrant discrimination by white officers against Black privates. In some instances actions were taken in direct response to Walter's reporting. But there were moments of heartbreak on this trip.

In Cairo Walter read a newspaper article about the lynching of a Black man in America, even as American soldiers were fighting and dying to defeat Hitler and his Aryan dogma. On a sand-swept airfield in northern Africa, Walter discovered a propaganda leaflet showing an elderly Black man being held by two white police officers while he was being beaten by a white man — an image from the Detroit race riot of 1943. In Arabic writing was an appeal to soldiers to fight Americans because of their hatred for dark-skinned peoples.

There were triumphant moments too. In the Battle of the Bulge, the Allies were so desperate for soldiers that, for the first time, the army placed Black platoons in white regiments. A white South Carolina soldier reported, "When I heard about it, I said I'd be damned if I'd wear the same shoulder patch they did. After that first day, when we saw how they fought, I changed my mind. They are just like any of the other boys to us." Speaking of Black soldiers who volunteered for combat in the Battle of the Bulge, General Eisenhower reported, "All my commanders reported that these volunteers did excellent work."

Walter interviewed members of the Ninety-Ninth Pursuit Squadron, the first all-Black unit of fighter pilots. These interviews were especially moving because Walter had a nephew who had fought as a pilot and had been shot down over Nazi-occupied territory, recently. Walter later wrote of his nephew, who died in that plane crash, "He hated war, he loathed killing. But he believed that Hitler and Mussolini represented the kind of hate he had seen exhibited in Georgia by the Ku Klux Klan and the degenerate political demagogues. He believed that the war would bring all of that hate to an end."

UPON RETURNING TO THE UNITED STATES, Walter wrote another book, *A Rising Wind*, with miraculous speed, about his experiences in the European theater, then dashed off to the Pacific theater. At one point, he was on the island of Guam, where the most noteworthy moment of his war correspondent work occurred. He met a Black soldier who had been court-martialed twice and was on trial a third time.

"For what were you court-martialed the first time?" Walter asked this prisoner.

"I sat down in a bus on a seat that wasn't for colored," he answered.

"What happened then?"

"They arrested me and put me in solitary confinement for five days on bread and water."

"And what was the charge the second time?"

"I went into a white restaurant and asked to be served food."

"What happened then?"

"The same sentence, sir. Solitary confinement on bread and water for five days."

Walter told this story on a radio news show, on the Columbia Broadcasting System. Mary White Ovington, who was now nearing eighty years of age and still fighting for the NAACP, although in a diminished capacity, remembered hearing Walter on CBS, from New York. She recalled, "It was then that the National Association for the Advancement of Colored People became a living power of sympathy and understanding that was felt around the world. . . . It was then that the NAACP became an international organization."

Walter traveled on to the Philippines. Flying low over territory that had recently been liberated from Japanese occupation, he felt his spine soak up the heavy vibration of the engines, his ears assaulted by the thundering noise in the non-pressurized cabin. Suddenly, he experienced the shock of his life — the plane colliding with antiaircraft fire from the ground. "We were hit," he recalled. "It's a strange thing — under circumstances like that you are very calm."

The plane was going down. He braced himself. His whole life did not flash before his eyes, like so often happens in storybooks. He was not a praying man, but he started to pray. He later remembered the moment: "I said, 'Please God, not yet. I'm not ready to die yet.'" Then shock and clarity came together in the image of a woman's face. He would never know why it happened, or from what crevice of his brain this image came to him. He started saying her name out loud.

"I was saying, 'Poppy, Poppy, Poppy.'"

When the plane hit the ground, Walter was thrown the length of it and knocked unconscious. Someone — he would never learn who — dragged him out of the wreckage. "When I came to," he recalled, "I had the feeling of someone moving away from me and the plane had already burst into flames."

He was left in a daze. Something had changed in him. He did not yet know what he was going to do about it.

THE YEAR 1945 saw history move at such a pace, reading the daily newspaper could feel like living a lifetime. On January 20, FDR inaugurated his unprecedented fourth term. Eighty-two days later he was dead of a cerebral hemorrhage. "Perhaps not since the dawn of history," State Department official Joseph Davies wrote in his diary, "has the passing of a great man been mourned contemporaneously by so many different nations, so many different religions and races, spread over the earth."

The vice president, Harry Truman, Democrat of Missouri, became the thirty-third president of the United States. Truman had never been governor of a state, never mayor of a city. He had no college degree and had never had the money to own his own home. Most Americans knew nothing about him, and his personal obscurity shocked the world. "Here was a man who came into the White House almost as though he had been picked at random off the street," recalled White House correspondent Robert G. Nixon.

The next four months saw the collapse of Nazi Germany, firebombings of Japanese cities that killed many thousands of civilians, the liberation of Nazi death camps, the suicide of Hitler, and the fall of Berlin. There was victory at Okinawa, the Potsdam Conference, the first atomic explosion, the nuclear destruction of Hiroshima and Nagasaki, and the dawn of the Cold War. When leaders of fifty nations gathered in San Francisco for the founding conference of the United Nations, Walter White attended as head of a delegation from the NAACP.

The guns fell silent, and when the most destructive war in human history ended, people across the globe mourned the dead and welcomed the peace. Black soldiers were riding a wave of patriotism and accomplishment. Walter could see a moment of great opportunity, but he knew progress would come at a grave cost. A large majority of those returning Black soldiers would be headed for their homes, back to the Jim Crow South. White later distilled his thinking into the following words:

> The increasingly shorter interval between wars had enabled the world to see all too vividly that once men have been taught that mass killing is both necessary and noble, it is almost impossible to unteach them in the art of murder. Blood lust and hatred cannot be shut off as simply as one turns off a faucet. . . . During the Second World War we heard many disturbing rumors that a number of Southern cities and towns and a few in the North had invested huge sums in machine guns, grenades, tear gas, armored trucks, and other riot-quelling equipment. This material was to be used, as some of the officials of these cities and towns frankly admitted, in case of trouble caused by two groups — Negro veterans and organized labor.

28

The blind soldier fought for me in this war. The least I can do now is fight for him. I have eyes. He hasn't. I was born a white man. And until a colored man is a full citizen like me, I haven't the leisure to enjoy that freedom that colored man risked his life to maintain, for me. I don't own what I have until he owns an equal share of it. Until somebody beats me and blinds me, I am in his debt.

— Orson Welles on Isaac Woodard, *The Orson Welles Commentaries* radio show, 1946

ON FEBRUARY 12, 1946, in the city of Augusta, Georgia, a Black soldier named Isaac Woodard Jr., age twenty-seven, signed papers and was officially discharged from the United States Army. With $44 in cash in his pocket, along with his honorable discharge certificate — which bore the mimeographed signature of President Harry S. Truman — Woodard headed for Augusta's bus station. He had been abroad for a long time, and now that he was home, he once again saw the familiar Colored Only and Whites Only signs all over the bus station. He boarded a Greyhound at roughly 8 p.m., bound for Winnsboro, South Carolina.

He had spent fifteen months serving his country in East Asia, earning a Good Conduct Medal and one Battle Star. Now he was headed home to reunite with his wife and children — on the final stretch of a journey that had taken him more than three years and halfway across the globe. He was still wearing the uniform of the United States Army.

Roughly an hour outside of Augusta, the bus driver — who was Caucasian — pulled over and stopped. Woodard walked to the front of the bus and asked if he could use a restroom. (In 1946 there would have been no bathroom on the bus.)

"Hell no," said the driver, according to future court testimony. "God damn it, go back and sit down. I ain't got time to wait."

Woodard did not appreciate the driver's tone. He must have felt empowered by the uniform he was wearing, and the shining battle medal pinned to the breast. "God damn it, talk to me like I am talking to you," Woodard said. "I am a man just like you."

The driver considered and said, "Go ahead then and hurry back."

On the road again, Woodard sat in his seat among fellow discharged soldiers, who would later testify that he was well behaved and causing no disturbance. At the next town the driver pulled over again and got off the bus. When he returned, he walked to Woodard's seat and said, "Get up, someone outside wants to see you."

Woodard did what he was told and walked off the bus into the night. Two white police officers were waiting.

"This soldier has been making a disturbance on the bus," the driver said.

Woodard tried to explain himself. "I was explaining to them," he later recounted, "what the bus driver said to me and what I said to him, but before I could explain it the police hit me with a billy [club] across my head and told me to shush up. So I hushed."

According to Woodard's testimony, one of the officers took him by the right wrist and twisted it behind his back, pushing him down the street toward an intersection. When the officer jerked Woodard's arm further behind his back, Woodard felt like his arm was going to break and instinctively struggled.

"Have you been discharged?" one of the two police officers asked.

"Yes."

"Don't say 'yes' to me, say 'yes sir.'"

"Yes, sir."

Woodard remembered being beaten at this point. "I had to do something so I grabbed his billy [club] and wrung it out of his hand, and when I did that some other officer throwed a revolver in my back and says, 'Drop that billy. If you don't I will drop you.'" Woodard dropped the club and the beating continued. One of the police officers drove the butt of a billy club into Woodard's face, repeatedly. That was the last thing Woodard remembered.

WHEN HE AWOKE, Woodard found himself lying in a bunk in a jail cell. He stared up at the ceiling but saw nothing. His eyes were swollen shut; he was entirely blinded and in excruciating pain. He had no idea where he was. An officer appeared and said, "All right, come on out. Let's go up and see what the judge has to say to you."

"I can't see," the prisoner said.

"You can feel, can't you?"

The officer took Woodard by the left arm and led him to a faucet so he could wash his eyes. Then the two walked to a courtroom where a judge was waiting.

The police officer said, "This soldier was making a disturbance on the bus last night, drunk and disorderly."

The judge asked, "Do you have anything to say?"

"Yes, sir." Woodard explained that he had not been drunk, that he had simply had words with the bus driver.

"Well, I will tell you," the judge said. "We don't have such stuff like that down here. I fine you fifty dollars and give you thirty days hard labor on the road."

Woodard said, "I will pay the fifty dollars but I don't have it all at the time."

"You have some money in your wallet though," the police officer said. Apparently, while Woodard was unconscious, the police had searched him, including inside his wallet. Woodard produced forty dollars from his wallet, and four singles from one of his pockets. He also had an army discharge check on him for $694.73.

"I see you have a check from the Government," the officer said. "Sign your name here."

Woodard refused. How could he sign anything, he said, if he could not see? "I goes back down," he recalled, "and in a few minutes, after I am back in the cell and laying down, the Chief of Police comes in and he says to me, 'We have some whiskey upstairs. . . . Take a drink.'" Woodard refused. The officer gave him a hot towel for his eyes. Later the police chief decided Woodard needed to go to a hospital. On the way out, Woodard asked, "What town is this?" He remembered the officer saying, "Aiken, South Carolina."

WOODARD SPENT TWO MONTHS IN A HOSPITAL BED, where doctors told him that he was permanently blinded. With the help of family, he then traveled north to the Bronx, New York, where his mother lived in a small apartment at 1100 Franklin Avenue. He had little money and no way to take care of himself or his wife and children financially. He was jobless and helpless.

Someone had the idea that perhaps the NAACP could be of assistance. So one day in the spring of 1946 a cousin of Woodard's took him to the association's headquarters, which had recently moved to a new location — 20 West Fortieth Street, across the street from Bryant Park and the New York Public Library. Walter White would never forget the scene when Woodard entered his office for the first time. The man wore dark glasses with round lenses, shielding his eyes.

"Faltering with the unsureness of the newly blinded," Walter recalled, "Woodard extended his hand into open space in greeting, pathetically attempting to find my hand through the sound of my voice. Not yet skilled enough, his hand wavered a full two feet away from where my hand was, in the manner of one feeling his way in the darkness of a strange place."

Woodard explained that he remembered seeing Walter when the association secretary was traveling in the Pacific theater during the war. "I saw you, Mr. White," Woodard said, "when you visited my outfit in the Pacific. I could see *then*."

Looking at Woodard, Walter felt a profound surge of emotion. It was impossible not to, impossible not to feel vengefulness, pity, and empathy, upon witnessing this man's face. There was so much mythology and symbolism in the act of blinding as punishment. And Woodard was not just any individual. He was a US Army veteran who had earned medals for bravery, in a war that was fought to defeat fascism and Hitler's racist ideology, a war fought for morality and justice. Woodard had come home to have this happen in his own country, while he was still wearing his uniform. Like so many violent tragedies in the past, this one, Walter White knew, presented opportunity.

Walter asked Woodard if he would tell his story in a sworn affidavit. He said yes. Walter fetched a stenographer, who typed as Woodard spoke.

"The policeman asked me was I discharged and when I said yes, that's when he started beating me with a billy club, hitting me across my head. After that I grabbed that billy, wrung it out of his hands. Another policeman came up and threw his gun on me, told me to drop the billy or he'd drop me. So I dropped the billy. He knocked me unconscious. He hollered, 'Get up.' When I started to get up he started punching me in the eyes with the end of his billy."

Walter wrote to Secretary of War Robert Patterson, addressing him as Bob as they had become good friends over the years, and Patterson wrote back immediately. Because Woodard was a civilian at the time of the incident, the War Department had no jurisdiction, nor was Woodard entitled to any injury benefits from the army. "Because of the serious nature of the facts alleged in this case," Patterson wrote Walter, "I have written a personal letter to Governor Ransome J. Williams of South Carolina." Who, as far as Walter was to learn, never commented publicly on the case.

Walter wrote J. Edgar Hoover of the FBI. He wrote US attorney general Tom Clark. Then he wrote a memorandum that went out to every branch of the NAACP. "If he can be treated so today," Walter wrote of Woodard, "other Negro veterans will be subjected to similar outrages in the future, as well as members of other minorities. The National Office, therefore, is seeking the aid of every branch in a nation-wide campaign of pressure upon the authorities and the stirring of public indignation so that Mr. Woodard's attackers will be brought to justice and punished to the full extent of the law." Walter's memo called for mass meetings, placards, handbills, sound trucks, speakers at veterans' facilities and churches, and a campaign of letter writing to President Harry Truman, Secretary Patterson, and General Omar Bradley of the Army, who was head of the Veterans Administration.

Then, in the summer of 1946, Walter lit up a firestorm in the press. The *Chicago Defender* ran a front-page headline on July 20: VETERAN'S EYES GOUGED OUT BY HATE-CRAZED DIXIE POLICE. The story showed a photo of Isaac Woodard being aided by his sad-faced mother. "For sheer bestiality and fascist terror the terrible story told by young Woodard is without parallel in all my experience," Walter was quoted as saying.

In Aiken, South Carolina — the location where Woodard claimed he had been beaten — authorities responded with bafflement. They had no record of anyone named Isaac Woodard being booked or beaten. They had no record of any prisoner being transferred to a hospital. They had no record of anyone named Woodard at all. Were they lying?

ONE DAY IN 1946, while the Woodard case was breaking, Walter had a speaking engagement in Westport, Connecticut, which was a handful of miles from where Poppy Cannon was living, in Redding. He telephoned her.

"Your office tells me that you are working at home today," he said. "How would you like to meet me at the train and have a late lunch?"

"Let me cook a sandwich here," she answered. "Or better still, I have some new peas. . . . I'll make you pea soup with champagne and then drive you to Westport."

They ate lunch on her porch on a sunny day under a branch of maple leaves, then went for a walk in the woods behind her house. She was embarrassed when she got them lost. When they found their way back to her house, Walter said abruptly, "Have you anything to drink around here?" He found a bottle of brandy and filled a water glass halfway, throwing it back as if it were a shot. She looked at him wide-eyed.

"I need this," he said. "There is something I've been wanting to tell you for a long time. Don't look so stricken."

"Don't say to me again that we mustn't see each other any more. I can't bear it."

"That wasn't what I had in mind," Walter said.

He told her he had been in a loveless marriage for more years than he could count. Poppy later recorded of this moment, "He told me how things had been between him and his wife for more than twenty years."

She instantly began to cry. "But I am glad," she said. "I am so relieved. We're not lost any more. I'm crying about all those years, all those wasted, crowded, empty years."

He returned to New York, and she began to write him long letters at his office in her almost illegible scribble, ending them with professions of love that seemed almost desperate. "As you may have gathered, my beloved," she wrote in one, "I love you — beyond all measure, beyond all reason, beyond all the words there are to tell!" In another she wrote, "When I think of you I wonder, darling, how any mortal man can be so perfect. In other words — I love you." She called the NAACP offices incessantly. The office switchboard operator grew so irritated that she said, "If that Mrs. Cannon calls Mr. White once more, I'll go crazy. She always wants to know where he is, where she can leave a message. She never takes, 'Mr. White is not in' without trying to track him down."

Even with all the phone calls, there appeared to be no gossip within the NAACP offices that anything in Walter's personal life was amiss. Evidence suggests, however, that his wife had begun to hear rumors — that she knew what was going on.

Walter was turning fifty-three that summer of 1946, but these had been hard years. Perhaps he knew then that he was not well. He would have his first heart attack in less than a year. The assistant secretary, Roy Wilkins, fearing for Walter's health, had been urging him to take his foot off the proverbial gas pedal. "[We] have been begging you to take a rest and slow down your many activities," Wilkins told Walter. "You must check your darting hither and yon. You are too valuable, you have too rich and necessary an experience to be lost to the cause."

But Walter could not slow down; he did not know how. If he was ever going to do something about his marriage, it was now or never.

IN 1946, the wave of postwar racial violence that Walter feared would come finally did. Just as had happened after the Great War, when Walter was starting out at the NAACP, Black veterans were returning from battle with pride and patriotism, hoping for full citizenship rights. Jim Crow had other things in mind.

On February 25, a Black woman named Gladys Stephenson went into a repair shop to have her radio fixed, in Columbia, Tennessee. The man who owned the shop, who was white, charged her a hefty amount, and when she got her radio back, it still did not work. With her nineteen-year-old son, James, by her side, she protested. When the shop owner and another white man began to beat and kick her, her son — who had just been discharged after three years in the navy — came to her rescue. He threw the radio repairman through the plate-glass window of his shop. When the police came, they arrested Mrs. Stephenson and James. The Stephensons were never charged with any crime, but soon after their apprehension, a mob of white men gathered at the edge of Columbia's Black neighborhood.

By darkness that night, police cars were blocking the roads. Streetlights were shot out. Black residents, many of them war veterans, had organized and were armed. The first of America's many postwar race riots began.

More than one hundred African Americans were arrested, and just two white Tennesseans (for drunkenness). Twenty-five of the Black defendants stood trial, in a courtroom before a white judge and an all-white jury. Thurgood Marshall represented the defendants, and Walter attended parts of the trial. "It is doubtful whether any other trial in the history of America was ever conducted under more explosive conditions," he recounted. "Open threats were made by the unshaven overall-clad spectators that the lawyers who dared defend Negroes would wind up in Duck

River." Outside in the streets, signs were posted: NIGGER, READ AND RUN. DON'T LET THE SUN GO DOWN ON YOU HERE. IF YOU CAN'T READ, RUN ANYWAY.

Marshall successfully got acquittals for all but one defendant. After the trial ended, Marshall was apprehended by police, accused of drunk driving, and driven in an unmarked car to Duck River, where through the car window he saw that a group of white men had gathered by the water — presumably to lynch him. Marshall's fellow lawyers had followed the unmarked police car, and seeing that there were eyewitnesses, the police ultimately let Marshall go. Walter believed that if it were not for the eye-witnesses, Thurgood Marshall would have never been heard from again.

Five months later, Walter was alerted to yet another tragedy. In Wal-ton County, Georgia, a mob of white men murdered four African Amer-icans — two men and their wives, one of the men having recently been honorably discharged from the US Army. Two weeks after that, a young Black man named John Jones, recently honorably discharged from the army, was tortured and lynched in Minden, Louisiana. The *Pittsburgh Courier*'s front-page headline: DIXIE "REIGN OF TERROR" SPREADS. The famed columnist Walter Winchell wrote Walter directly in disbelief over the Jones murder's sickening details; the slaying was "one of the most unbelievable stories I have ever come across in my 28 years of dealing with human cruelty," Winchell wrote Walter. "I shudder for America if it lets such cold-blooded savagery go unpunished."

From Walter's point of view, the nation was at war. All these cases had him working around the clock, and he found his only relief by the side of Poppy Cannon, the white woman he loved in secret. "It is as bad now as the Bloody Summer of 1919 at the end of the last war," he told Poppy. "There is the same tidal wave of violence." She recalled the mo-ment when he said this to her: "His face was chalky white. There was a blueness around his lips which was terrifying. His hands were never still. His cigarette case flipped open again and again and again."

"How can we stop it?" he asked her. "Who is to stop it?"

"There are a lot of decent people in this world. They can stop it."

"But they don't."

Ultimately, the story of Isaac Woodard went viral, by 1946 standards. It was the blinding of Isaac Woodard that sparked a national sensation and awakened the country's conscience as nothing had before.

IN THE SUMMER of 1946 Walter announced that he was offering a $1,000 reward for the name of the police officer who had blinded Woodard. Newspapers quoted witnesses on the bus the night of the incident saying Woodard's conduct was "proper at all times." Heavyweight champion of the world Joe Louis joined the protest.

"It's the same kind of thing Hitler did," Louis said from his training facility in Pompton Lakes, New Jersey. "We went over there and our boys fought and died to stop Hitler doing this. And we come back and see the same thing here. It's a doggone shame, that's what it is. It took hundreds of thousands of men to get Hitler. We gotta get together now. An Army, white and black."

Harlem's *New York Amsterdam News* ran story after story about the case. One showed photos of the blinded Woodard with his family, under the headline BLINDING OF ISAAC WOODARD, AMERICAN HERO. The *Atlanta Daily World:* BLINDING OF VET SHOCKS NATION.

Walter had the idea to reach out to the thirty-one-year-old Hollywood star Orson Welles, who hosted a national Sunday radio show called *Orson Welles Commentaries*. Welles put together a series of episodes pounding home the gory details of the Woodard story, and it was through these broadcasts that much of America heard the name Isaac Woodard for the first time.

"It was just another white man with a stick," Welles told his audience, "who wanted to teach a Negro boy a lesson to show a Negro boy where he belonged — in the darkness." In another broadcast, Welles told his listeners how the policeman who did this was still at large, his identity unknown. He called the man "Officer X" and even hired private investigators to find him.

YOUR BROADCAST ON ISAAC WOODARD CASE YESTERDAY WAS SUPERB, Walter told Welles by telegram, after one episode. OUR WARM THANKS.

A new witness came forward, saying, "The bus operator came into the bus with three police officers and pointed to Isaac Woodard. One of the policemen came into the back of the bus and took Woodard out. When they got him outside one of the policemen took out a blackjack and smashed Woodard across the head. . . . Then they carried him down the street. That is the last I saw of him."

On August 16 the NAACP helped launch a benefit for Woodard at Lewisohn Stadium, an outdoor amphitheater between 136th and 137th Streets in Harlem. Twenty thousand people attended. New York's new mayor, William O'Dwyer, gave the keynote speech. The *New York Amsterdam News* catalogued what it called "the million dollar list of dazzling stars" who attended: Orson Welles, bluesman W. C. Handy, radio personality Milton Berle, Cab Calloway and his band, Nat King Cole and his trio. The white folk singer Woody Guthrie performed a song he had written for this concert, "The Blinding of Isaac Woodard," and received what he called "the loudest applause I've ever got in my whole life."

"Nothing in the history of New York City approaches the appalling case of this young veteran," one reporter covering the event concluded. Another called the benefit "the greatest, most spectacular affair of its kind ever staged in the Harlem sector."

In the night's climactic moment, Isaac Woodard himself was led out onto the stage by the fighter Joe Louis. Walter White was on the stage with Woodard, who spoke so softly that the microphone barely picked up his cracking voice. But the packed theater was so quiet, everyone heard every word from Woodard's mouth, and countless in the stadium that night were reduced to tears. Poppy Cannon was in the crowd. "Sightless Isaac Woodard, returning war veteran of the Pacific, told quietly the story of his arrest and blinding by a policeman," she remembered. "He spoke only a little while but the story seemed long as history and old as evil. We sat in a paralysis of horror and pity."

Roughly one week after this benefit, a police officer finally came forward and solved the mystery. The beating had not occurred in Aiken, South Carolina, but in Batesburg, twenty-eight miles north. Under pressure due to the national outrage, Batesburg chief of police L. L. Shull admitted to the act, saying that Woodard was drunk and resisting arrest, even though witnesses attested otherwise. "I hit him across the front of the head after he attempted to take away my blackjack," Shull said. "I grabbed it away from him and cracked him across the head. . . . I was no harsher than was necessary to complete the arrest."

Demands for Shull's arrest came in newspaper editorials from all over the country, and from Orson Welles. "Officer X, we know your name now," Welles said on his radio show. "Now that we found you out we'll never lose you. You can't get rid of me, we have an appointment." The protest showed no signs of slowing down. A convict on death row named William Copeland, facing the electric chair, offered to give Woodard his eyeballs. A Philadelphia doctor named Henry L. Gowens offered to create a pair of plastic eyeballs for Woodard.

Walter knew the only way he could achieve justice was to go to the top, so he wrote to the White House. His meeting with the new president, Harry Truman, was scheduled for 11:45 a.m. on Thursday, September 19.

WALTER ARRIVED in the Oval Office with a delegation of six other civic leaders. The president's appointment calendar alerted him that a delegation was coming because of "concern over grave danger to [the] country caused by current wave of mob violence, particularly against Negro veterans." But Truman was otherwise unprepared for what was about to happen in his office that day. He sat behind his big desk, which had a wooden sign on it reading THE BUCK STOPS HERE!

Still new on the job, Truman was a mystery on the race question. His home state of Missouri was fully segregated. It was known that both sides of his family had supported the South in the Civil War and were slave owners. Newspapers had even published rumors that Truman had been a member of the KKK back in the 1920s. The story was proven false, but still, many in Washington believed that Truman would ally with the southern powerhouses of his own Democratic Party on the race question. He had appointed James Byrnes — a South Carolina politician who had actively opposed the federal anti-lynching bill—as secretary of state, and Byrnes had become Truman's most trusted advisor. When Truman became president, South Carolina senator Burnet Maybank had confided in a friend, "Everything's going to be all right—the new President knows how to handle the niggers."

Truman was about to prove Senator Maybank dead wrong.

The president sat with his elbows resting on the arms of his chair and his fingers interlocked on his stomach, listening to Walter speak. Summoning all the poignancy he could, Walter told the story of the recent lynchings of four black Americans, two married couples, in rural Walton County, Georgia. Their names were George and Mae Murray Dorsey, and Roger and Dorothy Malcom. George Dorsey had served his country in the army, in wartime. His own countrymen had taken his life—and had gotten away with it.

Walter told the story of the recent lynching in Minden, Louisiana. The victim's name was John Cecil Jones. He had also served his country in the army during the war. His own countrymen had taken his life—and had gotten away with it.

Finally, Walter told the story of the blinding of Isaac Woodard. As he spoke, he could see the president's face reddening. At the time, the end of the summer of 1946, Truman was presiding over the nation's transformation from a wartime to a peacetime economy. He faced crippling crises—a housing shortage that saw endless numbers of war veterans homeless, labor strikes that threatened to cripple the economy, and questions over what should be done with the atomic bomb. Truman had not known the details of the Woodard case. He was shocked.

"My God!" he said. "I had no idea it was as terrible as that! We've got to do something!"

With those words, the modern civil rights movement began.

29

From Frederick Douglass to Walter White, the value of Negro speakers and writers is that they have acted as a kind of thorn in the side of American democracy — not only working for racial equality but for real democracy for all American people.
— Langston Hughes, 1948

WITH WALTER AND HIS DELEGATION IN THE OVAL OFFICE, Truman came up with the idea to create a federal committee to study the field of civil rights in America.

"I'll create it by executive order," he said, "and pay for it out of the President's contingent fund."

The next day the president wrote a letter to his attorney general, Tom Clark. "I had as callers yesterday some members of the National Association for the Advancement of Colored People," Truman wrote. He was "alarmed at the increased racial feeling all over the country," and asked for a special commission to uncover the facts. The attorney general immediately launched an investigation into the Isaac Woodard case. G-men dispatched to Batesburg, South Carolina, and began a pressure campaign to force local authorities to arrest L. L. Shull, the chief of police, who had admitted to assaulting Woodard.

Events moved quickly. Eight days after Walter's meeting with Truman, the federal Justice Department made the bold move of filing a case against Shull. Grounds were shaky; because no federal anti-lynch law or any such applicable law existed, did federal prosecutors have jurisdiction?

States' rights advocates and southern politicians were apoplectic. But the Justice Department pushed forward anyway. Shull, a big man at six feet and well over two hundred pounds, was indicted.

This was news — that a white police officer would have to stand trial for beating a Black man in a southern state. Woodard's case, and its national spotlight, had no precedent in the nation's history.

Shull was tried in a courtroom in Columbia, South Carolina, before an all-white jury and a white judge named J. Waties Waring, a man who had lived his entire life in the traditions of the Deep South. The segregated courtroom held a crowd of Black spectators on one side and white on the other. Woodard sat daily in the courtroom, his eyes hidden behind dark sunglasses. At one point, the prosecutor asked Woodard to remove his glasses and show the jury his face. A reporter present described the scene: "Woodard turned in their direction and took off his glasses. His eyes were shrunken back into his head and nearly closed." When directly asked about the incident, Officer Shull said that he had been forced to assault Woodard: "I had no intention of hitting him in the eyes. I am sorry I . . ." He paused. "Caused him to be blind."

Woodard took the stand and told his story. His attorney said to him, "It has been charged here this morning that you were cursing and disorderly and drunk on the bus between Augusta and Batesburg. I will ask you whether or not that statement is true."

"The only thing is true is when I cursed that bus driver after he cursed me."

"Were you drunk on that bus?"

"No, sir."

"Were you disorderly on the bus?"

"No, sir."

"Had you had a drink while you were on the bus?"

"No, sir."

At one point a defense attorney shouted that if Shull was found guilty, "then let this South Carolina secede again," and even barked racial epithets at the judge. In the end, the trial displayed so much bigotry, Judge Waring later said, "I was shocked by the hypocrisy of my government . . .

in submitting that disgraceful case." When the jury found Shull innocent, a crowd of white South Carolinians applauded, from its own side of the courtroom.

Shull walked free that day. But the story of the blind soldier opened the eyes of countless white people to America's darkest secret, for the first time — one of them being the president of the United States.

On December 5, 1946, one month after the Shull verdict, President Truman issued Executive Order 9908, creating the President's Committee on Civil Rights, exactly as he told Walter White that he would. The committee consisted of prominent figures of the white and Black races, and Truman chose as its head Charles Wilson, the CEO of General Electric, one of the largest corporations in the world. Truman gave the group specific marching orders: "You have a vitally important job. We are none of us entirely familiar with just how far the Federal Government under the Constitution has a right to go in these civil rights matters. I want our Bill of Rights implemented in fact. We have been trying to do this for 150 years. We're making progress, but we're not making progress fast enough."

The group set to work on a report that, when completed in 1947, would be called *To Secure These Rights.* In its largest brushstrokes, it called for destroying the gap between what America was supposed to be, as defined in its founding documents, and America in reality. In other words, it spelled out exactly what had been the overall mission of the NAACP through its entire existence. An excerpt from the document's introduction:

> Our American heritage . . . teaches that to be secure in the rights
> he wishes for himself, each man must be willing to respect the
> rights of other men. This is the conscious recognition of a basic
> moral principle: all men are created equal as well as free. Stem-
> ming from this principle is the obligation to build social insti-
> tutions that will guarantee equality of opportunity to all men.
> Without this equality freedom becomes an illusion. . . . We abhor
> the totalitarian arrogance which makes one man say that he will
> respect another man as his equal only if he has "my race, my re-
> ligion, my political views, my social position." In our land men

are equal, but they are free to be different. From these very differ-
ences among our people has come the great human and national
strength of America.

Walter later described *To Secure These Rights* as "without doubt the
most courageous and specific document of its kind in American history."

"WHILE WALTER WAS WORKING ON THE PRESIDENT," Roy Wilkins later remembered, "Thurgood Marshall was working on the courts."

In 1946 a nine-year-old girl named Sylvia Mendez was turned away
from the Orange County public school system in California because she
was Mexican American. With the help of NAACP lawyers, Mendez sued.
The court ruled that California public schools "must be open to all children by unified school association regardless of lineage," and that Mendez's rights to education were protected by the Fourteenth Amendment.
The school district appealed the case in federal court — and lost. *Mendez
v. Westminster* became a landmark case, and two months after its comple-
tion, California's governor, Earl Warren, signed a bill ending segregation
in public schools, making California the first state to do so.

Each education case created precedent and proven tactics for the
next one, and using education as the linchpin, the association began a
direct assault on segregation itself. The NAACP brought the case of Ada
Lois Sipuel, a young woman who was denied admission to the University of Oklahoma's law school, and won. The association helped a student
named Heman Marion Sweatt sue the Board of Regents of the University
of Texas. The United States Supreme Court ruled in Sweatt's favor, and he
was given admission to the university's law school.

At the same time, the NAACP's legal arm was challenging voting laws.
In 1944 Thurgood Marshall and the NAACP had brought a case to the Supreme Court in the name of Lonnie Smith, a Black dentist and NAACP
member in Houston who attempted to vote in the Democratic primary in
Texas and was turned away. Smith sued, and the Supreme Court decided
in *Smith v. Allwright* that his Fourteenth and Fifteenth Amendment rights

had been violated. *Smith v. Allwright* was the most influential case yet for Black voters who had been disenfranchised in the South, going back to Walter White's childhood.

South Carolina's governor, Olin D. Johnston, issued a stark statement following the *Smith v. Allwright* ruling, "for the purpose," he said, "of safeguarding our elections." "We will have done everything within our power to guarantee white supremacy in our primaries and in our State in so far as legislation is concerned," Johnston said. "Should this prove inadequate, we South Carolinians will use the necessary methods to retain white supremacy in our primaries and to safeguard the homes and happiness of our people. White supremacy will be maintained in our primaries. Let the chips fall where they may!"

When the very next election cycle arrived, in 1946, a Black man named George Elmore attempted to vote in a Democratic primary in Governor Johnston's state of South Carolina. When Elmore was turned away, he sued with the help of Thurgood Marshall and the NAACP. Elmore's case landed on the desk of Judge J. Waties Waring, the same judge who had presided over the Isaac Woodard trial. In *Elmore v. Rice,* Judge Waring ruled in Elmore's favor.

"For too many years," Waring wrote in his decision, "the people of this Country and perhaps particularly of this State have evaded realistic issues. . . . Racial distinctions cannot exist in the machinery that selects the officers and law-makers of the United States; and all citizens of this State and Country are entitled to cast a free and untrammeled ballot in our elections."

In Georgia, Governor Eugene Talmadge announced a "holy war" against would-be Black voters in 1946, saying, "We will fix it so the Negro vote can't amount to anything. . . . As long as I am Governor of Georgia, no Negro will vote." But Black Georgians were already beginning to vote in 1946 (one, a World War II veteran named Maceo Snipes, was shot and killed for doing so). The courts were opening the doors to polling stations in Walter's home state.

Walter and his colleagues had spent their careers pushing boulders up a proverbial mountain, and for the first time they could see the mountain-top. Sudden and monumental strides in education rights, voting rights, and political power compounded to force the country to begin to reconsider its national identity. The signs could be seen even in unexpected places. One day in 1946, members of Congress held a press conference for a young white war hero from Mississippi, in Washington, to highlight stories of the country's victory and patriotism. In front of a crowd of reporters, Mississippi senator Theodore Bilbo asked the young soldier, "Captain, I suppose you had the usual trouble with the niggers overseas, didn't you?"

The soldier shocked Bilbo and the crowd. "No, Senator, I didn't," he said. "On the contrary, I learned something — that Negroes can fight just as well and die as bravely as white Americans. And I've been shocked on getting home to Mississippi to see something I've looked at all my life but never really saw before — those signs, 'White' and 'Colored.' What's more, Senator, I'm worried about this whole business of segregation. On the train coming up here I asked to be seated in the diner with a Negro Captain of Infantry. He was one of the most intelligent men I've ever talked with. We've got to do something about this race question, because what we've been doing isn't right."

Even in the field of sport, America was changing. In 1945 baseball manager Branch Rickey announced that his Brooklyn Dodgers had signed Jackie Robinson — star of the Negro League — to a minor-league contract with the Montreal Royals. The only "colored" players in professional baseball were a few who claimed to be "American Indians," or Cubans — light enough to pass for white. That was not Jackie Robinson. On April 15, 1947, Robinson debuted with the Dodgers, breaking the color line in Major League Baseball. Walter became fast friends with Robinson, who told him once of one of his favorite memories of that rookie year with the Dodgers — the time an opposing team scooted a black cat onto the ball field in an attempt to intimidate him.

"I was so angry," Robinson told Walter, "my immediate impulse was to use my bat on the fellows who were taunting me. But then I remembered my promise to Branch Rickey not to lose my head. Thinking I would be rattled, the pitcher threw a nice fat pitch right down the middle, and I leaned into it for a home run."

THE SAME WEEK that Robinson played his first major-league game, Walter visited the White House again to see Truman, at 11:30 a.m. on April 9. America was gearing up for election season. The 1948 presidential election would be the first of the postwar era, the first of the atomic age, the first to feature an election-night television broadcast. The two major political parties would compete to chart their visions for the postwar world. Truman had come out in support of pioneering civil rights policies, but it was hard to tell just how far he would go. Walter asked him if he would appear at the NAACP's national convention, which was set to be held in Washington in two months' time. It had never happened before — the president of the United States addressing the association in person.

Both Walter and Truman understood how much was at stake. Truman had inherited the presidency upon FDR's death. He had not yet declared whether he would run in 1948, whether he would attempt to win the presidency in his own right. His support of civil rights policies was threatening to shatter his Democratic Party, as the Solid South would seek to destroy him if he campaigned against Jim Crow. To steer the Democratic Party in the direction of civil rights in the 1948 election would be, in Walter's opinion, "nothing short of political suicide" for the president.

There was a counterargument, however. Voting rights cases in Texas and South Carolina had begun to open doors to African Americans, and far more Black voters were going to register to vote in 1948 than in any presidential election in decades, perhaps ever. Black power was strengthening, and prescient politicians were realizing the value of those voters — if not in 1948, then certainly in the future.

In the Oval Office, Truman stunned Walter by agreeing to appear in person at the NAACP's national convention in June. Truman said, "Send me a memorandum of the points you think I ought to emphasize in my speech." Walter replied that if Truman said half the things Walter wanted the president to say, the southern Democrats would attempt to run him out of the country. When Truman laughed out loud, Walter felt a genuine friendship blossom. The two men had roughly the same color skin, and they stood about the same height. When they shook hands, they literally saw eye to eye.

Meanwhile, the date was set for June 29, 1947 — what would be, thus far, the most important day of Walter White's professional life.

30

Our immediate task is to remove the last remnants of the barriers, which stand between millions of our citizens and their birthright. There is no justifiable reason for discrimination because of ancestry, or religion. Or race, or color.

—Harry Truman, NAACP speech at the base of the Lincoln Memorial, June 29, 1947

WITH THE 1947 NAACP NATIONAL CONVENTION in Washington approaching, Walter finally heeded the advice of his colleagues and took a vacation on the island of Saint Croix in the Caribbean. It was there that he suffered his first heart attack.

As he lay in a hospital bed, a doctor slipped a sphygmomanometer on his arm and measured his blood pressure at 194/120 — terrifying numbers. Walter spent six days horizontal. An electrocardiogram showed nothing fundamentally wrong with his heart. But when he contacted his friend and physician Louis T. Wright, who was also an NAACP board member, Wright ordered him to cancel all speaking engagements and to stay away from the office.

Walter wrote to Wilkins in New York. "*Very confidentially,*" his note began (his italics), "I had a rather severe heart attack in St. Croix." Dr. Wright had recommended "that I go to a sanitarium for six weeks," Walter wrote, "but I think I have talked him out of that. It appears to be a situation created by lack of rest and not having taken any vacation for several years."

Wilkins wrote back immediately. "I was shocked to have your letter," he wrote, "although I had been prepared for it."

When Walter returned to the office, he faced a crushing load of work. The amount of planning that had to go into the national convention and to Truman's appearance proved staggering. The NAACP was going to host the president at the same location where Marian Anderson had sung to seventy-five thousand people eight years earlier. The location would provide just the kind of historic drama that Truman's speech needed.

On June 6 the NAACP announced that it was holding the "largest mass meeting in [the] nation's history." "Focal point of the gigantic meeting will be the June 29th closing session of the NAACP annual convention at the Lincoln Memorial in Washington, DC, where 100,000 spectators are expected to assemble to hear President Harry S. Truman deliver a major declaration of government policy. . . . Walter White, NAACP executive secretary, declared in New York today that the June 29th meeting will be the most significant in the Association's 38 years."

News that the president would appear shocked the southerners of the Democratic Party, as expected. Meeting privately with several of them in the White House, Truman explained that he himself was from a family that had sided with the Confederates in the Civil War, and that he came from a part of Missouri where Jim Crow was in force. "But my very stomach turned over when I learned that Negro soldiers, just back from overseas, were being dumped out of army trucks in Mississippi and beaten," Truman told Democratic Party leaders. "Whatever my inclinations as a native of Missouri might have been, as President I know this is bad. I shall fight to end evils like this."

The association arranged for a special train to travel from Houston on the Missouri-Pacific line, making stops in Arkansas, Mississippi, Oklahoma, Missouri, and Ohio to pick up passengers and carry them to the nation's capital. Truman's speech would be carried live over the CBS, NBC, ABC, and Mutual radio networks, starting at 4:30 eastern time, while the State Department would broadcast it in countless nations around the globe. Nine days before the event, Walter announced that former First Lady Eleanor Roosevelt would speak, as well as the president.

On June 29 the crowds began to turn out early. They were young. They were old. They were Black. They were white. They came in military uniform. They came in wheelchairs, casualties of war. They made up the biggest gathering in the NAACP's history. Fleet Admiral Nimitz, commander of the US Navy, was there. So too was Senator J. Howard McGrath of Rhode Island, the new chief of the Democratic National Committee. The ambassadors from Belgium, Yugoslavia, Nicaragua, and the Philippines were in the crowd, as well as under secretary of the interior Oscar Chapman, labor leaders A. Philip Randolph and William Green, civil rights leader Mary McLeod Bethune. Thurgood Marshall was there, as was his mentor, Charles Houston.

Among all those luminaries sat a huge majority of everyday Black Americans who had come hoping to experience the magic of the American presidency, in hopes that it might shine on them as it did the white people sitting next to them.

It was a broiling afternoon, so hot it seemed that even the statue of Lincoln was sweating. Behind the memorial, away from the crowds, Walter met with Truman and Eleanor Roosevelt and the three walked toward the stage, trailed by a retinue of military aides. Mrs. Roosevelt walked in the middle, awkwardly towering in height over both Truman and Walter, who was wearing a gray double-breasted suit with a white pocket square and black leather shoes. On the stage, Walter sat with Truman on his right and the former First Lady on his left. An American flag waved in a breeze behind them. The chorus from Howard University began the program with "Lift Every Voice and Sing," followed by "The Star-Spangled Banner."

After Eleanor Roosevelt's speech, Walter approached the podium and looked out on an awesome sight. Rows of people sat in chairs, with the Lincoln Memorial Reflecting Pool behind them and, on the horizon, the Washington Monument reaching up to the sky. The crowd seemed to sprawl for eternity, but as Walter stood at the podium, he heard absolute silence. He began.

"There are 100,000 people here today at the foot of Abraham Lincoln in Washington," Walter said, his voice riding the radio waves worldwide. "I am told that between 30 and 40 million other Americans may be listening to the radio at this hour. Countless others listen overseas via short wave broadcast. We are gathered together because of our deep concern for human rights."

Walter told the story of how the NAACP was born, thirty-eight years earlier. "Look what has been done in a single generation," he said. "Six hundred thousand Americans — Negro and white — are banded together in 1,509 branches of the NAACP. They have helped to work a quiet, bloodless revolution." Walter told of the twenty-four Supreme Court cases the NAACP had won. He talked about education, about due process of the law, about all the progress he had seen in his lifetime. "We welcome to this struggle, whose outcome will help to determine the future of mankind, every citizen who believes that the Bill of Rights means what it says."

He waited a moment for the applause to die down. Then he said into the microphone: "Ladies and gentlemen: The President of the United States."

"WE ALL CRANED forward," remembered Wilkins. Truman walked quietly to the podium holding his speech in his hands. As Walter looked on from his seat, Truman spoke the words that Walter White had always dreamed he would hear a president of the United States speak. It was almost as if Walter had written the speech himself.

"I should like to talk to you briefly about civil rights and human freedom," Truman said. "It is my deep conviction that we have reached a turning point in the long history of our country's efforts to guarantee freedom and equality to all our citizens. Recent evils in the United States and abroad have made us realize that it is more important today than ever before to ensure that all Americans enjoy these rights. And when I say all Americans — I mean *all* Americans."

Truman was no FDR; he had never been a brilliant public speaker. He spoke in plain intonations that made him seem like he might have been someone in the crowd rather than the man chosen to stand and speak historic words. He continued:

Many of our people still suffer the indignity of insult, the harrowing fear of intimidation, and, I regret to say, the threat of physical injury and mob violence. The prejudice and intolerance in which these evils are rooted still exist. The conscience of our nation, and the legal machinery which enforces it, have not yet secured to each citizen full freedom from fear.

We cannot wait another decade or another generation to remedy those evils. We must work, as never before, to cure them now . . .

For these compelling reasons, we can no longer afford the luxury of a leisurely attack upon prejudice and discrimination. There is much that state and local governments can do in providing positive safeguards for civil rights. But we cannot, any longer, await the growth of a will to action in the slowest state of the most backward community.

Our national government must show the way.

As Walter listened, he thought of the great man of stone sitting behind him, watching over, and Lincoln's Gettysburg Address. "I did not believe that Truman's speech possessed the literary quality of Lincoln's speech," he recalled, "but in some respects it had been a more courageous one in its specific condemnation of evils based upon race prejudice . . . and its call for immediate action against them."

When Truman finished, he turned, took a few steps, and shook Walter's hand as the crowds applauded. "There it was," recorded Wilkins. "An unequivocal pledge. For the first time, the President was putting himself and the government where they should have been all along: at the head of the parade, not on the sidelines." Turning to Walter, Truman asked if his speech was a success. Smiling, Walter said that, indeed, it was.

"I said what I did because I mean every word of it," Truman told Walter. "And I am going to prove that I do mean it."

Not long after, Truman officially announced his plans to run for another term in 1948.

• • •

THE FIGHT for the soul of the Democratic Party climaxed at the Democratic National Convention in Philadelphia in July 1948. The northern Democrats were going all out for civil rights. The Solid South would fight for white supremacy. Northern Democrats were going to stump for Black voting rights, in hopes of courting those votes. The Solid South was going to continue its fight against Black enfranchisement.

At the convention the Democrats would have to compose an official plank, which would say: *This is what we stand for, and this is where we are going as a party in this new postwar world.* In anticipation, Alabama's Democratic Campaign Committee put out a statement: "Shall we continue as chattels under the leadership of the present National Democratic Party and of Walter White, a New York mulatto, or shall we be freemen under the doctrine of Thomas Jefferson and practiced by Robert E. Lee?"

Weeks before the convention, Walter suffered his second heart attack. He had to fight to regain his health in time to catch a train from New York to the City of Brotherly Love, so he could testify before the Democrats' plank committee. "When Walter and I reached the city, the Dixiecrats were already talking war," remembered Wilkins, referring to the southern faction of the Democratic Party by what was about to become its nickname. Walter and his assistant secretary went before the platform committee on July 8, four days before the convention began, and made their pitch for the party to include in the 1948 plank a historic civil rights program.

"The day of reckoning has come," Walter told the committee, "when the Democratic Party must decide whether it is going to permit bigots to dictate its philosophy and policy or whether the party can rise to the height of Americanism that alone can justify its continued existence."

Wilkins remembered the moment, "I was proud of him that day." Not long after a heart attack, "he was more than ready to fight."

Four days later the first televised Democratic National Convention opened proceedings. From the start, the whole affair smacked of defeat and discontent. The battle over civil rights was tearing the party apart, and the seam was the Mason Dixon Line. Nobody believed, under these circumstances, Truman had any shot at winning, except Mr. Truman himself. When he and the Democrats announced their official plank, it spelled out support for the right to equal opportunity in employment, equal treatment of all races in the military, and "security of person" (the lawful right not to be lynched). It was a major victory for Walter, who was ecstatic. He put out a statement to the press: "Real Americanism won at Philadelphia yesterday." The party's southern base was appalled.

On the final night of the convention, July 14, during the final session of resolutions leading up to Truman's acceptance speech, Philadelphia Stadium was jammed. Without warning, protesters took control of the night. A delegate from Georgia demanded to be heard.

"The south is no longer going to be the whipping boy of the Democratic Party," he belted out in a southern accent, his voice hoarse. "And you know that without the south you cannot elect a President of the United States. You shall not crucify the south on the cross of civil rights."

A crowd of southern leaders paraded out of the building — pushing and shoving, waving Confederate flags. One voice shouted, "Mississippi has gone home!" South Carolina's young governor, Strom Thurmond, stepped up onto the stage and declared, "Our fight is the fight of every American who does not want to be subjected to federal police control!"

When the Solid South of the Democratic Party walked out the door that night, a historic shift in the power structure of the political parties began. Alabama, Georgia, South Carolina, Mississippi, Louisiana — all these states that had voted Democrat in every presidential election going back to the nineteenth century — would ultimately become the Solid South of the GOP, just as Walter White had predicted in 1930.* When northern Democrats argued that the 1948 plank was not much different from FDR's in 1944, in terms of civil rights, Strom Thurmond famously replied, "Yeah, but that S.O.B. Truman really means it."

After the convention the southern Democrats bolted and created their own political party — the States Rights Democrats, or the Dixiecrats — with their own candidate, Strom Thurmond, who declared at the new

---

* Each of these states cast their electoral votes for the Republican Donald Trump in 2016 and 2020, with the exception of Georgia in the latter contest.

group's hastily concocted national convention in Birmingham, Alabama, "I want to tell you, ladies and gentlemen, that there's not enough troops in the Army to force the Southern people to break down segregation and admit the Negro race into our theaters, into our swimming pools, into our homes, and into our churches. . . . These uncalled for and these damnable proposals [Truman] has recommended under the guise of so-called civil rights . . . I'll tell you . . . The American people . . . had better wake up and *oppose* such a program because the next thing will be a totalitarian state in these United States!"

The Democrats' fears were now realized; their party was in shambles. The nation prepared for what all believed would be one of history's most lopsided elections, in favor of the Republican Thomas Dewey, governor of New York. All five major pollsters counted Truman out. *Newsweek* magazine polled fifty political experts; zero predicted a Truman victory. As Congressman L. Mendel Rivers of South Carolina put it, "Harry Truman is a dead bird."

Walter White, meanwhile, used all his power to get Black voters to the polls, and while he did not openly campaign for Truman (the NAACP was, according to its charter, nonpartisan), the association's tacit support for him was obvious. Writing to all branches, Walter told members, "Exercise of the franchise by the Negro voter throughout the United States will be more important in 1948 than ever before in the history of this country."

DURING HIS 1948 CAMPAIGN, Truman became the first major presidential candidate to hold a rally in the spiritual home of Black America, Harlem. Liberals championed him as a race crusader; cynics said he was groveling for Black votes. His real motivation he made clear in a letter to Walter White early in the campaign.

"This country and its people have one great goal in the conduct of our national affairs — the development of a moral order based on freedom and equality," Truman wrote Walter on June 19. "That is the only way in which lasting peace can be brought to the world. That is the only way to

fulfill our hopes for a more perfect democracy in our own country. Freedom and equality are not easily won. . . . But the people as a whole are determined to win them. We will never cease trying to win them. And I, for
one, will never lose confidence that we can win them."

On July 26 Truman stunned the nation when, with almost no warning, his White House issued Executive Orders 9980 and 9981. The first
created a system of "fair employment practices" within the federal government, "without discrimination because of race, color, religion, or national origin." Simply stated: any American who paid taxes would be as
eligible for federal employment as any other, no matter the color of their
skin. Executive Order 9981 was the historic one, however. With the swipe
of a pen, Truman desegregated the United States military.

Walter found out about the executive orders when a White House aide
called the NAACP offices and dictated their language over the phone. It
was a victory he had been fighting for, for nearly a decade. Telegrams
came in from newspapers wanting a reaction. Walter said that the two
orders would "restore faith in the Democratic process at home and re-
build American prestige abroad. That one president has had the courage
to tackle these problems is gratifying."

Weeks later Walter flew to Paris to attend United Nations meetings as
a consultant to the American delegation. He mailed his absentee ballot
from France. On the day he mailed it, he sat down to a lunch with friends.

"Well," he told them, "I've just cast my ballot for the next President."

"Dewey, of course," said one at the table.

"Certainly not," said Walter. "I said the next President — Harry Truman."

"You don't really believe that," said the labor leader Jim Carey, who
was present.

"Mark my words. Harry Truman is going to win — because of his stand
on civil rights, the stand they told him would mean political suicide. He'll
win by the margin of the Negro vote in states like Ohio and California."

On November 3, 1948, Truman won the biggest upset in American
presidential electioneering history. His stand on civil rights cost him four

states in the South, all of which went to the breakaway Dixiecrats. But he earned a vast majority of the Black vote in places where it counted. And he won.

Following the election, the NAACP put out a statistical report showing that "Negro voters supported President Truman overwhelmingly . . . that in several cases the Negro vote held the balance of power which swung a city or a state into the Truman column." The president, meanwhile, was in Key West, Florida, taking a break. His aide Philleo Nash sent him his own report on the Black vote in 1948, showing that "your majority in the Negro districts is the highest ever."

31

I am not white. There is nothing within my mind or heart which tempts me to think I am.

— Walter White, "Why I Remain a Negro," 1948

WALTER'S AUTOBIOGRAPHY, *A Man Called White,* appeared in 1948, to rave reviews. The book told the story of his life and times, but the reviewers seized on the extraordinary irony of his racial identity. The *New York Times:* "Mr. White is a Negro only because of his state of mind — physically he is always considered a white man except by those who know him. His appearance has, in fact, often put his life in danger during his investigations of racial conflicts, since to the whites he is a Negro bent upon enforcing the law, while to the Negroes who do not know him he is a white man in Negro territory."

His autobiography would outsell all of his other books combined. But at the moment he was reaching his zenith among the literati, his private life was fully coming apart. Gladys had been living a separate life for years, and Walter had begun to hear rumors that she too was having an affair. His health was further compromised by brutal insomnia. He knew that an announcement of a divorce and revelations about a white paramour would destroy his public persona, harm the association, and offend many of his family and friends.

He also had his children to think about. Walter Jr. turned twenty-one in 1948 and was in the army. Jane had recently graduated from Smith

College and had begun a career on the stage. (Ironically, she debuted in the play *Strange Fruit,* a term originated by a poet writing about the lynching of Thomas Shipp and Abram Smith in Marion, Indiana, which Walter had investigated in 1930.) Walter already felt a distance from his children, due to his workaholism, his late nights and travel. But that was not abnormal for a family man of his generation. The scandal of interracial adultery, for a public figure, would not be normal at all. The kids were grown up — old enough to form their own opinion of their father's betrayal.

Walter stiffened his resolve and chose a day when he would ask Gladys for a divorce. She was scheduled to fly to Mexico to visit a sister living there, and he thought it wise to tell her before she left, so she would have time to think things over, away from him. On the chosen morning, he told his wife of twenty-seven years that he wanted a divorce, and that he had heard rumors that she had been unfaithful. He later remembered how her face stretched wide with horror. "As long as I live I shall remember the stricken ashen look on her face this morning," he wrote. "Her eyes became frightfully tired and sad as though she were looking down an endless corridor."

Details about the inner workings of their marriage are sparse. But a letter exists that Walter wrote to Poppy, in which he quotes his wife's reaction: "Now I realize your suspicious and difficult attitude all these years have been due to listening to lies about me," she told him, according to Walter's account. "You certainly do not show much trust or faith in me. I also have heard stories during the past few years of our married life time which I would not think of letting touch me. . . . But I can now see you have harboured thoughts of distrust about me for years. I have never thought of divorce — but I can read between the lines that it is the thing you want. . . . [If] you had a little more faith in me you would not have the slightest doubt."

A couple of days later he confessed to Gladys what she apparently already knew — his own infidelity. She left for Mexico City, where legally she could obtain a divorce without his presence. Walter began leaking the news to his most trusted friends and family. The reactions were, in almost every case, not what he had hoped.

"I couldn't believe the tragic news when I heard it," Walter's sister Helen wrote him on May 20, 1949.

You didn't ask my opinion but I am going to give it to you. First because I am your sister . . . and also because I love you.

For thirty one years you have been the idol of our race. We have watched you grow and now to my thinking you have reached the top of the ladder. And for Gladys' sake, please, please don't fall in the pit. Please don't think that Gladys will take it lying down. . . . We have known for years long before Momma died that you and Gladys didn't get along. . . . Divorce Gladys if you want to, but please don't tear down your life's work and do something that will ruin you for the rest of your life. From the President of the United States to the lowest people on earth . . . both races respect and envy you, but if you take the step you plan to take, your name will be mud.

Walter's sister Madeline wrote him on the same day.

When you became the leader and spokesmen for 10,000,000 Negroes you sacrificed any private life you have had; the little people in the alleys and slums might not know who is President or even who Abraham Lincoln was but they all know, and worship, Walter White. One of the man [main] reasons for this worship and allegiance is the fact that you fell in love with and married a person of Gladys' complexion. They believed anything you told them. You were one of them. You personified the doctrine of Race. Can you afford to cast this aside?

The NAACP is your life. . . . When you give that up you will be lost. . . . Can you afford to destroy what you have been 31 years building up? People will desert it like rats leaving a drowning ship.

· · ·

ON MAY 9, 1949, AT 3:30 P.M., the NAACP's board of directors gathered in a conference room at the Fortieth Street headquarters for their monthly meeting. With Wilkins next to him, Walter led the group through his report. At the end, he stood and announced — with no prior warning — his desire to step down.

"My chief reason for this step," he told them, reading from a letter in his hand, "is because I have been warned again, following a physical check-up last Wednesday that I am 'riding for a fall' if I continue my present schedule. I have been told that I am in for very serious trouble if I do not change my pattern of work. It has become apparent that thirty-one years of work have taken their toll." Walter read aloud for several minutes. He finished with these words: "No human being to my knowledge has been blessed so abundantly in being able to work with so loyal and able a Board of Directors, staff, and membership."

His request for a separation left the room silent. Ultimately the board took an impromptu vote and refused to accept his resignation, granting him instead a year's leave of absence so he could improve his health, with full pay. Walter never mentioned his impending divorce or his plans to remarry. He did, however, request in a June 24 memorandum to have a portion of his paycheck made payable to Gladys, and mailed to her directly.

When the association announced that Walter would be leaving for a year, the Black press all but canonized him. "For more than 25 years," the *Afro-American* proclaimed, "the word of Walter White has been accepted as the voice of colored America." Now the association faced the task of finding "a successor to Moses."

Walter, meanwhile, had his own announcement to make: he was taking off on a trip around the world as a member of a new ABC News radio team, for a program called *America's Town Meeting of the Air*. A group of prominent figures would stop in major cities to host symposiums that would be aired over the ABC radio network.

What Walter did not announce was that he was going to bring Poppy Cannon with him. He did tell his successor, the new acting secretary of the NAACP. Before leaving, he called Wilkins into his office.

"Roy," Walter said, "there's something I've been meaning to tell you. Gladys and I are divorced. We haven't been getting along for some time. Gladys went down to Mexico, and the divorce went through."

Wilkins could not believe what he was hearing. "They had seemed a perfect match to me," he recalled. He expressed how sorry he was.

"I thought you should know," Walter said. Then he lapsed into a silence. He knew that a storm was coming.

On July 6, 1949, Walter and Poppy Cannon, along with a witness, appeared before a judge in a dusty office in downtown Manhattan. The judge married them, seemingly unaware that they were an interracial couple, that their union would be illegal in roughly half of the forty-eight states. Raindrops pounded on the windows during the ceremony, and when it was done, the witness—a friend of the bride's named Helen—burst into tears.

"It was such a beautiful wedding!" she said. The bride and groom looked at her, tacitly acknowledging the irony. It was the least romantic wedding setting they could imagine.

Three days later the newlyweds took off on a Pan American Boeing Stratocruiser to begin their round-the-world adventure, this being an era when even domestic air travel still seemed exotic. The iterinary was ambitious: London, Paris, Rome, Berlin, Vienna, Tel Aviv, Alexandria, Karachi, New Delhi, Manila, and Tokyo. Given Walter's precarious health, he did not know if he would make it home alive.

ON JULY 2, 1949, the *Chicago Defender* ran a newspaper column by Walter White, its opening line reading: "When you read this column its writer will have commenced a world tour as one of twenty or more representatives of American organizations and segments of the population who will participate in a 'round the World Town Meeting of the Air.'"

On that same day a photograph of Gladys White appeared in the *Afro-American* under the title "'Heavens, No!' Said Mrs. White." The article was all of about one hundred words and took its title from Gladys herself. When asked if the rumor was true—that she had obtained a divorce in Mexico—she responded, "Heavens, no! Is that what's being said about us?"

Within days, the White family saga became a national gossip sensation, mostly in the African American press. The *New York Amsterdam News:* "Walter White's Divorce Starts Tongues Wagging; Hint Top Leader to Wed a White Woman." The *Afro-American* ran a photo of Walter, Gladys, and their two kids under the headline "Walter Whites Divorced"; the photo was captioned, "Here's the White Family During Happier Days." The *Pittsburgh Courier:* "Gossip Circles Walter White," followed days later by "Another Courier Scoop! Walter, Poppy Married!" The *New York Daily News:* "Walter White Wed July 6 to Editor 'Poppy.'" The *New York Age:* "From coast-to-coast they're talking these days about two things: 1) The Mexican divorce of Mrs. Gladys Powell White and 2) The linking of Walter White's name in an interracial romance with Mrs. Poppy Cannon, divorcee and well-known freelance writer."

"Did Walter White Marry His White Sweetheart?"

"Bride Can't Be Located."

"Leadership of Walter White in Doubt."

The first paparazzi photo of the newlyweds together — snapped while they were traveling — appeared in the *Afro-American:* "First Photo of Walter White and New Bride." The first articles about Poppy Cannon White detailed her surprising story. She had been married already three times and had three children, one from each marriage. She had graduated from Vassar and worked as an advertising executive at the Peter Hilton Agency on Madison Avenue, on major accounts such as Heinz and Gillette. She was the food editor of *Mademoiselle* magazine. All of which made her an extraordinarily modern woman circa 1949. She was forty-three years old, a dozen years younger than Walter.

Walter and his newlywed wife, meanwhile, had checked in to their hotel in London, and in the days before international television and international newspapers, they had no knowledge of what was being said about them. They traveled on to Rome, and at one point a *New York Times* reporter caught up with them by phone in their hotel room.

"So this is it," Walter said into the phone, expecting probing questions about the scandal.

The reporter instead asked about the prevalence of communism in

NAACP branches, as the McCarthy-era Red Scare was in its infancy and making news. Walter answered the questions, and the *Times* man thanked him. "You're a newspaper man yourself, Mr. White. You know how to give a story. You know what we want."

"The hell I do!" Walter said under his breath.

In the United States the gossip columnists turned to Gladys's side of the story. Newspapers reported rumors that she was having an affair with the actor Fredric March, star of the movie *Christopher Columbus,* which was in theaters at the time. March was white and married to the costar in that film, Florence Eldridge. Gladys claimed to be "out of town" and was not taking interviews, but her son, Walter Jr., called the rumor "ridiculous." He said, "So far as I know, and so far as mother knows, the rumor is false." The rumor seemed to stem from a photo of Gladys with the actor; there is no evidence of any truth to it.

Following the initial shock of the scandal came a wave of Black resentment. Letters arrived by the bagful from indignant NAACP members, arguing that Walter was playing right into the hands of the bigots, lynchers, and demagogues who for generations had made excuses for their violent actions by claiming that Black men were after their white women. The writer J. Robert Smith teed off on Walter in the *Los Angeles Sentinel,* an African American paper: "It will take us another 50 years to convince the white man that this is not true when our leader has so betrayed us." C. C. Spaulding, president of one of the largest Black-owned companies, Mutual Life Insurance, wrote: "He has given credence . . . to the inaccurate charge of the white South that the highest aspiration of Negroes is to invade the white race."

Even members of the White family had choice words. "The selfishness is unbelievable," his sister Alice wrote in a letter to Walter. "Now you are telling . . . all the world that all this race pride and work for the Negroe [sic] race was only to advance your interest — and you had no real interest in them. You want a white woman to share the rest of your days. . . . I am glad moma [sic] and papa are not here to suffer this disgrace. However it will make them both turn over in their graves."

Walter was still acting secretary of the NAACP, but his critics were out for blood. The Black newspaper publisher and association board member Carl Murphy wrote to a friend that Walter's marriage "has so weakened his usefulness that the association will assume a grave risk in attempting to keep him in office. . . . The public believes Mr. Walter White, as an outstanding leader of the country and as executive of our Association, has done the wrong thing in marrying across racial lines. That bitterness is more pronounced with women than men." Murphy dug the knife in deeper in an editorial for the *Afro-American,* writing that Walter had "tossed away" his thirty-year career. "The race itself," Murphy wrote, "is to blame for permitting a man who wanted to be white so bad to be their spokesman for so long."

32

Some folks want to climb Everest, others to be president. Fine, right
now, is to be allowed to walk to the bathroom to clean my teeth,
shave, shower, etc., all by myself.

— Walter White to the NAACP staff after another heart attack, 1954

IN SEPTEMBER 1949 Walter returned to the NAACP office and staged a
press conference to clear the air. Reporters packed in and found him sitting at a desk covered in papers, hands fidgeting, cigarette hanging from
his lips. He was accustomed to having the nation's most powerful journal-
ists from the most influential newspapers and radio stations pepper him
with questions. These, however, were gossip columnists.

"Do you feel that the press handled the report of your divorce and
marriage fairly?" asked Lillian Scott of the *Chicago Defender*.

"My wife and I are pleased," Walter said, "and we are grateful to the
overwhelming majority of the press in America, as well as Europe and
Asia, for their accurate, dignified, even warmly sympathetic treatment of
the news of our marriage. As for a small minority of newspapers, which
for whatever motives has exploited the news of our marriage, I have only
this to say: In this country, we, fortunately, have freedom of expression —
a freedom which I certainly uphold."

"Do you feel that your interracial marriage has weakened your leadership among Negroes?"

"Time alone will provide the answer."

Another writer asked, "Some sections of the Negro press have stated that they feel it is improper for the head of the NAACP to be married to a white woman. Would you comment on this?"

Walter had anticipated this question, and when he answered it, he laid out his entire philosophy on race in a concise declaration. Everything he had done, and all that he stood for, was imbued in these few words. "Throughout my entire life, I have lived by one principle — that there is but one race, the human race. I have fought and always will fight against any artificial barriers among the peoples of the world based on race, creed, color or caste."

At the office, Walter had a lot of work to do to regain the trust of the NAACP board of directors and a broad swath of Black America too. In a jolting blow, Eleanor Roosevelt resigned from the board, and while she initially claimed that Walter's conduct had nothing to do with it, she bluntly wrote him that "your marriage created a problem for the organization, and that was one of the reasons I felt I should resign." He convinced her to withdraw her resignation, but he did not yet know if she would support him in his efforts to remain chief executive. Meanwhile, angry mail poured into the office from all over the country.

"Self-respecting Negroes are disgusted with him and all his foolish words," read one letter with an illegible signature. "As far as many Negroes are concerned Mr. White has already out lived his usefulness as a leader," read another, signed by one S. K. Bryson. The influential southern newspaper the *Dallas Express* spoke for many when it stated in an editorial, "In the deep South nobody will be able to think of Walter again, or his actions or statements, as pure, unadulterated Negro thinking, acting, or feeling. . . . If Walter comes back now, [the NAACP] will have a Negro as secretary with a white covering."

His yearlong leave of absence was officially ending on June 1, 1950. Roy Wilkins was running the day-to-day operations as acting secretary. On May 8 the board gathered to decide upon Walter's future. He was not invited to the meeting. Eleanor Roosevelt led a fight to keep him on, and the board voted, 16–10, to allow him to continue. "There was still plenty of lingering anger over what he had done," recorded Wilkins, who was demoted from acting secretary to "administrator."

Walter and his new wife moved into a Manhattan apartment, spending weekends at her home in Connecticut. His family life was destroyed; his kids would not talk to him. Walter Carl Darrow White, who through much of his life had been called Walter Jr., changed his name to Carl Darrow, wanting to disassociate from his father entirely. Walter had a niece from Atlanta named Rose Martin, who he helped get into Smith College in Massachusetts and thought of him "as a second father," as she put it. She came to live with Walter and Poppy for a short time right after Walter's divorce. "His children turned against him," she remembered. "Because he divorced his wife. He was very hurt by it."

When Walter returned to work full-time, it was quickly apparent that he would never again wield the influence he once did. Like his health, his power was slipping away.

WALTER'S HEART HAD WEAKENED to the point where he wondered with each beat if another would come. One day he was smoking a cigarette and began to cough. He could not stop. Sitting next to him was J. Waties Waring, the judge who had presided over the trial of Isaac Woodard, who had ruled in favor of Black voting rights in the controversial South Carolina case *Elmore v. Rice*, and who had since become one of Walter's closest friends. Waring said, "Walter, whenever you light a cigarette you ought to say, 'Here's to you, Jimmy Byrnes. Here's to you, Strom Thurmond. Here's to you, Senator Eastland.' For let me tell you, that when you die, they're going to declare a national holiday."

Walter stamped out his cigarette. He never lit another again.

Sensing that his time was short, he set out to write a final book. Diving into the research, typing the pages, he must have known he would not live to see it published. He merely hoped he would live long enough to type the manuscript's last sentence and the period at the end. While he worked at the association office as much as he could, he spent more time in Connecticut writing, until his role at the NAACP was little more than a figurehead. He never lost his sense of humor. At one point, after another heart attack, he joked with his colleagues in a letter he wrote while convalescing at New York Hospital: "They've kept me 'sedated' to such a degree the dope problem in New York City ought to have been solved this past month—they gave it all to me."

This quiet life he lived for four years, until the manuscript was completed and turned in.

There remained one final triumph of his lifetime, however, besides his last book. On May 17, 1954—"decision day"—the Supreme Court issued its ruling on *Brown v. Board of Education of Topeka*. A Black man named Oliver Brown had sued the board of education of Topeka, Kansas, after his daughter Linda Brown, a third grader, was denied entrance to one of the city's all-white public schools. Thurgood Marshall and the NAACP fought the case brilliantly, all the way to the Supreme Court. *Brown v. Board of Education* was the climactic case that Marshall had been building for twenty years, and while it named a single defendant, it actually consisted of five different school segregation cases that the Supreme Court ruled on collectively. On decision day, Chief Justice Earl Warren issued the court's ruling, and the phone in Walter's New York office rang, soon after, with the news.

For fifty-eight years, ever since *Plessy v. Ferguson*—the Supreme Court's "separate but equal" ruling of 1896—public education in the United States mostly consisted of white and Black schools. Now the court's nine justices decided unanimously: "We conclude that in the field of public education the doctrine of 'separate but equal' has no place. Separate educational facilities are inherently unequal." Separate but equal, the Court ruled, violated the Fourteenth Amendment rights of minority students, and thus began the end of legal segregation in public schools.

That night Walter and Poppy appeared at a party at the home of Justice Waring, now living in New York City. When they walked in, they were greeted warmly by the small crowd. Walter was asked to speak on *Brown v. Board of Education*. One of the guests had with her a newfangled machine that could record sound, and as Walter started to speak, she switched on the tape recorder. He told the story of his day, the minutiae that one never thinks about, until one realizes that one is living through a historic moment in time, and the little details take on extraordinary significance. Then he turned to the Supreme Court ruling.

"My first thought went back to the decision we won in the Arkansas riot case [which Walter had investigated in Phillips County in 1919]. . . . We won that Arkansas case just as we have won this particular case — against precedent. . . . We won against terrific odds." He paused. "All of you in this room know what this fight has meant." He looked around at the familiar faces, everyone silent. He continued.

> If I may be a little personal, and I ask your forgiveness for it, I can't help thinking of the number of times in the last thirty-five years of the struggle when some of my very closest friends told me that I was a damn fool — for believing that within a reasonable period of time we could really — smash — segregation — in America. It wasn't pleasant to have to listen to people who told you that you were idiotic . . . and stupid. . . . But yet we together have created a miracle. A miracle has been passed in America today. . . . Where do we go from here? . . . The decision we won today is meaningless unless we can smash residential segregation, unless we can smash segregation and discrimination in jobs. . . . Right now the rest of the world is looking at us in America with very great skepticism.

Walter paused again. With his voice full of pathos, he said, "There are some of us who will not be around much longer. . . . But there will be new people coming into the struggle and they have to complete the fight in which today we won possibly the greatest victory that has been won since the infamous Dred Scott decision."

A FEW MONTHS later, on March 21, 1955, Walter took a morning train to the office. He had been out sick for some time, and Wilkins was surprised to see him. Wilkins later recalled: "Who but Walter would make a point of stopping by the office before going home to die?"

Back in Connecticut later that afternoon, Walter walked into his bedroom to find his wife there. His papers were all over the place, and he apologized; he had been spending so much time at home, his work trailed behind him like exhaust from a car. He said, "I promised you yesterday to put these out of sight in the other room. But don't worry, pretty soon I'll be taking this stuff all back to the office."

Walter's young stepdaughter, Claudia, walked in, wearing an outfit she had purchased for the upcoming Easter holiday. "The heels are too high," her mother said. "And the suit is too old for you."

"Walter doesn't think so, do you Walter?" the girl asked.

"I plead the Fifth Amendment," he answered. He picked up the manuscript for his next book and walked out of the room. Poppy then heard a strange noise. She followed and found him kneeling on the floor, seized with pain.

"Oh, Walter, don't!" she said. "You mustn't do that."

Claudia ran out of the house to fetch a neighbor, who was a doctor. He came rushing in with his medical bag. He knelt over Walter, who was now lying on the floor.

"Shouldn't we send for oxygen?" Poppy said, panicked. "Mustn't we get an ambulance?"

The doctor looked at her and shook his head. She later recalled a "most terrible, unendurable, never-to-be-broken stillness," one that was shattered by the doctor's next words.

"It's too late, now."

Epilogue

The job of curing and preventing man's mistreatment of another
man because of his race or color in the United States or, for that
matter, anywhere else in the world is not done. But we are on
our way.
— Walter White, the final two sentences of his posthumously
published book *How Far the Promised Land?* (1955)

THE WORLD THAT WALTER WHITE LEFT UPON HIS DEATH, at age sixty-one,
would have been unrecognizable to his childhood eyes. He was probably already a teenager the day he first saw the miracle of a motorcar ride
past. His world of 1955 was one of hydrogen bombs and television sets, jet
planes and rocket power. But in one sense it was the same as the one he
was born into. It was a world in which human beings of different skin colors lived in proximity to one another. Just before he died, he hammered
out these words on his typewriter:

"All the peoples of the world are in the same boat now. Today that ves-
sel is unseaworthy because we have not yet mastered the science of living together. Through a major leak caused by color prejudice the waters
of hate are rushing in. Our survival may depend on how swiftly and ex-
pertly that leak is caulked."

For his funeral, eighteen hundred mourners appeared at Saint Martin's Episcopal Church in Harlem. His death, as expected, kept the obituary writers busy. The *New York Times:* "Walter White was the adviser
of statesmen and soldiers, in peace and war." The *Washington Post:* "He

gave his life to a heroic cause now well on its way to triumph." In a personal telegram to Poppy Cannon White, President Eisenhower said, HIS DEVOTED SERVICE TO HIS RACE OVER A PERIOD OF 40 YEARS WAS TIRELESS AND EFFECTIVE. PERMIT ME TO EXPRESS TO YOU MY PERSONAL SYMPATHIES IN YOUR LOSS. Vice President Nixon said he was privileged to know Walter, "not only in his official capacity but also as a personal friend." Senator Hubert Humphrey of Minnesota, a rising star of the Democratic Party, said that the NAACP man "literally gave his life for the welfare of his people."

Months after Walter's death, the Viking Press posthumously published his final book. It was called *How Far the Promised Land?*, and its purpose, he explained on page 1, was "to tell how democracy works in the United States." This was Walter's most optimistic book; it catalogued the progress the Black race had made in America in recent years — in law, education, economics, politics, and spirit — all results of "the long, heartbreaking struggle" that had defined his life. In his final chapter he wrote of the progress made in the fight against lynching.

"It would have been impossible a quarter of a century ago," he concluded, "or, for that matter, a decade ago, to write a book on the status of the American Negro without devoting at least one voluminous chapter to lynching. That such a chapter no longer needs to be included reflects the changing pattern of race relations in the United States."

On August 28, 1955 — in between the time of Walter's death and the publish date of *How Far the Promised Land?* — a fourteen-year-old Black child named Emmett Till walked into Bryant's Grocery Store and Meat Market in the town of Money, Mississippi. The facts of what happened in that store are disputed, and the brutality of what occurred next need not be catalogued here.

At Emmett Till's funeral, the Till family insisted on an open casket. A photo was taken of the fourteen-year-old boy lying there, with his parents standing by him. His father's eyes stare straight into the camera lens. His mother's are upon her son. *Time* magazine later called that photo one of the one hundred "most influential images of all time." Publicity of the crime — and the fact that no one was ever convicted, even after two men confessed to the murder — caused such national outrage, the name Emmett Till stands out generations later unlike any of the victims of the lynchings and beatings that Walter White investigated. It was the moment that Walter had chased his whole life but never lived to see, when America finally, en masse, faced its darkest secret, and mourned.

MONTHS AFTER Walter's death, in 1955, Martin Luther King Jr. led the Montgomery, Alabama, bus boycott to protest the arrest of Rosa Parks, who refused to give up her seat on a city bus so a white passenger could sit down. As quickly as MLK rose to fame as the new face of the civil rights movement, Walter's story became a thing of the past. His legacy faded into obscurity with remarkable speed. It was said that he was not Black enough for the new generation of civil rights fighters. He would have appeared strangely miscast in the pantheon of these leaders in the television age.

Did his decision to marry a white woman damage his legacy? Almost certainly. That the name Walter White — to almost anyone living in the year 2021 — refers to the main character of the television series *Breaking Bad* speaks volumes. Had he not chosen to marry Poppy Cannon late in life, there seems little doubt his legacy would have been treated better by history. Would he, if he could look back from now, regret the move? Who can say?

As I write this in 2021, I can only wonder what he would think of our world today. The NAACP still lives and breathes, and its mission has changed little. Walter would recognize other truths about America too. Throughout his life, he had fought for a federal anti-lynching law, and that fight continues. In 2019 the Emmett Till Antilynching Act passed the House of Representatives by a vote of 410–4. But just as it did in Walter's time (on numerous occasions), the US Senate blocked the bill, due mainly to the objection of one senator, Rand Paul of Kentucky, who said in explanation that he wanted the bill changed and made "stronger." There remains no federal anti-lynching law.

In Walter's time, countless Black voters were not permitted to vote. Today they can, but the suppression of their votes remains an ongoing fight in the politics of America. In Walter's time, there was Isaac Woodard,

Mary Turner, Thomas Shipp, Abram Smith, and so many others. Today there is George Floyd, Breonna Taylor, and Ahmaud Arbery. In Walter's time there was the KKK. Today the forces of white supremacy in America remain strong and outwardly vocal. Walter would have been heartbroken to see on his television screen insurrectionists breaking into the US Capitol and parading a Confederate flag through its hallways, as they did on January 6, 2021; he would have been over the moon to learn that a Black man had been voted to the United States Senate from his home state of Georgia, as Raphael Warnock was in 2021.

During the years it took me to write this book, I found that people who heard the rudiments of Walter White's story kept asking me the same question. Was he Black? Or not? I never could come up with an answer. So I will let Mr. White do the honors: *"I am one of the two in the color of my skin; I am the other in my spirit and my heart. It is only a love of both which binds the two together in me. . . . I am white and I am black, and know that there is no difference. Each casts a shadow, and all shadows are dark."*

Acknowledgments

This book says my name on the cover and I am responsible for everything in it. It was not an easy book to write. My hope is that if Walter White were alive today, he would find it to be fair and factual.

I would like to thank Rakia Clark, my editor, who helped to make this book so much better than it would have been had she not dug her hands into the manuscript and graced it with her empathy, knowledge, attention to detail . . . the list goes on. Thank you, Rakia, you are a superstar. I want to thank Margaret Wimberger, Ivy Givens, Megan Wilson, Katie Tull, Kelly Shi, and Jennifer Freilach at Mariner Books/HarperCollins for their amazing work. All of you are the best at what you do and I am proud to get the opportunity to work with you.

I decided when I was six years old that I was going to be an author, and it might not have ever happened if it were not for my agent of fifteen years — Scott Waxman of the Waxman Literary Agency. Thank you also to Susan Canavan and Ashley Lopez at the Waxman Literary Agency. You are all a pleasure to work with and top-notch in every way.

In my years of writing nonfiction, I have found that archivists are the unsung heroes of this field. These are the people who care for the documentation that makes up the building blocks of history. For this book, I visited Yale University's Beinecke Rare Book & Manuscript Library, which houses the Walter F. White and Poppy Cannon Papers, as well as smaller Walter White archives held at the New York Public Library's main location on Forty-Second Street and Fifth Avenue, and the Schomburg Center for Research in Black Culture, in Harlem. I also found valuable documents in the W.E.B. Du Bois papers, which are housed at the

University of Massachusetts but are accessible digitized online, and in the Truman Presidential Library in Independence, Missouri, which is, frankly, one of the greatest places on earth.

By far, the most important collection for me was the NAACP archives. These papers offer such a vivid and critical window into our national heritage. Without the archivists responsible for them, this book never could have been written, especially during the COVID pandemic, when libraries shut their doors to all of us. The NAACP archives are fully digitized and reachable online.

I want to also thank Professor Kenneth Janken at the history department of the University of North Carolina for his book *White: The Biography of Walter White, Mr. NAACP,* which should be the go-to place for anyone who wants to keep on reading about Walter.

WAY BACK ON JANUARY 1, 1994, I moved to New York City to try to make it as a writer in the good old American literary tradition. Working nights in kitchens to pay the bills, I began graduate work briefly at Columbia University and then at NYU, where I researched American literature of the 1920s and '30s, the literature of the American Depression, the emerging school of 1920s urban sociology, the Harlem Renaissance, and the art of writing biography. When I left graduate school to work in journalism, I thought I would never touch on much of that thinking again. All of it came alive again in *White Lies,* as I never imagined it could. It was almost as if all that graduate work at NYU's English Department was specifically undertaken for the writing of this book so many years later.

I would like to thank my family. My father, Judge David S. Baime, who was one of my greatest inspirations, passed away while I was finishing the very last draft of *White Lies.* Dad, I miss you every day. Thank you for all that you did for me. I am going to sign a copy of this book, address it to you, and put it in the mail: To Judge David S. Baime, Heaven.

Thank you, Michelle, Clay, and Auds. Nothing I can say here can express what you mean to me, and how proud I am of you. To the rest of my family — so many of you who have always been there for me — I will say (as we do in our long family tradition): *Love! Love! Love!*

In the end, I hope this book might open some eyes to the truths of our nation's past. I hope it might contribute, even if for one single reader, to a new idea of patriotism and to what it means to be American, in the future.

Notes

Much of this book was mined from the NAACP archives. Because these archives are available online through the archival database tool ProQuest, each of the endnotes that refer to these archives lists a code that corresponds to the file in which the source is to be found. Each NAACP archive endnote is instantly searchable using the last seven digits of the code, including the hyphen. The archive itself can be found and used for free through the New York Public Library's website, as well as other libraries.

Introduction

PAGE

1 *"I am a Negro"*: Walter White, *A Man Called White: The Autobiography of Walter White* (Athens and London: University of Georgia Press, 1995), p. 3.

2 *"was the perfect economy-size"*: E. J. Kahn Jr., "The Frontal Attack — II," Profiles, *New Yorker,* September 11, 1948.
"the Smith & Wesson Line": Walter White, "Smith and Wesson Line," letter to the editor, *Time,* July 22, 1929.
"Walter White was a New": David Levering Lewis, *When Harlem Was in Vogue* (New York: Penguin Books, 1997), pp. 130, 136.

3 *"enigma of a black man"*: E. J. Kahn Jr., "The Frontal Attack — I," Profiles, *New Yorker,* September 4, 1948.
"White, the nearest approach to": "Walter White, 61, Dies in Home Here," *New York Times,* March 22, 1955.
"a man whose life, in fuller": Ralph J. Bunche, foreword to *How Far the Promised Land?*, by Walter White (New York: Viking Press, 1955), pp. ix, xi.

Chapter 1

5 *"Have you ever witnessed"*: James Weldon Johnson, *The Autobiography of an Ex-Colored Man* (n.p.: Digireads Publishing, 2016), p. 87.
"My first introduction to": Walter White to Richard Halliday, June 8, 1926, NAACP archives, file 001469-009-0488.
"light-skinned Negroes": Walter White, *A Man Called White: The Autobiography of Walter White* (Athens and London: University of Georgia Press, 1995), p. 5.
"I don't think they would": White, *A Man Called White,* p. 6.

6   *"If God is omnipotent"*: White, *A Man Called White*, p. 15.

"I am the girl's father": "Father Begged to Settle Case with Negro," *Atlanta Constitution*, September 22, 1906.

7   *"At first it was a gentle"*: Walter White, *Flight* (Baton Rouge: Louisiana State University Press, 1998), p. 72.

"Down he went": White, *Flight*, p. 73.

"There goes another": White, *A Man Called White*, p. 9.

"The fifteen slow successive": "Governor Calls All Troops Out," *Atlanta Constitution*, September 23, 1906.

8   20 BLACKS SLAIN IN ATLANTA: "20 BLACKS SLAIN IN ATLANTA RACE RIOTS," *St. Louis Post-Dispatch,* September 23, 1906.

30 NEGROES SLAIN: "30 Negroes Slain, Streets Run Blood," *Los Angeles Times,* September 23, 1906.

"We turned out the lights": White, *A Man Called White*, p. 10.

"My father," he recalled: Walter White to Richard Halliday, June 8, 1926, NAACP archives, file 001469-009-0488.

9   *"That's where that nigger"*: White, *A Man Called White*, p. 11.

"in a voice as quiet": White, *A Man Called White*, p. 11.

"You're not to fire": It Seems to Heywood Broun, *Nation*, May 21, 1930.

"Mother characteristically plunged": White, *A Man Called White*, p. 14.

"Then, in Atlanta, as in many": Poppy Cannon, *A Gentle Knight: My Husband Walter White* (New York: Popular Library, 1956), p. 161.

10   *"The white man and the"*: Mark Bauerlein, *Negrophobia: A Race Riot in Atlanta, 1906* (San Francisco: Encounter Books, 2001), p. 25.

"I call that particular change": Cited in C. Vann Woodward, *The Strange Career of Jim Crow* (Oxford: Oxford University Press, 1974), pp. 77–78.

11   *"I recall the first time"*: Charles Houston to Walter White, October 31, 1929, NAACP archives, file 001469-012-0281.

12   *"Compounded of fear"*: Walter White, "Outline Article for Pittsburgh Courier," Walter White Papers, box 22, folder 193, Beinecke Rare Book & Manuscript Library, Yale University.

"Those who have been": Walter White, *How Far the Promised Land?* (New York: Viking Press, 1955), p. 65.

"This is white man's country": Bauerlein, *Negrophobia*, p. 22.

13   *"As a boy there in the darkness"*: White, *A Man Called White*, pp. 11–12.

"After that night": It Seems to Heywood Broun.

Chapter 2

14   *"Atlanta University was a"*: Kenneth Janken, *White: The Biography of Walter White, Mr. NAACP* (New York: New Press, 2003), p. 19.

15   *"Mr. Astor"*: Poppy Cannon, *A Gentle Knight: My Husband Walter White* (New York: Popular Library, 1956), p. 136.

"There I talked with": Walter White to Eugene Saxton, August 23, 1923, NAACP archives, file 001469-007-0405.

"Despair and consternation": Walter White, *A Man Called White: The Autobiography of Walter White* (Athens and London: University of Georgia Press, 1995), p. 19.

16 *"hopeless"*: Walter White, "Outline Article for Pittsburgh Courier," Walter White Papers, box 22, folder 193, Beinecke Rare Book & Manuscript Library, Yale University.

"There are so many things": Edgar A. Toppin, "Walter White and the Atlanta NAACP's Fight for Equal Schools, 1916–1917," *History of Education Quarterly* 7, no. 1 (Spring 1967).

17 *"too young and too hot-headed"*: Thomas Dyja, *Walter White: The Dilemma of Black Identity in America* (Chicago: Ivan R. Dee, 2008), p. 38.

"I want to plead guilty": Toppin, "Atlanta NAACP's Fight."

"I do not wish to plead": Toppin, "Atlanta NAACP's Fight."

"If the NAACP does no more": Janken, *White: The Biography,* p. 25.

"so packed with eager-faced": White, *A Man Called White,* p. 33.

18 *"Tell them about the NAACP"*: White, *A Man Called White,* p. 34.

"We have got to show": White, *A Man Called White,* p. 34.

"From the whole group": James Weldon Johnson, *Along This Way: The Autobiography of James Weldon Johnson* (New York: Da Capo Press, 2000), p. 316.

19 *"colored people" that "they may"*: Patricia O'Toole, *The Moralist: Woodrow Wilson and the World He Made* (New York: Simon & Schuster Paperbacks, 2018), p. 171.

"inevitable ascendancy": David Levering Lewis, *W.E.B. Du Bois: The Fight for Equality and the American Century, 1919–1963* (New York: Henry Holt, 2000), p. 353.

"It is like writing history": A. Scott Berg, *Wilson* (New York: G. P. Putnam's Sons, 2013), p. 349.

20 *"The exercises were held"*: "Klan Is Established with Impressiveness," *Atlanta Constitution,* November 28, 1915.

MOTHER, DO LYNCHERS GO: "The NAACP's Silent Parade," *Blackbird: An Online Journal of Literature and the Arts* 16, no. 2 (Fall 2017).

"a war to make the world": "Nation's War Plan," *New York Times,* May 6, 1917.

21 *"My dear Mr. White"*: James Weldon Johnson to Walter White, October 7, 1917, Walter White Papers, box 3, folder 105, Beinecke Rare Book & Manuscript Library, Yale University.

"You realize my position here": Walter White to James Weldon Johnson, October 10, 1917, Walter White Papers, box 3, folder 105, Beinecke Rare Book & Manuscript Library, Yale University.

"I made some inquiries about": James Weldon Johnson to Walter White, January 5, 1918, Walter White Papers, box 3, folder 105, Beinecke Rare Book & Manuscript Library, Yale University.

"Sodom and Gomorrah": White, *A Man Called White*, p. 35.

22 *"Your mother and I have"*: White, *A Man Called White*, p. 37.

Chapter 3

23 *"Indeed," Johnson said*: James Weldon Johnson, *Black Manhattan* (New York: Da Capo Paperback, 1991), pp. 3–4.

25 *"All the sales clerks knew"*: Walter White, *A Man Called White: The Autobiography of Walter White* (Athens and London: University of Georgia Press, 1995), p. 39.
"Of the real leader the": James Weldon Johnson, *The Selected Writings of James Weldon Johnson*, vol. 1 (Oxford: Oxford University Press, 1995), p. 121.
"In New York you can see": Ann Douglas, *Terrible Honesty: Mongrel Manhattan in the 1920s* (New York: Noon Day Press, 1996), p. 17.

27 *"We were a group of"*: Mary White Ovington, *The Walls Came Tumbling Down* (New York: Schocken Books, 1970), p. 105.
"No organization like ours": David Levering Lewis, *W.E.B. Du Bois, 1868–1919: Biography of a Race* (New York: Owl Books, 1993), p. 494.
"We were desperately": Mary White Ovington, *Black and White Sat Down Together* (New York: Feminist Press at the City University of New York, 1995), p. 69.
"The object of this publication": *Crisis* 1, no. 1 (November 1910): 10.
"the Fighting Saint": Ovington, *The Walls Came Tumbling*, p. vii.

28 *"Virtue is never solitary"*: Jonathan Rosenberg, *How Far the Promised Land? World Affairs and the American Civil Rights Movement* (Princeton: Princeton University Press, 2006), p. 22.
"A mob of more than 1,500": "Mob Burns Negro, Urged On by Woman," *New York Times*, February 13, 1918.
THOUSANDS OF COLORED MEN: NAACP telegram to Hon. T. C. Rye, February 14, 1918, NAACP archives, file 001527-017-0790.
SPEAKING IN BEHALF OF MILLIONS: John R. Shillady to President Woodrow Wilson, February 13, 1918, NAACP archives, file 001527-017-0790.

29 *"Under the decisions of the Supreme"*: William C. Fitts to the NAACP, February 16, 1918, NAACP archives, file 001527-017-0790.
"without being requested": Gov. Tom C. Rye to John Shillady, February 21, 1918, NAACP archives, file 001527-017-0790.
"I asked permission to go to the scene": White, *A Man Called White*, p. 40.
"heavy-jowled and strikingly": Ovington, *The Walls Came Tumbling*, p. 114.

30 *"Eventually, however, he gave"*: White, *A Man Called White*, p. 40.
"My self-confidence steadily": White, *A Man Called White*, p. 40.
"the finest hotel in the south": "Hotel Patten," *Atlanta Constitution*, March 31, 1908.
"There is one bank": Walter White, "The Burning of Jim McIlherron: An N.A.A.C.P. Investigation," *Crisis* 16, no. 1 (May 1918): 16–20.

31 *"very great excitement"*: Walter White to John Shillady, February 18, 1918, NAACP archives, file 001527-017-0790.

"leisurely of manner": White to Shillady, February 18, 1918.

"Even when they boasted": White, *A Man Called White,* p. 41.

"Nothing contributes so much": Walter White, "I Investigate Lynchings," *American Mercury,* January 1929.

Chapter 4

32 *"known to be a fighter"*: Walter White, "The Burning of Jim McIlherron: An N.A.A.C.P. Investigation," *Crisis* 16, no. 1 (May 1918): 16–20.

"At this point": White, "Burning of Jim McIlherron."

33 *"One of them pointed his"*: White, "Burning of Jim McIlherron."

"frantic": White, "Burning of Jim McIlherron."

"A wide iron bar": White, "Burning of Jim McIlherron."

34 *"The statements of onlookers"*: White, "Burning of Jim McIlherron."

"I got all the information": Walter White to John Shillady, February 18, 1918, NAACP archives, file 001527-017-0790.

35 *"We come as a delegation"*: James Weldon Johnson, *Along This Way: The Autobiography of James Weldon Johnson* (New York: Da Capo Press, 2000), p. 323.

"We were surprised that": Johnson, *Along This Way,* p. 324.

"seek an opportunity": Johnson, *Along This Way,* p. 324.

36 *"The facts I uncovered"*: Walter White, *A Man Called White: The Autobiography of Walter White* (Athens and London: University of Georgia Press, 1995), p. 42.

"Your organization is a fighting": Henry Mims to John R. Shillady, July 5, 1918, NAACP archives, file 001423-019-0730.

"I want you to know": Oscar Baker to NAACP, April 18, 1918, NAACP archives, file 001427-011-0473.

"Mass Meeting . . . N.A.A.C.P.": NAACP flyer for White speaking engagement on December 3, 1918, NAACP archives, file unknown, document in the author's possession.

"Splendid meeting [in Jacksonville]": Walter White to James Weldon Johnson, November 12, 1918, NAACP archives, file 001412-024-0447.

"the best speech I have": Walter White to John R. Shillady, January 20, 1919, NAACP archives, file 001412-024-0447.

"In New Orleans I had one": Walter White to James Weldon Johnson, January 20, 1919, NAACP archives, file 001412-024-0447.

"Mr. Walter F. White, Assistant": James Weldon Johnson to T. L. McCoy, October 8, 1918, NAACP archives, file 001423-018-0492.

37 *"The Negro race is today"*: Walter White to E. O. Smith, June 20, 1918, NAACP archives, file 001423-019-0671.

"We have been deprived": "Reports of the Branches," November 1918, NAACP archives, file 001527-001-1121.

"raging in our city": "Reports of the Branches," November 1918.

38 *"I reached the scene shortly"*: Walter White, "I Investigate Lynchings," *American Mercury,* January 1929.

"The stores were well stocked": White, "I Investigate Lynchings."

"You'll pardon me": This dialogue is from White, "I Investigate Lynchings."

39 *"Little by little"*: White, "I Investigate Lynchings."

"[Spratling] declares that none": Walter White, "Memo Re: Brooks-Lowndes Counties Lynchings of May, 1918," NAACP archives, file 001527-010-0231.

40 *"The other end was tied"*: Walter White, "The Work of a Mob," *Crisis* 16, no. 5 (September 1918): 221–23.

"Members of the mob": White, "Work of a Mob."

"You're a government man": Dialogue from White, "I Investigate Lynchings."

41 *"with an air of great mystery"*: Dialogue from White, "I Investigate Lynchings."

"I reached Atlanta this": Walter White to John R. Shillady, July 9, 1918, NAACP archives, file 001527-010-0231.

"Below are given some of": "Memorandum for Governor Dorsey from Walter F. White," July 10, 1918, NAACP archives, file 001527-010-0231.

42 *"We are enclosing for your"*: John R. Shillady to Woodrow Wilson, July 28, 1919, NAACP archives, file 001527-010-0231.

"I allude to the mob spirit": Woodrow Wilson statement, July 26, 1918, Library of Congress book/printed material, https://www.loc.gov/item/rbpe.24101800/.

"The governor of the state": "Courage and Cowardice," *Chicago Defender,* June 1, 1918.

43 *"The details of the murder of"*: C. P. Dam to Walter White, September 13, 1918, The Mary Turner Project, Mary Turner Documents, http://www.maryturner.org /images/CPDam.pdf

"So far as I am able": Hugh M. Dorsey to John R. Shillady, August 27, 1928, NAACP archives, file 001527-010-0231.

Chapter 5

45 *"furnished the first sight"*: Cited in David Levering Lewis, "We Return Fighting," in *The Harlem Reader: A Celebration of New York's Most Famous Neighborhood,* ed. Herb Boyd (New York: Three Rivers Press, 2003), p. 19.

"For the final mile": David Levering Lewis, *When Harlem Was in Vogue* (New York: Penguin Books, 1997), p. 5.

46 *"The great test of the"*: "Baker's Democracy and the Colored Soldiers," *Evening Post* (New York), February 3, 1918.

"a credit to their organizations": Newton D. Baker to W.E.B. Du Bois, April 29, 1918, published in *Crisis* 16, no. 2 (June 1918).

"This is the country": W.E.B. DuBois, "Returning Soldiers," *Crisis* 18, no. 1 (May 1919): 13.

47 *"The negroes will come"*: Mark Robert Schneider, *"We Return Fighting": The Civil Rights Movement in the Jazz Age* (Boston: Northeastern University Press, 2002), p. 15.

"Our organization was like": Mary White Ovington, *Black and White Sat Down Together* (New York: Feminist Press at the City University of New York, 1995), pp. 88, 90.

"His head [looked] like": Alessandra Lorini, *Rituals of Race: American Public Culture and the Search for Racial Democracy* (Charlottesville: University Press of Virginia, 1999), p. 132.

48 *"We are a nation disgraced"*: Cameron McWhirter, *Red Summer: The Summer of 1919 and the Awakening of Black America* (New York: St. Martin's Griffin, 2011), p. 36.

"Arrangements are well": Minutes of the Meeting of the Board of Directors, March 10, 1919, NAACP archives, file 001412-001-0654.

"The famous auditorium was": James Weldon Johnson, *Along This Way: The Autobiography of James Weldon Johnson* (New York: Da Capo Press, 2000), p. 337.

"the stains of Disenfranchisement": Johnson, *Along This Way,* p. 337.

49 *"The facts concerning the"*: W.E.B. Du Bois, *Dusk of Dawn* (Oxford: Oxford University Press, 2007), p. 132.

"May 2, Warrenton": "The Lynching Industry, 1919," *Crisis* 19, no. 4 (February 1920).

50 JOHN HARTFIELD WILL BE: "John Hartfield Will Be Lynched by Ellisville Mob at 5 O'clock This Afternoon," *Jackson (MI) Daily News,* reprinted in the *New Orleans States,* June 26, 1919.

"powerless to prevent it": "John Hartfield Will Be Lynched."

"Before the very gates": "After WWI, a Burst of Race Riots," *Washington Post,* July 17, 2011.

"I spent three hours": Walter White to Mary White Ovington, August 7, 1919, NAACP archives, file 001412-024-0467.

51 *"I ducked as a bullet"*: Walter White, *A Man Called White: The Autobiography of Walter White* (Athens and London: University of Georgia Press, 1995), p. 45.

"All three of these I expect": Walter White to Mary White Ovington, July 30, 1919, NAACP archives, file 001412-024-0467.

"It is not possible to": Walter F. White, "Election Day in Florida," *Crisis* 21, no. 3 (January 1921): 106–109.

"an unusual tenseness": White to Ovington, July 30, 1919.

Chapter 6

53 *"Do you think there is"*: Dialogue from Mary White Ovington, *The Walls Came Tumbling Down* (New York: Schocken Books, 1970), pp. 172–73, and *Black and White Sat Down Together* (New York: Feminist Press at the City University of New York, 1995), p. 91.

54 *"armed uprising"*: "Mobbing of John R. Shillady: Statement by the National Association for the Advancement of Colored People," October 1919, https://archive .org/stream/mobbingofjohnrshoonati/mobbingofjohnrshoonati_djvu.txt.

"remarked that he felt": Dialogue is from "Mobbing of John R. Shillady."

"You don't see my point": Cameron McWhirter, *Red Summer: The Summer of 1919 and the Awakening of Black America* (New York: St. Martin's Griffin, 2011), p. 165.

55 *"Shillady was the only"*: "Mobbing of John R. Shillady."

"I believe in Texas for": "Hobby Favors Intervention," *Gazette Times* (Pittsburgh), September 3, 1919.

56 *"These radical leaders"*: "Blames Race Riots on Negro Leaders," *New York Times*, August 26, 1919.

57 *"No, not tonight, but"*: Pablo Correa, "Spectacle Lynching and the NAACP's Push for Anti-Lynch Legislation" (dissertation, Florida State University, 2018).

"the turning point in the": James Weldon Johnson, *Black Manhattan* (New York: Da Capo Paperback, 1991), p. 246. Also James Weldon Johnson, "The Riots: An N.A.A.C.P. Investigation," *Crisis* 18, no. 5 (September 1919): 241–43.

"If we must die": "If We Must Die," Claude McKay, https://www.poetryfoundation .org/poems/44694/if-we-must-die.

58 *"Scattered clashes today"*: "Six More Are Killed in Arkansas Riots," *New York Times*, October 3, 1919.

"[I am] exceedingly anxious": Kenneth Janken, *White: The Biography of Walter White, Mr. NAACP* (New York: New Press, 2003), p. 51.

"I purposely led him": White, *A Man Called White*, p. 49.

"I am delighted that": White, *A Man Called White*, pp. 49–50.

"The cause of the Phillips": Walter White, "'Massacring Whites' in Arkansas," *Nation*, December 6, 1919.

59 *"As I stepped from the train"*: Walter White, "I Investigate Lynchings," *American Mercury*, January 1929.

"According to Pratt": White, "'Massacring Whites.'"

60 *"Plantation owners . . . sought"*: Henry Louis Gates Jr., *Stony the Road: Reconstruction, White Supremacy, and the Rise of Jim Crow* (New York: Penguin, 2020), p. 17.

"Get the hell out": White, "'Massacring Whites.'"

"advancing the intellectual": White, "'Massacring Whites.'"

"Do you believe in God?": White, "'Massacring Whites.'"

61 *"a plot to massacre whites"*: "The Arkansas Cases," *Crisis* 25, no. 5 (March 1923): 220–21.

"under order to shoot": Francine Uenuma, "The Massacre of Black Sharecroppers That Led the Supreme Court to Curb Racial Disparities of the Justice System," *Smithsonian*, August 2, 2018.

"I was never able to fix": White, *A Man Called White*, p. 49.

"Why, Mister," said the ticket: Dialogue from White, "I Investigate Lynchings."

62 *"The court room was thronged"*: Walter White to George Wickersham Esq., March 9, 1923, NAACP archives, file 001527-020-0852.
"There is not a civilized": David Levering Lewis, *W.E.B. Du Bois: A Biography, 1868–1963* (New York: John Macrae/Holt Paperback, 2009), p. 389.
"You have it in your power": J. E. Spingarn to Charles H. Brough, included in a November 17, 1919, NAACP press release, NAACP archives, file 001446-001-0205.
"I don't know where I can get": Scipio A. Jones to Walter White, March 25, 1921, NAACP archives, file 001527-008-0232.

Chapter 7

64 *"these years were not all"*: Walter White, *A Man Called White: The Autobiography of Walter White* (Athens and London: University of Georgia Press, 1995), p. 43.
"Frequently, [the Johnsons'] apartment": White, *A Man Called White*, p. 43.
"I am an all-or-nothing man": Poppy Cannon, *A Gentle Knight: My Husband Walter White* (New York: Popular Library, 1956), p. 228.

65 *"The whole world revolves"*: Ann Douglas, *Terrible Honesty: Mongrel Manhattan in the 1920s* (New York: Noon Day Press, 1996), p. 15.
"It seems rather like a": Johnson, *Black Manhattan*, p. 260.

66 *"They took fright, they"*: Johnson, *Black Manhattan*, p. 150.
"with one dollar and fifty": David Levering Lewis, *When Harlem Was in Vogue* (New York: Penguin Books, 1997), p. 96.
"It is a quite certain, but": Robert E. Park and Ernest W. Burgess, *The City* (Chicago: University of Chicago Press, 2019), pp. 2–3.
"The New Negro": "The New Negro — What Is He?" *Messenger,* August 1920.

67 *"The New Negro, unlike the"*: Lewis, *When Harlem Was in Vogue*, p. 24.
"I need the smell of carbon": Cannon, *Gentle Knight*, p. 195.
"Everything White did": Lewis, *When Harlem Was in Vogue*, p. 130.
"world leader and a negro": "Marcus Garvey Doggedly Pushes His Pet Hobby," *Philadelphia Tribune,* August 7, 1920.

68 *"What is good for the white"*: "Marcus Garvey Doggedly."
"one of the most remarkable": Johnson, *Black Manhattan*, p. 251.
"the luxurian vegetation of our": Robert A. Hill, ed., *The Marcus Garvey and Universal Negro Improvement Association Papers,* vol. 3 (Berkeley: University of California Press, 1984), p. 319.
"Negro nation": Lewis, *When Harlem Was in Vogue*, p. 40.
"As far as I am aware": Lewis, *When Harlem Was in Vogue,* p. 39.
"Being a race leader dawned upon": E. David Cronon, *Black Moses: The Story of Marcus Garvey* (Madison: University of Wisconsin Press, 1969), p. 6.

69 *"There's a young man here"*: Lewis, *When Harlem Was in Vogue,* p. 34.
"The man spoke": Johnson, *Black Manhattan*, p. 253.
"Send Us a Dollar": Advertisement in *Negro World,* December 17, 1921.

"Fellowmen of the Negro Race": The NAACP collected issues of the *Negro World,* included in NAACP archives, file 001421-035-0645.

70   *"There were gorgeous uniforms"*: Johnson, *Black Manhattan,* p. 254.

"The world has made being": Tony Martin, *Race First: The Ideological and Organizational Struggles of Marcus Garvey and the Universal Negro Improvement Association* (Dover, MA: Majority Press, 1976), p. 23.

"Garvey was the first Negro": Lewis, *When Harlem Was in Vogue,* p. 39.

"It is a little difficult": "Marcus Garvey," *Crisis* 21, no. 2 (December 1920): 58–60.

71   *"does not deal with such"*: Marcus Garvey to Walter White, October 16, 1920, NAACP archives, file 001527-018-0751.

"Is this Marcus Garvey really": Edgar Collins [estimated, signature slightly illegible] to James Weldon Johnson, March 12, 1921, NAACP archives, file 001527-018-0751.

"John's physical condition": White, *A Man Called White,* pp. 46–47.

"I am of the opinion that": memorandum to the Board of Directors, George Crawford, November 19, 1919, NAACP archives, file 001446-001-0205.

"broke," Walter recalled. "We owed": White, *A Man Called White,* p. 47.

"Our empty treasury began": White, *A Man Called White,* p. 52.

72   *"He is a respectable businessman"*: Ruth Crowd Wilkerson to James Weldon Johnson, undated, NAACP archives, file 001422-005-0001.

"Nigger, we are here": "Ku Klux Klan Is Spreading Over Indiana," *Indianapolis Ledger,* July 1, 1922.

"You niggers are getting too": "Ku Klux Klan" to "Redmond the Druggist," October 16, 1921, NAACP archives, file 001422-005-0001.

"The activities of the Ku": A. C. MacNeal to Walter White, April 9, 1921, NAACP archives, file 001422-005-0001.

73   *"The modern Knights of the Ku"*: "Ku Klux Klan to Organize Here," undated news clipping, NAACP archives, file 001422-005-0001.

"Your inquiry has been received": Walter White's application to the KKK, September 21, 1920, NAACP archives, file 001422-004-0705.

Chapter 8

75   KILL TWO WHITES AND SIX: "Kill Two Whites and Six Negroes in Florida Riot," *New York Times,* November 4, 1920.

76   *"My resolution," he announced*: "Demands Inquiry on Disenfranchising," *New York Times,* December 6, 1920.

77   *"There is no question of course"*: George Holden Tinkham to Walter White, January 12, 1921, NAACP archives, file 001422-027-0973.

78   *"to bring all pressure possible"*: Walter White to George Holden Tinkham, January 11, 1921, NAACP archives, file 001422-027-0973.

"This committee must inquire": This dialogue is from "Rep. Tinkham Is 'Tight,'" *Afro-American* (Baltimore), January 21, 1921. Also: *Apportionment of*

Representatives, Committee on the Census, House of Representatives H.R. 14498, H.R. 15021, H.R. 15158, and H.R. 15217, Washington, DC: US Government Printing Office, 1921.

"Mr. Chairman," Larsen said: Apportionment of Representatives.

79 *"In Orlando, a like band":* Affidavit from Alexander Akerman, undated, NAACP archives, file 001422-004-0705.

"In my county," he said: Apportionment of Representatives.

80 *"I suppose you have seen by":* Walter White to Moorfield Storey, January 4, 1921, NAACP archives, file 001422-027-0973.

"We are told that the Ku": "Imperial Wizard Explains Object of Ku Klux Klan," *Democrat-Reporter* (Linden, AL), January 20, 1921.

81 *"The Chairman [Mary White Ovington]":* Minutes of the Meeting of the Board of Directors, January 10, 1921, NAACP archives, file 001412-001-0809.

"As a leading citizen": Walter White, *A Man Called White: The Autobiography of Walter White* (Athens and London: University of Georgia Press, 1995), p. 54.

82 *"I wrote the Klan on plain":* White, *A Man Called White,* p. 54.

"letters threatening my life": White, *A Man Called White,* p. 55.

The N.A.A.C.P. vs. The K.K.K.: N.A.A.C.P. vs. The K.K.K., undated pamphlet, NAACP archives, file 001422-005-0354.

"fighting fire with fire": Walter White to Alben L. Holsey, February 11, 1921, NAACP archives, file 001422-005-0001.

"met by armed resistance": Walter White to Mary Christine DeBardeleben, February 19, 1921, NAACP archives, file 001422-005-0001.

"laugh the Klan out of": Walter White to Alben L. Holsey, February 21, 1921, NAACP archives, file 001422-005-0001.

83 *"That the Ku Klux problem":* "Shadow of Ku Klux Klan Grows Larger in Congress and Nation," *New York Times,* December 10, 1922.

"Negro named Walter White": White, *A Man Called White,* p. 56.

"No Kluxer will ever put": White, *A Man Called White,* p. 56.

Chapter 9

84 *"the single worst incident of":* "Tulsa Race Massacre," Oklahoma Historical Society, https://www.okhistory.org/publications/enc/entry.php?entryname=TULSA%20 RACE%20MASSACRE.

85 *"Nab Negro for Attacking":* Scott Ellsworth, *Death in the Promised Land: The Tulsa Race Riot of 1921* (Baton Rouge: Louisiana State University Press, 1982), p. 48.

"It depends on where you": William Danforth Williams, interview, 1921 Tulsa Race Massacre, Tulsa Historical Society & Museum, https://soundcloud.com/user -604183945.

"They ran the whole county": W. R. Holway, interview, 1921 Tulsa Race Massacre, Tulsa Historical Society & Museum, https://soundcloud.com/user-604183945.

"So they all started away": Williams interview.

85 *"a dozen or more" aircraft:* "Tulsa Shooting Stirs Memories of Race Riot," CNN Wire Service, October 4, 2016.
"After twenty-four hours of ": "Series of Fierce Combats," *New York Times,* June 2, 1921.
"I arrived in Tulsa while": Walter White, "I Investigate Lynchings," *American Mercury,* January 1929.
"I might have been a thug": White, "I Investigate Lynchings."

86 *"Now you can go out":* White, "I Investigate Lynchings."
"You say that your name is White?": Dialogue from White, "I Investigate Lynchings."

87 *"Detachments of guardsmen":* "Nine White, 65 Negroes Killed in Tulsa Race Riot," *Saint Louis Post-Dispatch,* June 1, 1921.

88 *"in ashes. . . . As far as one":* Mark Robert Schneider, *"We Return Fighting": The Civil Rights Movement in the Jazz Age* (Boston: Northeastern University Press, 2002), p. 159.
"The look in their eyes": Quoted in *Report on Tulsa Race Riot of 1921,* Oklahoma Commission to Study the Tulsa Race Riot of 1921, https://archive.org/details /ReportOnTulsaRaceRiotOf1921/page/n3/mode/2up.
"No matter whether it was": "Taft Charges Riot at Tulsa Was Due Largely to Whites," *Washington Post,* June 6, 1921.
"Despite the demagogues": "Harding Says Negro Must Have Equality in Political Life," *New York Times,* October 27, 1921.

89 *"There is a lesson in":* Walter White, "The Eruption of Tulsa," *Nation,* June 29, 1921.
"More than a hundred anonymous": White, "I Investigate Lynchings."

90 *"It is . . . our desire to launch":* Walter White to L. C. Dyer, May 15, 1918, NAACP archives, file 001529-011-0530.
"The real trouble with this": Merrill Moores to Walter White, May 17, 1918, NAACP archives, file 001412-019-0718.

91 *"The entire machinery of the":* James Weldon Johnson, *Along This Way: The Autobiography of James Weldon Johnson* (New York: Da Capo Press, 2000), p. 362.
"I am directed to say that": Secretary to the President to James Weldon Johnson, June 9, 1921, NAACP archives, file 001412-016-0229.
"There was intense excitement": Johnson, *Along This Way,* p. 366.
"I am opposed to mob": Philip Dray, *At the Hands of Persons Unknown: The Lynching of Black America* (New York: Modern Library, 2003), p. 264. Also *Congressional Record: Proceedings and Debates of the Sixty-Seventh Congress of the United States of America* (Washington, DC: US Government Printing Office, 1922), pp. 197–99.
"I am pouring into them": Kevin C. Murphy, "Uphill All the Way: The Fortunes of Progressivism, 1919–1929," academic paper, Columbia University, 2013.
"monstrous attempt to federalize": Dray, *At the Hands,* p. 265.

92 *"Sit down, you niggers!":* Dialogue from Johnson, *Along This Way,* p. 366.

"You who are supporting this": Congressional Record, Proceedings and Debates of the Second Session of the Sixty-Seventh Congress of the United States of America (Washington, DC: US Government Printing Office, 1922), pp. 1718–21.

93 *"a wave of thanksgiving"*: Johnson, *Along This Way*, p. 366.

"If the Senate of the United": "I'll Sign Dyer Bill — Harding," *Chicago Defender*, February 18, 1922.

"scores of officials of the": "Many Officials Ku Klux Klansmen," *Christian Science Monitor*, May 9, 1922.

94 *"Ku Klux Klan Growing by"*: "Ku Klux Klan Growing by Leaps and Bounds in Delaware," *Wilmington Advocate*, July 1, 1922.

"We are in politics from the": "300 Klan Women Robed and Masked Parade in Atlanta," New York *Evening Post*, November 22, 1922.

"We must use every effort": Walter White to Bishop John Hurst, February 7, 1921, NAACP archives, file 001422-005-0001.

"I hope your act will . . . become": Hearings Before the Committee on the Judiciary, House of Representatives, H.R. *10210, 10235, 10379, 10616, 10650, 11089*, December 11 and 16, 1919 (Washington, DC: US Government Printing Office).

"one of the most efficiently": "Anti-Lynching Bill Dead," *Austin Evening Statesman*, December 3, 1922.

FILIBUSTER KILLS ANTI-LYNCHING: "Filibuster Kills Anti-Lynching Bill, *New York Times*, December 3, 1922.

95 *"The Shame of America"*: The ad is pictured in Schneider, *"We Return Fighting,"* p. 191.

"The ad is great": Schneider, *"We Return Fighting,"* p. 190.

"From December 4, the day": James Weldon Johnson, "An Open Letter to Every Senator of the United States," December 13, 1922, NAACP archives, file 001529-015-0299.

"The campaign for federal": White, *A Man Called White*, pp. 42–43.

Chapter 10

96 *"The NAACP is religion"*: Robert L. Zagrando and Ronald L. Lewis, *Walter F. White: The NAACP's Ambassador for Racial Justice* (Morgantown: University of West Virginia Press, 2019), p. 50.

"Surely," he whispered: Konrad Bercovici, *Around the World in New York* (New York: Century, 1924), p. 222.

97 *"There are few Negroes of"*: Walter White, "Crossing the Color Line," manuscript, Walter White Papers, Schomburg Center for Research in Black Culture, Manuscripts, Archives and Rare Books Division.

"What sort of a looking": Walter White, "Exploits of a Colored Investigator of Lynchings," New York *Evening Post*, April 8, 1922.

"'It's a Cinch to Pass'": "'It's a Cinch to Pass for White' Says Author," *Afro-American* (Baltimore), February 7, 1923.

"*I have personally investigated*": Walter White to Eugene Saxton, August 23, 1923, NAACP archives, file 001469-007-0405.

98 "*I have to have something*": Poppy Cannon, *A Gentle Knight: My Husband Walter White* (New York: Popular Library, 1956), p. 168.

"*With Walter,*" one confidant: Cannon, *Gentle Knight*, p. 182.

"*Walter was just an impossibly*": Oral history of Arthur Spingarn, Ralph J. Bunche Oral History Project, March 6, 1968, quoted in Kenneth Janken, *White: The Biography of Walter White, Mr. NAACP* (New York: New Press, 2003), p. 138.

"*considered by many of her*": E. J. Kahn Jr., "The Frontal Attack—II," Profiles, *New Yorker,* September 11, 1948.

99 "*Mr. Johnson intimated to me*": Walter White to Moorfield Storey, May 7, 1925, NAACP archives, file 001412-024-0606.

"*Nowhere in the city except*": Konrad Bercovici, "The Black Blocks of Manhattan," *Harper's Monthly Magazine,* October 1, 1924.

"*Grace and I entertained*": James Weldon Johnson, *Along This Way: The Autobiography of James Weldon Johnson* (New York: Da Capo Press, 2000), p. 379.

100 "*Although his fingers looked*": Roy Wilkins, *Standing Fast: The Autobiography of Roy Wilkins* (New York: Da Capo Press, 1994), p. 156.

"*Night after night there*": "The Caucasian Storms Harlem," Rudolph Fisher, *American Mercury,* August 1927.

"*You had rights that could*": Rudolph Fisher, "The City of Refuge," *The New Negro: Voices of the Harlem Renaissance,* ed. Alain Locke (New York: Touchstone, 1997), p. 58.

"*one of the best-known figures*": Bercovici, "Black Blocks of Manhattan."

101 "*The movement became more*": James Weldon Johnson, *Black Manhattan* (New York: Da Capo Paperback, 1991), p. 255.

"*the Sublime Order of the Nile*": Johnson, *Black Manhattan*, p. 254.

102 "*I gave everybody a chance*": David Levering Lewis, *When Harlem Was in Vogue* (New York: Penguin Books, 1997), p. 38.

"*This open ally of the Ku*": W.E.B. Du Bois, "The American Scene," *Crisis* 28, no. 21 (May 1924): 7–9.

"*Knowing the power and influence*": "Garvey's Klan Parley Revealed by Imperial Giant of Ku Klux," *New York Amsterdam News,* February 14, 1923.

"*The sense of this interview*": Walter White to Louis R. Glavis, August 28, 1924, NAACP archives, file 001421-035-0844.

103 "*Universal Negro Improvement*": Ad appearing in *Negro World,* October 8, 1921.

"*You Work Hard For Your*": *Negro World* ad.

"*This would be a calamity*": W.E.B. Du Bois, "Marcus Garvey," *Crisis* 21, no. 3 (January 1921): 112–15.

"*Marcus Garvey is, without*": Du Bois, "The American Scene."

"*Be careful, or we may*": E. David Cronon, *Black Moses: The Story of Marcus Garvey* (Madison: University of Wisconsin Press, 1969), p. 109.

"All the troubles we have had": Marcus Garvey, *The Marcus Garvey and Universal Negro Improvement Association Papers,* vol. 9, ed. Robert A. Hill (Berkeley: University of California Press, 1995), p. 324.

104 *"Let me tell you somebody"*: Cronon, *Black Moses,* p. 108.

"Within ten years of": Johnson, *Black Manhattan,* p. 256.

"The central idea of Garvey's": Johnson, *Black Manhattan,* p. 258.

"Collapse of the Garvey": Walter White, *How Far the Promised Land?* (New York: Viking Press, 1955), p. 222.

105 *"He has a gorgeous baritone"*: Walter White to Roland Hayes, December 26, 1924, NAACP archives, file 001469-008-0354.

"would always be able to": Lewis, *When Harlem Was in Vogue,* p. 138.

"Gladys and I sat up late": Walter White to Essie and Paul Robeson, September 28, 1925, NAACP archives, file 001469-009-0250.

106 *"I want to have a talk with"*: Walter White to Countee Cullen, April 14, 1924, NAACP archives, file 001469-007-0584.

"Walter, I am really doing my": Lewis, *When Harlem Was in Vogue,* p. 138.

"Although there is no single": James Weldon Johnson, *The Selected Writings of James Weldon Johnson,* vol. 1, ed. Sondra Kathryn Wilson (Oxford: Oxford University Press, 1995), p. 249.

107 *"It dances"*: Lewis, *When Harlem Was in Vogue,* p. 59.

"the first negro work I have": Lewis, *When Harlem Was in Vogue,* p. 59.

"This play looks to me": H. L. Mencken to Walter White, March 13, 1922, Walter White Papers, box 4, folder 137, Beinecke Rare Book & Manuscript Library, Yale University.

"I said that Stribling's": Walter White, *A Man Called White: The Autobiography of Walter White* (Athens and London: University of Georgia Press, 1995), p. 65.

"Why don't you do the": White, *A Man Called White,* p. 65.

108 *"I started to write"*: White, *A Man Called White,* p. 66.

"The accumulation of experience": Lewis, *When Harlem Was in Vogue,* p. 132.

Chapter 11

109 *"Now," he explained in a cover*: Walter White to Eugene Saxton, August 23, 1923 [this letter is likely misdated], NAACP archives, file 001469-007-0405.

110 *"as conservative and respectable"*: Walter White to H. L. Mencken, October 17, 1923, quoted in Charles F. Clooney, "Walter White and the Harlem Renaissance," *Journal of Negro History* 57 (July 1972).

"Boni and Liveright": Kenneth Janken, *White: The Biography of Walter White, Mr. NAACP* (New York: New Press, 2003), p. 108.

"We have gone over the": Eugene Saxton to Walter White, August 16, 1923, NAACP archives, file 001469-007-0405.

111 *"The principal reason we have"*: Walter White to Eugene Saxton, August 19, 1923, NAACP archives, file 001469-007-0405.

"If in fact a trial is dominated": Decision by Justice Oliver Wendell Holmes, *Moore et al. v. Dempsey,* Keeper of Arkansas State Penitentiary, Decided February 19, 1923, https://www.law.cornell.edu/supremecourt/text/261/86.

"I am writing within five": Walter White to Louis Marshall, June 25, 1923, NAACP archives, file 001412-024-0606.

112 ELAINE RIOTERS FREED: "Elaine Rioters Freed," *Pittsburgh Courier,* June 30, 1923.

"It was my first chance to": Roy Wilkins, *Standing Fast: The Autobiography of Roy Wilkins* (New York: Da Capo Press, 1994), p. 53.

"Look around you, sir": Wilkins, *Standing Fast,* p. 54.

"Ten thousand black people rose": Wilkins, *Standing Fast,* p. 54.

113 *"as good meals as any club"*: Mary White Ovington, *The Walls Came Tumbling Down* (New York: Schocken Books, 1970), p. 194.

"one of the most significant": Harold Bloom, *The Harlem Renaissance* (Philadelphia: Chelsea House Publishers, 2004), p. 174.

"What American literature": David Levering Lewis, *When Harlem Was in Vogue* (New York: Penguin Books, 1997), pp. 93–94.

114 *"the most sporting editor"*: "Race Authors in Dinner to Praise Jessie Fauset for New Novel on Negro," *Pittsburgh Courier,* March 29, 1924.

"the greatest novel yet written": "The American Negro Enters Literature," *Literary Digest International Book Review* 4 (December 1925–November 1926): 253.

"It manages to make civilization": Freda Kirchwey, "What Is the Solution?," review of *The Fire in the Flint, New York Herald,* September 28, 1924.

"one of the foremost novelists": "Walter White to Write for the Courier," *Pittsburgh Courier,* March 6, 1926.

115 *"splendidly courageous, rather"*: Alfred Knopf publicity literature, March 16, 1926, NAACP archives, file 001469-009-0596.

"The Fire in the Flint *and"*: Sinclair Lewis to Joel Spingarn, September 6, 1924, Joel Spingarn Papers, Manuscripts and Archives Division, New York Public Library.

"'The Fire in the Flint held me'": Eugene O'Neill to Walter White, October 12, 1924, NAACP archives, file 001469-008-0354.

"one of the younger writers": "'The Fire in the Flint' Draws Fire," *New Journal and Guide,* October 8, 1924.

"unfair, unjust, and thoroughly": "Georgia Calls Walter White's Novel 'A Book of Lies,'" *Afro-American* (Baltimore), December 6, 1924.

"To those who are intelligently": "Georgia Calls."

"I am glad to say": Walter White to Moorfield Storey, October 15, 1924, NAACP archives, file 001469-008-0148.

"Your idea of dramatizing": Eugene O'Neill to Walter White, October 24, 1924, NAACP archives, file 001469-008-0354.

116 *"The acid test which proves"*: Undated and unsigned speech manuscript written by

someone who claims to have "known Mr. White more or less intimately for thirty years," NAACP archives, file 001422-035-0395.

"*the wildest in U.S. history*": Jack Shafer, "1924: The Wildest Convention in U.S. History," *Politico,* March 7, 2016.

"*Mac! Mac! McAdoo!*": Shafer, "1924."

117   "*The Klan has a large following*": NAACP, "Negro Vote May Be Made Anti-Klan; Power in 1924 Election, Says NAACP," press release, November 9, 1923, NAACP archives, file 001422-019-0948.

"*As far as the eye could*": "40,000 Klansmen Parade in Washington as 200,000 Spectators Look On Quietly," *New York Times,* August 9, 1925.

118   SIGHT ASTONISHES CAPITAL [*sic*]: "40,000 Klansmen Parade."

"*Get the damn niggers*": Alan Mallach, *The Divided City: Poverty and Prosperity in Urban America* (Washington, DC: Island Press, 2018), p. 77.

119   "*Homicide warrants were*": "Seek 10 Arrests in Race War," *World* (New York), September 11, 1925.

FULLEST INFORMATION POSSIBLE: James Weldon Johnson, telegram to Rev. R. L. Bradby, September 11, 1925, NAACP archives, file 001521-002-0923.

5,000 INFURIATED PEOPLE: Telegram quoted in Detroit branch of the NAACP to James Weldon Johnson, September 12, 1925, NAACP archives, file 001521-002-0923.

"*It will be necessary to have*": W. Hayes McKinney to NAACP national headquarters, September 14, 1925, NAACP archives, file 001521-002-0923.

Chapter 12

120   "*I have been almost forced*": Walter White to Claude McKay, May 20, 1925, NAACP archives, file 001469-009-0020.

121   "*Judge Jayne tells me that*": Walter White to James Weldon Johnson, September 17, 1925, NAACP archives, file 001521-002-0923.

"*I pointed out that this*": White to Johnson, September 17, 1925.

"*The bearer of this letter*": To Whom It May Concern from the City of Detroit, September 16, 1925, NAACP archives, file 001521-002-0923.

122   CONFERENCES ALL DAY: Walter White, telegram to James Weldon Johnson, September 16, 1925, NAACP archives, file 001521-002-0923.

"*Here is the story of the*": White to Johnson, September 17, 1925.

"*We'll throw no stones*": White to Johnson, September 17, 1925.

"*About 2000 whites around house*": Statement of O. H. Sweet, September 12, 1925, NAACP archives, file 001521-002-0923.

123   "*Under Michigan statutes*": White to Johnson, September 17, 1925.

"*from one of Detroit's oldest*": White to Johnson, September 17, 1925.

"*Splendid work on your part*": James Weldon Johnson, telegram to Walter White, September 17, 1925, NAACP archives, file 001521-002-1030.

"The evidence shows no act": Kevin Boyle, *Arc of Justice: A Saga of Race, Civil Rights, and Murder in the Jazz Age* (New York: Henry Holt, 2004), p. 193.

124 *"For a good cause and the"*: Boyle, *Arc of Justice*, p. 220.

"Though I suffer and am torn": Boyle, *Arc of Justice*, p. 220.

"one of the best trial men": White to Johnson, September 17, 1925.

"I am convinced more than": White to Johnson, September 17, 1925.

"No case of this kind has": Walter White, undated and unnamed manuscript, p. 4, NAACP archives, file 001521-003-0372.

"without a roof over his": Walter White to Fay Lewis, January 18, 1926, NAACP archives, file 001469-009-0418.

125 *"Several other lawyers, somewhat"*: Walter White, *A Man Called White: The Autobiography of Walter White* (Athens and London: University of Georgia Press, 1995), p. 75.

"I have got to go to Detroit": Walter White to Blanche Knopf, October 8, 1925, NAACP archives, file 001469-009-0281.

"Thank God! We can now": White, *A Man Called White*, p. 74.

"The importance of the case": White, *A Man Called White*, p. 74.

126 *"It is our separate and collective"*: William E. Davis, Dr. O. H. Sweet, Leonard C. Moore, Chas. B. Washington to W. Hayes McKinney, legal counsel NAACP, September 29, 1925, NAACP archives, file 001521-002-1164.

127 *"listened with deep sympathy"*: White, *A Man Called White*, p. 75.

"I mean your race": Dialogue from E. J. Kahn Jr., "The Frontal Attack — I," Profiles, *New Yorker*, September 4, 1948.

128 NATIONAL OFFICE OF NAACP: Walter White telegram to Dr. O. H. Sweet, October 9, 1925, NAACP archives, file 001521-002-1164.

"Did the defendants shoot": Dialogue from White, *A Man Called White*, p. 76.

"I am going to get $5,000": "Mich. Murder Trial Starts Friday: Dr. Sweet and Others Go on Trial October 30," *New York Amsterdam News*, October 28, 1925.

129 *"Dr. Sweet [Judge Murphy said] has the same right"*: Michael Hannon, *The people v. Ossian Sweet, Gladys Sweet, et al. (1925), The People v. Henry Sweet (1926)*, 2010, University of Minnesota Law Library, http://moses.law.umn.edu/darrow/trialpdfs /SWEET_TRIALS.pdf.

"Here at last is 'Flight'": Walter White to Blanche Knopf, October 29, 1925, NAACP archives, file 001469-009-0281.

"The city of Detroit prosecutor has been": "Darrow Starts Quiz of Jurors in Dr. Sweet's Case," *Chicago Defender*, November 7, 1925.

"I don't give a God damn": White, *A Man Called White*, p. 78.

"We are not ashamed": State of Michigan in the Recorder's Court for the City of Detroit, No. 30317, NAACP archives, file 001521-003-0919.

130 *"Well, I hadn't counted accurately"*: "Darrow Bares Conspiracy in Sweet Case," *Chicago Defender*, November 14, 1925.

"*When I opened the door*": David E. Lilienthal, "Has the Negro the Right of Self-Defense?" *Nation,* December 23, 1925.

"*In connections with the*": "Klan's Hand Seen in Detroit Race Friction," *New York Amsterdam News,* September 23, 1925.

"*Are Negroes to be forced*": Walter White, "Negro Segregation Comes North," *Nation,* October 21, 1925.

131 "*At last all the testimony*": White, *A Man Called White,* p. 78.

"*A deep silence fell*": Lilienthal, "Has the Negro the Right."

"*Clarence Darrow, the greatest*": "Director of Branches" to "My Dear Rev.," December 3, 1925, NAACP archives, file 001521-001-0811.

"*from the point of view of*": NAACP, "Darrow Will Draw Huge Crowd at Sweet Case Meeting Dec. 13 in Salem M.E. Church," press release, December 4, 1925, NAACP archives, file 001521-001-0811.

132 "*The sooner you people find*": "2 Negro Audiences Applaud Darrow," *World* (New York), December 14, 1925.

"*The only weapon the Negro*": "Darrow Jeers 'Noble Nordics' Before Negroes," *New York Herald Tribune,* December 14, 1925.

Chapter 13

134 "*I did not find a town*": Mary White Ovington, *The Walls Came Tumbling Down* (New York: Schocken Books, 1970), p. 223.

135 "*Negro illiteracy had fallen*": Roy Wilkins, *Standing Fast: The Autobiography of Roy Wilkins* (New York: Da Capo Press, 1994), p. 73.

"*This new phase of things*": Alain Locke, "The New Negro," in *The New Negro: Voices of the Harlem Renaissance,* ed. Alain Locke (New York: Touchstone, 1992), p. 10.

136 "*This volume aims to document*": Locke, "The New Negro," p. xxv.

"*The real pride of a people*": James Weldon Johnson, "Some New Books of Poetry and Their Makers," September 7, 1918, *The Selected Writings of James Weldon Johnson,* vol. 1 (Oxford: Oxford University Press, 1995), pp. 272–73.

137 "*It is a book of surprises*": "From Cotton Field and Levee to the Streets of Harlem," *New York Times,* December 20, 1925.

"*on the edge, if not already*": Henry Louis Gates Jr., "Black Creativity: On the Cutting Edge," *Time,* October 10, 1994.

"*Things are certainly moving*": Walter White to Claude McKay, May 20, 1925, NAACP archives, file 001469-009-0020.

138 "*The Sinclair Lewis business is*": Blanche Knopf to Walter White, September 29, 1925, NAACP archives, file 001469-009-0250.

"*I slit them open eagerly*": Walter White, "The Spotlight," *Pittsburgh Courier,* July 3, 1926.

"*less important and persuasive*": "Black and White: Flight," *New York Times,* April 11, 1926.

"'*Flight' is not perfect*": Book review, *Pittsburgh Courier,* May 1, 1926.

"It is a pleasure to be able": Carl Van Vechten, "A Triumphant Negro," *New York Herald Tribune,* April 11, 1926.

"Reactions to criticisms are": White, "The Spotlight."

139 *"I can imagine no job which"*: Walter White to Ethel Bodient Gilbert, October 6, 1926, NAACP archives, file 001469-010-0329.

"I am too new at the game": Walter White to John Haynes Holmes, May 6, 1926, NAACP archives, file 001469-010-0002.

"In telling of Mimi": White to Holmes, May 6, 1926.

"Some of the critics have": White to Holmes, May 6, 1926.

140 a *"blow to the face"*: Typed manuscript review, December 1926, W.E.B. Du Bois Papers, Special Collections and University Archives, University of Massachusetts Amherst Libraries, https://credo.library.umass.edu/view/full/mums312-b228-i023.

"We have been in communication": Signature illegible, "Secretary to Mrs. B. W. Knopf" to Walter White, March 3, 1927, NAACP archives, file 001469-010-0630.

"By the way, do you know": Walter White to Jim Tully, May 7, 1926, NAACP archives, file 001469-010-0002.

"Evidently, things have been moving": Walter White to Jim Tully, June 9, 1926, NAACP archives, file 001469-010-0002.

Chapter 14

144 *"This charge excluded"*: "South Carolina Court Grants New Trial to 3 Charged with Murder," *New York Age,* June 5, 1926.

"If not for the NAACP": Mark Robert Schneider, *"We Return Fighting": The Civil Rights Movement in the Jazz Age* (Boston: Northeastern University Press, 2002), p. 323.

"Now this is no idle threat": James L. Quinby to James Weldon Johnson, October 12, 1926, NAACP archives, file 001527-016-0461.

145 *"Did you know that"*: Quinby to Johnson, October 12, 1926.

"The guilty parties that pulled": A. H. Johnson to James Weldon Johnson, October 12, 1926, NAACP archives, file 001527-016-0461.

"As you perhaps know, I am": N. J. Frederick to James Weldon Johnson, October 11, 1926, NAACP archives, file 001527-016-0461.

"everything possible will be": "Public Condemns Aiken Affair," *New York Amsterdam News,* October 20, 1926.

146 *"We should be glad indeed"*: W. P. Beazell to Walter White, October 17, 1926, NAACP archives, file 001527-016-0461.

"I am leaving New York": Walter White to Bishop John Hurst, October 22, 1926, NAACP archives, file 001527-016-0461.

147 *"Whenever the Constitution"*: "A Story Much Older Than Ol' Strom," *Washington Post,* December 20, 2003.

"I don't recall any man": Walter White, *A Man Called White: The Autobiography of Walter White* (Athens and London: University of Georgia Press, 1995), p. 57.

"I will go with you if": Dialogue from Walter White, "I Investigate Lynchings," *American Mercury,* January 1929.

"If the Klan would molest": White, *A Man Called White,* p. 57.

148 *"I show you this so that"*: White, "I Investigate Lynchings."

"very extensive business of": Walter White to Gov. Thomas G. McLeod, October 26, 1926, NAACP archives, file 001527-016-0461.

"Mr. White," this man said: "'Unknown Parties' Who Lynched Three in South Carolina Known," *New York Amsterdam News,* November 3, 1926.

149 *"Let your man see me at"*: A. H. Johnson to James Weldon Johnson, October 12, 1926, NAACP archives, file 001527-016-0461.

"We had to waste fifty": White, "I Investigate Lynchings."

"My dear Gov. McLeod": White to McLeod, October 26, 1926.

152 *"pussyfooter" who "will do nothing"*: Walter White, "Shambles of South Carolina," *Crisis* 33, no. 2 (December 1926): 72–75.

"My God, I wish this was over": Schneider, *"We Return Fighting,"* p. 330.

"most daring of his investigations": "NAACP Won Notable Legal Fights in 1926," *Afro-American* (Baltimore), January 8, 1926.

"Mrs. Hurst was not joking": Bishop John Hurst to Walter White, November 2, 1926, NAACP archives, file 001469-010-0362.

"Is that true?": Claude E. Sawyer to Walter White, November 23, 1926, NAACP archives, file 001527-016-0710.

"So far as I can remember": Walter White to Colonel Claude E. Sawyer, December 2, 1926, NAACP archives, file 001527-016-0710.

153 *"The result of this dramatic"*: "NAACP Won Notable Legal Fights in 1926," *Afro-American* (Baltimore), January 8, 1926.

"This is the man the crackers": Schneider, *"We Return Fighting,"* p. 332.

154 *"a few rather incoherent words"*: "Lowman and White NAACP Speakers Here," *Philadelphia Tribune,* April 2, 1927.

Chapter 15

155 *"Why don't you look where"*: Walter White, *A Man Called White: The Autobiography of Walter White* (Athens and London: University of Georgia Press, 1995), p. 3.

156 *"the most elaborate production"*: "'Deep River,' Native Opera, Lost $100,000," *Pittsburgh Courier,* November 13, 1926.

"Good Lord, man": Walter White to Sinclair Lewis, November 5, 1926, NAACP archives, file 001469-010-0362.

"I got it!": Walter White to Joel Spingarn, March 12, 1927, Joel E. Spingarn Papers, box 12, New York Public Library Archives & Manuscripts.

157 *"I am much disturbed"*: Joel Spingarn to Walter White, October 23, 1926, NAACP archives, file 001469-010-0362.

"Mr. Darrow has tentatively": Minutes of the Meeting of the Board of Directors, March 14, 1927, NAACP archives, file 001412-002-0122.

"This fellowship [Ovington said]": Walter White to Mary White Ovington, March 12, 1927, NAACP archives, file 001469-010-0630.

158 *"White is literally the"*: Kenneth Janken, *White: The Biography of Walter White, Mr. NAACP* (New York: New Press, 2003), p. 82.

159 *"We have known for"*: Helen Martin to Walter White, May 20, 1949, Walter White Papers, box 10, folder 62, Beinecke Rare Book & Manuscript Library, Yale University.

"From the day I set foot": James Weldon Johnson, *Along This Way: The Autobiography of James Weldon Johnson* (New York: Da Capo Press, 2000), p. 208.

"the most delicious luncheon": Walter White to James Weldon Johnson, August 16, 1927, Walter White Papers, box 3, Beinecke Rare Book & Manuscript Library, Yale University.

"If you are lucky enough to": Ernest Hemingway to "a friend," 1950, *A Moveable Feast* (New York: Collier Books, 1964), title page.

160 *"It's the one place worth"*: White, *A Man Called White*, p. 92.

"We found just the villa": White to Johnson, August 16, 1927.

"Imagine coming four or five": White to Johnson, August 16, 1927.

"she could cook like": White, *A Man Called White*, p. 93.

"Lovely as this place is": White to Johnson, August 16, 1927.

Chapter 16

162 *"the lynching industry"*: The term is mentioned throughout White's writings, and chapter 2 of his book *Rope and Faggot* is called "The Extent of the Industry." See Walter White, *Rope and Faggot: A Biography of Judge Lynch* (Notre Dame, IN: University of Notre Dame Press, 2001).

163 *"where leaders of the mob"*: White, *Rope and Faggot*, p. 4.

"We took the government": "North Carolina Historical Commission, Bulletin No. 1," 1907. Also Charles Austin Beard, *Contemporary American History, 1877–1913* (New York: MacMillan, 1914), p. 8.

"The lyncher and the legislator": White, *Rope and Faggot*, p. 102.

164 *"In the South we believe"*: Desmond King, "The Segregated State? Black Americans and the Federal Government," in *Democracy and North America*, ed. Alan Ware (New York: Routledge, 2013), p. 81.

"No person," he wrote, "who is familiar": White, *Rope and Faggot*, p. 43.

"Until very recent times": White, *Rope and Faggot*, p. 8.

"mobbism has inevitably": White, *Rope and Faggot*, p. viii.

165 *"For two and a half centuries"*: White, *Rope and Faggot*, p. 62.

"For more than two hundred years": White, *Rope and Faggot*, p. 63.

"Nobody . . . believes the old thread-bare": Ida Wells-Barnett quoted in "Women of Color Calling Out White Feminism in the Nineteenth Century and the Digital

Age," Paige V. Banaji, *Feminist Connections: Rhetoric and Activism Across Time, Space, and Place*, eds. Katherine Fredlund, Kerri Hauman, and Jessica Ouellette (Tuscaloosa: University of Alabama Press, 2020), p. 221.

"*Lynching has always been*": White, *Rope and Faggot*, p. 82.

166   "*it was at this point that*": White, *Rope and Faggot*, p. 86.

"*Ku Kluxery is the Southern*": White, *Rope and Faggot*, p. 11.

"*Before the wide eyes of the*": W.E.B. Du Bois, "The Shape of Fear," *North American Review*, June 1926.

167   "*I think you have done a*": James Weldon Johnson to Walter White, March 1, 1928, NAACP archives, file 001469-011-0107.

"*The terrace of our villa*": Walter White to Richetta Randolph, December 12, 1927, NAACP archives, file 001412-024-0663.

168   "*With painful frequence*": Walter White, *A Man Called White: The Autobiography of Walter White* (Athens and London: University of Georgia Press, 1995), p. 95.

"*Although I have thought of*": Charles Studin to Walter White, February 21, 1928, NAACP archives, file 001469-011-0107.

Chapter 17

170   "*I have been asked by*": Walter White to Bishop John Hurst, July 18, 1928, NAACP archives, file 001469-011-0107.

171   "*The Negro is being kicked*": White to Hurst, July 18, 1928.

"*I firmly believe that if ever*": White to Hurst, July 18, 1928.

"*Establish office in New York*": "Analysis of Possible Effect of Negro Vote in the 1928 Election," undated, NAACP archives, file 001469-011-0107.

172   "*the Negro vote unquestionably*": "Analysis of Possible Effect."

"*Eventually it appears to me*": Walter White to Moorfield Storey, July 22, 1928, NAACP archives, file 001469-011-0107.

"*is dependent for success*": White to Storey, July 22, 1928.

"*If Gladys and I had no*": Kenneth Janken, *White: The Biography of Walter White, Mr. NAACP* (New York: New Press, 2003), p. 132.

"*If Smith is elected, the NAACP*": David Levering Lewis, *When Harlem Was in Vogue* (New York: Penguin Books, 1997), p. 206.

173   "*be president of all the people*": Walter White, *A Man Called White: The Autobiography of Walter White* (Athens and London: University of Georgia Press, 1995), p. 100.

"*I know Negroes distrust*": White, *A Man Called White*, p. 100.

"*Can't you — won't you*": White, *A Man Called White*, p. 101.

174   "*time and space were eliminated*": "Television Test Links New York and Washington," *Christian Science Monitor*, April 8, 1927.

175   "*Everyone was a broker*": John Steinbeck, "I Remember the Thirties," in *The Thirties: A Time to Remember*, ed. Don Condon (New York: Simon & Schuster, 1962), p. 23.

"It was impossible to get": Daniel Okrent, "Wayne B. Wheeler: The Man Who Turned Off the Tap," *Smithsonian,* May 2010.

"Alcohol played a part": Ann Douglas, *Terrible Honesty: Mongrel Manhattan in the 1920s* (New York: Noon Day Press, 1996), p. 23.

176 *"We turned over to that"*: Kenneth Whyte, *Hoover: An Extraordinary Life in Extraordinary Times* (New York: Vintage Books, 2017), p. 369.

177 *"I had no idea who he"*: Poppy Cannon, *A Gentle Knight: My Husband Walter White* (New York: Popular Library, 1956), p. 21.

"nothing more than a gizzard": Dialogue from Cannon, *Gentle Knight,* pp. 22–24.

178 *"all of whom," she recalled*: Cannon, *Gentle Knight,* p. 24.

"Let me add a word of warning": Walter White to Poppy Cannon, June 17, 1932, NAACP archives, file 001469-015-0296.

Chapter 18

179 *"This book should be read"*: E. J. Kahn Jr., "The Frontal Attack — II," Profiles, *New Yorker,* September 11, 1948.

"It is with a distinct jolt": "The Reign of Lynch Law in the United States," *New York Times,* May 12, 1929.

"the most thorough exposition": J. A. Rogers, "Rambling Ruminations," *New York Amsterdam News,* January 8, 1930.

"The well-balanced Southerner": "Threaten Tar and Feather for Author," *Philadelphia Tribune,* July 18, 1929.

180 *"If anyone ever needed a"*: "Threaten Tar and Feather."

"disturbed by the fatigue": B. Joyce Ross, *J. E. Spingarn and the Rise of the NAACP* (New York: Athenaeum, 1972), p. 123.

181 *"I blithely accepted the"*: Walter White, *A Man Called White: The Autobiography of Walter White* (Athens and London: University of Georgia Press, 1995), p. 103.

"Presently I grew puzzled": Rudolph Fisher, "The Caucasian Storms Harlem," *American Mercury,* August 1927.

182 *"a sort of New York institution"*: James Weldon Johnson, *Black Manhattan* (New York: Da Capo Paperback, 1991), p. 212.

"The idea is this: We want": Walter White to Bill Robinson, October 7, 1929, NAACP archives, file 001421-008-0434.

"Will you be good enough to": Walter White to Florenz Ziegfeld, October 22, 1929, NAACP archives, file 001421-008-0434.

"The fundamental business of": A. J. Baime, *The Accidental President: Harry S. Truman and the Four Months That Changed the World* (New York: Houghton Mifflin Harcourt, 2017), p. 68.

183 *"night off"*: "NAACP Sponsors First Sunday Night Benefit at Downtown Theatre," *New York Amsterdam News,* December 11, 1929.

"A mixed audience": "NAACP Sponsors."

"[It] certainly was a gala": "From the Front Row," *Afro-American* (Baltimore), December 21, 1929.

Chapter 19

184 *"Confirmation was inevitable"*: Walter White, *A Man Called White: The Autobiography of Walter White* (Athens and London: University of Georgia Press, 1995), p. 105.

185 *"The Republican Party in North"*: "Report of the Acting Secretary (For the April Meeting of the Board)," 1930 (otherwise undated), NAACP archives, file 001412-008-1393.

"A few hours later," Walter: White, *A Man Called White*, p. 105.

186 *"stands his best chance of"*: Walter Francis White, "The Negro and the Supreme Court," *Harper's Monthly Magazine*, December 1931.

"The Constitution is what the": "Judgeship Offer for Vote for Parker Is Charged," *New York Times*, May 6, 1930.

"inimical to the political": Affidavit sent out to be signed by petitioners, undated, NAACP archives, file 001422-036-0564.

187 *"At first a trickle"*: White, *A Man Called White*, p. 107.

"The attempt to put Judge": "Chicagoans Hear White on Parker," *Chicago Defender*, May 3, 1930.

"It was a thrilling battle": Mary White Ovington, *The Walls Came Tumbling Down* (New York: Schocken Books, 1970), p. 253.

NEGRO VOTERS WILL HOLD THEIR: Roy Wilkins, *Standing Fast: The Autobiography of Roy Wilkins* (New York: Da Capo Press, 1994), p. 91.

COUNTRYWIDE FIGHT ON PARKER: Wilkins, *Standing Fast*, p. 91.

"To me," Wilkins recalled, "the most intriguing": Wilkins, *Standing Fast*, p. 91.

188 *"taking a most active part"*: "Hoover Exerts Strong Pressure for Judge Parker," *Atlanta Constitution*, May 5, 1930.

"There is not, in my judgment": *Confirmation of Hon. John J. Parker to Be an Associate Justice of the Supreme Court of the United States: Hearing Before the Subcommittee of the Committee on the Judiciary*, United States Senate, 71st Congress, 2d Session (April 5, 1930) (letter submitted by O. Max Gardner), (Washington, DC: US Government Printing Office, 1930).

"My name is Walter White": All the hearing dialogue is from *Hearing Before the Subcommittee*.

189 *"became incensed"*: White, *A Man Called White*, p. 106.

"hell-raising political vampires": *Hearing Before the Subcommittee*.

"Yes: The negro must have": *Hearing Before the Subcommittee*.

"In the event of a tie vote": Walter White to Vice President Charles Curtis, May 7, 1930, NAACP archives, file 001422-027-0278.

"For confirmation — 39": White, *A Man Called White*, p. 110.

190 WALTER WHITE IS HERO: "Walter White Is Hero of Judge Parker's Defeat," *Afro-American* (Baltimore), May 17, 1930.

NEGRO STAR IN ASCENDANT: "Negro Star in Ascendant," *Philadelphia Tribune,* May 29, 1930.

"the NAACP had come of age": Kenneth W. Goings, *The NAACP Comes of Age: The Defeat of Judge John J. Parker* (Bloomington: Indiana University Press, 1990).

"The victory made White": Wilkins, *Standing Fast,* p. 92.

Chapter 20

191 *"James," she said, "I wish"*: Dialogue from James Cameron, *A Time of Terror: A Survivor's Story* (Milwaukee: Life Writes Press, 2016), pp. 42–46.

192 *"Tonight," the sheriff said*: Cameron, *A Time of Terror,* p. 53.

193 *"I started running away from"*: Cameron, *A Time of Terror,* pp. 58–59.

"The sheriff didn't say read": Cameron, *A Time of Terror,* p. 60.

"I had had enough": Cameron, *A Time of Terror,* p. 60.

KU KLUX KLAN IS SPREADING: "Ku Klux Klan Is Spreading Over Indiana," *Indianapolis Ledger,* July 1, 1922.

"the Hoosier State initiated more": Cynthia Carr, *Our Town: A Heartland Lynching, a Haunted Town, and the Hidden History of White America* (New York: Three Rivers Press, 2007), p. 60.

194 *"I believe that if Jesus"*: Carr, *Our Town,* p. 75.

"Hi, there! How ya feeling": Dialogue from Cameron, *A Time of Terror,* p. 64.

195 *"It was indescribable"*: Cameron, *A Time of Terror,* p. 69.

"You'll never get": Cameron, *A Time of Terror,* p. 75.

196 *"Don't shoot! There are women"*: Carr, *Our Town,* p. 18.

"Smith fared no better": Carr, *Our Town,* p. 18.

"James Cameron is in here": Cameron, *A Time of Terror,* p. 89.

"They surged forward in one": First-person remembrances from Cameron, *A Time of Terror,* pp. 91–93.

198 *"I am sorry, son"*: Cameron, *A Time of Terror,* p. 100.

"The night was one of horrors": F. K. Bailey to Walter White, August 8, 1930, NAACP archives, file 001527-011-0501.

Chapter 21

199 NEGRO SECTION THREATENED WITH: R. L. Bailey, telegram to Walter White, August 8, 1930, NAACP archives, file 001527-011-0501.

UTILIZE EVERY POSSIBLE RESOURCE: Walter White, telegram to Hon. Harry G. Leslie, August 8, 1930, NAACP archives, file 001527-011-0501.

200 INDIANA MOB OF 10,000: "Indiana Mob of 10,000 Lynches Two Negroes; Beats Wrong Man as Third Alleged Killer," *New York Times,* August 8, 1930.

"Mr. White," she wrote: F. K. Bailey to Walter White, August 8, 1930, NAACP archives, file 001527-011-0501.

STATE TROOPS BEING RUSHED: L. O. Chasey, telegram to Walter White, August 8, 1930, NAACP archives, file 001527-011-0501.

"In what manner will it": Walter White to F. K. Bailey, August 11, 1930, NAACP archives, file 001527-011-0501.

201 *"Even though you are coming":* Mrs. W. T. (Flossie) Bailey to Walter White, August 12, 1930, NAACP archives, file 001527-011-0501.

"He was lying there in": Cynthia Carr, *Our Town: A Heartland Lynching, a Haunted Town, and the Hidden History of White America* (New York: Three Rivers Press, 2007), p. 126.

"She flew at the prostrate": Carr, *Our Town,* p. 126.

"Hardin about 50": Walter White's handwritten notes/reporter's pad, White Papers, Notebooks, 1930, undated, box 35, folders 359–63, Beinecke Rare Book & Manuscript Library, Yale University.

202 *"People had been going":* This dialogue from handwritten notes/reporter's pad, White Papers, Notebooks, 1930, undated, box 35, folders 359–63, Beinecke Rare Book & Manuscript Library, Yale University.

"mingled in the crowd trying": White's handwritten notes.

"somewhat strange," he later wrote: Carr, *Our Town,* p. 143.

"a timid, blustering official": Walter White, "Sheriff's Fears Permitted Indiana Lynchers," *World* (New York), August 24, 1930.

"impossible to get the witnesses": Walter White to Hon. James Ogden, September 22, 1930, NAACP archives, file 001527-011-0610.

203 *"No notorious N":* Walter White's handwritten notes.

"Many gruesome white crimes": Walter White's handwritten notes.

"It is my earnest desire": Merrill "Jack" Edwards to Walter White, August 16, 1930, NAACP archives, file 001527-011-0501.

204 *"The two most formidable":* Walter White to Hon. James Ogden, August 22, 1930, NAACP archives, file 001527-011-0565.

"Hell only knows when there": White to Ogden, August 22, 1930.

205 *"The evidence against the lynchers":* "A State Matter," *Indianapolis Times,* undated clipping, NAACP archives, file 001527-011-0610.

"If so-called Negro leaders": Letter "To Mrs. Bailey, from Chicago, Ill.," unsigned, August 20, 1930, NAACP archives, file 001527-011-0565.

207 *"The Indiana law against":* Walter White to Hon. James Ogden, September 22, 1930, NAACP archives, file 001527-011-0610.

208 *"They are scared to death":* F. K. Bailey to Walter White, August 30, 1930, NAACP archives, file 001527-011-0610.

"Every decent citizen must": Herbert Hoover to Sam H. Reading, September 23, 1940 (this letter was released to the press by the White House), *Public Papers of*

the Presidents of the United States: Herbert Hoover, January 1 to December 31, 1930* (Washington, DC: US Government Printing Office), p. 301.

209 *"There was really no sincere":* Mrs. M. T. "Flossie" Bailey to Walter White, May 5, 1931, NAACP archives, file 001427-007-0469.

"Really, Mr. White," she wrote: Katherine "Flossie" Bailey to Walter White, July 13, 1931, NAACP archives, file 001427-007-0469.

"Black bodies swinging in the": "Strange Fruit," performed by Billie Holiday, composed by Abel Meeropol, https://www.youtube.com/watch?v=-DGY9HvChXk.

Chapter 22

210 *"Senator McCulloch was":* NAACP, untitled press release, November 2, 1930, NAACP archives, file 001422-025-0705.

211 *"The telephone rang and":* Walter White, *A Man Called White: The Autobiography of Walter White* (Athens and London: University of Georgia Press, 1995), p. 112.

"A number of persons fastened": White, *A Man Called White,* p. 113.

NEGROES AT FEVER HEAT: B. E. Dickinson, telegram to Walter White, November 3, 1930, NAACP archives, file 001422-025-0705.

PROTECTION AT POLLING BOOTHS: Walter White, telegram to C. E. [White got the name wrong] Dickinson, November 3, 1930, file 001422-025-0705.

212 *"All the senators who voted":* "Finish of the Parker Fight," editorial, *Crisis* 41, no. 12 (December 1934): 311.

"White politicians, Republican": White, *A Man Called White,* p. 113.

"I was promoted from acting": White, *A Man Called White,* p. 115.

"I am simply overwhelmed": "New NAACP Executive Director Is Busy Man," *Pittsburgh Courier,* May 2, 1931.

213 *"She never was comfortable":* Kenneth Janken, *White: The Biography of Walter White, Mr. NAACP* (New York: New Press, 2003), p. 83.

"a little ridiculous to refer": It Seems to Heywood Broun, *Nation,* May 21, 1930.

214 *"Many thanks for the articles":* Janken, *White: The Biography,* p. 17.

"Dad did have guns and": Janken, *White: The Biography,* p. 17.

215 *"How would you like your":* Dialogue from E. J. Kahn Jr., "The Frontal Attack — I," Profiles, *New Yorker,* September 4, 1948.

"I am writing to you personally": Walter White to Roy Wilkins, February 26, 1931, NAACP archives, file 001469-013-0411. Also: Roy Wilkins, *Standing Fast: The Autobiography of Roy Wilkins* (New York: Da Capo Press, 1994), p. 104.

216 *"The NAACP was the most militant":* Wilkins, *Standing Fast,* p. 105.

"feeling happier than I could": Wilkins, *Standing Fast,* p. 106.

"the NAACP's wealthy maiden": Wilkins, *Standing Fast,* p. 106.

217 *"a man whose gift, life":* "Many Laud Retiring NAACP Secretary at Pennsylvania Hotel Dinner," *Afro-American* (Baltimore), May 23, 1931.

"one of the most distinguished": White, *A Man Called White,* p. 115.

"He rescued me from Georgia": "Many Laud Retiring NAACP Secretary."

"The luckiest break I got": "Many Laud Retiring NAACP Secretary."

"Worry over money," remembered: Mary White Ovington, *The Walls Came Tumbling Down* (New York: Schocken Books, 1970), p. 244.

218 *"have completely exhausted"*: Walter White to William Pickens, April 2, 1935, NAACP archives, file 001412-026-0308.

Rent cost $1,401.60: Budget figures from Minutes of the Meeting of the Board of Directors, December 8, 1930, NAACP archives, file 001412-002-0287.

"Look Doc, your office": Juan Williams, *Thurgood Marshall: American Revolutionary* (New York: Three Rivers Press, 1998), p. 167.

"At present time," he wrote: David Levering Lewis, *W.E.B. Du Bois: A Biography 1868–1963* (New York: Henry Holt, 2009), p. 539.

219 *"Do you know who this man"*: Dialogue from "First Draft of the Story of My Father's Death," Walter White, White Papers, box 24, folder 221, Beinecke Rare Book & Manuscript Library, Yale University.

"Dinginess, misery, and": White, *A Man Called White*, p. 136.

"On the meagre salary of": White, "My Father's Death."

"I feel like a watermelon": White, *A Man Called White*, p. 136.

220 *"We talked about everything"*: White, *A Man Called White*, p. 137.

"The vigil during the day": White, *A Man Called White*, p. 136.

"And then," he remembered, "Father": White, *A Man Called White*, p. 137.

221 *"I am at the station"*: Poppy Cannon, *A Gentle Knight: My Husband Walter White* (New York: Popular Library, 1956), p. 11.

Chapter 23

222 *"His face was so pulled"*: Poppy Cannon, *A Gentle Knight: My Husband Walter White* (New York: Popular Library, 1956), p. 12.

"My father is dead": Dialogue from Cannon, *Gentle Knight*, pp. 12–13.

223 *"That day," she wrote, "Walter wept"*: Cannon, *Gentle Knight*, p. 15.

"Your way is clear": Cannon, *Gentle Knight*, p. 29.

224 *"investigate the expenditure"*: Minutes of the Meeting of the Board of Directors, December 21, 1931, NAACP archives, file 001412-002-0350.

"We have all had considerable": Kenneth Janken, *White: The Biography of Walter White, Mr. NAACP* (New York: New Press, 2003), pp. 166–67.

225 *"I wish to express my"*: Herbert J. Seligmann to Walter White, December 22, 1931, W.E.B. Du Bois Papers, Special Collections and University Archives, University of Massachusetts Amherst Libraries, https://credo.library.umass.edu/view/full/mums312-b060-i004.

"I do want you to know": Jeanette Randolph to Dr. Du Bois, Mr. Seligmann, Mr. Pickens, Mr. Bagnall, Mr. Wilkins, December 22, 1931, W.E.B. Du Bois Papers, Special Collections and University Archives, University of Massachusetts Amherst Libraries, https://credo.library.umass.edu/view/full/mums312-b060-i003.

"The memorandum which you": J. E. Spingarn to W.E.B. Du Bois, December 29, 1931, W.E.B. Du Bois Papers, Special Collections and University Archives, University of Massachusetts Amherst Libraries, https://credo.library.umass.edu /view/full/mums312-b060-i007.

"He's just a badly brought": Janken, *White: The Biography,* p. 172.

"It grieves me": B. Joyce Ross, *J. E. Spingarn and the Rise of the NAACP* (New York: Athenaeum, 1972), p. 142.

226 *"Dear Mr. Spingarn: I will"*: W.E.B. Du Bois to J. E. Spingarn, December 31, 1931, W.E.B. Du Bois Papers, Special Collections and University Archives, University of Massachusetts Amherst Libraries, https://credo.library.umass.edu/view/full /mums312-b060-i008.

"The pall of office politics": Roy Wilkins, *Standing Fast: The Autobiography of Roy Wilkins* (New York: Da Capo Press, 1994), pp. 116–17.

"If Du Bois was a visionary": David Levering Lewis, *W.E.B. Du Bois: A Biography 1868–1963* (New York: Henry Holt, 2009), p. 535.

227 *"More than ten thousand"*: White, *A Man Called White,* p. 127.

229 *"1932 marked the emergence"*: White, *A Man Called White,* p. 139.

Chapter 24

230 *"I do not often envy other"*: Quoted in *To Extend and Amend the Office of the President to Reorganize the Executive Branch of the Government Under Chapter 9 of Title 5, United States, Hearing on S. 893 Before the Committee on Governmental Affairs,* United States Senate, 1st Session, May 6, 1981 (Washington, DC: US Government Printing Office, 1981), p. 54.

"I have looked into the": Arthur Meier Schlesinger, *The Crisis of the Old Order, 1919–1933,* vol. 1 of *The Age of Roosevelt* (Boston and New York: Mariner, 1985), p. 430.

"I dream of a world of black": "Walter White Gives NAACP Stewardship," *Afro-American* (Baltimore), May 28, 1932.

231 *"the greatest political revolt"*: NAACP, "'Greatest Negro Political Revolt' Predicted by Negro Association Chief," press release, October 17, 1932, NAACP archives, file 001427-007-0731.

"The Negro in America today": "Pro-Parker Senator on 'Spot' at Confab of Indiana NAACP," *Pittsburgh Courier,* October 22, 1932.

"plain and unequivocal declaration": NAACP, "NAACP Asks Hoover & Roosevelt for Plain Declaration on Negro," press release, September 16, 1932, NAACP archives, file 001422-027-0914.

"Will you in word and deed": "NAACP Asks Hoover."

"The questions are of great": NAACP, "Can Hoover & Roosevelt Evade Negro Asks World Tomorrow Editorial," press release, NAACP archives, file 001422-027-0914.

232 *"Philadelphia has always been"*: Isadore Martin to Walter White, November 12, 1932, NAACP archives, file 001422-021-0827.

"Go home and turn Lincoln's": Bruce M. Stave, *The New Deal and the Last Hurrah: Pittsburgh Machine Politics* (Pittsburgh: University of Pittsburgh Press, 1970), p. 34.

"The seismic shift of Negro": Roy Wilkins, *Standing Fast: The Autobiography of Roy Wilkins* (New York: Da Capo Press, 1994), pp. 92–93.

"The 1932 election will be a": NAACP, "Blind Allegiance of Negroes to Republicans Ended Says White," press release, November 9, 1932, NAACP archives, file 001422-021-0827.

233 *"a fine lesson for the whole"*: Philip Dray, *At the Hands of Persons Unknown: The Lynching of Black America* (New York: Modern Library, 2003), p. 334.

"That lynching in Maryland": James Weldon Johnson to Walter White, October 30, 1933, James Weldon Johnson Papers, box 24, file 542, Beinecke Rare Book & Manuscript Library, Yale University.

234 *"He probably needs no introduction"*: Testimony dialogue from *Hearings on S. 1978 Before a Subcommittee of the Committee on the Judiciary,* United States Senate, February 20 and 21, 1934, 73rd Congress, 2d session (Washington, DC: US Government Printing Office, 1934), pp. 10–15.

235 *"It was a great occasion"*: Walter White to James Weldon Johnson, February 28, 1934, James Weldon Johnson Papers, box 24, file 543, Beinecke Rare Book & Manuscript Library, Yale University.

"Both Senators Costigan": Walter White to Marvin McIntyre, April 14, 1934, NAACP archives, file 001412-026-0104.

"I talked with Mrs. Roosevelt": Walter White to James Weldon Johnson, May 8, 1934, James Weldon Johnson Papers, box 24, file 543, Beinecke Rare Book & Manuscript Library, Yale University.

236 *"The virtue of womanhood"*: "Dixie Senators Again Defend Lynching Evil," *Chicago Defender,* April 20, 1935.

"The underlying motive": Kenneth Janken, *White: The Biography of Walter White, Mr. NAACP* (New York: New Press, 2003), p. 224.

237 *"The thinking colored people"*: W.E.B. Du Bois, "Segregation," *Crisis* 41, no. 1 (January 1934).

"created a furor in Negro": Walter White, untitled and undated manuscript, Walter White Papers, box 26, folder 273, Beinecke Rare Book & Manuscript Library, Yale University.

"until my own eyes convinced": David Levering Lewis, *W.E.B. Du Bois: The Fight for Equality and the American Century, 1919–1963* (New York: Henry Holt, 2000), p. 38.

"The puzzle was why Dr.": Wilkins, *Standing Fast,* p. 163.

CAN YOU ARRANGE FOR SPACE: Walter White, telegram to W.E.B. Du Bois, January 9, 1934, W.E.B. Du Bois Papers, Special Collections and University Archives, University of Massachusetts Amherst Libraries, https://credo.library .umass.edu/view/full/mums312-b195-i1278.

238 *"I have your article on"*: W.E.B. Du Bois to Walter White, January 10, 1935, W.E.B.
     Du Bois Papers, Special Collections and University Archives, University of
     Massachusetts Amherst Libraries, https://credo.library.umass.edu/view/full
     /mums312-b195-i281.
     "If . . . the NAACP has conducted": W.E.B. Du Bois, "Segregation in the North,"
     Crisis 41, no. 4 (April 1934).
     "For the first time in its": "Fight within NAACP," *Philadelphia Tribune*, April 12,
     1934.
     "A brilliant student of": "What Garvey Thinks of DuBois," *Afro-American*
     (Baltimore), January 7, 1921.
     "I wish you would write": Walter White to James Weldon Johnson, May 7, 1934,
     James Weldon Johnson Papers, box 24, file 543, Beinecke Rare Book & Manuscript
     Library, Yale University.

239 *"Confidentially," the association board chief*: Joel Spingarn, Memorandum to
     the Secretary from the Chairman of the Board: Confidential, January 10, 1934,
     NAACP archives, file 001421-030-0178.
     "has been growing increasingly": Janken, *White: The Biography,* p. 172.
     "Frankly," the president's press: Doris Kearns Goodwin, *No Ordinary Time:
     Franklin & Eleanor Roosevelt: The Home Front in World War II* (New York: Simon
     & Schuster Paperbacks, 1994), p. 164.
     "I think I should have": Goodwin, *No Ordinary Time,* p. 164.
     "I turned in desperation to": White, *A Man Called White,* p. 168.

240 *"Shortly afterwards, the"*: Dialogue from White, *A Man Called White,* pp. 169–70.

241 *"Looks tired and is working"*: Diary of Roy Wilkins, January 4, 1934, excerpted in
     Wilkins, *Standing Fast,* p. 138.
     "In thirty-five years of": Minutes of the Meeting of the Board of Directors, June 11,
     1934, NAACP archives, file 001412-002-0570.
     "I believe we were limping": Wilkins, *Standing Fast,* p. 155.

Chapter 25

242 *"Child Brutally Beaten"*: "False Rumors of a Black Puerto Rican Boy's Death
     Sparks Harlem Riot of 1935," *New York Daily News,* March 18, 2015.

243 COLORED STORE: "Rages: Mischief Out of Misery," *Time,* April 1, 1935.
     "This sudden breach of the": "Report of Subcommittee Which Investigated the
     Disturbance of March 19th," May 29, 1935, Law and the Struggle for Racial Justice
     Exhibit, Selected Materials from the Riesenfeld Rare Books Center, University of
     Minnesota Law Library, http://moses.law.umn.edu/racial-justice/harlemriot010
     .html.

244 *"[I] could very easily"*: Langston Hughes, *The Big Sea: An Autobiography* (New
     York: Hill and Wang, 1993), p. 320.
     "Gone was the almost": George Schuyler, *Black No More* (Mineola, NY: Dover
     Publications, 2011), p. 52.

"Perhaps few of us realize": J. E. Spingarn to the Board of Directors of the National Association for the Advancement of Colored People, December 1, 1930, Joel Spingarn Papers, box unknown, document in the author's possession, Schomburg Center for Research in Black Culture, New York Public Library.

"When I joined the Association": David Levering Lewis, *W.E.B. Du Bois: The Fight for Equality and the American Century, 1919–1963* (New York: Henry Holt, 2000), p. 315.

245 *"a calamity"*: Minutes of the Meeting of the Board of Directors, June 12, 1933, NAACP archives, file 001412-002-0508.

"the dismal decade of the": Walter White, *A Man Called White: The Autobiography of Walter White* (Athens and London: University of Georgia Press, 1995), p. 141.

GOOD LUCK, *a Chicago:* Frances Williams, telegram to Walter White, April 27, 1935, NAACP archives, file 001529-008-0301.

"held spellbound": NAACP, "Sidelights on Senate Anti-Lynching Bill Fight," press release, April 27, 1935, NAACP archives, file 001529-008-0301.

"Crowded galleries laughing": Walter White, handwritten "Notes to G.S.S. for inclusion in April 26 press story for fight for anti-lynching law," undated, NAACP archives, file 001412-026-0308.

"Called the political football": "Predict Congress Will Pass Anti-Lynch Bill This Week," *Chicago Defender,* June 20, 1936.

246 *"My dear Mr. President"*: Walter White to Franklin Roosevelt, May 6, 1935, NAACP archives, file 001412-026-0344.

"Does America expect": NAACP, "White Raises Question of Negro's Patriotism in Next War," press release, April 27, 1935, NAACP archives, file 001529-008-0301.

"the first significant mixed": "1st Big NY Mixed Bout Draws 15,000 Negroes and 1,300 Police," *New York Times,* June 26, 1935.

247 *"Walter White was a man"*: Poppy Cannon, *A Gentle Knight: My Husband Walter White* (New York: Popular Library, 1956), p. 126.

"Walter White is conducting": Quoted in "The NAACP and Walter White," *Atlanta Daily World,* August 9, 1936.

248 *"Isn't it amazing," he wrote:* Walter White telegram to Eleanor Roosevelt, November 4, 1936, NAACP archives, file 001422-022-0611.

"One Negro, whose name has": *Congressional Record: Proceedings and Debates of the Third Session of the Seventy-Fifth Congress of the United States of America,* vol. 83, part 1 (Washington, DC: US Government Printing Office, 1938), p. 310.

"dapper": "The Congress: Black's White," *Time,* January 24, 1938.

249 *"apostle of human liberty"*: "Doctor Walter White — Apostle of Human Liberty," *Atlanta Daily World,* July 7, 1939.

"The nation owes Walter": "Walter White Lauded as Lynch Rate Drops," *Afro-American* (Baltimore), June 18, 1938.

"In Mr. White we have": "Who's Who: Walter White, the Crusader," *Afro-American* (Baltimore), March 23, 1935.

"*Modest, genial Walter White*": "Did Walter White Enter via Kitchen?," *Afro-American* (Baltimore), February 12, 1938.

"*Observers are now asking*": "Who Caused FDR's Lynching Stand?," *Afro-American* (Baltimore), April 2, 1938.

"*the White House of Negro*": Kahn, "Frontal Attack — II" Profiles, *New Yorker,* September 11, 1948.

"*My life is an open book*": "Filibusters Pry into White's Skeleton Closet," *Afro-American* (Baltimore), January 29, 1938.

Chapter 26

250 "*We had a giant banner*": Roy Wilkins, *Standing Fast: The Autobiography of Roy Wilkins* (New York: Da Capo Press, 1994), pp. 174–75.

251 "*There was a lanky, brash*": Walter White, *A Man Called White: The Autobiography of Walter White* (Athens and London: University of Georgia Press, 1995), p. 154.

"*What's at stake here is*": "One Man vs. Racial Injustice: U.S. Supreme Court Justice Thurgood Marshall Has Spent a Lifetime Fighting the White Establishment to Secure Equal Rights for Black People," *Los Angeles Times,* January 14, 1990.

"*In those days,*" *Wilkins recorded*: Wilkins, *Standing Fast,* pp. 161–62.

252 "*If somebody calls you*": Juan Williams, *Thurgood Marshall: American Revolutionary* (New York: Three Rivers Press, 1998), p. 15.

"*exposure to Walter White*": Williams, *Thurgood Marshall,* p. 101.

"*Don't lay a hand on him*": Williams, *Thurgood Marshall,* p. 103.

253 "*To remain as a member*": Victoria Garrett Jones, *Marian Anderson: A Voice Uplifted* (New York: Sterling, 2008), p. 74.

"*Marian was so heartbroken*": White, *A Man Called White,* p. 180.

254 "*Oscar,*" *Walter said,* "*wouldn't it be*": Dialogue from oral history of Oscar L. Chapman, August 2, 1972, Truman presidential archives, https://www.trumanlibrary.gov/library/oral-histories/chapman6#282, pp. 282–83.

"*No member of that audience*": White, *A Man Called White,* p. 184.

"*I could not run away from*": Susan Stamberg, "Denied a Stage, Marian Anderson Sang for a Nation," NPR, April 9, 2014.

"*Marian Anderson is singing this*": "80 Years Ago Marian Anderson Performed for Some 75,000 People at the Lincoln Memorial," *All Things Considered,* NPR, April 9, 2019.

"*She sang these religious*": Chapman oral history, p. 289.

255 "*Tears streamed down the*": White, *A Man Called White,* pp. 184–85.

"*one of the most important*": Stamberg, "Denied a Stage."

"*aerial attacks*": A. J. Baime, *The Arsenal of Democracy: FDR, Detroit, and an Epic Quest to Arm an America at War* (New York: Houghton Mifflin Harcourt, 2014), p. 62.

"*Every time you flicked on*": Wilkins, *Standing Fast,* p. 175.

256 *"You would think"*: Arthur M. Schlesinger, *The Coming of the New Deal: The Age of Roosevelt, 1933–1935* (New York: Mariner, 1986), p. 512.

257 *"The thing is we've got to"*: Dialogue from Doris Kearns Goodwin, *No Ordinary Time: Franklin & Eleanor Roosevelt: The Home Front in World War II* (New York: Simon & Schuster Paperbacks, 1994), pp. 168–69.

 "The policy of the War": "The White House Jim Crow Plan," *Crisis* 47, no. 11 (November 1940).

 WE REPUDIATE: Walter White, telegram to Franklin Roosevelt, October 10, 1940, NAACP archives, file 001434-025-0002.

258 *"Negroes will be considered"*: Goodwin, *No Ordinary Time*, p. 246.

 "We have not had a Negro": Goodwin, *No Ordinary Time*, p. 247.

 "It is not the policy of this": Goodwin, *No Ordinary Time*, p. 247.

 "our getting introduced in": Walter White to Bill Hastie and Thurgood Marshall, October 2, 1940, NAACP archives, file 001434-024-0168.

 "to make a full and complete": Senate Resolution 75, 77th Congress, 1st Session, February 19, 1941, NAACP archives, file 001434-024-0168.

259 *"The success of this March"*: NAACP, letter "To all branches," May 12, 1941, NAACP archives, file 001434-024-0168.

 "When I got into the": Goodwin, *No Ordinary Time*, p. 250.

 "Mr. President," Randolph said: Dialogue from Goodwin, *No Ordinary Time*, pp. 251–52.

260 *"to provide for the full and"*: Executive Order 8802, Prohibition of Discrimination in the Defense Industry, June 25, 1941, General Records of the United States Government, National Archives, available at https://www.archives.gov/historical-docs/todays-doc/?dod-date=625#:~:text=In%20June%20of%201941%2C%20President,to%20enforce%20the%20new%20policy.

 "the author of President": "Walter White," *New York Times*, March 23, 1955.

 "one of the most significant": "President's Committee Meets," *Pittsburgh Courier*, July 26, 1941.

 "Meanwhile," Walter recorded, "Hitler's": White, *A Man Called White*, p. 189.

Chapter 27

261 *"Air raid! This is no shit!"*: A. J. Baime, *The Arsenal of Democracy: FDR, Detroit, and an Epic Quest to Arm an America at War* (New York: Houghton Mifflin Harcourt, 2014), p. 123.

 "Though 13 million American": "Negro Leaders Promise Unity in Defense Effort Against Japan," *Atlanta Daily World*, December 10, 1941.

 "I have never seen a": "Rogers Says: Walter White Listed Southern Demagogues at New York Protest," *Pittsburgh Courier*, June 27, 1942.

262 *"The long expected riot"*: White, *A Man Called White*, p. 225.

 "President Roosevelt or Cleopatra": Nat Brandt, *Harlem at War: The Black Experience in WWII* (Syracuse, NY: Syracuse University Press, 1996), p. 189.

"But does Mr. White know": White, *A Man Called White,* p. 233.

"Roy Wilkins and I rode": Walter White, "People and Places: The Harlem Riot," *Chicago Defender,* August 14, 1943.

263　*"Wild-eyed men and women"*: White, *A Man Called White,* p. 236.

"I have lived in Harlem": White, *A Man Called White,* p. 239.

"I'd rather see Hitler or": Baime, *Arsenal of Democracy,* p. 157.

264　*"spineless"*: Walter White, "People, Politics, and Places: The Truth About the Red Cross," *Chicago Defender,* December 29, 1945.

"There is definite fear": L. C. Barrett to Walter White, July 3, 1943, NAACP archives, file 001459-028-0078.

"It should be realized by": J. L. LeFlore to Walter White, July 6, 1943, NAACP archives, file 001459-028-0078.

"It is our feeling that any": Arthur L. Gray to Walter White, July [no other date listed], 1943, NAACP archives, file 001459-028-0078.

"Even the balcony was packed": "Here to Yonder: Walter White's First Twenty-Five," *Chicago Defender,* June 10, 1944.

"White has tenderly cultivated": E. J. Kahn Jr., "The Frontal Attack — I," Profiles, *New Yorker,* September 4, 1948.

265　*"that it is an American organization"*: "Here to Yonder."

"As the Second World War": Roy Wilkins, *Standing Fast: The Autobiography of Roy Wilkins* (New York: Da Capo Press, 1994), p. 186.

266　*"You have no idea," she wrote*: Poppy Cannon, *Gentle Knight: My Husband Walter White* (New York: Popular Library, 1956), p. 32.

"I remember looking at him": Cannon, *Gentle Knight,* p. 28.

"I'm quite free at last": Cannon, *Gentle Knight,* p. 28.

"Dear General [A. D.] Surles": Walter White to Major General A. D. Surles, September 18, 1944, NAACP archives, file 001439-013-0009.

267　*"to go right up to the battlefronts"*: Walter White to J. Edgar Hoover, September 23, 1943, FBI FOIA file of Walter White.

"Negro" box as his race: White's press correspondent identification and application are from Walter White Papers, box 36, file 371, Beinecke Rare Book & Manuscript Library, Yale University.

"No sooner had I been billeted": White, *A Man Called White,* p. 242.

268　*"You are an idiot"*: Walter White, *A Rising Wind* (Garden City, NY: Doubleday, Doran, 1945), p. 53.

"War vehicles of every imaginable": Walter White, "People and Places," *Chicago Defender,* April 15, 1944.

"When I heard about it": White, *A Man Called White,* p. 250.

"All my commanders reported": White, *A Man Called White,* p. 250.

269　*"He hated war, he loathed"*: White, *A Man Called White,* p. 365.

"For what were you court-martialed": Dialogue from Mary White Ovington, *The Walls Came Tumbling Down* (New York: Schocken Books, 1970), p. 280.

"It was then that the National": Ovington, *Walls Came Tumbling,* p. 280.

270 *"We were hit," he recalled:* Cannon, *Gentle Knight,* p. 105.

"I said, 'Please God'": Cannon, *Gentle Knight,* p. 105.

"When I came to": Cannon, *Gentle Knight,* p. 105.

"Perhaps not since the dawn": Diary of Joseph Davies, April 19, 1945, Joseph Edward Davies Papers, box 1:16, Manuscript Division, Library of Congress, Washington, DC.

"Here was a man who came": Robert G. Nixon, oral history, October 19, 1970, Truman presidential archives, https://www.trumanlibrary.gov/library/oral-histories/nixon3, p. 159.

271 *"The increasingly shorter interval"*: White, *A Man Called White,* p. 308.

Chapter 28

273 *"Hell no," said the driver:* Dialogue from Isaac Woodard testimony, Plaintiff's Bill of Exceptions No. 1, in the Circuit Court of Kanawha County, West Virginia, November 10, 1947, NAACP archives, file 001532-030-0073.

275 *"Faltering with the unsureness"*: Walter White, *A Man Called White: The Autobiography of Walter White* (Athens and London: University of Georgia Press, 1995), p. 327.

"I saw you, Mr. White": White, *A Man Called White,* p. 327.

276 *"The policeman asked me"*: Orson Welles, *Obediently Yours,* excerpted in the documentary *The Blinding of Isaac Woodard,* American Experience, WGBH 2021, aired on PBS March 30, 2021, https://www.pbs.org/wgbh/americanexperience/films/blinding-isaac-woodard/.

"Because of the serious nature": Robert Patterson to Walter White, June 17, 1946, NAACP archives, file 001532-028-0706.

"If he can be treated so": Walter White, memorandum to NAACP branches, July 25, 1946, NAACP archives, file 001532-028-0706.

277 VETERAN'S EYES GOUGED: "Veteran's Eyes Gouged Out by Hate-Crazed Dixie Police," *Chicago Defender,* July 20, 1946.

"Your office tells me that": Dialogue from Poppy Cannon, *A Gentle Knight: My Husband Walter White* (New York: Popular Library, 1956), p. 36.

278 *"As you may have gathered"*: Poppy Cannon to Walter White, date unknown, Poppy Cannon Papers, box 12, folder unknown (unable to access due to COVID pandemic), Beinecke Rare Book & Manuscript Library, Yale University.

"When I think of you": Cannon to White, date unknown.

"If that Mrs. Cannon calls": Roy Wilkins, *Standing Fast: The Autobiography of Roy Wilkins* (New York: Da Capo Press, 1994), pp. 204–205.

"[We] have been begging you": Roy Wilkins to Walter White, March 11, 1947, Wilkins, *Standing Fast,* p. 197.

279 *"It is doubtful whether any"*: White, *A Man Called White,* p. 314.

280 NIGGER, READ AND RUN: White, *A Man Called White*, p. 314.

"one of the most unbelievable": Philip Dray, *At the Hands of Persons Unknown: The Lynching of Black America* (New York: Modern Library, 2003), p. 376.

"It is as bad now as the Bloody": Dialogue from Cannon, *Gentle Knight*, p. 30.

281 *"proper at all times"*: "Blinded Vet Loses $50,000 Suit," *Afro-American* (Baltimore), November 22, 1947.

"It's the same kind of thing": "Joe Louis Speaks Out Against Terror Wave," *Chicago Defender*, August 31, 1946.

BLINDING OF ISAAC WOODARD: "Blinding of Isaac Woodard, American Hero," *New York Amsterdam News*, August 17, 1946.

BLINDING OF VET SHOCKS NATION: "Blinding of Vet Shocks Nation," *Atlanta Daily World*, July 21, 1946.

"It was just another white": Welles, *Obediently Yours*.

YOUR BROADCAST ON ISAAC: Walter White, telegram to Orson Welles, July 29, 1946, NAACP archives, file 001532-028-0706.

282 *"The bus operator came into"*: "S.C. Sheriff Admits Hate Blinding of Isaac Woodard," *Chicago Defender*, August 24, 1946.

"the million dollar list": "Music Events: Million Dollar List of Stars Head Woodard Benefit Program," *New York Amsterdam News*, August 17, 1946.

"the loudest applause I've": "'Blinding of Isaac Woodard': 1946 Racist Police Violence Case Gets Fresh Attention," *People's World*, March 10, 2021.

"Nothing in the history": "Million Dollar List of Stars."

"Sightless Isaac Woodard, returning": Cannon, *Gentle Knight*, p. 30.

283 *"I hit him across the front"*: "Negro Ex-GI Blinding Laid to Policeman," *Baltimore Sun*, September 27, 1946.

"Officer X, we know": Welles, *Obediently Yours*.

"concern over grave danger": Daily Appointments of Harry S. Truman, September 12, 1946, Harry S. Truman Papers, Truman presidential archives, https://www .trumanlibrary.gov/calendar/search?body_value_op=word&comment_keywords =&page=47.

284 *"Everything's going to be"*: A. J. Baime, *Dewey Defeats Truman: The 1948 Election and the Battle for America's Soul* (New York and Boston: Houghton Mifflin Harcourt, 2020), p. 21.

"My God!" he said: White, *A Man Called White*, p. 331.

Chapter 29

285 *"I'll create it by executive"*: Walter White, *A Man Called White: The Autobiography of Walter White* (Athens and London: University of Georgia Press, 1995), p. 331.

"I had as callers yesterday": Harry S. Truman to Attorney General Tom Clark, with attached memo to David Niles, September 20, 1946, President's Committee on Civil Rights, Research Files, Harry S. Truman Library & Museum, National

Archives, https://www.trumanlibrary.gov/library/research-files/letter-harry-s
-truman-attorney-general-tom-clark-attached-memo-david-niles.

286 *"Woodard turned in their"*: "Freedom for Woodard Attacker Protested," *Chicago Defender,* November 16, 1946.

"I had no intention of hitting": "Freedom for Woodard Attacker."

"It has been charged here": Dialogue from Isaac Woodard testimony, Plaintiff's Bill of Exceptions No. 1, In the Circuit Court of Kanawha County, West Virginia, November 10, 1947, NAACP archives, file 001532-030-0073.

"then let this South Carolina": "Police Chief Acquitted in Blinding of Veteran," *Pittsburgh Post-Gazette,* November 6, 1946.

"I was shocked by the hypocrisy": Richard Kluger, *Simple Justice: The History of* Brown v. Board of Education *and Black America's Struggle for Equality* (New York: Vintage Books, 2004), p. 298.

287 *"You have a vitally"*: Remarks to Members of the President's Committee on Civil Rights, January 15, 1947, Public Papers of Harry S. Truman, Harry S. Truman Library and Museum, National Archives, https://www.trumanlibrary.gov/library /public-papers/9/remarks-members-presidents-committee-civil-rights.

"Our American heritage": "To Secure These Rights: The Report of the President's Committee on Civil Rights," Public Papers of Harry S. Truman, Harry S. Truman Library and Museum, National Archives, https://www.trumanlibrary.gov/library/ to-secure-these-rights.

288 *"without doubt the most"*: White, *A Man Called White,* p. 333.

"While Walter was working": Roy Wilkins, *Standing Fast: The Autobiography of Roy Wilkins* (New York: Da Capo Press, 1994), p. 194.

"must be open to all children": "Background: Mendez v. Westminster Re-Enactment," United States Courts (website), https://www.uscourts.gov/educational-resources/ educational-activities/background-mendez-v-westminster-re-enactment.

289 *"We will have done everything"*: White, *A Man Called White,* p. 90.

"For too many years": Nadine Cahodas, *Strom Thurmond and the Politics of Southern Change* (Macon, GA: Mercer University Press, 1994), p. 116.

"holy war": "Talmadge Prepares to Bar Negroes from Voting in Georgia Primaries; Calls His Nomination a 'Mandate,'" *St. Louis Post-Dispatch,* August 11, 1946.

290 *"Captain, I suppose you had"*: Walter White, *How Far the Promised Land?* (New York: Viking Press, 1955), p. 172.

"I was so angry": White, *How Far the Promised Land?,* p. 184.

291 *"nothing short of political"*: White, *How Far the Promised Land?,* p. 174.

"Send me a memorandum": White, *A Man Called White,* p. 348.

Chapter 30

293 "Very confidentially": Walter White to Roy Wilkins, March 8, 1947, Roy Wilkins, *Standing Fast: The Autobiography of Roy Wilkins* (New York: Da Capo Press, 1994), pp. 196–97.

294 *"I was shocked to have"*: Roy Wilkins to Walter White, March 11, 1947, Wilkins, *Standing Fast.*

"largest mass meeting in": NAACP, "Largest Mass Meeting in Nation's History Planned by NAACP," press release, June 6, 1947, NAACP archives, file 001412-011-0807.

"But my very stomach": National Park Service, "Truman & Civil Rights," Harry S. Truman National Historic Site, https://www.nps.gov/hstr/planyourvisit/upload /civil-rights.pdf.

296 *"There are 100,000 people"*: Walter White, address given at the Lincoln Memorial, June 29, 1947, President's Committee on Civil Rights, Research Files, Harry S. Truman Library & Museum, National Archives, https://www.trumanlibrary.gov /library/research-files/address-given-walter-white-lincoln-memorial.

"We all craned forward": Wilkins, *Standing Fast,* p. 198.

"I should like to talk to": Truman's NAACP address, June 29, 1947, Truman Library Institute, trumanlibraryinstitute.org/historic-speeches-naacp/.

297 *"I did not believe that"*: Walter White, *A Man Called White: The Autobiography of Walter White* (Athens and London: University of Georgia Press, 1995), p. 348.

"There it was," recorded Wilkins: Wilkins, *Standing Fast,* p. 199.

"I said what I did because": White, *A Man Called White,* p. 348.

298 *"Shall we continue as"*: Walter White, "People, Politics, and Places," *Chicago Defender,* May 29, 1948.

"When Walter and I reached": Wilkins, *Standing Fast,* p. 201.

"The day of reckoning": Wilkins, *Standing Fast,* p. 201.

"I was proud of him": Wilkins, *Standing Fast,* p. 201.

299 *"security of person"*: 1948 Democratic Party Platform, American Presidency Project, University of California, Santa Barbara, https://www.presidency.ucsb.edu /documents/1948-democratic-party-platform.

"Real Americanism won at": Walter White, "Statement to Associated Press," July 15, 1948, NAACP archives, file 001459-021-0570.

"The south is no longer": "11 States Support Georgian," *Atlanta Constitution,* July 15, 1948.

"Mississippi has gone home!": "Truman and Barkley Nominated; Two Dixie Delegations Walk Out," *Los Angeles Times,* July 15, 1948.

"Our fight is the fight": "Delegates Look for Spectacle and Find One," *Chicago Daily Tribune,* July 15, 1948.

"Yeah, but that S.O.B. Truman": Carl Rowan, "Harry Truman and the Negro: Was He Our Greatest Civil Rights President?," *Ebony,* November 1959.

300 *"I want to tell you, ladies"*: A. J. Baime, *Dewey Defeats Truman: The 1948 Election and the Battle for America's Soul* (New York and Boston: Houghton Mifflin Harcourt, 2020), p. 159.

"Harry Truman is a dead": Baime, *Dewey Defeats Truman,* p. 172.

"Exercise of the franchise": Walter White to Branch Officers, January 26, 1948, NAACP archives, file 001459-018-0280.

"This country and its people": Harry Truman to Walter White, with Related Material, June 19, 1948, Harry S. Truman and Civil Rights, Research Files, Harry S. Truman Library & Museum, National Archives, https://www.trumanlibrary .gov/library/research-files/harry-s-truman-walter-white-related-material.

301 *"fair employment practices"*: Executive Order 9980, Regulations Governing Fair Employment Practices Within the Federal Establishment, July 26, 1948, Executive Orders, Harry S. Truman Library & Museum, National Archives, https:// www.trumanlibrary.gov/library/executive-orders/9980/executive-order-9980.

"restore faith in the": "Truman Proclamation Splits Negro Leaders," *Los Angeles Sentinel,* July 29, 1948.

"Well," he told them: Dialogue from Poppy Cannon, *A Gentle Knight: My Husband Walter White* (New York: Popular Library, 1956), p. 35.

302 *"Negro voters supported"*: NAACP, "NAACP Publishes Survey of Negro Presidential Vote," press release, January 27, 1949, NAACP archives, file 001459-018-0280.

"your majority in the Negro": Philleo Nash to Harry Truman, November 6, 1948, 1948 Election Campaign Collection, Research Files, Harry S. Truman Library & Museum, National Archives, https://www.trumanlibrary.gov/library/research -files/philleo-nash-harry-s-truman.

Chapter 31

303 *"Mr. White is a Negro"*: "Mr. White's Story of Dedication," *New York Times,* September 26, 1948.

304 *"As long as I live I shall remember"*: Randy Stakeman and Jackson Stakeman, "Walter White's Divorce and Remarriage," Walter White Project, https://scalar.usc .edu/nehvectors/stakeman/marriage-divorce-and-remarriage.

"Now I realize your suspicious": Kenneth Janken, *White: The Biography of Walter White, Mr. NAACP* (New York: New Press, 2003), p. 331.

305 *"I couldn't believe the"*: Helen Martin to Walter White, May 20, 1949, Walter White Papers, box 10, folder 62, Beinecke Rare Book & Manuscript Library, Yale University.

"When you became the": Madeline White to Walter White, May 20, 1949, Walter White Papers, box 7, folder 225, Beinecke Rare Book & Manuscript Library, Yale University.

306 *"My chief reason for this"*: Minutes of the Meeting of the Board of Directors, May 9, 1949, NAACP archives, file 001412-003-0879.

"For more than 25 years": Janken, *White: The Biography,* p. 337.

307 *"Roy," Walter said, "there's"*: Wilkins, *Standing Fast,* p. 204.

"It was such a beautiful": Poppy Cannon, *A Gentle Knight: My Husband Walter White* (New York: Popular Library, 1956), p. 43.

"When you read this column": "World Town Meeting of the Air Gets Underway," *Chicago Defender,* July 2, 1949.

" 'Heavens, No!' ": " 'Heavens, No!' " Said Mrs. White," *Afro-American* (Baltimore), July 2, 1949.

308 *"Walter White's Divorce"*: "Walter White's Divorce Starts Tongues Wagging," *New York Amsterdam News,* July 16, 1949.

"Walter Whites Divorced": "Walter Whites Divorced," *Afro-American* (Baltimore), July 16, 1949.

"Gossip Circles Walter White": "Gossip Circles Walter White," *Pittsburgh Courier,* July 23, 1949.

"Another Courier Scoop!": "Another Courier Scoop! Walter, Poppy Married!" *Pittsburgh Courier,* July 30, 1949.

"Walter White Wed July": "Walter White Wed July 6 to Editor 'Poppy,'" *New York Daily News,* August 14, 1949.

"From coast-to-coast they're": "Mrs. Walter White Denies Link with Noted Movie Star," *New York Age,* July 16, 1949.

"Did Walter White Marry": "Did Walter White Marry His White Sweetheart?" *New York Amsterdam News,* undated, NAACP archives, file 001451-024-0081.

"Bride Can't Be Located": "Bride Can't Be Located," undated newspaper clipping, NAACP archives, file 001451-024-0081.

"Leadership of Walter White": "Leadership of Walter White in Doubt," undated newspaper clipping, NAACP archives, file 001451-024-0081.

"First Photo of Walter": "First Photo of Walter White and New Bride," *Afro-American* (Baltimore), August 27, 1949.

"So this is it": Dialogue from Cannon, *Gentle Knight,* p. 57.

309 *"out of town"*: "Mrs. White's Love Rumors Called Untrue," *St. Louis Voice,* July 14, 1949.

"It will take us another": "California Writer Raps Walter White for Taking White Bride," *Los Angeles Sentinel,* undated clipping, NAACP archives, file 001451-024-0081.

"He has given credence": "C. C. Spaulding Chides Walter White for His Recent Marriage," undated newspaper clipping, NAACP archives, file 001451-024-0081.

"The selfishness is unbelievable": Janken, *White: The Biography,* pp. 337–38.

310 *"has so weakened his usefulness"*: Carl Murphy to Palmer Weber, August 31, 1949, NAACP archives, file 001451-023-0895.

"tossed away": Simon Topping, "All Shadows Are Dark: Walter White, Racial Identity, and National Politics," in *Long Is the Way and Hard: One Hundred Years of the NAACP,* eds. Kevern Verney and Lee Sartain (Fayetteville: University of Arkansas Press, 2009), p. 6.

Chapter 32

311 *"Do you feel that the"*: Dialogue from "Walter White Sweats Out Press Quiz on Marriage," *Chicago Defender,* October 1, 1949.

312 *"your marriage created a"*: Eleanor Roosevelt to Walter White, March 29, 1950, Eleanor Roosevelt, *It Seems to Me: Selected Letters of Eleanor Roosevelt,* eds. Leonard C. Schlup and Donald W. Whisenhunt (Lexington: University of Kentucky Press, 2005), p. 144.

"Self-respecting Negroes are": Illegible signature to NAACP, October 14, 1949, NAACP archives, file 001451-021-0664.

"As far as many Negroes are": S. K. Bryson to NAACP, October 15, 1949, NAACP archives, file 001451-024-0081.

"In the deep South nobody": Kenneth Janken, *White: The Biography of Walter White, Mr. NAACP* (New York: New Press, 2003), p. 350.

"There was still plenty of": Roy Wilkins, *Standing Fast: The Autobiography of Roy Wilkins* (New York: Da Capo Press, 1994), pp. 212, 205.

313 *"as a second father"*: Author's telephone interview with Rose Palmer, June 3, 2021.

"Walter, whenever you light": Poppy Cannon, *A Gentle Knight: My Husband Walter White* (New York: Popular Library, 1956), p. 169.

314 *"They've kept me 'sedated'"*: Walter White to "Dear Folks," November 14, 1954, NAACP archives, file 001451-023-0149.

"We conclude that in the": Transcript of *Brown v. Board of Education* 347 U.S. 483 (1954), Supreme Court of the United States, https://www.ourdocuments.gov /print_friendly.php?flash=false&page=transcript&doc=87&title=Transcript+of +Brown+v.+Board+of+Education+%281954%29.

315 *"My first thought went"*: Cannon, *Gentle Knight,* pp. 193–95.

"Who but Walter would": Wilkins, *Standing Fast,* p. 220.

316 *"I promised you yesterday"*: Dialogue from Cannon, *Gentle Knight,* pp. 209–10.

Epilogue

317 *"All the peoples of the"*: Dialogue from Cannon, *Gentle Knight,* p. 28.

"Walter White was the": "Walter White," *New York Times,* March 23, 1955.

"He gave his life to a heroic": "Walter White," *Washington Post,* March 24, 1955.

318 HIS DEVOTED SERVICE TO HIS: "Walter White Eulogized by Leaders," *Washington Post,* March 23, 1955.

"not only in his official": Janken, *White: The Biography,* p. 361.

"literally gave his life for": "Walter White Eulogized by Leaders," *Washington Post,* March 23, 1955.

"to tell how democracy works": Walter White, *How Far the Promised Land?* (New York: Viking Press, 1955), p. 3.

"the long, heartbreaking struggle": White, *How Far the Promised Land?,* p. 3.

"It would have been impossible": White, *How Far the Promised Land?,* p. 229.

"most influential images of": "The Most Influential Images of All Time: 100 Photos," *Time,* http://100photos.time.com/.

319 *"stronger"*: "Rand Paul Holds Up Anti-lynching Legislation as He Seeks Changes to Bill," CNN, June 3, 2020, https://www.cnn.com/2020/06/03/politics/rand-paul -lynching-legislation/index.html.

320 *"I am one of the two in"*: Walter White, *A Man Called White: The Autobiography of Walter White* (Athens and London: University of Georgia Press, 1995), p. 366.

Index